LEGITIMIZING HUMAN RIGHTS NGOs

LEGITIMIZING
HUMAN RIGHTS NGOs

Lessons from Nigeria

By

Obiora Chinedu Okafor

Africa World Press, Inc.

P.O. Box 1892
Trenton, NJ 08607

P.O. Box 48
Asmara, ERITREA

Africa World Press, Inc.

P.O. Box 1892
Trenton, NJ 08607

P.O. Box 48
Asmara, ERITREA

Book design: Saverance Publishing Services
Cover design: Roger Dormann

Library of Congress Cataloging-in-Publication Data

Okafor, Obiora Chinedu.
    Legitimizing human rights NGOs : lessons from Nigeria / by Obiora Chinedu Okafor.
        p. cm.
    Includes bibliographical references and index.
    ISBN 1-59221-285-9 (hardcover) -- ISBN 1-59221-286-7 (pbk.)
    1. Non-governmental organizations--Nigeria. 2. Human rights--Nigeria. 3. Non-governmental organizations--Africa. I. Title.

JZ4841.O38 2005
323.06'0669--dc22

2005026474

To the evergreen and loving memory of my late father and mentor

Ichie F. Okwu-Okafor, *Agundu n'Ukpo* (1930-2004)

TABLE OF CONTENTS

ACKNOWLEDGMENTS

To borrow a little from Upendra Baxi's extensive repertoire of mellifluous prose, it is an understatement to say that this book has been "long in the making." Inspired by the pioneering progressive human rights scholarship of Baxi, Makau Matua, Shedrack Gutto and Joe Oloka-Onyango, the empirical research that grounds this book began in 1998, more than seven years ago!

Starting with a small pilot study that was generously supported by a Carleton University SSHRC small grant, the project was able to proceed with much intensity for the bulk of the next four years because of a major "standard research grant" from the Social Sciences and Humanities Research Council of Canada (SSHRC). As importantly, the last two years of the project, during which the bulk of the writing and editing was completed, proved to be a success story in large part because I was awarded a York University SSHRC small grant. The project also benefited much from some of the data and insights that I gained from the conduct of another research project that was very generously funded by the Social Sciences Research Council of New York. As such, I am most grateful to all the aforementioned institutions for helping to make this book possible.

My numerous research associates and assistants deserve special mention here for the very high quality and effectiveness of their work. Adila Abusharaf (my post-doctoral research associate), Shedrack Agbakwa, Bernard Assan, Amandi Esonwanne, Chinedu Idike, Rhoda Kargbo, Pius Okoronkwo, and Richelle Samuel (research assistants) provided invaluable help. So did my numerous Nigerian colleagues, including but not limited to R.A.C.E Achara, Okey Ajunwa, Peter Eze, Sam Nwatu, Tony Okeke, Ugochukwu Okezie, Chike Okoye, and Ugochukwu Ukpabi.

I must also express my deep gratitude to the many students (too numerous to name) who participated in the human rights courses that I taught at various institutions over the last thirteen years. Their keen and sharp minds always drove me toward ever more perfect scholarship and contributed in no small measure to the refinement of almost all of the arguments made in this book.

My colleagues at Osgoode Hall Law School of York University (especially Susan Drummond, Shelley Gavigan, Jinyan Li, Ikechi Mgbeoji, Iain Ramsay, Craig Scott, Rob Wai, and Toni Williams) also deserve to be acknowledged in the same way for their extraordinary support and inspiration. So do my own former teachers, especially the late Ivan Head, the late Gaius Ezejiofor, Karin Mickelson, Obinna Okere, Wes Pue, and Kofi Quashigah.

Solomon Ukhuegbe, my esteemed former colleague in the Nigerian professorate, deserves special mention for taking the time from his busy schedule to read through critical portions of the earlier drafts of this book, and for making important criticisms and commendations. I am also grateful to Boniface Ahunwan, Sam Amadi, Antony Anghie, Obijiofor Aginam, Basil Enwegbara, James Gathii, Bonny Ibhawoh, Pablo Idahosa, Ilwad Jama, Sylvia Kanga'ra, Karin Mickelson, Joel Ngugi, Celestine Nyamu, Paul Ocheje, Balakrishnan Rajagopal, Ugochukwu Ukpabi, Bibhas Vaze, Kamoji Wachira, and Ken Wiwa for indulging me with the various conversations and arguments that helped shape and refine this book.

The book would definitely have not seen the light of day without the tremendous support and sacrifice of my family. My wife Atugonza; our children Ojiako and Mbabazi; my mother Lechi; and my siblings Ogo, Okey, Ada, Ojiugo, and Chibuzo - all richly deserve my deepest gratitude in this respect and my fondest regards as always.

Last (but by no means least) on this list of acknowledgments is my publisher, Africa World Press. I wish to express special thanks to Kassahun Checole (the publisher and chief executive) and to Damola Ifaturoti (the senior editor) at the press for their touching interest in the whole project.

Thank you one, thank you all!

This book is dedicated to the evergreen and loving memory of my recently deceased father, hero, and role model, Ichie F. Okwu Okafor (Agundu n'Ukpo). I can only hope that I will some day match his rare combination of scholarly genius, humanist ethos, and diligent struggle.

TABLE OF ACRONYMS

BAOBAB	Baobab for Women's Rights
CAPP	Community Action for Popular Participation
CD	Campaign for Democracy
CDHR	Committee for the Defense of Human Rights
CLEEN	Center for Law Enforcement Education
CLO	Civil Liberties Organization
CRP	Constitutional Rights Project
EMPARC	Empowerment and Action Research Center
ERA	Environmental Rights Action
HURILAWS	Human Rights Law Service
HRA	Human Rights Africa
HRM	Human Rights Monitor
IHRHL	Institute for Human Rights and Humanitarian Law
MOSOP	Movement for the Survival of Ogoni People
MRA	Media Rights Agenda
PRAWA	Prisoners' Rehabilitation and Welfare Action
SERAC	Social and Economic Rights Action Center
SRI	Socio-Economic Rights Initiative [formerly Shelter Rights Initiative]
TMG	Transition Monitoring Group
UAD	United Action for Democracy
WACOL	Women's Aid Collective
WOTCLEF	Women Trafficking and Child Labor Eradication Foundation
WRAPA	Women's Rights Advancement and Protection Alternative

CHAPTER 1

THE CONCEPTUAL FRAMEWORK
AND METHODOLOGY
OF THE STUDY

1. THE RESEARCH PROBLEM

The community of self-described human rights nongovernmental organizations[1] that has operated in Nigeria since the mid-1980s has (in largely unacknowledged and yet highly innovative ways) exerted a measure of influence on state and society in Nigeria, even in the harsh context of military rule. However, despite the location of these NGOs in Africa's vastly most populous country and in spite of their important status as one of the largest and most dynamic communities of NGOs in Africa, very little comprehensive, systematic, and/or detailed work has thus far been undertaken regarding the nature of this NGO community; nor has there been similar work on the extent of the impact that this NGO community has had within Nigeria and the reasons for the limited extent of their success. In particular, despite the obviously *modest* extent of the impact that this NGO community has had within Nigeria, even less scholarly work has been done regarding the exposure of the linkages among the conceptual and institutional orientations of this community, on the one hand, and the limited character of their success in mobilizing popular resistance within Nigeria, on the other hand. To put it succinctly, very little systematic work (and certainly no comprehensive study) has been done regarding the *popular legitimization crisis* that afflicts this important NGO community. As the literature review in section 2 of this chapter shows, virtually all of the existing commentaries on the character of this NGO community have either become outdated or taken the form of hypothetical essays. And where this has not been the case, such commentaries have been far too brief to be comprehensive. The relative neglect of this important NGO community is even more consequential given the fact that an understanding of both the character of this community and the nature of the popular legitimization crisis that seems to afflict it should provide some guidance toward the understanding of other NGO communities elsewhere in Africa (and even in the rest of the so-called third world).[2]

In this light, the first broad objective of this book is to map the nature, impact, and limitations of the Nigerian NGO community.[3] The book will, therefore, analyze the origins, developmental path, composition, structure, geopolitical location, programs, methods, and funding regime of this NGO community. It will also assess the impact that this NGO community has had within Nigeria and account for the palpable inability of this otherwise dynamic and creative NGO community to acquire the kind of popular validation that it requires if it is to develop into a much more influential movement. In this last sense, nothing less than a systematic investigation of, and explanation for, the popular legitimization crisis that seems to afflict this NGO community is entailed.

The other broad objective of the book is to contribute in an indirect way to human rights NGO theory. By explicating the ways in which the conclusions drawn from the empirical study of this NGO community offers an insight into the limitations of the model of human rights NGO activism that is currently dominant around the world, the book will make an important contribution to knowledge. In effect, this study will provide empirical confirmation for many of the conceptual critiques of the dominant model of NGO activism that have been offered over the years by a small college of critical human rights scholars.[4]

All in all, this study will demonstrate (and not just theorize) the intimate and intricate linkages among the conceptual and institutional orientations of this NGO community and the popular legitimization crisis that seems to afflict it.

To this end, the sequence of analysis will proceed as follows: First, an attempt is made in chapter 2 to understand the origins, general character, and developmental history of this NGO community. Second, chapter 3 is devoted to an analysis of the nature and consequences of the composition, structure, and geopolitical location of this NGO community. Third, chapter 4 identifies, classifies, and analyzes the nature and consequences of the programmatic and methodological orientations of this NGO community. Fourth, chapter 5 analyzes the structure and effects of the funding regime of this NGO community. Fifth, an attempt is made in chapter 6 to explore the nature and extent of the influence that this NGO community has exerted within Nigeria. Sixth, chapter 7 is devoted to articulating the linkages among the conceptual and institutional problems that have faced this NGO community, and the popular legitimization crisis that seems to afflict it—a crisis that has hindered severely its capacity to optimize its influence. Chapter 8 concludes the book and outlines the recommendations that are entailed by the findings discussed elsewhere within it.

At a broad theoretical level, this book draws quite significantly from *TWAIL* human rights scholarship.[5] It is therefore steeped in a rich tradition of scholarship regarding the place of human rights activism in African and other so-called third world societies.[6] Three major examples will serve to illustrate this point. The sensitivity of TWAIL scholarship (and related work) to the existence and significance of a continuous and unbroken history of popular resistance to oppression in African and other third world societies[7] is reflected in this book's sustained inquiry into, and concern for, the relative inability of the NGO community in Nigeria to attract widespread validation and commitment among ordinary Nigerians.[8] The sensitivity of TWAIL scholarship to the question of the place of the poor, the abused, and the vulnerable within the structures and processes of the very human rights NGOs that claim to speak for them is reflected in this book's sustained attention to the extent to which these NGOs have been inclusive or exclusive of ordinary Nigerians. And the sensitivity of TWAIL scholarship to the global context in which human rights struggles are waged even within third world societies is reflected in this book's sustained concern with the extent to which this NGO community has been mostly oriented toward foreign (rather than local) actors.

Furthermore, parts of this book are, in a broad sense, steeped in the emergent tradition of *constructivist* human rights theory.[9] This constructivist approach maps, analyzes, and theorizes the range of ways in which human rights activists have contributed, and can contribute, to the alterations in understandings and in logics of appropriateness that have occurred, and that can occur, in particular contexts. The sensitivity of constructivism to this alternative narrative of the mechanics of human rights transformations (one that differs significantly from the dominant approach to the study of the "effectiveness" of human rights activism) is reflected in this book's preferred approach to the question of assessing the extent to which the NGO community has exerted influence within Nigeria.

2. LITERATURE REVIEW

That the work of NGOs has over the last half century or so become a key factor in both international and domestic efforts to promote and protect human rights is no longer in doubt. The relevant literature is replete with studies of the nature of the "international human rights movement", as well as with evidence for, and affirmations of, this truism.[10] Yet that body of literature has also recognized that this widespread effort at disseminating what might be styled a "human rights culture" has only been partially successful. As Paulin Houtondji has noted, nowhere in the world is respect for human rights a "mass cultural fact."[11]

Similarly, the importance of human rights NGOs to the struggle for social justice on the African continent has not escaped scholarly enquiry and analysis.[12] But here again, the literature has tended to be even less assured as to the gains that have been made in the transformations of any of these African polities into what Makau Mutua has referred to as a "human rights state."[13]

What have been far less available in the relevant literature, however, have been sufficiently detailed and systematically articulated overviews of the character, impact, and limitations of specific national communities of these NGOs in Africa. Yet, such systematic and detailed overviews are necessary to understand more adequately the overall impact and broad limitations of each such NGO community. Similarly, the existing body of literature on the domestic NGOs that operate in Africa is much thinner than that relating to the activities of their "international" or foreign counterparts. What is more, even those general commentaries on such domestic NGOs that currently exist tend to be subsumed within the literature that focuses on the rather broad category of "civil society."[14] Claude Welch's commendable 1995 work on human rights NGOs in Africa stands virtually alone as *the* book-length treatment of this question.[15] However, concerned as this book is with the human rights NGOs that operate in the fifty-four or so countries of the second largest continent in the world, and based as it is on a study of only four national NGO communities in Africa, it is of necessity pitched at so general a level as not to provide a sufficiently detailed portrait of any one of the national NGO communities with which it is concerned. What is more, the book is now quite dated. Similar comments apply to Pita Agbese's very important 1993 article on the confrontation between human rights advocates in Nigeria and the then-ruling military junta.[16]

Based as it is on a systematically articulated overview of the NGO community in Nigeria (a group of NGOs that has been described as one of the most dynamic, creative, and important in Africa[17]), the current study is a significant step in the direction of closing the afore-described gap in the scholarly literature – of affording interested observers a far more detailed and much more adequate account of the broad character, impact, and limitations of this particular NGO community than has ever been available.

3. MAJOR RESEARCH QUESTIONS

The major research questions, entailed by the research problems that are articulated in section 2, are as follows:

i. What are the origins of the NGO community? In what directions has this community developed over the years?

ii. What is the nature of the composition, structure, geopolitical location, programs, methods, and funding regime of each of the NGOs that constitute this community? What overall patterns are decipherable in terms of the nature of these organizations? What factors have shaped the nature of these organizations? What is the overall character of the NGO community in Nigeria?

iii. What are the conceptual and institutional problems that face this NGO community? How have these problems arisen? Why are they significant?

iv. In what ways and to what extent has this NGO community been influential within Nigeria?

v.   What kinds of linkages are observable among the conceptual and insti-
       tutional problems that afflict this NGO community (on the one hand),
       and its capacity to achieve influence within Nigeria (on the other hand)?

vi.   Does analysis of these linkages demonstrate the existence of a popular
       legitimization crisis within this NGO community? And if so, how is this
       legitimization crisis best understood?

vii. What lessons can be learnt from a study of this NGO community? To
       what extent do the findings of the study confirm or challenge conven-
       tional scholarly wisdom?

4. SUMMARY OF THE EXPECTED RESULTS:

This book will demonstrate, among other things, that:

i.   The NGO community in Nigeria has, on the whole, enjoyed *modest*
       success. It has contributed to the significant, albeit equally modest,
       transformations that have certainly occurred in Nigeria in the nature and
       character of judicial thinking and action, in terms of legislative process
       and legislation, and concerning executive thinking and action. It is indeed
       a significantly creative, dynamic, influential and courageous activist com-
       munity.

ii.   There have been many significant, even serious, problems with both the
       nature of these organizations and their preferred mode(s) of human
       rights activism. These problems have limited, sometimes severely, their
       capacity to attract and secure the widespread allegiance of Nigeria's
       teeming population of dispossessed and abused persons.

iii. These NGOs were largely founded by elite, urbanized, Lagos-based civil
       rights lawyers (and other such professionals) who were—during the rel-
       evant period—mostly focused on undermining military rule in Nigeria,
       and who marginalized too often other equally important human rights
       issues related to gender, socio-economic rights, and minority/environ-
       mental claims.

iv.   The great majority of these NGOs lack an active and effective member-
       ship base; rarely canvass the local population for members and other
       resources; are too often run and controlled by extremely powerful
       founder/CEOs (who are not controlled by an effective board, and are
       rarely elected by or answerable to an active membership); lack democra-
       tized internal decision-making structures; have offices and projects that
       are located almost always either in the Lagos area or in some other large
       urban centre; and do not for the most part have offices or project loca-
       tions in the rural areas where most Nigerians live and work.

v.   These NGOs tend to set agendas and mount programs that are focused
       on, centered in and targeted at urban Nigeria, and tend to marginalize
       rural- or grassroots-centered agendas. What is more, rarely do these
       agendas speak adequately to the priorities of the ranks of the most
       impoverished and abused underclass in Nigeria.

vi. The funding structure of the NGO community, which is in general characterized by a situation where almost every dollar that is spent by each of these organizations is raised from foreign sources has, by their own admission, provided an incredibly powerful *disincentive* to their engaging in the notoriously difficult task of canvassing the local population for funds, members, and other resources, and has thus contributed to the conceptual and physical distance that can often be observed between these NGOs and most ordinary Nigerians.

vii. Partly as a result of its very conceptual and institutional character, the NGO community in Nigeria has faced a popular legitimization crisis almost since its inception. It has been unable to develop fully its potential of becoming a highly influential player within the Nigerian polity.

viii. To optimize its relevance to Nigerians, most of the organizations that constitute this NGO community will have to re-invent their institutional and conceptual praxis. In sum, these entities will have to pay much more attention to the admittedly far more difficult process of popular mobilization and legitimization (via canvassing the local population for members, funds, and other resources; treating much more with the grassroots and rural Nigeria; and ceding some real power to an active and engaged membership base).

Thus, overall, the study is expected to conclude that despite the fact that this NGO community has enjoyed a modest measure of success (an achievement that is largely attributable to its dynamism, creativity, and courage under successive military regimes), a highly significant gap still exists between its actual achievements and its optimal potential to contribute to the transformation of the Nigerian polity. The study is also expected to find that the existence of this gap between its level of attainment and its real potential is significantly attributable to the fact that the very character of its conceptual and institutional praxis has worked in various ways to distance the community from most of the very same Nigerian masses whose enthusiastic support is imperative for its success. Thus, the study is expected to conclude that this NGO community is in fact afflicted with a popular legitimization crisis. More generally, the study is expected to challenge to some degree the widespread tendency in the human rights literature to regard the currently dominant human rights NGO model as unproblematic, even in the context of its application within African countries such as Nigeria.

5. METHODOLOGY

The study is based on a purposefully selected sample of twenty diverse and representative domestic human rights NGOs in Nigeria. This sample size was considered adequate given the fact that the number of functional self-described human rights NGOs in Nigeria, was during the period of the study, estimated at fewer than one hundred. For instance, a 1994 survey conducted by the Swedish NGO Foundation and the International Human Rights Internship Program was based on thirteen such NGOs in Nigeria, and even then at least two of the organizations surveyed were really generalist research institutions.[18] Purposeful, rather than random, samples were used mainly because of the need to capture the geographical, issue area, gender, and historical diversity of the community. Using a random sample might have resulted in a list of study subjects that consisted entirely of civil/political rights NGOs (when a number of socioeconomic rights NGOs existed), or that might have completely excluded women's groups. Again, although most of the NGOs of concern to us are located in the Lagos area of Nigeria, not all of them are. There was therefore the risk of missing certain of the useful insights that were garnered from including in the sample some NGOs that are located outside the Lagos area.

Given the nature of its objectives, and its interdisciplinary nature, the study could not but have adopted a variety of methods. The methods of "data collection" that were employed were intimately linked to the specific research questions that were being investigated. The principal sources of the evidence relied upon in this study are interviews and documents. To some extent, the study also relied, wherever possible, on the verified and verifiable contents of existing scholarly literature.

The staff of the relevant NGOs provided most of the oral and documentary evidence that is relied upon in this book. The veracity of this information was always crosschecked against other relevant sources. In virtually all cases, fact-finding visits were made to the offices of the relevant NGO. In one or two cases, for practical reasons, only telephone interviews were conducted with the staff of the relevant NGOs. During such visits, unstructured interviews were conducted with both senior and junior activists and relevant documents were collected. In many cases, where there was a real need to update data, or to clarify ambiguities in either previous interview responses or in documents already collected and analyzed, follow-up visits were made to these NGOs; failing that, telephone interviews were conducted with the relevant activists.

The evidence regarding the extent to which this NGO community has influenced executive processes and action in Nigeria was in the main collected by locating, examining, and cross checking the relevant public documents, mainly government gazettes, proposed legislation (especially government-sponsored bills), enacted legislation, and informational bulletins. The interview technique was not utilized extensively in this case because most of the relevant information already existed in the public domain. Interviews with NGO activists also revealed useful information in this regard. Such information was, of course, always cross checked. The evidence regarding the extent to which these NGOs had influenced legislative behavior in Nigeria was in the main collected by interviewing the relevant members of parliament as well as staff of the relevant NGOs. Relevant *hansards* (records of parliamentary proceedings) were also collected and examined. So were actual copies of proposed and enacted legislation. The evidence regarding the extent to which these NGOs have influenced judicial reasoning in Nigeria was obtained principally by collecting and examining case reports. Interviews were also conducted with the relevant NGO activists and, where necessary and possible, with some judges.

At this juncture, a note of caution must be sounded regarding the methodological difficulties associated with locating, mapping, and assessing human rights NGO influence. On the one hand, NGOs do have a bit of an incentive to overstate their own influence; for the more influential they have been in the past, the more likely they are to attract much-needed donor funding for their ongoing and future projects. On the other hand, government officials have tended to be highly skeptical regarding the achievements of these NGOs.[19] What is more, as Susan Dicklitch has argued, because of the mystical, venerable, quality that human rights NGOs tend to posses – the moral plateau to which they have now climbed in our time – it is sometimes difficult to develop a realistic and balanced understanding of the exact roles that NGOs have really played in given contexts.[20] As such, in attributing a given level of influence to these NGOs, the author has had to take care to make reasoned judgments, backed as much as possible either by independent evidence and/or by his own observations in the field. While this method cannot provide a one hundred percent guarantee against the attribution of mistakenly higher or lower level of influence in any given context, it does lower the risk of error to an acceptable level.

6. THE BENEFITS OF THE STUDY

As the first detailed systematic study of one of the most important national communities of human rights NGOs in Africa, this book is likely to interest and benefit a wide range of actors. In particular, academics, research institutions, foreign aid workers, charities, human rights activists, judges, lawyers, journalists, government officials, and members of parliament, not just in Nigeria, but also in other parts of Africa and around the world.

In an atmosphere of scarce resources, when both NGOs and donors alike must be taken to be even more interested in a systematic account of the successes and failures of decades of NGO-centered human rights activism in Nigeria and elsewhere, this book should provide a guide to these diverse actors as they ponder and assess the gains and losses of the last two decades. The book should also be useful to them as they work toward the transformation of the existing human rights NGO movement into a much more influential and effective player within Nigeria and elsewhere.

7. THE PERIOD OF CONCERN

This study is limited in a temporal sense. It is restricted to the study of the nature, status, impact, and problems of the human rights NGO community in Nigeria between 1987 and 2001. The adoption of 1987 as the start off date was done advisedly. For it was not just the year in which the CLO – Nigeria's oldest contemporary self-described human rights NGO – was founded; it was also the year in which the African Commission on Human and Peoples' Rights – a crucial resource for these NGOs – became functional for the first time. The year 2001 was chosen as a convenient cut off date against which the validity of the propositions and arguments advanced here would be assessed. It was also the year in which the bulk of the fieldwork on which this study is founded was concluded.

NOTES

1.   Hereinafter referred to as NGOs. Laurie Wiseberg has defined a human rights NGO as:

> [A] private association which devotes significant resources to the promotion and protection of human rights, which is independent of both governmental and political groups that seek *direct* political power, which does not itself seek such power.

See L.S. Wiseberg, "Protecting Human Rights Activists and NGOs: What More Can Be Done?" *Human Rights Quarterly* 13 (1991): 525 at 529. Emphasis added. Although Martin Olz's definition is not all that different, it is somewhat more specific. According to Olz:

> Generally, for an NGO to be considered as human rights NGO it should be of private character and its work should be guided by the idea of international human rights as set forth in the UN Declaration of Human Rights, the International Covenant of Civil and Political Rights, the International Covenant on Economic, Social and Cultural Rights, and other instruments of international law. Some scholars expand this definition to also include any group which is active in a single country and relies solely on the domestic legal order. This encompasses human rights centers at universities, grassroots organizations and social institutions of churches.

See M.A. Olz, "Nongovernmental Organizations in Regional Human Rights Systems" Columbia Human Rights Law Review 28 (1997): 307.

2.   See U. Baxi, *The Future of Human Rights* (New Delhi: Oxford University Press, 2002), 124; M. Mutua, "A Discussion on the Legitimacy of Human Rights NGOs in Africa," *Africa Legal Aid Quarterly* (October-December 1997): 28; C.A. Odinkalu, "Why More Africans Don't Use the Human Rights Language," *Human Rights Dialogue* (2000): 3; and J. Ihonbvbere, "Where is the Third Wave? A Critical Evaluation of Africa's Non-Transition to Democracy," *Africa Today* 43:4 (1996): 343 at 358.

3.   Hereinafter referred to as the "NGO community."

4.   For example, see M. Mutua, "The Politics of Human Rights: Beyond the Abolitionist Paradigm" *Michigan Journal of International Law* 17 (1996): 591; Odinkalu, *supra* note 2 ; Gutto, *infra* note 12 ; and Baxi, *supra* note 2.

5. The acronym *TWAIL* stands for the third world approaches to international law movement. For detailed explanations of this approach, see M. Mutua, "What is TWAIL?" *ASIL Proceedings* (2000): 31; and J. Gathii, "Alternative and Critical: The Contribution of Research and Scholarship on Developing Countries to International Legal Theory" *Harvard International Law Journal* 41 (2000): 263.

6. For example, see Baxi, *supra* note 2; I. Shivji, *The Concept of Human Rights in Africa* (London: CODESRIA, 1989); P. Houtondji, "The Master's Voice—Remarks on the Problem of Human Rights in Africa" in UNESCO, ed., *Philosophical Foundations of Human Rights* (Paris: UNESCO, 1986), 319; M. Mutua, "Savages, Victims and Saviours: The Metaphor of Human Rights" *Harvard International Law Journal* 42 (2001): 201; ibid., "Abolitionist Paradigm," *supra* note 4; Odinkalu, *supra* note 2.; Gutto, *infra* note 12; E.K. Quashigah and O.C. Okafor, eds., *Legitimate Governance in Africa: International and Domestic Legal Perspectives* (The Hague: Kluwer Law International, 1999); O.C. Okafor, "Re-Conceiving Third World Legitimate Governance Struggles in our Time: Emergent Imperatives for Rights Activism" *Buffalo Human Rights Law Review* 6 (2000): 1; J. Oloka-Onyango and S. Tamale, "'The Personal is Political' or Why Women's Rights are Indeed Human Rights: An African Perspective on International Feminism," *Human Rights Quarterly* 17 (1995): 691; A. Anghie, "Francisco Vitoria and the Colonial Origins of International Law" *Social and Legal Studies* 5 (1996): 321; and J.T. Gathii and C.I. Nyamu, "Reflections on United States-Based Human Rights Work on Africa" *Harvard Human Rights Journal* 9 (1996): 285.

7. See C.A. Odinkalu, "Human Rights Language," 3 (arguing that: "From the child soldier, the rural dweller deprived of basic health care, the mother unaware that the next pregnancy is not an inexorable fate, the city dweller living in fear of the burglar, the worker owed several months' arrears of wages, and the activist organizing against bad government, to the group of rural women seeking access to land so that they may send their children to school with its proceeds, *people are acutely aware of the injustices inflicted upon them*"). See also Swedish NGO Foundation, "The Status of Human Rights Organizations in Sub-Saharan Africa: Overview-Introduction," http://www1.umn.edu/humanrts/africa/intro.htm (visited 20 October 2000).

8. Ibid., 4.

9. This approach is exemplified by the work of Kathryn Sikkink and her collaborators. See M.E. Keck and K. Sikkink, *Activists Beyond Borders* (Ithaca, NY: Cornell University Press, 1998); T. Risse, S.C. Ropp, and K. Sikkink, eds., *The Power of Human Rights: International Norms and Domestic Change* (Cambridge, U.K.: Cambridge University Press, 1999); K. Sikkink, "Human Rights, Principled Issue-Networks, and Sovereignty in Latin America" International Organization 47:3 (1993): 411.

10. For example, see Baxi, *supra* note 2; Keck and Sikkink, ibid.; Risse, Ropp, and Sikkink, eds., ibid.; Sikkink, ibid.; D.C. Thomas, "International NGOs, State Sovereignty, and Democratic Values," Chicago Journal of International Law 2:2 (2001): 389, 392; L. Amede Obiora, "Symbolic Episodes in the Quest for

Environmental Justice" Human Rights Quarterly 21 (1999): 464, 471; C.R. Epp, *The Rights Revolution: Lawyers, Activists, and Supreme Courts in Comparative Perspective* (Chicago: University of Chicago Press, 1998), 205; W. Korey, *NGOs and the Universal Declaration of Human Rights: A Curious Grapevine* (New York: St Martin's Press, 1998); M. Cameron, R.J. Lawson, and B.W. Tomlin, eds., *To Walk without Fear: The Global Movement to Ban Landmines* (Toronto: Oxford University Press, 1998); H.J. Steiner and P. Alston, *International Human Rights in Context: Law, Politics, Morals* (New York: Oxford University Press, 2000); and W. Over, *Human Rights in the International Public Sphere: Civic Discourse for the 21st Century* (Samford, CN: Ablex Publishing Corporation, 1999).

11. See Houtondji, *supra* note 6.

12. For example, see C. Welch, Jr., *Protecting Human Rights in Africa: Roles and Strategies of Non-Governmental Organizations* (Philadelphia: University of Pennsylvania Press, 1995); M. Mutua, "The Politics of Human Rights: Beyond the Abolitionist Paradigm in Africa," *Michigan Journal of International Law* 17 (1996): 591; C.A. Odinkalu, "Human Rights Language" *supra* note 2; S. Ndegwa, *The Two Faces of Civil Society: NGOs and Politics in Africa* (Hartford, CN: Kumerian Press, 1996); S.B.O. Gutto, "Non-Governmental Organizations, People's Participation and the African Commission on Human and Peoples' Rights: Emerging Challenges to Regional Protection of Human Rights," in B. Andreassen and T. Swineheart, eds., *Human Rights in Developing Countries Yearbook 1991* (Oslo: Scandinavian University Press, 1992), 33; E. Osaghae, "The Role of Civil Society in Consolidating Democracy: An African Perspective," *African Insight* 27 (1997) 15; T. Shaw, "Popular Participation in Non-Governmental Structures in Africa: Implications for Democratic Development in Africa" *Africa Today* 37 (1990): 5; J. Ihonbvere, "A Critical Evaluation of Pro-Democracy Movements in Africa" *Journal of Asian and African Studies* 31 (1996): 125; S. Dicklitch, *The Elusive Promise of NGOs in Africa: Lessons From Uganda* (Houndmills, UK: Macmillan Press, 1998); and E. Sandberg, *The Changing Politics of Non-Governmental Organizations and African States* (Westport, CN: Praeger, 1994).

13. See M. Mutua, "Hope and Despair for a New South Africa: The Limits of Rights Discourse" *Harvard Human Rights Journal* 10 (1997): 63.

14. For example, see A. Ikelegbe, "The Perverse Manifestation of Civil Society: Evidence from Nigeria," *Journal of Modern African Studies* 39 (2001): 1; A. Ikelegbe, "Civil Society, Oil and Conflict in the Niger Delta Region of Nigeria: Ramifications of Civil Society for Regional Resource Struggle" *Journal of Modern African Studies* 39 (2001): 437; J. Ihonbvere and O. Vaughan, "Nigeria: Democracy and Civil Society: The Nigerian Transition Programme, 1985–1995" in J.A. Wiseman, ed., *Democracy and Political Change in Sub-Saharan Africa* (London: Routledge, 1995), 71-72; N. Kasfir, "Civil Society, the State and Democracy in Africa" Commonwealth and Comparative Politics 36 (1998): 123; Ndegwa, *supra* note 12; and Osaghae, *supra* note 12.

15. See Welch, *supra* note 12.

16. See P.O. Agbese, "The State versus Human Rights Advocates in Africa: The Case of Nigeria," in E. McCarthy-Arnolds, et al, eds., *Africa, Human Rights and the Global System: The Political Economy of Human Rights in a Changing World* (Westport, CN: Greenwood Press, 1994).

17. See T.M. Shaw, "Africa in the New World Order: Marginal and/or Central?" in A. Adedeji, ed., *Africa Within the World* (Ijebu Ode, Nigeria: ACDESS, 1993); M. Brunner and W. Sutinger, "Nigeria," in P. Baer, H. Hey, J. Smith, and T. Sineheart, eds. , *Human Rights in Developing Countries* (The Hague: Kluwer Law International, 1995); and Agbese, *supra* note 16.

18. See Swedish NGO Foundation and International Human Rights Internship Program, *Non-Governmental Organizations in Sub-Saharan Africa* (Stockholm and Washington, D.C., 1994).

19. See Chapter 6, infra.

20. See S. Dicklitch, "Action for Development in Uganda" in Welch. ed., *NGOs and Human Rights: Promise and Performance* (Philadelphia: University of Pennsylvania Press, 2001), 182.

CHAPTER 2

THRIVING UNDER FIRE:
THE ORIGINS, GENERAL CHARACTER, AND DEVELOPMENT OF THE HUMAN RIGHTS NGO COMMUNITY IN NIGERIA

1. INTRODUCTION

As Isa Chiroma has noted: "During the 1980's [the contemporary] non-governmental human rights movement developed in Nigeria....Due to the NGOs' activities, awareness and knowledge of human rights in the country is being monitored."[1] This emergence in the latter half of the 1980s of Nigeria's contemporary human rights NGO community is, in general, consistent with the broader trend on the rest of the African continent.

It must be emphasized however that the genealogy (even history) of human rights activism in Nigeria is several decades longer than that of the current phase of institutionalized human rights campaigns in that country. For instance, the 1929 Aba women's struggle against specific forms of colonial repression (otherwise referred to as the Aba women's revolt) was by any reasonable measure an exceedingly important human rights campaign.[2] It is only as a result of what Upendra Baxi has aptly referred to as "genesis amnesia"[3] that such anticolonial human rights struggles can be almost completely ignored in the mainstream accounts of the historical development of the international human rights movement. As such, the current institutionalized phase of human rights activism in Nigeria is only a part of an unbroken and continuous history of similar activist struggles that date back to precolonial times. The current phase of human rights activism in Nigeria did not emerge as a sudden volcanic eruption.

What is new, however, is the emergence within Nigeria of self-described human rights NGOs who have adopted the communicative symbols of the post-world war II human rights movement, namely: a particular version of the *language* of rights. As one important report on the status of human rights NGOs in Africa has concluded:

> Human rights activism in Africa is long-standing. For decades, concerned individuals, including lawyers, journalists, trade unionists and members of religious organizations, have monitored and reported upon human rights violations, often in the most hazard-

ous of circumstances. However, what is new for many African countries is …[the more recent emergence] of open and *self-professed* human rights organizations.[4]

As such, since the concern here is to understand these more contemporary activist groups, the focus of this book on the period between 1987 and 2001 is appropriate. Consequently, this chapter does not attempt to offer a complete account of the origins, general character, and development of human rights activism in Nigeria. What it does offer is an account of the latest phase of a long-standing and historically continuous struggle.

The main objectives of this chapter are twofold. The first is to show that the contemporary human rights NGO community in Nigeria[5] was, for the most part, founded and developed by an extremely resourceful and mostly urbanized group of *civil rights* activists who were also mostly lawyers; and then these NGOs were founded largely in response to the increasingly worsening state of human rights in Nigeria at the time (especially under the Ibrahim Babangida-led military junta that seized power in 1985). The second objective of the chapter is to highlight the broad purposes that have animated these groups and offer a sketch of the developmental path that this NGO community has traveled on the way to its present position within the Nigerian polity.

In an attempt to understand the origins, general character and development of this NGO community, this study relies on a classification of the NGOs that constitute this community which is founded on their varying substantive focus. The focus of these NGOs ranges from civil/political rights, through social/economic rights and women's rights, to minority/environmental rights. As such, I will treat those NGOs that I have found to be civil/political rights-centered as "civil/political rights NGOs," and so on.

2. THE ORIGINS, GENERAL CHARACTER, AND DEVELOPMENT OF CIVIL/POLITICAL RIGHTS NGOS IN NIGERIA

At the outset, the first generation of the NGOs that constitute this NGO community were entirely focused on the promotion and protection of the specific kinds of human rights norms that are usually referred to as "civil/political rights" (for example: freedom of expression, freedom of association, and the right to liberty and the security of the person). The concentration of these first generation NGOs on this narrow band of human rights is attributable to a number of factors. These factors include: the perception that the increasing abuse of civil rights under successive military regimes in Nigeria ought to be the priority of the struggle; the conceptual poverty of much conventional human rights philosophy at that time (which, at its best, relegated social/economic rights to second-class status); and the perceived pressure to conform to the broad agenda of the foreign donors that provided the vital funds that kept these NGOs afloat.

As importantly, many second- and third-generation NGOs have also adopted a similar focus. As such, this NGO community now constitutes of a large number of civil/political rights groups. From the Civil Liberties Organization (CLO) to the Constitutional Rights Project (CRP), from the Committee for the Defense of Human Rights (CDHR) to the Center for Law Enforcement Education (CLEEN), from Media Rights Agenda (MRA) to the Institute for Human Rights and Humanitarian Law (IHRHL), from Community Action for Popular Participation (CAPP) to the Human Rights Law Service (HURILAWS), and from Human Rights Monitor (HRM) to Human Rights Africa (HRA), these civil/political rights NGOs have, in the mode of traditional Western-based NGOs been mainly concerned with the documentation, publicity, and litigation of the violations of the civil/ political rights violations that were attributable to the various military and civilian regimes that ruled Nigeria between 1987 and 2001. As such, most of these groups have not focused on other human rights questions that squarely concern gender, minorities, social/economic rights, and the environment. It is for this reason that the groups treated in this section will be classified as civil and political rights NGOs.

In order to better understand the origins and development of these civil/political rights NGOs, a representative sample consisting of the eleven NGOs listed in the preceding paragraph will now be examined in some detail.

2.1. THE CIVIL LIBERTIES ORGANIZATION (CLO)

Founded in October 1987 by Olisa Agbakoba and Clement Nwankwo (both of whom are Lagos-based lawyers), the CLO is easily the oldest member of the extant NGO community.[6] It is also the most established and institutionalized of these NGOs. With its national headquarters in Lagos and with zonal offices spread across the entire country, it is also one of the largest such organizations in Nigeria.[7] While Olisa Agbakoba served as its first president, Clement Nwankwo was its founding secretary. Its current president is Ayo Obe, a well-known female human rights activist. Abdul Oroh, an activist journalist, served as its executive director between 1987 and 2002.[8] He is now an elected member of Nigeria's parliament.[9] Its current executive director is Ubani Chima, himself a former student leader and highly respected human rights activist.

According to Clement Nwankwo, who is now one of Nigeria's most notable human rights activists, the CLO was established in response to the declining state of human rights under the regime of General Ibrahim Babangida.[10] Another senior CLO activist has offered a similar account of that group's foundational impetus.[11] This activist has also noted that the "rights consciousness" of the CLO's founding members, the deplorable state of Nigerian prisons, and the assassination of Dele Giwa (an independent journalist of national renown) were important factors that shaped the conception and formation of the CLO.[12] Both accounts are supported by the findings of Bonny Ibhawoh's recent report on the work of Nigerian human rights NGOs.[13]

In any case, it is hardly surprising that the CLO was established during the Babangida regime, given that government's dictatorial character and orientation. For instance, despite its early profession of respect for human rights, that regime soon became notorious for the arrests and detentions of independent journalists and other vocal opponents of its policies, the promulgation of several draconian decrees, and the arbitrary cancellation of the results of the 12 June 1993 presidential election – widely regarded as the freest and fairest election in Nigerian history.[14]

The CLO's stated major purpose is the defense, and expansion of the scope of the *civil liberties* of all persons resident in Nigeria.[15] This humanist objective is pursued by the investigation of human rights abuses and the publication of reports of their findings. The CLO also engages in education, in public enlightenment campaigns, and in the use of the law courts to seek redress for persons whose rights have been violated.[16] The organizational objectives of the CLO are set out in its current Constitution, which came into force on the 10 December 1995. Since this is Nigeria's foremost human rights NGO, these objectives will be set out in their complete form as follows: [17]

- To promote the principles and practice of human rights in Nigeria as enshrined in the Constitution of the Federal Republic of Nigeria, and in accordance with the African Charter on Human and Peoples' Rights and the Universal Declaration of Human Rights

- To monitor the condition of human rights and civil liberties in Nigeria and to issue reports and bulletins thereon

- To monitor the extent of compliance with the principles of human rights in Nigeria by the government and its agencies and bodies, including the police and other security agents, the judiciary, prison authorities, and others.

- To publish books, magazines, periodicals, newspapers, pamphlets, and other materials on human rights

- To raise the level of human rights consciousness in Nigeria by organizing workshops, seminars, symposia, public talks, lectures, and other activities and by [issuing] publications

- To sponsor and/or support programs, and/or to support activities that have the aim of promoting or propagating human rights, democracy, and good government in Nigeria

- To promote and propagate the human rights of any disadvantaged class or group

- To raise funds and establish trust funds, and to receive donations or contributions for the protection and achievement of the objects of the organization

- To organize and provide legal assistance in respect of cases involving the abuse or violation of the human rights of any person
- To establish an institute to undertake research on human rights issues
- To cooperate with organizations within and outside Nigeria that profess objectives similar to those of the CLO in the defense and promotion of human rights, good government, democracy and a healthy environment.

Despite its liberal use of the broader term "human rights" to describe its objectives, it bears reemphasis at this stage that in both its conceptual orientation and in its practice, the CLO has, at least for most of its existence, generally focused on civil/political rights, mostly (though not entirely) to the exclusion of economic and social rights, etc. And although it now engages in some social/economic rights struggles, this aspect of its work remains comparatively less developed. A similar conclusion applies with respect to its work on gender issues and on minority/environmental rights. Most instructive in this connection is the very name and style that was assigned to it by its founders. Named the Civil Liberties Organization, this body was clearly conceived as an organization that would focus mainly on the promotion and protection of civil liberties. Even today, the bulk of its work, even when they relate to gender, ethnic minorities, and environment, is focused on the promotion and protection of civil/political rights.

Significantly, however, the CLO has now expanded its agenda to include previously neglected or deemphasized aspects of the human rights struggle. For instance, its 2000 Annual Report includes a column for its women's rights projects, as well as an entry for its Niger Delta monitoring project (a minority/environmental rights program).[18] However, of the fourteen or so entries on this list of the CLO's year 2000 projects, only one appears to deal squarely with social/economic rights issues.[19]

This situation should not surprise any serious observer of the Nigerian and international human rights scenes, as even the most established of the large Western human rights NGOs are indictable on the same score. Was it not as recently as the mid-1990s that Amnesty International and Human Rights Watch decided to end decades of their conceptual and practical exclusion of social/economic rights from their respective institutional agendas?[20] As such, the marginalization of the struggle for such rights in the CLO's activist agenda tends to reflect a broader global human rights context in which a traditional Liberal human rights ideology (that tended to accord second class status to social/economic rights) once reigned supreme. Moreover, the fact that this Liberal ideology of human rights dominates the thinking and broad agenda of the foreign donors that support the NGO community in Nigeria could not but have helped shape and cement the proclivity of these NGOs toward a concentration on the promotion and protection of civil/political rights. What is more, the CLO was born at a time when the struggle against military dictatorship and the interconnected campaign for democratic rights was beginning to assume an all-important position within Nigeria.[21]

As shall become clear in sections 3 - 6 of this chapter, it was in part the relative incompleteness of the CLO's agenda that inspired the formation of several other human rights NGOs devoted to social/economic rights, gender issues, and minority/ environmental rights. Indeed, it was former CLO staff who formed many of these younger NGOs. However, while the CLO's narrow focus on civil/political rights can explain (at least in part) the formation of separate and distinct platforms to advance struggles for other sub-categories of human rights – i.e., those other than civil/political rights – it hardly explains the proliferation of civil/political rights NGOs in Nigeria! In fact, civil/political rights NGOs constitute by far the most numerous subset within the extant NGO community. Their proliferation, and the consequent fragmentation of the Nigerian human rights movement, is explained in more detail in chapters three and seven, but suffice it to say that internal rivalries and competition related to power, position, resources, and sometimes principles have fueled the proliferation of this and other kinds of NGOs in Nigeria.[22] While proliferation is not in itself a negative feature of human rights NGO communities (for some desirable forms of specialization may in fact arise there from), it is very clear that but for what Upendra Baxi has aptly referred to as "market logic,"[23] it would not seem sensible in the Nigerian context to have dozens (even hundreds) of extremely small and more personalized human rights bodies that are mostly based in the same cities, pursue the same broad objectives, and compete for the same pool of resources. This phenomenon is even more worrisome when it is realized that many of the founders of the newer, smaller, and more personalized human rights bodies resigned from the CLO or one of the other groups in order to found "their own" group.[24]

We will now turn to an analytical consideration of the origins, general character, and development of other civil/political rights NGOs. This exercise begins with an examination of the Constitutional Rights Project, the oldest and most established of the organizations that were founded by former CLO activists.

2.2. THE CONSTITUTIONAL RIGHTS PROJECT (CRP)

The CRP was established in 1990 by Clement Nwankwo, himself a cofounder of the CLO.[25] Nwankwo served as the CRP's executive director for the twelve formative years of its existence between 1990 and 2002. He remains a member of the CRP's board of trustees. Its current executive director is Mr. Yinka Lawal – a long time CRP lawyer. Based in Lagos, and with offices in other parts of the country, the CRP is currently the second largest and most established human rights NGO in Nigeria, and is also second only to the CLO in terms of the scope of its national presence. The CRP has become one of Nigeria's most successful human rights NGOs.

It is not exactly clear why Nwankwo broke away from the CLO to found the CRP. Indeed, the very fact that he broke away from a successful organization that he cofounded is curious. What is more, both the CRP and the CLO have always had very similar objectives, and have always benefited from mostly the same broad pool of funding sources. Clearly, all could not have been well within the CLO at the time. This and similar issues will be dealt with in detail in chapter 3, but suffice it to mention that internal rivalries, dissatisfactions, and disagreements did contribute to the split that occurred in the CLO between Agbakoba and Nwankwo.[26] However, the split in the CLO that resulted in the formation of the CRP was not altogether worrisome as the worsening state of human rights under the then Babangida-led military junta ensured that there was at the time more than enough room and work for another major human rights group.[27]

The major objective of the CRP is to "promote respect for human rights and the rule of law in Nigeria."[28] In pursuing this objective, the CRP focuses on two main goals: "strengthening and promoting the independence of the judiciary and other democratic institutions in Nigeria" and "working towards ensuring that legislation affecting the rights and freedoms of Nigerians are in compliance with universal human rights standards."[29]

Just like its elder sibling—the CLO—the CRP is basically a civil/political rights NGO. As such, the comments already made about the CLO's historical (if evolving) emphasis on civil/political rights activism apply to the CRP as well. The explanations offered for the CLO's originally narrow substantive focus apply as well to the CRP. And like the CLO, the CRP has also evolved in the direction of taking other kinds of human rights issues a little more seriously. For instance, in 1999, the CRP investigated and published a report on the controversy around the operations of multinational oil companies in the Delta Region and the havoc their operations were wreaking on the environment.[30] Furthermore, as part of activities leading up to the Fourth World Conference on Women in China in 1995, the CRP organized a conference on the elimination of discrimination against Nigerian women.[31] Thus, although its work continues to reflect its civil liberties leanings, commendable efforts have been made to extend its reach (if not its grasp) to areas that were once ignored.

2.3. HUMAN RIGHTS AFRICA (HRA)

Tunji Abayomi, a prominent Lagos-based lawyer, founded the HRA in 1988.[32] It is one of the oldest and most well known of Nigeria's contemporary human rights NGOs. Yet it is also one of the least institutionalized of these bodies in terms of its organizational form. Like most of Nigeria's NGOs, HRA mainly functions from a relatively small office located in Lagos. It also has an office/library in Ota, near Lagos. However, unlike most other Nigerian NGOs, it describes itself as a continental human rights NGO based in Nigeria.[33] Thus, regardless of the extent of its actual grasp, HRA's geographical reach extends beyond Nigeria to the rest of the African continent, hence its name.

Like the CLO, the founders of HRA were motivated for the most part by the desire to curb significantly the abusive human rights climate that existed in Nigeria of the late 1980s. However, unlike other such NGOs, HRA chose to become what its founder has referred to as a "systematic value infuser." Such organizations seek to find ways of establishing channels of communication with the government in order to infuse human rights values within the regime. By contrast, "negative proclaimers" choose to adopt the strategy of highlighting and heralding the bad news about rights violations in the target country.[34] Indeed, Abayomi has, on this basis, explicitly distinguished HRA from the CLO and most other contemporary human rights NGOs that work in Nigeria.[35] Thus, in the view of its founder, the HRA was formed to fill a vacuum that existed in the praxis of the NGO community in Nigeria.

As would be expected, the content and orientation of HRA's organizational objectives were shaped by this motivating factor. The major purposes of HRA include support for the protection and preservation of human rights in Africa as established in the Universal Declaration of Human Rights, the African Charter of People's Rights, and the various rights provisions in the constitutions of the nations of Africa; and the sensitization of governments in Africa, where necessary and proper, in various ways deemed appropriate to the protection of the human rights of the peoples of Africa.[36] Other purposes that inspired the formation of the organization include serving as a link between African peoples and international bodies interested in the protection and preservation of human rights on the continent; educating Africans where necessary on their rights; and working with other Africans for the preservation of human dignity and respect for the human family on the continent.[37] Judged by its conceptual and practical orientation, HRA is a civil/political rights NGO. Its major focus has been the promotion and protection of this category of rights in Nigeria (and to a much lesser extent in other parts of Africa). The decision of HRA's founders to focus on this narrow band of rights is attributable to the same factors that shaped the CLO's original objectives and programs. These factors have already been discussed in section 2.1.

HRA's civil/political rights orientation has not altered to date. Like the other NGOs that are examined in this section of the chapter, HRA has continued to pursue its limited civil/political rights agenda without much expansion. As such gender, social/economic rights, and minority/environmental rights issues have not become as central to its work as they could be. For instance, a cursory look at its program outline for 1993 contains no planned activity/operation pertaining to environmental, women's or minority rights.[38] The same can be said for most of the more current versions of that document.

2.4. THE COMMITTEE FOR THE DEFENSE OF HUMAN RIGHTS (CDHR)

The CDHR was founded in 1989 by a group of activist intellectuals led by Femi Falana (a prominent, radical, Lagos-based lawyer) and Beko Ransome Kuti (an activist physician who has since left the CDHR to found and lead the Lagos-based Center for Constitutional Governance). Like most other such NGOs, the CDHR is based in Lagos. It is also one of the oldest human rights groups in the country. Its current president is Femi Falana.[39] Like HRA, the CDHR was not really an offshoot of the CLO—at least not in any direct way. While Falana and Ransome-Kuti may have collaborated with the CLO at one point or the other, they were never really employed by that organization.

Broadly speaking, the CDHR's roots are traceable, at least for the most part, to the groundswell of dissatisfaction with the poor human rights climate that was generated by the excesses of the Babangida military junta that ruled Nigeria at the relevant time of the CDHR's formation. More specifically, the all-too-frequent arrests and detentions of activist intellectuals and professionals by that military regime was direct impetus for the establishment of that NGO.[40] Another important reason adduced by the founders of the CDHR was their concern for the neglect and/or marginalization of social/economic rights issues in the praxis of virtually all the NGOs of this era.[41] As one of the brains behind that organization has put it:

> In 1989, one of our colleagues, Aborishade of NCP (National Conscience Party), was detained. At that time we were in the habit of forming ad hoc free-this-person-or-that-person-committee. We were forming one committee or another as a platform to mobilize and secure the release of detained activists or other persons. It was then felt that instead of forming ad hoc committees, a more permanent organization would be better and more appropriate to campaign for the freedom of detainees and also pay adequate attention to economic, social and cultural rights, which I felt was being neglected and marginalized. That was how we floated CDHR.[42]

The stated objectives of the CDHR include giving legal aid and assistance to poor victims of human rights violations, human rights education, campaigns (encompassing seminars, workshops, and publications), and actively promoting the restoration of genuine and popular democracy in Nigeria.[43] Although the CDHR has attempted to focus on both civil/political and social/economic rights issues, the former has featured much more prominently in its work.

As in the case of similar NGOs, this preponderance of civil/political rights activism in the CDHR's agenda can be partly explained by the global and local contexts in which it was formed. The reasons already offered with regard to the formation of the CLO apply here as well.

Nevertheless, given the dominant philosophical climate at the time of its birth, its status as a first-generation contemporary NGO, and the fact that the struggle against military dictatorship had at that time of its formation assumed priority status in the minds of most NGO-based human rights activists in Nigeria, it is remarkable that the CDHR did articulate social/economic rights activism as one important aspect of its agenda. However, even today, its gender-related and minority/environmental rights work has at best remained a minor aspect of its activist praxis. Its work in these areas has been limited to detailing the corruption that has characterized successive military governments, and highlighting the appalling state in which the public education system currently finds itself.[44] Only a small portion of its energies is therefore spent on promoting these other categories of rights.[45]

2.5. MEDIA RIGHTS AGENDA (MRA)

MRA was founded in 1993 by a group of activist professionals, journalists and lawyers, including Tive Donedo, Josephine Bamibele and Beko Ransome-Kuti [46] Like most other members of the NGO community in Nigeria, it is essentially a Lagos-based organization. Compared to other organizations such as the CLO and the CRP, the MRA is a young organization. Its current executive director is Edetaen Ojo.[47]

Like its older siblings, MRA was born in the context of sustained but increasingly rapacious military dictatorship in Nigeria. In particular, the founders of MRA were motivated by the desire to combat the determination of successive military regimes in Nigeria to harass and/or detain independent or opposing journalists, round up and seize copies of "offending" publications, close down independent newspaper houses, and curtail the freedom of information/expression in general.[48] While these kinds of human rights violations did not of course occur on a daily or weekly basis, they nevertheless occurred all too frequently.

The MRA is mainly dedicated to the creation of an ever more favorable climate in Nigeria for the effective practice of journalism as well as to the attainment of press freedom. Consequently, its major objectives are:

- To promote respect and recognition for freedom of expression for the press in Nigeria
- To provide protection and support for journalists and writers engaged in the lawful pursuit of their professional duties
- To promote the highest standards of professional ethics, integrity, training, and conduct in the journalism profession
- To bring about a conducive social and legal atmosphere for the practice of journalism in Nigeria and ensure the protection of the journalist's right not to be compelled to work against his or her conviction or disclose confidential sources of information[49]

As its objectives indicate, MRA is in the main a civil/political rights NGO. Its orientation toward civil/political rights activism is explained as well by the reasons already adduced with respect to the CLO, CRP, HRA and CDHR. However, MRA's civil/political rights activism is much more specialized than that of these other groups. As the word *media* in its name suggests, MRA's agenda and work focuses specifically on the media-related (civil/political) rights of journalists and of the general population of Nigeria. This is not to say that environmental activism or minority/women issues are entirely ignored in its work. Rather, the point is that MRA sees itself as mainly a media-focused organization. It is this medium that it utilizes as it strives to draw attention to environmental pollution, the abuse/oppression of minority groups, etc. What is done about the abuses/pollution it publicizes becomes less its concern.[50] In this sense then, although it seems to have benefited from the obvious advantages of specialization, MRA is not all that different from the more generalist NGOs (such as the CLO, the CRP, HRA, and CDHR). After all, do not these generalist NGOs also work to promote and protect media rights as part of their more generalist civil/political rights vocation?[51]

2.6. CENTER FOR LAW ENFORCEMENT EDUCATION (CLEEN)

CLEEN was founded in 1998 by Innocent Chukwuma (formerly a senior staff of the CLO).[52] It is thus one of the many NGOs that in effect broke away from the CLO. Like its elder siblings, CLEEN is based in Lagos. But quite unlike the CLO, it remains a small, noninstitutionalized, and highly specialized human rights body. Chukwuma continues to serve as its executive director.

Like virtually all its peers, the impetus for CLEEN's formation is in part attributable to the deplorable state of human rights in Nigeria under the military regimes of the 1980s and 1990s. However, as a "breakaway" NGO (in the sense of it being founded by a former CLO staff) at least some of the factors that have contributed to fragmentation within Nigeria's indigenous human rights NGO community also played a role in the formation of CLEEN. The desire of its founder to work in an NGO devoted solely to promoting the accountability of law enforcement officers and the strengthening of police-community relations is also cited as another reason for its formation.[53]

CLEEN's *raison d'être* is the planning and execution of human rights education programs for law enforcement personnel that assist "in reorienting their attitude and world view regarding their profession."[54] Its major objectives are:[55]

- To enhance the awareness of law enforcement agencies in Nigeria on the changing trends in law enforcement with regard to the liberties of individual members of the society (men, women and children)
- To promote cooperation between civil society and law enforcement agencies in the lawful discharge of their duties
- To encourage the use of alternatives to detention measures in dealing with juvenile suspects or offenders

Clearly, CLEEN is a civil/political rights NGO—at least in the sense that its agenda is vastly oriented in the direction of the promotion and protection of such rights through the medium of "law enforcement education." This NGO has not treated social/economic rights, and minority/environmental rights activism as its central concern. Its rather narrow civil/political rights orientation is also attributable, at least for the most part, to the factors already discussed in sections 2.1-2.5 above. However, having been born at a time when the dominant human rights ideology had begun a reversal of its historic neglect of social/economic rights, i.e., when the language of "indivisibility" had begun to gain currency, the relative marginalization of social/economic rights in CLEEN's agenda is slightly more surprising. This is not to suggest, however, that this NGO has not at all dealt with questions related to these other human rights issues. It has in fact sought to mainstream gender–sensitivity in its programs and activities. For instance, CLEEN is championing a campaign to abrogate some police regulations that discriminate against women in the police force. As it has noted:

> .... these discriminatory laws and practices violate Nigeria's obligations under international human rights law. For instance the police regulations that prevents women from getting married until two years of service and denial of special privileges to the married ones in recognition of their roles in family life, violates the International Covenant on Civil and Political Rights (ICCPR) which was ratified by Nigeria in 1993."[56]

In the end though, CLEEN was conceived of, and has continued to operate, mainly as a specialized civil/political rights NGO. Even when it has focused on gender issues it has almost always done so in terms of the promotion and protection of the relevant civil/political rights norms.

2.7. PRISONERS' REHABILITATION AND WELFARE ACTION (PRAWA)

Uju Agomoh, its founding and current executive director, established PRAWA in 1994.[57] Unlike most of the founders of the other major NGOs, Agomoh is female and has little or no formal legal training. She is, however, a very well educated social scientist. Nevertheless, though it runs an office in Enugu—the old capital city of the defunct Eastern region of Nigeria— PRAWA is much like other Nigerian NGOs in terms of being headquartered in Lagos.[58]

Again, while the establishment of PRAWA was definitely inspired by the broader social context that existed in Nigeria at the time, its more specific foundational impetus was the deplorable state of Nigeria's prisons.[59]

Its major objectives are (i) to promote and protect the human rights of prisoners and those persons that have survived their prison terms, and (ii) to help them reintegrate into the society.[60] PRAWA has carried out this task through:

- Training prison officers and other criminal justice agents on human rights and good practices
- Policy advocacy
- Research
- Public awareness campaigns
- Providing prison/community based-support services for target groups[61]

As its name suggests, and as its objectives reveal, it is a very specialized human rights NGO that is focused not only on the rights, but also the welfare of prisoners. Given its interest in the welfare of prisoners, PRAWA cannot be easily classified as a civil/political rights NGO that marginalizes social/economic rights activism. However, it has been classified as such because, as a detailed examination of its actual work and orientation suggests, commendable as its integrated focus on both civil/political and social/economic rights is, its civil/political rights activism nevertheless dominates (however slightly) its social/economic rights work. Thus, while PRAWA has not imagined itself or functioned as a classic civil/political rights NGO, for the purposes of this study, and for the reason already adduced, it does make sense to deal with it under this heading.

PRAWA's social/economic rights work has mainly related to the provision of valuable services such as free psychological, legal and social counseling, and job skills to prisoners and former prisoners.[62] This has, as it should, become an important part of its agenda and work. However, and quite understandably, being a highly specialized NGO, PRAWA's work has not been primarily devoted to gender-related or ethnic/minority rights-based activism. While it has of course not ignored gender issues altogether in the course of its work on prisoner's rights and welfare,[63] this has clearly not formed the principal focus of its agenda in the same way in which gender-related activism has formed the mainstay of the work of some other NGOs such as Baobab for Women's Rights (BAOBAB) and the Women's Aid Collective (WACOL).

2.8. THE HUMAN RIGHTS LAW SERVICE (HURILAWS)

HURILAWS was established in 1997. Although Mr. Olisa Agbakoba, (a prominent Lagos-based lawyer, human rights activist, and first president of the CLO) is widely regarded as the founder and principal agent behind the formation of HURILAWS, some of the credit for its formation is attributable to his staff lawyers.[64] This NGO operates out of a relatively small office in the Apapa area of Lagos.[65] Agbakoba has continued to serve as its senior counsel/CEO.[66] Prominent, although younger, Nigerian human rights lawyers such as Mr. Ndubuisi Obiorah and Mr. Sam Amadi have at one time or the other served as its key counsel.[67] Its current executive director and chief operations officer is Frances Ogwo, one of a minority of female top officers of mainstream human rights NGOs in Nigeria.[68] A relatively young, if already accomplished, organization, HURILAWS can to some extent be described as an offshoot of the CLO. Its founder and leader, as well as many of its staff have, at one point or another, been associated in some way with the CLO.

Aside from the obvious impetus given to its formation by the booming "market"[69] for human rights "products" generated by the poor human rights climate under successive military regimes in Nigeria (especially under the notorious Abacha regime) as well as by the readier availability of foreign funding for the execution of its programs, three other major factors seem to have led to the establishment of HURILAWS as a separate and distinct entity from the CLO, the "parent" group to which its founder belonged. The first relates to the coincidence of the creation of HURILAWS and the expiration of Agbakoba's term as the president of the CLO. It is noteworthy that HURILAWS was not established until Agbakoba had ceased to function as President of the CLO. Having left that office, Agbakoba was now free to take up the time-consuming task of creating and leading another organization. The second relates to his desire for autonomy. This is inferable from the very move to create yet another human rights organization instead of continuing to work within the more established structures of the CLO. This desire for autonomy is also inferable from the fact that HURILAWS is not a membership organization and is much less institutionalized than the CLO, leaving Agbakoba with almost complete control of its governance. Finally, he astutely identified a significant gap in the conception and execution of human rights activism in Nigeria. HURILAWS was thus intended to be a litigation and legislative advocacy-focused human rights law service NGO that applies its specialist expertise—in mounting court challenges and in influencing legislation—to the aid of other NGOs and the larger public. In fact, this is the official reason offered by HURILAWS for its establishment.[70]

Even though HURILAWS is devoted to the litigation of human rights claims and the exertion of influence over the legislative process, it has over time morphed into a more generalist NGO that is no longer easily distinguishable from its peers such as the CLO and the CRP. In its own words, its major objectives are:

- Establishing human rights legal standards and advancing the application of human rights norms through high-impact test cases
- Promoting legal and judicial reform through legislative advocacy
- Providing legal assistance to disadvantaged persons, communities and groups
- Advancing the application of international legal instruments on human rights in Nigerian law
- Advancing the application of social and economic rights in Nigerian law through legislative advocacy and constitutional litigation
- Facilitating collaboration with national and international NGOs to promote good governance through law in Africa
- Undertaking any other programs, activities, and initiatives that would secure and enhance the above objectives[71]

When these objectives are considered alongside the nature of its actual programs, now stretching from litigation, through monitoring and research, to working for the creation of specialized human rights commissions, the increasingly more general character of this NGO becomes clear. This fact will become even clearer when its programs are considered in detail in chapter 4 as part of the discussion of the typology and programs of the NGO community in Nigeria.

As importantly, the nature of the vast majority of its objectives and projects betrays its basic civil/political rights orientation. Although its objectives clearly mention its intention to pursue social/economic rights activism, its actual practice in this area has been sparse. While it has not totally ignored gender issues and minority/environmental rights, these have neither been the focus of its agenda nor formed the mainstay of its programs. A good example of its nontraditional or non–civil/political rights-based activist work is its efforts toward the protection of children, the provision of more effective social security for the elderly, and the creation of a specialized gender equality commission within the Nigerian government. In its own words:

> HURILAWS is promoting the enactment of legislation for the establishment of a Commission on Gender Equality to promote gender equality and advance women's human rights in Nigeria. The CGE will be responsible for monitoring the level of compliance in the public and private sectors to achieve gender equality. The CGE will also lobby government to enact legislation to prohibit the abuse of women and children and penalizing such abuse with appropriate sanctions. Widening the social safety net for elderly pensioners by introducing inflation-index pension adjustments[72]

In the end, though, the orientation of this body has tended to reflect the traditional civil/political rights emphasis of most member units of the broader Nigerian and international human rights movement.

2.9. COMMUNITY ACTION FOR POPULAR PARTICIPATION (CAPP)

CAPP was founded in 1993 by a group of activists led by Mr. Emma Ezeazu.[73] Unlike most of its peers, CAPP is headquartered in Abuja, Nigeria's administrative capital. Ezeazu himself has roots in the CLO. Until recently Ezeazu served as CAPP's executive director.[74] Its current executive director is Mr. Clement Wasah.

The reasons for the formation of CAPP are not dissimilar from those that led to the formation of the CLO and many of the other NGOs discussed thus far. In this particular case, an added impetus was the desire to form a specialized NGO that would emphasize popular or grassroots participation in Nigeria's governance.[75] As CAPP itself has affirmed:

> As a community development and democracy project, the CAPP has been concerned with the development of necessary structures

for grassroots and community participation in the political processes of Nigeria. *A central plank of the engagement of the organization
revolves around popular empowerment education.* The objective of the
involvement is to ensure that for them [i.e., the masses] to be
masters of their destiny they must play active part in the political
process in the country.[76]

While some other groups have sporadically done similar work, none of
these other NGOs had either become specialized in such work or carried it
on in a sustained way. In this sense the establishment of CAPP did fill a significant gap. In addition, since relatively few NGOs are based in the Northern
regions of Nigeria, choosing Abuja as its headquarters did set CAPP apart
from most of its peers in terms of the main geographical focus of its work.

Yet CAPP is very much like most of its peers in at least one sense.
At its core, it is a civil/political rights NGO. Its major focus has not been
social/economic rights. And while it has not been inattentive to gender questions and issues, the promotion and protection of women's rights has not
to date been the corner stone of its activist vocation. Similarly, while it has
not neglected the question of minority/environmental rights, the promotion
and protection of these kinds of rights has not its way into its main agenda.
According to its own documentation, the major purposes of CAPP are the:

- Development and enhancement of popular structures at the community
  levels to ensure the right of the people to take part in the government of
  their country
- Promotion of democratic norms and human rights at the community
  level to ensure that the will of the people shall be the basis of authority
  of government
- Encouragement of the poor and powerless to take part in the government of their communities and country
- Promotion of community and grassroots perspective in national devel-
  opment policies
- Promotion of dialogue, understanding, and collaboration across com-
  munities to eliminate intercommunal violence and hatred
- Promotion of women's participation in local government
- Campaign against corruption and abuse of office at the community and
  local government level
- Monitor the implementation of people's projects at the grassroots level
- Provision of legal aid
- Campaign against degradation of community environment[77]

The nature of its objectives buttresses the arguments made above regarding
its classification as in the main a civil/political rights NGO.

2.10. HUMAN RIGHTS MONITOR (HRM)

HRM was founded in 1992 by a group of activists led by Festus Okoye, a prominent lawyer and former head of the CLO's Northern Office in Kaduna.[78] It is one of the few major human rights NGOs that are based in Nigeria's Northern states. It is also one of the so-called breakaway NGOs that were in effect founded by former CLO activists.

Although the factors that led to the formation of HRM are not entirely different from those already discussed with respect to the other NGOs, one distinguishing factor deserves mentioning. This is the relative dearth of such NGOs in the Northern states of Nigeria. While HRM's offices are in Kaduna (the former capital of the defunct Northern region), the vast majority of the kind of NGOs that are of interest in this study are located in and around Lagos.

HRM's stated objectives are :

- To defend freedom of thought and expression, due process, and equal protection under the law
- To provide free legal assistance to indigent victims of domestic violence
- To educate labor unions, student unions, and professional bodies on the laws governing their trades and professions
- To empower Nigerian citizens to understand and defend their fundamental rights
- To lobby and campaign for the promulgation of human rights and people–oriented legislation
- To promote the principles of accountability and transparency in the public and private sectors of the society
- engage in programs that will strengthen the legal system and guarantee a free and independent judiciary and other democratic institutions
- investigate human rights abuses and issue reports on human rights situations especially on women, children, the Area Courts, the Police and other paramilitary organs and institutions[79]

As these objectives indicate, HRM's work is, for the most part, oriented toward the promotion and protection of civil/political rights. Like most other NGOs of its kind, its main focus has not been the advancement of either social/economic rights or minority/environmental rights claims.

2.11. THE INSTITUTE FOR HUMAN RIGHTS AND HUMANITARIAN LAW (IHRHL)

A former CLO operative, Mr. Anyakwe Nsirimovu, founded this organization in 1988.[80] Unlike the vast majority of such NGOs, the IHRHL is based in Port Harcourt (the capital city of Rivers State, a coastal southeastern state). The factors that led to its formation are similar to those of other groups discussed earlier. It should be noted however that at the very beginning Anyakwe Nsirimovu had to fund the organization with his own personal resources.[81] However, Anyakwe Nsirimovu's desire to create an organization different from the others in terms of its concentration on research, makes the IHRHL's substantive focus slightly different (at least in theory) from those of its peers in the NGO community in Nigeria.

In addition, the IHRHL's explicit inclusion of the promotion and protection of *humanitarian law* as a major part of its agenda makes it distinguishable from other NGOs. Its goal of advancing respect for human rights in Nigeria is pursued through "structural human rights education, research, documentation and public interest advocacy."[82] All in all though, it is clear from the manner in which it has been described above that like most NGOs in Nigeria, the IHRHL remains civil/political rights-centered in its orientation. It has also ventured into the area of minority/environmental rights. But for the most part, gender issues have not formed the core of its concerns. Neither have minority/environmental rights really been its main focus. It is in this sense then that it does make sense to categorize the IHRHL as in the main a civil/political rights NGO.

2.12. AN OVERVIEW OF THE ORIGINS, GENERAL CHARACTER AND DEVELOPMENT OF CIVIL/POLITICAL RIGHTS NGOS IN NIGERIA:

Overall, the history of this generation of civil/political rights NGOs in Nigeria dates back to the birth of the CLO in 1987. From that date onwards, and through the 1990s, several other similar groups were formed to prosecute very similar objectives. These NGOs tended to be founded by a generation of young, male, indigenous, activist lawyers.[83] These activists (and the NGOs they founded) were almost always based in Lagos, Nigeria's largest city and economic capital. Remarkably, former CLO staff established the majority of the younger civil/political rights NGOs. The major factor that led to the establishment of most of the older NGOs was the worsening status of human rights under the successive Nigerian military regimes. This was certainly the major factor in the formation of the CLO. However, a key impetus for the formation of the younger NGOs tended to be the booming market[84] for human rights products that had been generated by the poor human rights climate under successive military regimes in Nigeria, especially under the notorious Abacha regime, and which had been fueled in part by the readier availability of the foreign funding that they sought in order to execute their programs. As with all other human institutions, other factors such as internal rivalries, disagreements, disappointments, and the changing post-cold war international climate, contributed to the establishment and proliferation of these NGOs. As their categorization as civil/political rights NGOs suggests, each of these organizations tended to focus much more on the actualization of these subset of rights than on other kinds of human rights. The relative narrowness of the substantive focus of these kinds of NGOs is attributable to a number of factors such as the perceived need to tackle as a priority the ills of military rule, the neglect of social/economic rights by the dominant ideologies of human rights,[85] and the perceived need to conform to the substantive agendas of the donors on whom these NGOs relied so heavily for their financial survival. Happily, most such NGOs have, over time, evolved to focus and take on the task of promoting and protecting a fuller complement of human rights.

The next sub-section focuses on a consideration of the origins and development of the next subgroup of human rights NGOs—those that I refer to as "social/economic rights NGOs". Subsequent sections of this chapter will be devoted to the consideration of similar issues related to the gender-focused and the minority/environmental rights NGOs.

3. THE ORIGINS, GENERAL CHARACTER AND DEVELOPMENT OF SOCIAL/ECONOMIC RIGHTS NGOS IN NIGERIA

Very few of the entities that constitute the NGO community in Nigeria can be accurately described as social/economic rights NGOs (in the sense that they regard social/economic rights activism as central to their praxis). Yet, as small as their number is virtually none of these socioeconomic rights NGOs was established until fairly recently. The later emergence of such groups on the Nigerian human rights scene is not at all surprising, given the historical marginalization of social/economic rights within the global and local human rights praxis.[86] This is not of course to suggest that the many other kinds of organizations that have fought for the kinds of values and norms that would today be regarded as social/economic rights claims are all that new to the Nigerian socio-political scene. Hundreds of such organizations dot, and have always dotted, the Nigerian sociopolitical landscape. Most such groups antedate the self-described human rights NGOs. However, from the mid-1990s or so, Nigerians witnessed the advent of self-described socioeconomic rights NGOs that employed the dominant global language of rights.

Not surprisingly, these emergent NGOs set themselves up as *partial* alternatives to the mainstream civil/political rights NGOs that had hitherto tended to marginalize social/economic rights activism. While they were as interested in the struggle against the military dictatorships of that era, they were at the very least as interested in ameliorating the serious denials of social/economic rights that occurred in the country. The Socio-economic Rights Initiative (SRI), the Social and Economic Rights Action Center (SERAC), and the Empowerment and Action Research Centre (EMPARC), are the principal members of this subset of Nigerian human rights NGOs. As their names suggests, the work of these bodies is mainly oriented in the direction of social/economic rights activism.

Sections 3.1–3.3 below explore the origins, general character and development of each of these NGOs.

3.1. THE SOCIO-ECONOMIC RIGHTS INITIATIVE [FORMERLY THE SHELTER RIGHTS INITIATIVE] (SRI)

The SRI was founded in 1995 by Eze Onyekpere (a lawyer and former member of the CLO's staff), Ray Onyegu (a Lagos based lawyer), and Dr. Dom Okoro (a social scientist).[87] All three activists continue to serve as its executive directors.[88] The SRI, which operates from a single but large office in the Surulere area of Lagos, is one of the new breed of self-professed human rights groups in Nigeria. Like many other such NGOs, the SRI has substantial roots in the CLO. But unlike most of its peers, the SRI was conceived as an organization that will help plug what at the time was one of the most obvious gaps in the conceptual and practical orientation of the NGO community in Nigeria, namely, the relative neglect of social/economic rights activism.[89] The SRI itself claims that its formation was a response to the "fact that human rights work in Nigeria concentrated on civil and political liberties to the neglect of economic, social and cultural rights. A lacuna existed in the socio-economic rights sector, which SRI set out to fill."[90] Accordingly, the conceptual dissatisfaction of its founders with the blind spots within the NGO community in Nigeria partly explains the impetus for the formation of the SRI. As has already been shown in section 2 of this chapter, the agenda and programs of the CLO and of many other NGOS have to this day maintained a highly significant civil/political rights bias. It was the urgent need to help redress this lopsidedness in the activist agenda of this NGO community that in part motivated the SRI's founders. Other obvious reasons include the need for an autonomous vehicle with which to pursue their different vision of human rights activism (hence the formation of a separate organization); and some level of personal dissatisfaction with their lot within their previous workplaces—hence their choice not to pursue their socio-economic rights activism within their former organizations. The repressive atmosphere created by very long periods of military rule in Nigeria and the availability (even if initially in trickles) of some foreign funding for their work cannot also be ruled out as important factors that shaped the decision of these activists to found the SRI.

The SRI's main objective is the promotion of due process and basic standards with regard to economic, social, and cultural (ESC) rights claims. It claims to recognize the "indivisibility of all human rights and fundamental freedoms" and thus "sets out to achieve its objects through advocacy, action research, investigation and reports on rights abuses."[91]

Since its formation (and despite an international conceptual and funding context that was relatively biased against social/economic rights activism) the SRI has remained faithful to its specialized objectives and has not departed from its dedication to the cause of social/economic rights. As shall be made clear in subsequent chapters, the Nigerian human rights scene has been the richer for it.

3.2. THE SOCIAL AND ECONOMIC RIGHTS ACTION CENTRE (SERAC)

The SERAC was founded in 1995 by a group of activist lawyers led by Felix Morka (a former staff of the CLO). Morka, who is currently a doctoral student at Harvard Law School, had returned from a stint as an LL.M. student at the same law school in order to found this organization. The SERAC operates out of a single but relatively large office in the Ilupeju area of Lagos, but maintains a U.S. liaison office. Unlike the vast majority of other human rights NGOs, the SERAC's founders were concerned by the continued neglect that social/economic rights activism had suffered at the hands of both Nigerian and foreign human rights groups, and the serious problems that could be attributed to this marginalization of socioeconomic rights. The formation of the SERAC was thus a practical move to help ameliorate this undesirable situation. Thus, a major impetus for the creation of the SERAC was this dissatisfaction with the conceptual underpinnings and programs of most NGOs in the country. Other obvious factors that shaped the decision to form that organization were the serious abuses committed by Nigeria's successive military rulers, the organization's ability to secure some foreign funding for its work (however meager it was in the beginning), the perceived need on the part of its founders for an autonomous activist platform, and Morka's obvious felt need to depart from his job at the CLO.

The SERAC has as its main objective the promotion and protection of social and economic rights in Nigeria. It pursues this objective by researching, monitoring and documenting Nigeria's social and economic rights situation, and by providing "legal assistance to individuals or groups seeking to assert their social and economic rights" and also by "litigating in the public interest."[92] In addition:

> The organization seeks to expand access to and enhance individual's and communities' participation in the design and implementation of social and economic policies and programs which affect them....the promotion of the rights of marginalized sectors of the population (e.g., women, children, the aged, ethnic minorities, people living with HIV/AIDS, and persons with disabilities) to be treated based on the principles of non-discrimination and equality.[93]

Like the SRI, SERAC has since its establishment weathered successfully the negative storms related to a local and international environment that has been more or less hostile to social/economic rights activism. In so doing, it has remained true to its chosen vocation and greatly enriched the Nigerian human rights scene.

3.3. THE EMPOWERMENT AND ACTION RESEARCH CENTER (EMPARC):

This NGO was founded in 1992 by a group of activists led by Ms. Adetoun Ilumoka (a former law teacher at the University of Jos, Nigeria).[94] The EMPARC is run from a main office located in the Isolo area of Lagos but also operates a resource center near Ibeju-Lekki, a suburb of Lagos. Unlike most such NGOs, the EMPARC's leadership did not break away from the CLO or from any of the older groups. The EMPARC is also unlike most Nigerian NGOs in at least one other sense; its leadership is female. However, like most of its peers, its leader is a lawyer. Interestingly though, the legal background of its leader has not translated into an excessively legalistic conception of its activist vocation. In fact, the EMPARC emphasizes nonlegalistic paths toward the empowerment of Nigerians.

As might therefore be expected, an important motivation for the formation of the EMPARC was the dissatisfaction of its leaders with the much more legalistic, much more rightscentric approach that remains customary within the extant NGO community in Nigeria.[95] Another was the obvious neglect during the relevant period of social/economic rights issues within this community.[96] As well, the excesses of successive military dictatorships, including the abuse of the public treasury by government officials and their cronies, contributed significantly to the decision to found the EMPARC.[97]

The EMPARC is thus "dedicated to empowering groups and communities to improve their living conditions and to participate actively in the making and implementation of policies affecting their lives."[98] This is so especially as regards "health and social justice issues."[99] It seeks to fulfill this mission through what it describes as "action research" and through training and advocacy campaigns.[100]

While the EMPARC has continued to function effectively since it was founded, and while it has remained true to its objectives, its operations have now been scaled down.[101] This descaling of its operations is linked to the increasing sense of dissatisfaction among its leaders with the level of progress that the NGO community has so far made.[102] As shall be made clear in subsequent chapters of this book, there is an increasing sense of dissatisfaction among many politically educated activists with the standard modes in which human rights activism has proceeded in Nigeria. From the formation of specialized social/economic rights NGOs, through the descaling of operations by the EMPARC, to the attempt by many senior activists to seek elective office, a trend is beginning to emerge—one that may or may not be sustained—but one that reveals varying levels of unease with the current state of NGO-driven human rights activism in Nigeria.

4. THE ORIGINS, GENERAL CHARACTER, AND DEVELOPMENT OF WOMEN'S RIGHTS NGOS IN NIGERIA

Relatively few members of the NGO community in Nigeria can be accurately described as "women's rights NGOs," i.e., in the sense that they regard women's rights activism as the main focus of their praxis. While the genealogy of women's activism in Nigeria is a long and rich one (dating as far back as the Aba women's revolt of 1929 and even earlier), the formation of *institutionalized* women's NGOs in the country has a shorter history.[103] It was not until 1958 that the first such NGO, the National Council of Women's Societies (NCWS), was formed.[104] What is more, the operational history of the self-professed women's human rights NGOs that speak and deploy the language of rights, and that are modeled on groups like CLO and Amnesty International, is even shorter. Though the establishment of the CLO back in 1987 heralded the birth of the extant NGO community in Nigeria, most such NGOs have been lax in adopting gender-based activism as one of their central or major objectives. As such, a gap has existed in the matrix of human rights activism in Nigeria, one that the older and more established groups had initially sought to fill by setting up their own in-house women's rights projects. However, this gap was more adequately plugged by the establishment of a number of specialized women's rights NGOs such as Boabab for Women's Rights (BOABAB), the Women's Aid Collective (WACOL), and the Women's Rights Advancement and Protection Alternative (WRAPA). Given the dominance of the Nigerian human rights scene by male activists, and by the NGOs founded by these male activists, the more recent emergence of these women's rights NGOs groups is not at all surprising.

While many more of them exist,[105] this section deals with the origins, general character, and development of a regionally representative sample of the indigenous women's rights NGOs that operate in Nigeria: BAOBAB (based in Lagos), WACOL (based in Enugu), and WRAPA (based in Abuja).

4.1. BAOBAB FOR WOMEN'S HUMAN RIGHTS (BAOBAB)

BAOBAB was founded in 1996 by a group of female human rights activists led by the late Hajira Usman and Ayesha Imam (a women's rights scholar and the 2002 winner of the John Humphrey Human Rights Prize awarded by the Montreal-based International Center for Human Rights and Democratic Development).[106] Though headquartered in Lagos, BOABAB operates a network of outreach groups and centers around the country, making it one of the few really nationwide human rights NGOs in Nigeria.[107] While Ayesha Imam served as its first executive director, its current executive director is Sindi Meda-Gould.[108] Unlike most Nigerian human rights groups, BAOBAB is not an offshoot of the CLO or any other older human rights NGO. Though one or two of its cadres may have been employed at the CLO, most of its founders or leaders do not have deep roots in that organization.

BAOBAB grew out of a research project on the status of women's human rights in Muslim-majority countries around the world in which several Nigerian women participated.[109] At the end of that project, Imam and Usman decided to establish BAOBAB to advance the status of women's rights all over Nigeria (and not just in Nigeria's Moslem-dominated states).[110] As such, the core motivation for BOAOBAB was neither the struggle against military dictatorship (as was the case with many civil/political rights NGOs) nor the historic neglect of social/economic rights (as was the case with the social/economic rights NGOs). While these factors could not but have featured in the consciousness of the activists who came together to found this group they were not the main reasons for this organization's inception. Rather, BAOBAB's founders were largely motivated by a desire to advance the status of women in Nigeria. While BAOBAB's specialized activist agenda does of course entail and involve working for the advancement of civil/political and social/economic rights, it is on the rights of women that it focuses. In addition, it is also clear that the availability of some foreign funding for its programs and the increasing gender sensitivity of these donors played a role in the decision to set up this NGO. Dependent as they are on foreign funding (see chapter 5) it would have been impractical to assume the huge staffing and infrastructural costs of setting up a new organization without some assurance of the probability of securing vital funding. And such funding was hardly available from domestic sources. This much is made clear in chapter 5.

As part of its objectives, BOABAB works (a) to promote and protect the rights of women throughout Nigeria, (b) to create awareness on gender perspectives, (c) to conduct research on reproductive and sexual rights education in the country, (d) to raise the status of women through socioeconomic empowerment, and (e) to combat, and educate women on, sexually transmitted diseases such as HIV/AIDS. [111]

To this day, BAOBAB has remained true to its specialist vocation and has concentrated on working toward the advancement of the rights of all Nigerian women. Yet, while its work has aimed at the entire country and has in fact affected parts of it, BAOBAB has now gained international renown for its courageous work in defense of women's rights in the ten or so so-called "sharia states" located in the Northern portion of Nigeria.[112]

4.2. WOMEN'S AID COLLECTIVE (WACOL)

WACOL was established in 1997–1998 by Joy Ezeilo.[113] A law teacher, women's rights activist, and key participant at Nigeria's 2005 political reform conference, Ezeilo possesses deep roots in the broader women's movement in Nigeria. She also serves as WACOL's executive director/CEO.[114] WACOL is registered with the Nigerian Corporate Affairs Commission as a non-profit organization, and with the Nigerian Federal Ministry of Justice as a charity.[115] Unlike most Nigerian human rights groups, WACOL is not a Lagos-based outfit. Rather, it is based in Enugu, a major Eastern Nigerian city, and maintains a branch office in Abuja, and another in Port Harcourt, another major

Eastern Nigerian city.[116] Like BAOBAB, it is not an offshoot of the CLO in any meaningful sense. It is therefore, in this respect, quite unlike most other such NGOs. It is better described as an offshoot of an organization known as Women in Nigeria (WIN), to which its founder belonged in the period immediately before WACOL's inception. Like BAOBAB, it was founded and has always been dominated by female activists.

As it was with BAOBAB, the founders of WACOL were less motivated by the general struggle against military dictatorship (the focus of the civil/political rights NGOs) than they were inspired by the need to advance women and children's rights.[117] Similarly, their major motivation was not a concern for redressing the historic neglect of social/economic rights (the focus of the social/economic rights groups). Of course, neither factor can be dismissed as entirely irrelevant to WACOL's formation.[118] The point, however, is that the major impetus for the formation of this specialized body was the perceived inadequacy in the broad conceptual orientation of the rest of the NGO community in Nigeria, which had tended to suffer from what might be styled "a gender deficit."[119] Additionally, as with BAOBAB, it seems clear enough that its ability to attract funding from foreign donors and the trend toward gender sensitivity in the work of such donors played an important role in shaping the decision to establish this NGO.[120] In WACOL's case, seed money from the MacArthur Foundation's office in Nigeria greatly facilitated the realization of the dream of its founder to establish an effective women's right group.[121] And as will be clear in chapter 5, such funding was not as readily available from local sources.

WACOL is governed by the vision of a society free from violence and abuse, where sexual and reproductive health rights of women and adolescents are recognized in law and in practice.[122] It sees its mission as helping women and adolescents in need and working towards gender equality and human rights for all citizens of Nigeria.[123] It employs the following strategies, among others, to carry out its mission:

- Advocating for the reproductive health rights of women and adolescents
- Providing legal advice and other support services to women and children and victims of human rights abuses
- Providing shelters /safe homes where abused women can stay on short term basis, particularly at peak crises periods
- Research on human rights, sexual and reproductive health rights of women and adolescents in particular
- Facilitating community participation in designing and implementing effective and meaningful strategies that will protect women and adolescents from rape, sexual abuse and exploitation, unwanted pregnancies, early marriages, STDS/HIV/AIDS, and gender discrimination
- Lobbying for women's issues, particularly for legislative changes and the enforcement of legal and police protection[124]

During its young life, WACOL has remained steadfast in its commitment to women's rights advocacy, and has thus maintained its specialized focus. Of recent, its work on reproductive rights has assumed centre stage. It remains to be seen, however, how, and in what directions, it will develop in the years to come.

4.3. WOMEN'S RIGHTS ADVANCEMENT AND PROTECTION ALTERNATIVE (WRAPA)

WRAPA was founded in 1999 by Fati Abubakar—a female high court judge.[125] One of the youngest and least well-known NGOs, WRAPA operates from a large suite of offices in Abuja, a northern city that serves as Nigeria's administrative capital.[126] WRAPA's current secretary-general/CEO is Saudatu Mahdi, a female activist.[127] Justice Abubakar is the chair of its board of trustees.[128]

Like BAOBAB and WACOL, it is one of a small but fast-growing minority of NGOs founded, led and dominated by women. As its full name suggests, WRAPA is a specialized NGO that focuses on the advancement and protection of women's rights.[129] As such, while the concern to improve the general human rights climate in Nigeria could not but have played an important role in shaping the decision to establish WRAPA, its main and immediate foundational impetus was the need to advance women's rights in Nigeria.[130] As importantly, other factors such as the clout of its founder (the wife of one of Nigeria's military heads of state), the availability of foreign funding for its programs, and the increasing gender sensitivity of donors played an important role in shaping the decision of its founders to establish this NGO.

Thus far, WRAPA has maintained its specialized focus and has not become as generalist as most other NGOs. Specialization does, of course, have its advantages; but as a relatively youthful organization, it will be some time before it can achieve the status and renown of NGOs like the CLO or SERAC.

5. THE ORIGINS, GENERAL CHARACTER, AND DEVELOPMENT OF MINORITY/ ENVIRONMENTAL RIGHTS NGOS IN NIGERIA

As with the other groups of specialized NGOs in Nigeria, only relatively few of Nigeria's self-described human rights NGOs can be accurately styled "minority/ environmental rights NGOs" (in the sense that they regard minority and/ or environmental rights activism as the main focus of their praxis). While activism regarding minority/environmental issues is not at all new to Nigeria (as minority rights activism was a source of much national discomfort even before Nigeria gained its independence from Britain),[131] the contemporary emergence within Nigeria's self-professed NGO community of organizations specifically dedicated to the promotion and protection of minority/environmental rights is a more recent phenomenon. Since the CLO's birth in 1987, the vast majority of NGOs have not, as we have seen, adopted minority/environmental rights activism as their central objective.

This gap in the matrix of human rights activism in Nigeria was in the beginning tentatively filled by the various "Niger Delta" or "environmental rights" projects established within some of the older NGOs. Even though many of these projects still exist, the minority/environmental rights deficit within the NGO community in Nigeria has been largely filled by the emergence of a number of autonomous groups such as the now famous Movement for the Survival of Ogoni People (MOSOP) and Environmental Rights Action (ERA).

The later emergence of these minority/environmental rights groups on the Nigerian human rights scene is not at all surprising. It tends to reflect the short shrift that minority rights and environmental rights issues have received at the hands of successive military and civilian regimes in Nigeria, as well as the more recent exponential rise in the levels of popular consciousness about the degradation of the environment in the oil-rich Niger Delta region of Nigeria. As this region is home to hundreds of minority groups, there has been a deep interconnection between minority rights activism and the defense of environment in Nigeria.

While a number of minority/environmental rights NGOs exist in Nigeria, this section only deal with the origins and development of a representative sample of the major groups:[132] namely, MOSOP and ERA.

5.1. THE MOVEMENT FOR THE SURVIVAL OF OGONI PEOPLE (MOSOP)

Though MOSOP was founded in 1990 as the umbrella minority/ environmental rights organization of the Ogoni minority ethnic group of Nigeria's Niger Delta region,[133] the struggle of the Ogoni for better treatment within the Nigerian state and for the protection of their environment from devastating pollution is much older.[134] At the very least, it dates back to the early 1960s, a few years after oil was discovered in the area.[135] As a prominent Ogoni writer has put it: "There had been periodic riots, protests, and letter-writing campaigns since the 1960s, but most of these fizzled out after the leaders were intimidated into silence or bought off ....Our people had accepted their status as second-class citizens."[136] MOSOP was established largely through the efforts of Ogoni elders and intellectuals and, in particular, as a result of the work of the late Ken Saro-Wiwa, a prominent Ogoni writer and intellectual who later became its president.[137] While Dr. G.B. Leton was its first leader, its current president is Mr. Ledum Mittee, a prominent Port Harcourt-based lawyer.[138] MOSOP's headquarters is located in Port Harcourt, Nigeria's oil capital.[139]

Three major factors shaped the emergence of MOSOP. The first is the deep-seated resentment felt by most Ogoni people regarding the unfairness of their status within the country. As one Ogoni has put it:

> Like most of the minority groups in Nigeria, the Ogoni suffered from the discrimination and chauvinism of the larger ethnic groups. There were few Ogoni in key government positions or

within the management structure of the same oil industry that derived such rich rewards from our land. Seventy percent of Ogoni university graduates were unemployed, and many of them had to leave the country in search of opportunities.[140]

The second factor relates to the massive exploitation and devastation of the Ogoni environment over three decades by the oil industry, especially by Shell (the company with the largest oil interests in the Ogoni area), with the Ogoni getting very little in return. In consequence, MOSOP was envisaged as:

> ...a vehicle to challenge those companies to clean up our environment, to compensate our people for the damage done, and force them to pay a fairer rent for the land....Shell was not only flouting Nigeria's environmental laws, but also paying lip service to its own commitment to a clean and safe environment.[141]

The last major factor was the vision and extraordinary zeal with which its founder, the late Ken Saro-Wiwa, approached the struggle. As his own son has put it and as a lot of other more independent assessors have noted:

> In many respects...[the late Ken Saro-Wiwa] was MOSOP. He set up the organization, and he wrote, published, and persuaded the Ogoni people to sign the Ogoni bill of rights, which set down a list of our demands from the oil companies and the government. He was tried and tested in the battle against the conspiracy of silence in Nigeria, and he was responsible for wooing the international media and skeptical nongovernmental organizations to the struggle.[142]

Thus, even though the broader battle against military dictatorship could not but have markedly affected Saro-Wiwa as he thought through the task of creating MOSOP, that was not the immediate, proximate "cause" of his decision to help set up that organization.[143]

As might be expected, the major objectives of MOSOP were to secure environmental justice for the Ogoni people and improve their social, economic, and political status within the Nigerian state. MOSOP was formed with the twin goals of securing from the Nigerian government the political, economic and environmental rights of all Ogoni on the one hand, and on the other, demanding from the Shell Corporation that "it bypass the central government, engage immediately in environmental impact assessment of its past activities[,] and raise its standards to best practice."[144]

To this day, and despite the execution of Ken Saro-Wiwa and many other prominent Ogoni by the notoriously dictatorial Abacha regime, MOSOP continues to wage a relentless struggle for a fairer union with Nigeria's other constituent peoples and polities.[145] It has remained focused on its *raison d'être* and continues therefore to contribute to the much-needed struggle to restructure and redefine the relationships among Nigeria's constituent units so hastily agglomerated without their consent into the political shell that is

Nigeria.[146] It is much to the credit of MOSOP activists – and especially
of the late Ken Saro-Wiwa – that minority/environmental rights activism
has gained exponentially in prominence within the Nigerian human rights
arena. To put it metaphorically, today most well-dressed NGO activists adorn
themselves (at least in part) in minority/environmental rights clothing. As
Samian dan Lawan has noted:

> Saro-Wiwa may not have perfected the strategy to fight the forces
> of oppression in that area [the Nigerian Niger Delta], but he
> seems to have opened the floodgate for more Saro-Wiwas and
> more Isaac Boros. In the Niger Delta zone now, *several interest
> groups* have sprung up, all battling to achieve the same result....
> Not all these are as daring as the "Egbesu Boys" [who sometimes
> deploy violent tactics] but from all of them come strident cries
> for fairness.[147]

5.2. ENVIRONMENTAL RIGHTS ACTION:

ERA was founded in 1993 by a group of former CLO staff led by
Nnimmo Bassey and Oronto Douglas (who in 2004 became a member of
cabinet of the Governor of Bayelsa state of Nigeria).[148] While ERA's main
office is located in Benin, in the southern mid-west of Nigeria, its operations
span the entire Niger Delta region of Nigeria. It is therefore unlike most
Nigerian human rights NGOs in this last respect. However, because it was
founded by activists who had been associated with the CLO, ERA is, like
most such groups, an offshoot of the CLO. Like MOSOP, ERA's operations
tend to incorporate both environmental and minority rights concerns. This is
so mainly because the most pressing environmental problems in Nigeria, the
problems related to oil pollution, tend to be of most direct concern to the
minority groups that inhabit the Niger Delta region.[149]

It is not exactly clear what led the founders of ERA to quit the CLO.
However, a number of factors apparently helped to shape their decision to
leave the CLO and to start a separate organization. For one, although the
main focus of the CLO has never been minority/environmental rights activism, it had not entirely neglected that aspect of its work either. After all, ERA
began life as a semi-autonomous CLO project located in Benin (away from
the CLO's headquarters in Lagos), albeit as an integral part of the CLO's
activities.[150] It seems therefore that one major reason for the establishment
of ERA as a completely autonomous and separate vehicle for minority/envi-
ronmental rights work in Nigeria was a desire for even more administrative
and financial autonomy than it already had within the CLO. Another obvious
impetus for its formation was the fact that despite the massive devastation
over time of the Niger Delta environment, and the abject poverty in which
most of its minority groups lived, little progress had been made toward
halting such wanton ecological devastation and ameliorating the poverty of its
mass populations.[151] This state of affairs made the local human rights scene

fertile for, and receptive to, the emergence of another specialized minority/ environmental rights group. What is more, although MOSOP existed before the inception of ERA, MOSOP's membership and focus was not in the least national. It was and still is basically restricted to ethnic Ogonis.

Thus, ERA is a highly specialized NGO that focuses on the promotion and protection of environmental rights, especially within the Niger Delta region of Nigeria. Its main objectives are (a) to spread environmental consciousness in the Niger Delta region, (b) to defend and protect the people of that region against industrial pollution, mainly from the activities of MNOCs; and (c) to protect human rights and promote participatory democratic development in the region.[152]

So far, ERA has remained committed to its specialist vocation and has not turned into a more generalist organization. As shall become clear in subsequent chapters, the NGO community in Nigeria has been enriched as a result.

6. AN OVERVIEW OF THE ORIGINS, GENERAL CHARACTER, AND DEVELOPMENT OF HUMAN RIGHTS NGOS IN NIGERIA

It should be apparent from the above discussion that most of the NGOs that we are concerned with fit somewhere within a four-pronged typology. While many are civil/political rights-oriented, a smaller number are social/ economic rights-focused. And while some are gender based, a few others are focused on the advancement of minority/environmental rights. Another notable feature of these groups that became more pronounced during the period under study is their increasing specialization. As Ibhawoh has noted:

> In the 1990s, there was a significant growth in the number of human rights NGOs in the country and the scope of their operations....Human rights NGOs began to emerge with mandates focused *on more specific agendas* such as economic and social rights, media rights, minority rights, issues of law enforcement and gender rights.[153]

It should also be clear from the discussion in this chapter that the NGO community in Nigeria dates back to the birth of the CLO in 1987, and that most of the NGOs that form this community were established between the late 1980s and late 1990s. Ibhawoh is also correct in observing that there was an upsurge in human rights NGO activism in Nigeria between 1985 and 1998 partly because of the dictatorial and repressive character of the military regimes of that era.[154] Nnamdi Aduba and Olu Onagoruwa have also expressed similar views.[155] However, as was noted, even though the 1980s and 1990s recorded an exponential growth in the number of self-professed human rights NGOs in Nigeria, the history of human rights activism in Nigeria antedates this more contemporary period by at least several decades. Similar trends have been noted with respect to the emergence of self-professed human rights NGOs within the broader African context[156], as well as on the global scene.[157]

Remarkably, most of these NGOs were established by lawyers or by groups with a substantial percentage of lawyers. This has contributed to the overwhelmingly legalistic character of such groups as well as to their historical neglect of social/economic rights activism.

Similarly, the vast majority of these organizations are based in Lagos (Nigeria's largest city) and do not have much of a presence in most other parts of the country. This has, as shall be demonstrated in chapter 3, tainted this NGO community with a Lagos (and indeed urban) bias. As importantly, most such groups were established by male activists, contributing in no small measure to the gender deficit that has historically characterized this NGO community. Moreover, many of the NGOs that form this community were established by activists who broke away from the CLO. While this kind of fragmentation has energized the NGO sector, it has not, as we shall see, been an unqualified blessing.

As has also been shown, the establishment of almost every civil/ political rights NGO in Nigeria was significantly motivated by the sorry status of human rights under successive military regimes in Nigeria. Nevertheless, far too many of them were also formed in order to achieve the desires of their founder(s) for administrative and financial autonomy from either the CLO or other such parent body; to address the dissatisfaction of its founders with their own circumstances within the relevant parent organization; and to gain separate and independent access to the available pool of foreign funding.[158] While some of these same factors also helped trigger the formation of many social/economic rights-focused, gender-focused, and minority/environmental rights-focused NGOs, the major conceptual differences between each of these groups and their parent organization (usually the CLO) provided plausible justifications for the fragmentation that occurred.

The next chapter examines closely the composition, structure, and geopolitical location of the same sample of NGOs considered in the present chapter, before moving on to an analysis, in chapter four, of the programs and methods of these groups. Following that, chapter 5 will be devoted to pertinent issues related to the funding regimes of these NGOs. Thereafter, chapter 6 assesses the extent to which these NGOs have or have not been influential within and without Nigeria. Chapter 7 offers a constructive critique of the praxis of these NGOs. The book concludes with an examination, in chapter 8, of the major arguments that its advances.

NOTES

1. I. H. Chiroma, "Human Rights and Military Rule in Nigeria: Issues and Options," in O.A. Obilade et al., eds., *Text for Human Rights Teaching in Schools* (Lagos: Constitutional Rights Project, 1999), 138 at 139. See also J.O. Ihonvbere,

"Are Things Falling Apart? The Military and the Crisis of Democratization in Nigeria" *Journal of Modern African Studies* 34 (1996): 193 at 201.

2. See J.N. Oriji, "The Aba Women's Revolt," in J.N. Oriji, ed., *Ngwa History* (New York: P. Lang, 1997); N. Nina, "Heroines of the Women's War," in B. Awe, ed., *Nigerian Women in Historical Perspective* (Ibadan: Sankore/Bookcraft, 1992) 75; J.N. Oriji, "Igbo Women from 1929-1960," *West Africa Review* (2000), on-line: http://www.westafricareview.com/war/vol12.1/orji.html (visited 29 May 03).

3. U. Baxi, *The Future of Human Rights* (New Delhi: Oxford University Press, 2002).

4. Swedish NGO Foundation, "The Status of Human Rights Organizations in Sub-Saharan Africa: Overview-Introduction," on line: http://www1.umn.edu/humanrts/africa/intro.htm (visited: 20 October 2000). Emphasis added.

5. Hereinafter referred to as the NGO community. In this study, the term *NGOs* refers to "Nigerian human rights NGOs."

6. See C. Nwankwo, "Human Rights and the Challenges of NGOs in Nigeria" in A.O. Obilade et al., eds., *supra* note 1, 258.

7. See Civil Liberties Organization, *Accounts and Activities for 2000* (Lagos: CLO, 2001), 7.

8. See Transcripts of Interview with OA, 20th August 2001 (on file with the author).

9. See http://www.odili.net/news/source/2003/apr/325/327.html (visited: 13 August 2003).

10. See C. Nwankwo, *supra* note 6, 258; and Interview with AO, 17 August 2001 (on file with the author). See also P.O. Agbese, "The State versus Human Rights Advocates in Africa: The Case of Nigeria," in E. McCarthy-Arnolds, D.R. Penna, and D.J. Cruz Sobrepena, eds., *Africa, Human Rights, and the Global System: The Political Economy of Human Rights in a Changing World* (Westport, CN: Greenwood Press, 1994), 162-63. The three citations above represent the testimony of the founders of the CLO and corroboration by another independent researcher other than myself.

11. See *Transcripts of Interview with OA*, 20 August 2001 (on file with the author).

12. Ibid.

13. See B. Ibhawoh, *Human Rights Organisations in Nigeria: An Appraisal Report on the Human Rights NGO Community in Nigeria* (Copenhagen, Denmark: The Danish Centre for Human Rights, 2001), 9.

14. O.N. Ogbu, *Human Rights Law and Practice in Nigeria: An Introduction* (Enugu: CIDJAP Press, 1999), 341-50

15. See Liberty (a CLO publication) 6:3 (1995): 5.

16. See *Accounts and Activities for 2000, supra* note 7.

17. Ibid.

18. See CLO, *Accounts and Activities for 2000, supra* note 7, 28. The following projects were listed:

    i. Legal Assistant Network

    ii. Democracy Action Projects/Liberty Magazine
   iii. Administration of Justice (Training of Lower Court Judges)
   iv. Campaigns and Monitoring Project
    v. Prison Watch and Penal Reforms
   vi. Human Rights Education for Religious Groups
  vii. Women Rights Projects
 viii. Annual Report – State of Human Rights in Nigeria
   ix. Human Rights Education with Trade Unions and other Social Groups
    x. Transparency and Accountability Project with Civil Society Groups
   xi. Police and Law Enforcement Project
  xii. Niger Delta Monitoring Project
 xiii. General Purpose and Capacity Building
 xiv. Academic Freedom and State Repression

19. Ibid.
20. See M. Mutua, "The Politics of Human Rights: Beyond the Abolitionist Paradigm in Africa," *Michigan Journal of International Law* 17 (1996): 591 at 599; M. Mutua; "The Ideology of Human Rights," *Virginia Journal of International Law* 36 (1996): 589 at 617-619; J. Power, "Like Water on Stone: The Story of Amnesty International," *Human Rights Quarterly* 24 (2002): 830; and C. E. Welch, Jr., "Amnesty International and Human Rights Watch: A Comparison," in C.E. Welch, Jr., *NGOs and Human Rights: Promise and Performance* (Philadelphia: University of Pennsylvania Press, 2001), 84 at 88, 99, 106-107.
21. O.N. Ogbu, *supra* note 14.
22. See A. Ikelegbe, "The Perverse Manifestation of Civil Society: Evidence from Nigeria," *Journal of Modern African Studies* 39 (2001): 1 at 10.
23. See Baxi, *supra* note 2. See also ibid., "Voices of Suffering and the Future of Human Rights" *Transnational Law and Contemporary Problems* 8 (1998): 125 at 159.
24. See Ikelegbe, *supra* note 22 at 10.
25. See C. Nwankwo, *supra*, note 6 at 258. See also Ikelegbe, *supra*, note 22 at 9.
26. This much is inferable from the available evidence.
27. See Ogbu, *supra* note 14.
28. See CRP, *The Crisis of Press Freedom in Nigeria* (Lagos: CRP, 1993)
29. Ibid.
30. See CRP, *Land, Oil, and Human Rights in Nigeria's Delta Region* (Lagos: CRP, 1999).
31. See ibid., *Eliminating Discrimination against Women* (Lagos: CRP, 1995).
32. See T. Abayomi, "Non-Governmental Organizations in the Protection and Promotion of Human Rights in Africa: Critique of Approach and Methods" in A.U. Kalu and Y. Osinbajo, eds., *Perspectives on Human Rights* (Lagos: Federal Ministry of Justice, 1992), 173 at 173-174.
33. Ibid.
34. Ibid.

35. Ibid.

36. See HRA, *Annual Report 1991/1992* (Lagos: HRA, 1992).

37. Ibid.

38. Ibid., 23.

39. CDHR, *1999 Annual Report on the Human Rights Situation in Nigeria* (Lagos: CDHR, 1999).

40. See transcripts of interview with FF, 25 August 2001 (on file with the author).

41. Ibid.

42. Ibid.

43. See CDHR, *1999 Annual Report, supra* note 36.

44. See ibid., 143-147, 160.

45. Ibid., 217.

46. See transcripts of interview with LA, 4 March 2003 (on file with the author)

47. See *Media Rights Monitor* 5:4 (April 2000)

48. See transcripts of interview with DT, 13 March 2000 (on file with the author)

49. See: http://www.internews.org/mra/mra_about.htm.

50. See interview with LA, *supra* note 46.

51. Indeed MRA and some of these other groups have sometimes collaborated to wage specific media rights struggles. For example, MRA has worked hand in hand with the CLO and a few other groups to push Nigeria's parliament to enact a freedom of information law and repeal the offensive press laws that survived the end of military rule in 1999. See *Media Rights Monitor* 5 (2000): 13.

52. See transcripts of interview with NV, 28 February 2003 (on file with author).

53. Ibid.

54. See *Law Enforcement Review* 8 (1999): 4.

55. Ibid.

56. See *Law Enforcement Review* 8 (1999): 21.

57. http://www.ngprawa.org/prawa/default.asp.

58. http://www.ngprawa.org/prawa/contact.htm.

59. PRAWA, *Overcrowding in Nigerian Prisons* (Lagos: PRAWA, 1999), 1-14. See also, ibid., *1998 Annual Report* (Lagos, PRAWA, 1999), 5–6.

60. See *About PRAWA* (PRAWA leaflet issued in Lagos, Nigeria, June 2001), (on file with the author).

61. Ibid.

62. http://www.ngprawa.org/prawa/programs/recass.htm.

63. For example one of the main subthemes for its 2002 Alternatives to Violence Project Conference was dubbed "The gendered face of violence." See http://www.ngprawa.org/prawa/programs/avp.htm#themes.

64. See transcripts of interview with AO, 17 August 2001 (on file with the author).

65. The author and one of his research assistants personally observed this fact. See also http://www.hurilaws.org (visited 07 May 2003).

66. HURLAWS, *The Governance Scorecard: Review of Democratic Governance in Nigeria* (Apapa: HURILAWS, 2000).

67. http://www.hurilaws.org/secretariat.htm (visited 07 May 2003).

68. Ibid.

69. For an excellent explanation of this concept in relation to human rights groups, see U. Baxi, *The Future of Human Rights* (New Delhi: Oxford University Press, 2002), 121.

70. See transcripts of interview with AS, 13 March 2000 (on file with the author).

71. See http://www.hurilaws.org/about%20us.htm (visited 27 February 2003)

72. See HURILAWS, *Annual Report and Accounts* (Lagos: HURILAWS, 1999), 12.

73. See CAPP, *Selling the Message* (Abuja: CAPP, 1999), 28–29.

74. See http://www.capp.kabissa.org (visited 28 February 2003).

75. See CAPP, *Selling the Message* (Abuja: CAPP, 1999), 30.

76. Ibid., 1.

77. Ibid., 28-29. See also http://www.isodec.org.gh/workshop-cd/organisations/pages/organisations/CAPP.htm (visited on 28 February 2003).

78. See transcripts of interview with OF (on file with the author).

79. See http://www.hrm.kabissa.org/ (visited on 28 February 2003).

80. See A. Nsirimovu, *Human Rights Education and Techniques in Schools* (Port Harcourt: IHRHL, 1994).

81. Ibid.

82. Ibid.

83. See O. Oko, "Lawyers in Chains: Restrictions on Human Rights Advocacy under Nigeria's Military Regimes," *Harvard Human Rights Journal* 10 (1997): 257, 289.

84. For an excellent explanation of this concept in relation to human rights groups, see U. Baxi, *supra* note 3, 121, 124.

85. For more on this point, see J. Oloka-Onyango, "Beyond the Rhetoric: Reinvigorating the Struggle for Economic and Social Rights in Africa," *California Western International Law Journal* 26 (1995): 1.

86. Ibid.

87. See SRI, *Economic, Social and Cultural Rights: A Compilation of International Standards* (Lagos: SRI, 2001), 352.

88. Ibid.

89. See http://www.srinitiative.org/saboutus.htm (visited 28 February 2003).

90. Ibid.

91. Ibid.

92. See: http://www.wangonet.org/serac/default.htm (visited 28 February 2003).

93. Ibid.

94. See EMPARC, *Five Year Report on Activities: 1992–1997* (Lagos: EMPARC, 1997).

95. See transcript of interview with IA, 11 July 2003 (on file with the author).

96. Ibid.

97. Ibid.

98. See EMPARC, *supra* note 94, 2.

99. Ibid., 5–8.

100. Ibid., 3.

101. Interview with IA, *supra* note 95.

102. Ibid., *supra* note 95.

103. On this historic revolt, see Oriji, "Igbo Women from 1929–1960," *supra* note 2.

104. See B. Ibhawoh, *Human Rights Organizations in Nigeria: An Appraisal Report on the Human Rights NGO Community in Nigeria* (Copenhagen, Denmark: The Danish Centre for Human Rights, 2001), 25.

105. See *Action Woman* (a WACOL publication) 1:1 (2002): 6.

106. See transcripts of interview with IO, 4 March 2003 (on file with the author).

107. Ibid.

108. Ibid.

109. Ibid.

110. Ibid.

111. Ibid.

112. See http://www.ichrdd.ca/frame.iphtml (visited 23 May 2003).

113. See WACOL, *Gender, Politics and the Law* (Enugu: WACOL, 1999).

114. Ibid.

115. See ibid., *The Reproductive Rights and Maternal Health Education and Advocacy Project* (Enugu: WACOL, 2001), 1.

116. See ibid., *Women's Socio-Economic and Legal Rights* (Enugu: WACOL, 2001), 12.

117. Ibid.

118. See ibid., *Gender, Politics and the Law*, *supra* note 113, 1–7.

119. See ibid., *supra* note 115, 1.

120. Ibid.

121. Ibid.

122. Ibid., v.

123. Ibid.

124. Ibid.

125. See transcripts of interview with MS, 7 March 2003 (On file with the author). See also http://www.wrapa.org/profile.htm (visited 18 March 2003).

126. Ibid.

127. Ibid.

128. Ibid.

129. Ibid.

130. Ibid.

131. Douglas Oronto, "A Community Guide to Understanding Resource Control," on-line: http://www.waado.org/NigerDelta/Essays/ResourceControl/Guide_

Douglas.html (visited 20 June 2003), stating that "the attempt by Isaac Boro, a former student union leader and ex-policeman, to declare a republic may have been propelled by the abundance of oil resources. The federal forces crushed the rebellion which lasted only twelve days."

132. See A. Ikelegbe, "Civil Society, Oil and Conflict in the Niger Delta Region of Nigeria: Ramifications of Civil Society for a Regional Resource Struggle," *Journal of Modern African Studies* 39 (2001): 437, 442–43.

133. See http://www.righttolivelihood.se/recip/saro-wiwa.htm (visited on 4 March 2003).

134. See K. Wiwa, *In the Shadow of a Saint: A Son's Journey to Understand His Father's Legacy* (South Royalton, VT: Steerforth Press, 2001), 51.

135. Ibid.

136. Ibid.

137. See Newswatch, 29 January 2001, on line: http://www.newswatchngr.com/editorial/allaccess/29012001/ng515.htm (visited 30 January 2001).

138. See www.newswatchngr.com/editorial/allaccess/2901200/ng515.htm (visited 4 March 2003).

139. See http://www.dawuda.net/mosop.htm (visited 4 March 2003).

140. See Wiwa, *In the Shadow of a Saint, supra* note 134 , 49.

141. Ibid.

142. Ibid., 51–52.

143. See also S. Cayford, "The Ogoni Uprising: Oil, Human Rights, and a Democratic Alternative in Nigeria," *Africa Today* 43:2 (1996): 183, 187.

144. See http://www.rightlivelihood.se/recip/saro-wiwa.htm (visited on 4 March 2003).

145. On the execution of the Ogoni nine and developments around it, see O.C. Okafor, "International Law, Human Rights and the Allegory of the Ogoni Question," in E.K. Quashigah and O.C. Okafor, eds., *Legitimate Governance in Africa: International and Domestic Legal Perspectives* (The Hague: Kluwer Law International, 1999).

146. O.C. Okafor, *Re-defining Legitimate Statehood: International Law and State Fragmentation in Africa* (The Hague: Martinus Nijhoff, 2000), 30–31, see also "After Martyrdom: International Law, Sub-state Groups, and the Construction of Legitimate Statehood in Africa" *Harvard International Law Journal* 41:2 (2000): 501, 506.

147. See S. dan Lawan, "Mayhem in the Niger Delta," *Democracy Review* (a CLO publication) (January-March 1999): 3–5.

148. See transcripts of interview with NP, 10th January 2003 (on file with the author).

149. Ibid.

150. Ibid.

151. See Ikelegbe, *supra* note 132, 440.

152. Ibid.

153. See B. Ibhawoh, *Human Rights Organizations in Nigeria: An Appraisal Report on Human Rights NGO Community in Nigeria* (Copenhagen, Demark: The Danish Centre for Human Rights, 2001), 14. Emphasis added.

154. Ibid., 9.

155. See N. Aduba, "The Protection of Human Rights in Nigeria" in O.A. Obilade, et al., eds., *supra* note 1, 109, 133; and *Newswatch*, 29 June 1992, 15.

156. See J. Harrington, "Practice Made Personal" Harvard Human Rights Journal 9 (1996): 333, 334.

157. See K. Sikkink, "Human Rights, Principled Issue-Networks, and Sovereignty in Latin America" *International Organization* 47 (1993): 411, 418.

158. For instance, see *Action Woman* 1:1 (2002): 25.

CHAPTER 3

INSIDE/OUTSIDE:
THE COMPOSITION, STRUCTURE, AND GEO-POLITICAL LOCATION OF THE HUMAN RIGHTS NGO COMMUNITY IN NIGERIA

1. INTRODUCTION

Given the overall objectives of this book, it is important at this juncture to undertake a detailed analysis of the institutional character of the NGO community in Nigeria.[1] That will be the focus of this chapter and the two that follow it. The present chapter will be devoted to an assessment of the composition, structure, and geopolitical location of the NGO community in Nigeria. In this connection, a passage from Chidi Odinkalu's seminal essay on human rights activism in Africa captures quite succinctly the basic character of most of the organizations that constitute the NGO community in Nigeria. According to this seasoned activist:

> Most human rights organizations are modeled after Northern watchdog organizations, located in an urban area, run by a core management without a membership base (unlike Amnesty International), and dependent solely on overseas funding.[2]

Thus, the main objectives of this chapter are twofold. The first is to map the composition of the organizations that form this NGO community as well as that of the NGO community itself. Are these NGOs membership organizations? Is the NGO community a popular or mass movement? Or are these NGOs constituted and run by what Odinkalu has referred to as "a core management without a membership base"[3] and assisted by a staff of "hired hands?" If these NGOs have members, then who are their members, and how are they chosen? How national is the distribution of their membership base? Who are the leaders of these NGOs, and how are they chosen? What is the composition of the broader human rights NGO community, and how nationally spread is it? The second objective of this chapter is to understand the structure and geo-political location of the groups that make up this NGO community. What is the administrative structure of each of these NGOs? How institutionalized are they? Who makes decisions for these organizations, and how are these decisions made? To what extent are these NGOs "one-person" shows that are characterized by personal rule? Do they operate out of an office in Lagos (Nigeria's largest city) or from a network of offices spread throughout the country? What presence do these NGOs have at the grassroots – especially among the majority rural population of Nigeria? Have these NGOs established coalitions and networks with like-minded groups? Have these NGOs fragmented into separate groups? Why has such fragmentation occurred?

These institutional questions deserve investigation because the composition, structure, and geopolitical location of such groups have been identified in several hypothetical essays as factors that have negatively affected the overall growth, development, and effectiveness of NGO communities in Africa. For instance, Odinkalu has decried what he sees as the tendency of these NGOs, with the possible exception of women's and faith-based groups, to exclude "almost by design" the very people whose welfare they claim to advance—resulting in their inability to acquire a sufficient degree of popular or grassroots legitimacy.[4] Makau Mutua has also reached a similar conclusion.[5]

In this vein, this chapter investigates systematically and by reference to the relevant empirical evidence, the charge that the composition, structure, and geopolitical location of these NGOs have tended to exclude the very people that these organizations claim to work for. To this end, a survey of each of the NGOs that are of concern to us in this book will be undertaken. To facilitate this survey, reliance will be placed on the classification of these groups that was developed in the previous chapter. In the end, a general assessment of the composition, structure, and geo-political location of the NGO community in Nigeria will be offered.

2. THE CIVIL/POLITICAL RIGHTS NGOS

This section considers the nature of the composition, structure and geo-political location of those NGOs that were categorized in chapter 2 as civil/political rights NGOs. The same sample of civil/political rights NGOs are assessed here.

2.1. THE CIVIL LIBERTIES ORGANIZATION (CLO)

Easily the most established and institutionalized of Nigeria's contemporary human rights NGOs, the CLO is a membership organization *par excellence*.[6] Anyone can apply to its secretariat in Nigeria to be enrolled as a member.[7] Presumably, however, only those who profess a commitment to its broad objectives will be able to obtain a membership in this organization. Significantly though, the CLO's membership has not been as active and dominant in the decision-making processes of its Lagos-based national unit as should be expected. This is so despite the characterization of its members by a senior CLO activist as "very active,"[8] and the impressive role often played by its membership in the functioning of the organization.

Though its main offices are located in Lagos, the CLO has over time managed to establish branches in all of the major geopolitical regions of the country, and in many states of the Nigerian federation, each with an impressive membership roll and an elected leadership.[9]

The Lagos unit – which has been the most dominant of all its units – is basically run by a "core management" consisting of its principal officers and senior staff.[10] While it is, broadly speaking, governed by its board of directors, its day-to-day activities are in practice overseen by an executive director who is appointed by the Board and is directly responsible to an executive management committee, comprising its President, Vice President, Treasurer and an elected staff representative.[11] Members of this committee are elected by a biannual national convention.[12] This convention is its highest decision-making organ and meets to discuss the state of the country as well as to offer general policy guidance and direction to the leadership[13]. Thus, far from being a system of "personal rule," the CLO's structure is robustly formalized and institutional in nature. And as shall soon be made clear, this has been a rare feature of the NGO community in Nigeria.[14]

Unfortunately, because of the fiscal and budgetary constraints it has had to grapple with, impressive as it is, the CLO's presence at the grassroots has nevertheless not been as significant as one would expect from an organization of such stature. Even the very small portion of its work that occurs in the rural areas is left to the often less endowed state branches and zonal offices.[15] Not surprisingly, it does not also have a significant membership base or body of followers among rural Nigerians. As such, its membership is drawn largely from a section of Nigeria's urban population – a relatively elite minority.

As importantly, the CLO's institutional development has been somewhat weakened by its inability to retain many of its most experienced and accomplished senior activists. The renowned activist Ubani Chima is almost alone among its most experienced cadres in remaining with the CLO till this day. As pointed out in chapter 2, it was many of these breakaway CLO members and staff who established many of the other competing NGOs in Nigeria. For instance, the CRP was founded by Clement Nwankwo, himself a cofounder of the CLO. HURILAWS was established by Olisa Agbakoba, the other cofounder and first president of the CLO. CLEEN, ERA and HRM were, among many other such groups, set up by breakaway CLO staff. However, rather than fragment completely as a result of the continual exodus of so many of its best hands, the CLO has managed to remain reasonably robust and dynamic.

It has even built coalitions with like-minded domestic groups. For instance, during the serious governance crisis that engulfed Nigeria in the 1990s, the CLO was an important partner within a coalition of NGOs called the Campaign for Democracy (CD). Indeed, the effective leader of the CD, Ubani Chima, was at the time and still remains a notable CLO activist. The CD organized strikes and demonstrations to protest the cancellation of the 12 June 1993 presidential election and campaigned against many of the human rights abuses of the time.[16] During the last days of the Abacha regime, the CLO was also a partner in the United Action for Democracy (UAD), which played a similar role as the CD.[17] Later on, the CLO became an important member of the Transition Monitoring Group (TMG).[18]

In addition to these domestic alliances, the CLO has also formed activist networks with some foreign human rights NGOs and institutions. Following the widespread incidence of human rights abuses in military-ruled Nigeria of the 1990s, the CLO collaborated with other prodemocracy groups in Nigeria to lobby the U.N. High Commissioner for Human Rights to visit Nigeria to investigate the country's human rights situation. [19] It is also noteworthy that the International Human Rights Law Group lent its support to this CLO-led initiative and lobbied NGOs in the United States and Western Europe on its behalf.[20] While the CLO's coalitions with foreign NGOs has tended to be unequal, the fact remains that they occur, and have for better or for worse helped to shape the structure of the CLO and the rest of the NGO community in Nigeria.[21]

2.2. THE CONSTITUTIONAL RIGHTS PROJECT (CRP)

Though it is one of the oldest and most established NGOs in Nigeria, the CRP can hardly be described as a quintessential membership organization. Although it is open to all who want to join, it has managed to attract fewer than one hundred nominal members in over twelve years.[22] The CAPP, a similar organization, which was formed many years after the CRP has over eight hundred members. What is more, its membership has not in general been of the active or dominant type. The CRP is led by an executive director who is directly assisted in the discharge of her/his functions by a retinue of senior staff, many of whom are lawyers.[23] In a formal sense, the governance of the CRP is done under the broad authority of its board of directors.[24] Unfortunately, however, it is difficult not to categorize the CRP as one of a vast majority of such NGOs whose governance structure, until quite recently, came too close to becoming a "one-person show". This was certainly the case between 1987 and 2002. As talented as he was, and as benevolently as his fifteen year reign came to be seen by many observers, the CRP's founding executive director was without doubt the dominant power within the organization until his commendable resignation in 2002. While the existence of a level of personal rule in the CRP during the relevant period does not, in and of itself, say a whole lot about the substantive quality of its governance arrangements, it is nevertheless a cause for concern. There is always the danger that without an active membership to account to, and without a dominant elected board of directors that is, in practice, capable of checking the executive director, most such chief executives would govern in a less than commendable fashion. Since the CRP has remained a dynamic organization all these years, there is not as much room as would otherwise be available to censure it on this score alone; but suffice it to say that its lack of a strong membership base has, as shall be made clear in subsequent chapters, hampered its ability to achieve its full potential.

As part of its drive to become more accessible to the Nigerian people the CRP has managed to establish two other offices beyond its Lagos base. It has established regional offices in Abuja (in the North) and Owerri (in the East).[25] But like its Lagos office, none of these regional offices has acquired a significant membership base.[26] They are in effect extensions of the main office in Lagos. Moreover, like its Lagos office, both regional offices are located in large urban centers. Abuja is Nigeria's capital city, while Owerri is the capital of Imo state. The eminently urban location of these regional offices mirrors the historical neglect and marginalization of the rural areas, not just by the CRP but also by virtually all other NGOs. It is also consistent with the largely urbanized character of its leadership and staff. This has, as shall also be made clear in subsequent chapters, also inhibited its ability to rise to its optimal potential.

Commendably, the CRP participates actively in (and sometimes even leads) the grand networks and coalitions that have been formed by NGOs in Nigeria. It was a part of the Campaign for Democracy (CD) and the United Action for Democracy (UAD), and for a time did play a leadership role within the Transition Monitoring Group (TMG).[27] It also enjoys observer status at the African Commission on Human and People's Rights.[28]

2.3. HUMAN RIGHTS AFRICA (HRA):

Like most other NGOs in Nigeria, HRA is not a membership organization. It replicates the "core management without a membership base" organizational model that has been characteristic of most such NGOs.[29] Even though it has a board of directors, it is in practice run by Tunji Abayomi, its founder, president, and CEO. Abayomi has served as CEO throughout the life of this organization. While he is assisted in the discharge of his duties by a number of senior staff, as well as by a founders' council,[30] his authority over the organization is, in effect, almost complete. Thus, like almost all of its peers, its governance system tends toward the "personal rule" model.

With its offices and operations located in Ota (in the Lagos axis) and in Lagos itself, HRA is for the most part an urban centered outfit. Like it peers, it is also run and governed by elite members of Nigeria's urbanized minority, with little direct input from rural Nigerians. It has few roots in rural Nigeria and does not normally work directly in these areas. It has therefore remained relatively distant (as an organization) from the "voices of suffering"[31] of the Nigeria's majority rural population. While the benefits of many of its projects could potentially "trickle down" to this rural population, and while its objectives may often coincide with theirs, its inability to engage directly with them has inhibited its development into an organization that is actively supported by most ordinary Nigerians.

To its credit, HRA has participated in broader cooperative alliances with other human rights groups.[32]

2.4. THE COMMITTEE FOR THE DEFENSE OF HUMAN RIGHTS (CDHR)

The CDHR is one of a small number of Nigerian human rights NGOs that command a significant membership base.[33] A large portion of its membership is composed of urbanized activists and university students.[34] Many are Lagos-based. Most are based in large urban centers. Membership is open to anyone, but presumably the organization reserves the right to refuse to enroll those prospective members it deems unsuitable upon reasonable grounds, e.g., secret police agents intent on spying on its members.

The organization is governed by a national executive committee (NEC) that, at least in theory, coordinates and supervises the CDHR's national secretariat.[35] The NEC is made up of the chairs and secretaries of all the state branches.[36] Although the NEC has responsibility for the proper functioning of the organization, it is the delegates to the biannual general conference of the organization that set policy and program direction.[37] The secretariat is headed by an executive director who is assisted by a small number of staff lawyers and activists.[38] In practice though, the founding members of the organization, some of whom still serve it in various capacities, exert a great deal of influence on its direction and operations.

Notwithstanding its significant membership base and spread, the CDHR has yet to establish a remarkable presence at the rural grassroots. Rather, it largely functions within urban Nigeria. Most of its offices and branches are located either in large urban centers or within universities. As has been noted in relation to other such NGOs, this urban bias has, overall, not been a beneficial feature of human rights activism in Nigeria.

The CDHR has, however, enhanced its profile and work by participating in most of the cooperative structures that have been set up by NGOs in Nigeria. It has participated in the CD, the UAD, and the TMG.[39] It has also formed other smaller and less elaborate alliances with both local and foreign NGOs. For instance, the CDHR once ran a joint training program with the Constitutional Rights Project (CRP) and often collaborates with Amnesty International and the U.S.-based Lawyers' Committee for Human Rights.[40]

2.5. MEDIA RIGHTS AGENDA (MRA):

As indicated in the previous chapter, MRA was founded by, and is composed of, activist professionals, lawyers, and journalists.[41] While its broad policy directions are set and governed by a board, its day-to-day operations are overseen by an executive director.[42] However, MRA is not a true membership organization.[43] In real terms, its membership has been virtually limited to the very group of activists that founded it. The other activists that are associated with it are, to put it rather bluntly, hired hands. These include its legal officers, administrative officers, and so on. MRA thus fits well within the organizational model of NGOs that Odinkalu refers as to as characterized by a "core management without a membership base."[44] As previously noted, this has been the preferred model within the NGO community in Nigeria.

Like most other NGOs of similar orientation, MRA is located in and functions almost exclusively within Lagos (Nigeria's largest urban centre).[45] Even though its reach is definitely national in the sense of the issues that concern it, its grasp falls far short of that: for although it sometimes organizes workshops and seminars in cities such as Abuja and Kano, it has no permanent presence in these places, and does not operate any office outside the Lagos area.[46] It has also not done much work in rural Nigeria. In addition, lacking a significant membership base, it has not optimally involved or engaged ordinary Nigerians (either rural or urban) in its work. Even its staff is dominated by members of Nigeria's urban minority. Again, this is not a situation that is peculiar to MRA. Most other NGOs in Nigeria have operated in this fashion. Yet, as a result, it has become an urban-centered organization that is not accountable in any real sense to ordinary Nigerians, be they urban or rural.

Nevertheless, MRA's decision-making structure has been influenced by the many coalitions/networks that it has formed with like-minded domestic and foreign groups. As coalition/network decisions are made jointly (however unequal the relative power of the participating NGOs), the decision-making structure of the participating organizations are themselves invariably reconfigured by participation in such coalitions, albeit temporarily and for specific projects only. Two out of a multitude of the examples of its efforts at building domestic coalitions will suffice. For one, MRA has been a part of an NGO coalition working for the passage of the Freedom of Information Bill currently before the National Assembly.[47] It has also cooperated with other Nigerian groups in its work at the African Commission on Human and Peoples' Rights regarding the Nigerian Press Council Decree.[48] A good example of its participation in coalitions with foreign NGOs is its working relationship with a group known as Article 19.[49]

2.6. CENTER FOR LAW ENFORCEMENT EDUCATION (CLEEN)

Like almost every other such organization that operates in Nigeria, CLEEN is not really a membership organization.[50] Probably one of the least institutionalized of Nigeria's human rights groups, CLEEN is composed of a board of directors, a secretariat managed by its executive director, Innocent Chukwuma, and a small administrative support staff.[51] Chukwuma has served in that capacity for as long as the organization has existed.[52] Though formally subject to the decisions of CLEEN's board, he is in charge of the day-to-day running of the organization and is, in practice, the CEO and controlling mind of this NGO.[53] Unrestrained by an active and dominant membership, he is in effect free to reign over CLEEN as he sees fit, subject only to the directives of the board. Yet there is no evidence that this board has been a powerful one. Thus, although there is no clear evidence that his rule over CLEEN has not been benign, its more personal character has not made for the deepening institutionalization of his organization with all the attendant benefits that might have accrued to it.

Again, the CLEEN is like most other such NGOs in terms of it being run from a single office located in the Lagos area and also in terms of it being governed by a largely urbanized activist cadre.[54] While the CLEEN's geographical reach is clearly intended to be national, it has not always succeeded in fulfilling this dream. Currently, its "Gender and Law Enforcement Program" provides it with a more national reach if not grasp.[55] Also, rarely have its projects been located in or targeted specifically at rural Nigeria. An exception to this overly urban focus of CLEEN has been its Community Police Forum, designed to give the general public a say in security and other law enforcement issues within their communities.[56] While the urbancentrism of its structures does taint it with a significant level of distance from the vast majority of the very populations on whose behalf it claims to work, it must be said to its credit that the very nature of its work – delivering human rights education to police officers – and the unitary command structure of the Nigerian police force does justify to some extent a single small secretariat. However, the near-exclusive urban location of almost all of CLEEN's educational operations cannot be similarly justified. After all, do not a significant number of police officers and formations serve in rural Nigeria? And is the task of educating such officers not advanced by the delivery of CLEEN's programs to Nigeria's rural population?

Commendably, the more personal character of CLEEN's decision-making structure has been ameliorated to some extent by its participation in external coalitions/networks. Domestically, it is a member of the Transition Monitoring Group,[57] and a partner in the Network on Police Reforms in Nigeria (NOPRIN).[58] Internationally, it is a member of the World Organization against Torture.[59]

2.7. PRISONERS' REHABILITATION AND WELFARE ACTION (PRAWA)

Replicating the preferred organizational model among NGOs in Nigeria, PRAWA is without a remarkable membership base.[60] Rather, it has different "membership ties," to various so-called "alternatives to violence" and "penal reform" clubs.[61] It is headed by an executive director and CEO who reports to a board of trustees, but who is in practice the undisputed leader of the organization. A management team comprised of PRAWA's deputy executive director, the heads of the various program units, and the head of the administration and finance unit supports the work of the CEO.[62] As PRAWA was founded by its current executive director, and as she is largely unrestrained by either an active membership or a sufficiently powerful board, it is not unreasonable to infer that benign as it may be, this NGO's governance structure, like that of almost all of its peers, is characterized by a level of "personal rule."

PRAWA currently functions from its main office in Lagos and a branch office in the New Haven area of Enugu. Both offices are thus located in large urban centers. Most of its operations are similarly located. As importantly, members of Nigeria's urbanized minority dominate the organization. However, as many of its activities are targeted at prisons and places of detention, they occur wherever such prisons are located. While some Nigerian prisons are located in rural areas, most are sited in urban centers. Nevertheless, like virtually all other such NGOs, the location of PRAWA's activities has tended to be far more urban than rural—with all the attendant consequences.

To its credit, PRAWA has built networks with like-minded organizations around the world in areas of prison reform and the rehabilitation and resettlement of former prisoners. For instance, in August 2002 it hosted the International Conference on Penal Abolition, attended by social and political groups from around world.[63] It has formed the Penal Reform Media Network (PERMNET) with the European Union and Penal Reform International.[64] And it has collaborated with the International Rehabilitation Council for Victims of Torture in setting up a number of centers for the treatment of victims of torture in Nigeria.[65]

2.8. THE HUMAN RIGHTS LAW SERVICE (HURILAWS)

Viewed from the perspective of the CLO's organizational form, HURILAWS is one of the least institutionalized of its peers. Founded by Olisa Agbakoba, one of Nigeria's brightest and most respected human rights activists and a cofounder of the CLO, it is structured like a typical Nigerian law office and is housed in the same suite of offices that houses Agbakoba's law firm. It, however, has reasonably separate offices and personnel.[66] Agbakoba serves as its senior counsel/CEO and undisputed leader, and he is assisted in his duties by an executive director, some senior legal officers, and a number of other legal officers.[67] None of these other officers has any "ownership" of HURILAWS; they are all "hired hands." As importantly, HURILAWS does not have a powerful board of directors and is not a membership organization.[68] Rather, it has a board of trustees whose role is limited to approving the organization's annual budget, and authorizing other programs/projects that the organization has to fund without donor assistance.[69] As HURILAWS is not governed either by a sufficiently powerful board or an active membership, its senior counsel is the effective decision-making authority of this organization. As such, one cannot be far off the mark if one characterizes its governance structure (however benign it has turned out to be) as characterized by a level of "personal rule."

HURILAWS' offices are located in the Apapa area of Lagos. It has no other office in the country, be it in an urban center or in a rural location. Similarly, its projects have been concentrated in urban locations, and its governance controlled by a largely urbanized cadre. However, as shall be made clear in chapter 4 of this book, it has undertaken several projects outside its Lagos base, although almost all of such projects have usually been located in another large urban center. As such, HURILAWS has not been free of the excessive urban bias that has afflicted most of its peers.

To its credit, HURILAWS has often cooperated with like-minded local and foreign groups to undertake particular projects. For instance, it has worked with the CLO and Transparency International (Nigeria) to launch a campaign to recover Nigerian government funds lodged in foreign banks by corrupt public officials.[70] It has also worked within the Transition Monitoring Group (TMG).[71] Internationally, it has forged cooperative relationships with the Legal Reform Centre in South Africa and Amnesty International.

2.9. COMMUNITY ACTION FOR POPULAR PARTICIPATION (CAPP):

Membership in CAPP is open to all Nigerians who share its goal of promoting respect for human rights and democratic norms in the country and the development and enhancement of popular structures at the community level to ensure the right of the people to take part in the government.[72] CAPP has over eight hundred registered members and is affiliated with over one hundred community associations.[73]

Formally speaking, CAPP's activities and decision-making are governed by its board of directors. This board sets policies and supervises their implementation by the Secretariat.[74] An executive director heads this secretariat.[75] The executive director is elected by the members of CAPP at its biannual congress. S/he is in charge of the day-to-day management of the organization.[76]

CAPP operates from an office in Abuja, Nigeria's administrative capital, and has offices in Kano, Plateau, Niger, and Kaduna states. However, none of these offices is independent. They are all directed from the head office in Abuja.[77] The location of CAPP's offices in large urban centers, the concentration of many of its activities and programs in these cities, and the domination of its staff by a largely urbanized activist cadre underlies the urbanized character of its administrative structure and *many* of its activities. A note of caution must be added though. CAPP is of course quite *unlike* most human rights NGOs in Nigeria in that it actually undertakes a very significant amount of work in the rural areas of the country. For instance, it has organized community and town hall meetings in the rural areas of some Northern Nigerian states, as well as in the Abuja area. Such community meetings have been aimed at promoting grassroots democracy and good governance within the target rural localities.[78] Additionally, it must be noted that the location of its offices in the Northern region of the country is out of pattern with the Lagos-centric location of most such NGOs. It geopolitical location in the North has contributed, albeit modestly, to the ongoing effort to spread human rights activism around the country.

As an integral part of the Nigerian and international human rights NGO community, CAPP has sometimes worked in concert with other domestic

and foreign groups. It was an important partner in the UAD and later participated in the TMG.[79]

2.10. HUMAN RIGHTS MONITOR (HRM)

The HRM is unlike the vast majority of its peers in the sense that it actually possesses a significant membership base. According to its records, it has
recruited two thousand five hundred members.[80] In a formal sense the governance of the organization is the overall responsibility of its membership and
its advisory board. The board is assisted by an executive committee of eight
(four men and four women). However, in real terms, the governance of HRM
is in the hands of its CEO. In Nigerian lingo, he is the *Oga,* i.e., the "boss." Like
most other such CEOs in Nigeria, he founded this NGO and he has served
continuously in that capacity from its inception to this day. Furthermore, he,
in effect, recruited HRM's advisory board, and he hires/fires its staff. And as
in most other such NGOs, the other activists tend not to have a significant
stake or "ownership" in this organization. However, the CEO's dominance of
HRM's governance is to some extent tempered by the broad policy guidelines
that are set annually by a congress consisting of its members.

To its credit, the HRM is also unlike most its peers in that its offices are
located in Kaduna, a large city in the North of the country, rather than in
or around Lagos.[81] It operates out of a single office on a prominent street
in that city and does not have any branch offices.[82] As has been noted with
respect to its peers, the location of HRM's office in a large urban center,
the concentration of its activities and programs in that and other cities, the
control of its governance structure by a cadre of largely urbanized activists,
and the urban character of its membership, all underlie the urbancentrism of
most of its human rights work.

The HRM's operational structures have also involved some external collaboration. It has been a critical part of the UAD as well as the TMG.[83]
Indeed, its executive director has served as the chair of TMG. HRM has also
been affiliated with the Penal Reform Coalition and the Network on Police
Reform in Nigeria.[84]

2.11. THE INSTITUTE FOR HUMAN RIGHTS AND HUMANI-
TARIAN LAW (IHRHL)

Founded and run by the same activist who has served as its executive director since its inception, the IHRHL is, like most other such NGOs, without
a membership base.[85] While the IHRHL is in theory governed by a board of
directors, in practice, the real power behind it, its oga, is its executive director.
In the discharge of his duties, the executive director is assisted by a small staff
of lawyers, librarians, etc, whom he hires and fires. Neither circumscribed
by a powerful board nor controlled by an active membership, the executive
director's reign over this organization can also be described as characterized
by a level of personal rule (however benign). This personal control of the
organization is ameliorated by the fact that the IHRHL's executive director

is formally answerable not only to a board of trustees which meets once or twice a year in order to makes broad policy decisions, but also to a board of management which oversees the day-to-day operations of the organization.[86]

Unlike most other such NGOs, the offices of the IHRHL are located in Port Harcourt, a large urban center in the Niger Delta region of Nigeria.[87] This, to some extent, differentiates this NGO from its peers, very few of which are located outside Lagos, and even fewer of which operate from head offices in the Niger Delta region of the country. Nevertheless, Port Harcourt is a large urban center and the IHRHL staff tend to belong to Nigeria's urbanized minority. What is more, the IHRHL's activities have not in general been mounted in or focused on rural Nigeria. As such this NGO is still much like its peers in its urban bias. That is not to say that it does not strive to reach out to the grassroots or to have a presence in those areas of the country where its expertise is most needed. For instance, it runs community legal advice centers in some states.[88] These centers are manned by paralegals and community activists who have been trained in basic legal issues.[89] These centers further serve as links between the communities in which they work and the head office, bringing to the attention of the head office community-level issues that may have national dimensions.[90]

The structure of the IHRHL is, like most other such organizations, characterized by a linkage to networks and coalitions that are ordinarily external to its core operations. IIHRHL played a very active role in the TMG; is a member of the Citizens' Forum for Constitutional Reform in Nigeria; and participates in the Penal Reform Coalition.[91] It has also worked in concert with the Geneva-based International Commission of Jurists and the New York-based Lawyers' Committee for Human Rights.[92]

3. THE SOCIAL/ECONOMIC RIGHTS NGOS

Here, issues related to the composition, structure, and location of those Nigerian human rights NGOs that, for stated reasons are categorized in chapter 2 as "social/economic rights NGOs," will be examined. These NGOs are the Socio-Economic Rights Initiative (SRI), the Social and Economic Rights Action Center (SERAC), and the Empowerment Action and Research Center (EMPARC).

3.1. THE SOCIO-ECONOMIC RIGHTS INITIATIVE [SHELTER RIGHTS INITIATIVE] (SRI)

Though formally subject to the control of its board of directors (which is currently chaired by an activist female High Court judge), this organization is in practice run by its three founders who serve as executive and associate executive directors and who by virtue of holding these offices constitute its executive management committee (EMC).[93] It is the duty of the EMC to see to the proper execution of whatever broad policy/operational decisions that are made by the board of directors.[94] Decision-making in this NGO is thus relatively collegial. In this sense, the SRI's governance arrangement is somewhat more institutionalized than is the custom among the NGO community in Nigeria. Commendably, membership in the SRI is open to all members of society who share its ideals and vision.[95] Thus far, however, it has not managed to create a significantly active or powerful membership base.

Located in and run from a relatively large single office in Lagos, the SRI is open to the same kinds of accusations of locational bias as its peers. Even though it has undertaken many projects outside Lagos, including a training workshop for high court judges held in the year 2000 which the present writer attended, almost all of these locations have been urban. Moreover, it is only occasionally that it has actively sought and included rural Nigerians in its work. What is more, it is run by a group of activists who are largely urbanized and socially elevated. While this lack of direct engagement with Nigeria's rural majority is probably a function of the unavailability of the resources needed to expand its outreach work, it has nevertheless lent some structural bias to its programs. Again, this is not a problem that is peculiar to the SRI; rather, it afflicts almost all of the NGOs in Nigeria. The redeeming quality of the SRI in this regard is the work that it has often done within and for the benefit of some poorer, local (if urban) communities.[96]

Laudably, the SRI's governance structure has on occasion admitted of the collaborative governance of one or more specific projects with one or more domestic or foreign institutions. For instance, it has worked with the UN Committee on Economic, Social and Cultural Rights and the UN Committee on the Elimination of all Forms of Discrimination against Women. It is also a member of the Habitat International Coalition and has worked with the Geneva-based Center on Housing Rights and Evictions.[97] Domestically, the SRI co-ordinates the Lagos state wing of the TMG and hosts the secretariat of the Nigerian Budget Group (which is composed of Nigerian civil society organizations involved in civil society oversight of the management and allocation of public expenditure in Nigeria).[98]

3.2. THE SOCIAL AND ECONOMIC RIGHTS ACTION CENTRE (SERAC)

The SERAC is not a membership organization.[99] Though formally governed by a board of directors, and though founded by a number of activists, SERAC is in practice run and controlled by its executive director. As SERAC's principal founder, he has had a powerful and certainly continuous hold over the affairs of the organization, one that has been strengthened by the absence of a significant membership base within this NGO.

Like the vast majority of its peer organizations, SERAC's offices are located in Lagos. SERAC, however, has the ambition of becoming national in its character and reach, hence its laudable attempts to register its presence in other parts of the country through educational workshops and seminars on economic and social rights issues (e.g., on the rights to adequate housing and education).[100] However, the fact remains that, thus far, it has not strayed very far from the largely urban-focus of the rest of the NGO community in Nigeria.

The SERAC is also run by a largely urbanized activist cadre. This has left it open to the same accusation of urban bias that has, with good reason, been leveled against most of its peers. Like the SRI, the SERAC's work does have a quality that redeems it to some extent from the dual charges of urban elitism and the absence of a real membership base. It works *with* and *within* local communities, disbursing microcredit where it is needed, mobilizing them for popular action, and sensitizing them to broader national issues. It has even set up field posts within these communities. And even when these communities have been located in urban areas, they have been among the most powerless and dispossessed populations of the country.[101]

Significantly, its governance arrangement has on occasion accommodated joint ventures with other like-minded groups, domestic and foreign. For instance, its has been part of an umbrella organization put together by BOABAB to specifically work on women's issues.[102] It has also worked with the SRI on behalf of the former residents of the Maroko shantytown who were forcibly evicted by the notorious regime of the then military governor of Lagos state, Colonel Raji Rasaki.[103] Its much celebrated collaboration with the New York-based Centre on Economic and Social Rights is a good example of its linkages with foreign NGOs.[104]

3.3. THE EMPOWERMENT AND ACTION RESEARCH CENTRE (EMPARC)

While the EMPARC originally set out to function as a collective, over time (and through no particular fault of its executive director) its organizational structure became more typical of NGOs in that the EMPARC developed into an organization that was led by one dominant executive director.[105] As at 2003, it had returned to its original collectivist structure. But though it is governed by its board, the real initiative and power within this organization continues to lie with its executive director.[106] And like most of its peers, it does not have a mass membership base.[107]

While its main offices are in Lagos, it does have a resource center in the semi-rural Ibeju-Lekki area of Lagos state. Conceived of as an action and research centre, it has concentrated on the empowerment of Nigeria's most powerless and dispossessed underclass in order to advance their socioeconomic status. As such, while many of its projects have been mounted within the highly urbanized Lagos area, and while its officers have been mostly drawn from Nigeria's urbanized minority, it has nevertheless understood the limitations of an urbancentered approach in the Nigerian context. As such, even though it has now wound down most of its operations, it has continued to maintain operations in its rural location.[108]

EMPARC has also participated in coalitions/networks of domestic and foreign human rights groups. For instance, it has participated actively in the Women's Global Network for Reproductive Rights and in local coalitions concerned with sustainable development and capacity building for young people.[109]

4. THE GENDER-FOCUSED NGOS

The organizations that will be considered here are Baobab for Women's Rights (BAOBAB), the Women's Aid Collective (WACOL), and the Women's Rights Advancement and Protection Alternative (WRAPA).

Since these organizations are not in institutional terms very different from the civil/political rights and social/economic rights NGOs already considered, their examination here will be relatively brief.

4.1. BAOBAB FOR WOMEN'S RIGHTS (BAOBAB)

Unlike most of its peers, BAOBAB is a reasonably national organization; with affiliated field committees and organs located in communities in about fourteen of Nigeria's thirty-six states.[110] Its main office in Lagos coordinates these field organs and provides them with information, resources, requisite training, and funding.[111] Although it has a board of directors that sets broad policies and approves new program initiatives, its day-to-day management is overseen by an executive director whose duties include the hiring/firing of most staff, the supervision of the various units of the organization, and the implementation of approved programs.[112]

Although its main offices are located in Lagos, its grasp is much more national than is normal within the NGO community in Nigeria. However, notwithstanding the fact that it has considerable presence in rural Nigeria, especially compared with some of the NGOs we have studied so far, it would be a mistake to think of this otherwise dynamic organization as a rural-centered NGO. Not only have most of its activities and projects been located in urban areas, most of its offices or contact groups are located in urban centers, and its governance structures are dominated by a cadre of largely urbanized and elite Nigerians.[113] As has been already noted, this sort of urban bias tends to be a weakness in the Nigerian NGO context.

BAOBAB has also on occasion worked in coalitions/networks with similar-minded organizations in pursuit of their common goals. For instance, BOABAB is part of the Coalition on Violence against Women.[114] It is also part of the Coalition for the Protection of Women's Rights under Religious and Customary Law, and it collaborates with the U.S.-based Women's Learning Partnership for Peace.[115] As a result of this collaboration, BOABAB has produced a leadership manual for women that it uses in training its outreach volunteers.[116] It also played a leading role in the preparation and submission by Nigeria's NGO community of a report on Nigeria's compliance with its obligations under the Convention for the Elimination of all Forms of Discrimination against Women (CEDAW) to the UN Committee responsible for monitoring the implementation of that convention.[117] What is more, BOABAB has operated an NGO support network around the country. It regularly supports affiliated or networked NGOs with advice, technical aid, and sometimes hands-on aid.[118] For instance, it has provided hands-on and technical support to WISSEA (Women for Independence, Self-Sufficiency and Economic Advancement), based in Kano. In this case, it did so largely by seconding one of its program directors to that organization.

4.2. WOMEN'S AID COLLECTIVE (WACOL)

In terms of composition, structure, and location, WACOL is much like most other NGOs in Nigeria. It does not have a significant membership base. However, it does have a board of directors that is charged with the broad governance of the organization. As might be expected, the real power within the organization lies with is its founder/executive director/CEO. It is this CEO that set up the board, hired its staff, and sourced the bulk of its funds. WACOL's executive director is assisted by a relatively large staff but, for the most part, supervises the day-to-day operations of the organization.

Worthy of mention here is the fact that WACOL is different from most of its peers in operating from a head office located in Enugu, and a branch office in Port Harcourt. Both cities are located in the old Southeastern region of Nigeria and are as such outside the typical Lagos location of most similar organizations. Despite this difference, WACOL is still somewhat typical of these NGOs in being run by a largely urbanized activist cadre, and in having the bulk of its operations run from, and mounted in, urban areas. In any case, the physical locations of its two offices are very urban. While it does have a number of important rural projects, especially in Rivers and Bayelsa states, and while it does not explicitly want to be urban-centered in orientation, rural-centered activism has thus far not been its major focus.[119]

WACOL has participated in networks and coalitions designed to enhance its own work. It has for instance been a notable participant in the Coalition on Violence against Women. It has also collaborated with the Swedish NGO Foundation and the International Human Rights Law Group.[120] As its leader, Joy Ezeilo, has put it, since "networking is critical for women's mobilization," WACOL "emphasises coalitions."[121]

4.3. THE WOMEN'S RIGHTS ADVANCEMENT AND PROTECTION ALTERNATIVE (WRAPA):

WRAPA was founded by Fati Abubakar, a high court judge.[122] As might be expected, Justice Abubakar continues to play a very prominent role in the governance of this organization. Indeed, she is the chair of its board of trustees.[123] In a sense, WRAPA is somewhat different from most of its peers, which are largely run on a day-to-day basis by the same persons who founded the given organization. In this case, Justice Abubakar is not its CEO. Rather, WRAPA's CEO is its secretary general, Saudatu Mahdi.[124]. While the board of trustees sets the broad policies of the organization, the secretary general supervises its day-to-day activities and operations.[125]

Unlike most of its peers, WRAPA does, at least in formal terms, view itself as a membership organization. As of December 2001, it had roughly 7,189 people on its membership rolls.[126] By October 2002, this number had grown to 11,217.[127] As interesting is the fact that its membership consists not just of women but also of many men and youths.[128] Furthermore, it is significant that at least 19 international subscribers have been attracted to its membership roll.[129]

While the location of its main office in Abuja, in the Northern part of the country, does differentiate it from most such NGOs in Nigeria, it is still much like most of these other groups in focusing the bulk of its attention on urban Nigeria, while paying far less direct attention to the needs of Nigeria's majority rural population. This is not of course to say that it has entirely neglected the rural areas. It has not. It has run a number of adult education and skills development workshops in some rural localities.[130] Much to WRAPA's credit as well, it has made considerable attempts to have its presence felt across the country. In this direction, branch offices have been opened or are slated to open in about thirty-six Nigerian states.[131]

WRAPA is, *inter alia*, a member of the Coalition against Violence against Women.[132]

5. THE MINORITY/ENVIRONMENTAL RIGHTS NGOS

The organizations considered here are the Movement for the Survival of Ogoni People (MOSOP), and Environmental Rights Action (ERA).

5.1. THE MOVEMENT FOR THE SURVIVAL OF OGONI PEOPLE (MOSOP):

Unlike most such NGOs in Nigeria, MOSOP is essentially a membership organization. However, its membership philosophy is different from the other NGOs discussed thus far in the sense that one need not register or pay dues to become or continue to be a member. Rather, every Ogoni, either at home in Nigeria or abroad is considered a member by virtue of his/her ethnicity.[133] As striking in the current context is the fact that MOSOP is in fact a grassroots organization and popular movement which consists of thousands of mostly rural dwelling Ogoni people working almost always in concert for the actualization of specific dreams regarding their status within Nigeria.[134] As we have seen earlier in this chapter, most NGOs in Nigeria have, to put it mildly, not been blessed with this kind of popular membership base. In this sense is MOSOP quite unique, at least when compared with most of its peers in the NGO community in Nigeria: for it is one of the few Nigerian NGOs that do not exclude from its membership the very people whose rights it wants to advance. Rather, it is closely connected to those whose voices Upendra Baxi has described as "voices of suffering."[135]

MOSOP is governed by an executive organ that consists of its president, vice-president, heads of its various units (including a women's unit), and its various representatives around the world.[136] These officers are directly responsible to its very active and vocal mass membership.[137] Again, unlike the vast majority of such NGOs, MOSOP's chief executive is to a significant extent constrained by the wishes of a vast and highly active membership. However, it cannot be denied that its top national leadership consists mostly of a largely urbanized cadre of activists. In this last sense, MOSOP marginally resembles the typical NGO in Nigeria.

While MOSOP's main offices are in Port Harcourt, the city closest in location to Ogoniland, its grassroots mobilization work is done in the villages and towns of Ogoniland.[138] Thus, while it does carry on some of its work outside Ogoniland (sensitizing the local and international populations to its struggles for the Ogoni), it is most unlike its peers in terms of the eminently rural and grassroots location of the bulk of its activities.

As commendably, MOSOP has tended to establish linkages with local and foreign groups in order to advance its cause. It has worked in alliance with the internationally recognized environmental NGO, Greenpeace, and with the British NGO, Oxfam.[139] As importantly, MOSOP represents the Ogoni people at the Unrecognized People's and Nations Organization.[140] Within Nigeria, MOSOP also aligns itself with other NGOs. For instance, during its darkest days, when the bulk of its leadership was either detained or had been tried and executed by the Abacha junta, legal counsel supplied by other NGOs greatly assisted MOSOP. These other groups also launched dedicated (though ultimately unsuccessful) campaigns to save the "Ogoni nine" (as the convicted leaders of MOSOP were referred to) from execution.

5.2. ENVIRONMENTAL RIGHTS ACTION (ERA):

Like MOSOP, ERA has an active membership base within the communities it works.[141] Like those of the NGOs examined thus far, its governance structure comprises, *inter alia*, of a board of directors that is charged with the responsibility of setting broad policies and overseeing the overall direction of the organization.[142] This board consists of seven rotating members. ERA's day-to-day operations are entrusted to an executive management committee (EMC) made up of the Executive Director, his deputy, the Programs Director and all the Program Managers.[143] This governing structure distinguishes it from most of the other NGOs we have studied so far in that its decisions are made in a somewhat collegial way. However, it needs to be kept in mind that ERA is still a very typical Nigerian NGO in the sense that its founders, who have for the most part served as its leaders since its formation, practically "run the show". There is no doubt that these founders are the ogas of this NGO.

The current restiveness of the Niger Delta minorities about the devastation of their environment by oil pollution has provided this organization with a great opportunity to mobilize and to serve as a genuine voice for its grassroots membership base.

ERA operates from an office in Benin City.[144] The location of ERA in a major urban center and its governance by a cadre of largely urbanized activists underlies the urban character of *some* of its work. Yet, ERA has *largely* worked in rural communities, mobilizing them to resist the pollution of their lands and—through media awareness campaigns, "environmental testimonies," and "alerts" from the field— to demand action from their government.[145]

As an integral part of the Nigerian and international human rights movement, ERA has on occasion worked within coalitions/networks of like-minded groups—both domestic and foreign in origin. For instance, ERA constitutes the Nigerian chapter of Friends of the Earth and is a member of the Federation of Community Organizations Opposed to the Dangerous Environmental Work of Oil MNCs. It is also serves the Co-coordinating Secretariat for Oil Watch Africa.[146]

6. AN OVERALL ASSESSMENT

Based on the evidence supplied and discussed above, and given the discussion in the preceding chapter, a number of important observations may be made regarding the composition, structure, and geopolitical location of NGOs in Nigeria. In general, the evidence discussed firmly supports Odinkalu's insightful hypothesis that these NGOs tend to be located in an urban area, are almost always controlled by a core management, and generally lack an active and powerful membership base.[147] In addition, some evidence of the proliferation of human rights NGOs in Nigeria and the consequent fragmentation of that community is implied in the analysis conducted both in this chapter and in the one that immediately precedes it.

First, virtually all of these NGOs are, in practice, controlled (with few effective internal checks) by a powerful founder/CEO, who is the oga (or undisputed boss) of his/her organizations). Without a powerful board of directors, and lacking an active and powerful membership, such founder/CEOs usually reign over their organizations largely unconstrained by the local community. Having thus largely excluded from their real ranks the very population of average Nigerians whose interests they want to advance, the governance systems within most of these NGOs tend to reflect the organizational architecture of the typical Nigerian law firm, i.e., where one oga "owns" the law firm and every other lawyer that works in the firm is a hired hand without any real stake in the organization. Since almost all of these NGO founder/CEOs are lawyers, it is possible that there is some relationship between the culture of personal rule in many of these NGOs and a similar culture within Nigerian law firms. However, an important factor that helps explain both cases is the underlying struggle for resources among actors in an atmosphere of relative scarcity.[148] Exclusive control of an autonomous unit of activity (be it an NGO or a law firm) ensures complete suzerainty over the resources that flow into that unit of activity. In a country where most people live below the poverty line, this is one very powerful incentive for the formation of, and exercise of a high degree of personal control over, such founder-headed autonomous units. However, in a few cases, two or three activists have shared power within a given NGO. Yet even in these few cases, the executive team is, because of the absence of an active membership and a powerful board, almost always without any really effective institutional checks on its power. A notable exception in this regard is the CLO – Nigeria's most institutionalized human rights organization. This group is one of the few

Nigerian human rights organizations to have been described by the *Swedish NGO Foundation's Study on the Status of Human Rights Organizations in Sub-Sahara Africa* as characterized by "strong institutional structures".[149] Therefore, on the whole Paul Wapner's conclusion that NGOs are *in general* "accountable to their members" is hardly applicable to the NGO scene in Nigeria.[150] Peter Spiro's guarded conclusion that, *in general*, even in the of cases where they are run as membership organizations, NGOs can hardly be said to be largely controlled by their membership, is much more reflective of the realities of the NGO scene in Nigeria.[151]

Second, a related, if somewhat obvious, observation concerning the composition of the major NGOs in Nigeria is that most of them are led and dominated by male activists. While a growing number of these groups are now led by women, that number remains obviously disproportionate to the number of female Nigerians, to the ratio of male-female impoverishment, and even to the number of female activists overall. This trend within the NGO community in Nigeria reflects a similar trend within the wider Nigerian society. For instance, in the first session of Nigeria's Fourth National Assembly (i.e., between 1999 and 2003), of the 109 seats in the Senate only 3 were occupied by women; only 12 of the 366 seats in the House of Representatives were occupied by women; and only 31 women were elected into the Houses of Assembly of the 36 states of the federation.[152] What is more, of the 50 ministers appointed by the President, only 6 were women.

Third, generally based in urban areas or centered on urban populations, almost all these NGOs can be accused of a significant (although varying) level of urban bias. And the majority of these groups are guilty of a sustained neglect of Nigeria's majority rural population. Their projects are usually mounted in the large urban centers; their activities are almost always focused on urban populations; and their leaders and employees are mostly drawn from the ranks of Nigeria's minority urban population. As one activist group has itself put it:

> Most human rights NGOs [in Nigeria] are urban-based, leaving the majority rural poor ignorant about their civic responsibilities. [Unlike most NGOs] Abuja-based CAPP has, however, commenced grassroots mobilization in several areas towards enhanced consciousness of rural dwellers about their surrounding.[153]

Furthermore, the vast majority of these NGOs are located in and operate from Lagos, Nigeria's largest city and economic capital, restricting enormously the geo-political reach (not to talk of grasp) of these organizations. While a few of them (like CAPP and the SERAC) have made significant efforts to extend their reach to more parts of the country, few, if any, of such efforts have been as successful as would be wished. Few NGOs have been able to extend their grasp beyond their immediate environs, usually Lagos or some other large urban centre. Perhaps only MOSOP is largely unassailable on these grounds. As Ibhawoh has put it:

...the approach to human rights activism in Nigeria has tended to be elitist and urban-centered. Although efforts have been made by a number of NGOs to reach out to the grassroots and rural populations, their success in this direction has been limited. Most NGOs are still based in urban areas and run by elites in a country where a vast section of the population live in rural areas.[151]

Fourth, it is also easily decipherable from the discussions in this chapter and from the one that precedes it that there has been a marked proliferation of NGOs in Nigeria in the period under study (1987–2001). A significant portion of that proliferation has been produced by the fragmentation of preexisting NGOs. And all kinds of NGOs in Nigeria – from civil/political rights groups to women's rights groups – have benefited or suffered from this proliferation. Such proliferation has definitely resulted in the speedy and vigorous growth of the NGO community in Nigeria: it has led to the creation of hundreds of new activist jobs and to the development of specialized and more technically competent groups. However, such proliferation has not been without its negative consequences, some of which (as shall be shown in chapter 7) have been quite damaging to the overall effectiveness of this NGO community. In the end though, the point is not that proliferation is a bad thing in and of itself. As Joy Ezeilo – a senior Nigerian human rights activist – has correctly noted:

> ...it depends on what people have in mind while forming [new] NGOs. What is the purpose of setting up [new] NGOs? How committed are the people involved? What are the issues they want to address? *Is the organization going to make a difference—do something that has not been done?*....When you see these things [that is new NGOs] coming up without any clear objectives, of course they will fall by the roadside when the chips are down.[155]

Lastly, almost every such NGO has participated in coalitions/networks with other similar groups, domestic and foreign, in order to strengthen its hand. Such coalitions/networks have included the Ubani Chima-led Campaign for Democracy (CD) and the Clement Nwankwo-led Transition Monitoring Group (TMG).[156] Participation in such coalitions/networks has (for specific issues and for the duration of particular campaigns) modified, a little, the typical personal mode of rule within these groups and has introduced a larger measure of democratic accountability to the operations of these organizations, as coalition decisions are much more likely to be made in a much more collegial manner (by agreement among the participating units). For many Nigerian human rights NGO leaders, unconstrained as they largely are by their own internal institutional arrangements, coalitions are one of the few fora at which they are held accountable by a powerful and active membership base.

Overall, it is quite clear from the discussion and analysis in this and the preceding chapters that Robert Fatton, Jr., was *partly* correct when he charged years ago that:

> "Civil society's plurality does not entail an automatic and equal representation of the whole polity [genders, classes etc]. Civil society is not the *all-encompassing* movement of popular empowerment ... portrayed in the reveling and exaggerated celebrations of its advocates."[157]

That the intentional or unintentional exclusion of the vast majority of Nigeria's vulnerable population from direct or indirect participation in the structures and governance of these NGOs does help explain the *limited* nature of the success that such groups have so far enjoyed in engendering a human rights transformation in Nigeria becomes rather apparent in chapter 7.

NOTES

1. See chapter 1 for a definition of these key terms.
2. See C.A. Odinkalu, "Why More Africans Don't Use the Human Rights Language" Human Rights Dialogue (2000): 3, 4.
3. Ibid.
4. Ibid.
5. M. Mutua, "A Discussion on the Legitimacy of Human Rights NGOs in Africa," *Africa Legal Aid Quarterly* (October-December 1997): 28.
6. See transcripts of follow up interview with OU, 20 March 2003 (on file with author).
7. Ibid.
8. Ibid.
9. Ibid.
10. Ibid.
11. Ibid.
12. Ibid.
13. Ibid. See also *Liberty* (a CLO publication) 11:5 (1999): 32.
14. See Swedish NGO Foundation, "The Status of Human Rights Organizations in sub-Saharan Africa; Overview-Characteristics and Problems of Human Rights NGOs" on-line: http://www1.umn.edu/humanrts/africa/charactr.htm (visited: 20 October 2000).
15. Interview with OU, *supra* note 6.
16. See Swedish NGO Foundation, *supra* note 14.
17. See B. Ibhawoh, *Human Rights Organizations in Nigeria: An Appraisal Report on the Human Rights NGO Community in Nigeria* (Copenhagen, Denmark: The Danish Centre for Human Rights, 2001), 11.
18. Ibid., 12.

19. See J. Gathii and C. Nyamu, "Reflections on United States-Based Human Rights NGOS' Work on Africa," *Harvard Human Rights Journal* 9 (1996): 285, 287-88.

20. Ibid.

21. Ibid., 295–96.

22. See transcripts of interview with OB, 11 March 2002 (on file with author). According to this activist, the CRP has about eighty-four members on its membership lists.

23. Ibid.

24. Ibid.

25. Ibid.

26. Ibid.

27. Ibid.

28. Ibid.

29. See Odinkalu, *supra* note 2.

30. See transcripts of interview with OD, 13 March 2000 (on file with the author).

31. I borrow athis expression from Upendra Baxi, see U. Baxi, *The Future of Human Rights* (New Delhi: Oxford University Press, 2002), 4 , 152.

32. See transcripts of interview with OD, 13 March 2000 (on file with the author).

33. See transcripts of interview with FF, 25 August 2001 (on file with the author).

34. See transcripts of interview with JS, 20 March 2003 (on file with the author).

35. Ibid.

36. Ibid.

37. Ibid.

38. Ibid.

39. Ibid.

40. Ibid.

41. Interview with AL, 4 March 2003 (on file with the author).

42. Ibid.

43. Ibid.

44. See C.A. Odinkalu, *supra* note 2 at 3-4.

45. See Interview with AL, *supra* note 41.

46. Ibid.

47. See *Media Rights Monitor* (an MRA publication) 5 (2000): 13.

48. See Media Rights Agenda, *A Harvest of Blooms* (Lagos: Media Rights Agenda, 2000), 16.

49. Interview with AL, *supra* note 41.

50. See transcripts of interview with JD, 28 March 2003 (on file with author).

51. Ibid.

52. Ibid.

53. Ibid.

54. Ibid.

55. Ibid. (This program is available in all the thirty-six states of the federation).
56. Ibid.
57. Ibid.
58. Ibid.
59. See www.cleen.kabissa.org/links.htm.
60. See www.ngprawa.org/prawa/about/membership.htm.
61. Ibid.
62. Ibid.
63. Ibid.
64. *PRAWA News* 2:3 (1999): 5.
65. Ibid., 27.
66. See transcripts of interview with OH, 28 March 2003 (on file with the author).
67. Ibid.
68. Ibid.
69. Ibid.
70. See HURILAWS, 1999 *Annual Report and Accounts* (Lagos: HURILAWS, 2000), 2–3.
71. See ibid., *The Governance Scorecard: Review of Democratic Governance in Nigeria* (Lagos: HURILAWS, 2000), 137.
72. See transcripts of interview with CW on 11 March 2003 (on file with the author).
73. See CAPP, *Selling the Message* (Abuja: CAPP, 1999), 28–29.
74. Ibid.
75. Ibid.
76. Ibid.
77. Ibid.
78. See B. Ibhawoh, *supra* note 17, 29.
79. See transcripts of interview with CW, *supra* note 72.
80. See record of email survey of 17 June 2003 (on file with the author).
81. Ibid.
82. Ibid.
83. Ibid.
84. Ibid.
85. See transcripts of interview with NA, 20 March 2003 (on file with the author).
86. Ibid.
87. Ibid.
88. Ibid.
89. Ibid.
90. Ibid.
91. Ibid.
92. Ibid.
93. See http:///www.srinitiative.org/saboutus.htm (visited 11 March 2003).

94. Ibid.

95. Ibid.

96. Some of these are discussed in Chapters 4 and 6 infra.

97. See http://www.srinitiative.org/saboutus.htm (visited 11 March 2003).

98. Ibid.

99. See transcripts of follow-up interview with NJ, 28 March 2003 (on file with the author).

100. Ibid. These seminars and workshops have been held in places such as Abuja, Port Harcourt, Kaduna, etc.

101. See transcripts of interview with AJI, 29 April 2002 (on file with the author).

102. See interview with NJ *supra* note 100.

103. See H. Hershkoff and A. McCutcheon, "Public Interest Litigation: An International Perspective," in M. McClymont and S. Golub, eds., *Many Roads to Justice: The Law-Related Work of Ford Foundation Grantees Around the World* (New York: The Ford Foundation, 2000), 283, 293.

104. See *Access Quarterly* [a SERAC publication] 1-2 (2000): 25.

105. See transcripts of interview with IA, 11 July 2002 (on file with the author).

106. Ibid.

107. Ibid.

108. See record of email of survey of IA, 13 June 2003 (on file with the author).

109. Ibid.

110. See transcripts of interview with DFB, 1 April 2003 (on file with the author.)

111. Ibid.

112. Ibid.

113. Ibid.

114. Ibid.

115. Ibid.

116. Ibid.

117. Ibid. See also *NGO's CEDAW Report for Nigeria* (Lagos: BOABAB, 1999).

118. See BOABAB, *Annual Report 1999* (Lagos: BAOBAB, 1999), 15.

119. See *Action Woman* (a WACOL publication) 1:1(2002): 26.

120. See WACOL, *Women's Socio-Economic and Legal Rights* (Enugu: WACOL, 2001), 2; and *Action Woman* (a WACOL publication) 1:1(2002): 8.

121. Ibid., 25.

122. See transcripts of Interview with MS, 7th March 2003 (on file with the author).

123. Ibid.

124. Ibid.

125. Ibid.

126. See *Daily Trust*, 17 January 2003, on-line: http://allafrica.com/stories/200301170355.html (visited 13 May 2003).

127. Ibid.

128. Ibid.
129. Ibid.
130. See transcript of Interview with MS, *supra* note 122.
131. Ibid.
132. Ibid.
133. See transcripts of interview with WJ, 1 April 2003 (on file with the author).
134. Ibid. See also S. Cayford, "The Ogoni Uprising: Oil, Human Rights and a Democratic Alternative in Nigeria" *Africa Today* 43:2 (1996): 183, 187.
135. See U. Baxi, *supra* note 31 at 152.
136. See transcript of interview with WJ, *supra* note 133.
137. Ibid.
138. Ibid.
139. Ibid.
140. Ibid.
141. See transcript of interview with NP, 10 January 2003 (on file with the author).
142. Ibid.
143. Ibid.
144. Ibid.
145. Ibid.
146. Ibid.
147. See Odinkalu, *supra* note 2.
148. Concerning NGOs, Andrew Ikelegbe and Bonny Ibhawoh have found this factor to be explanatory. See A. Ikelegbe, "The Perverse Manifestation of Civil Society: Evidence from Nigeria" *The Journal of Modern African Studies* 39 (2001): 1, 10; and B. Ibhawoh, *Human Rights Organizations in Nigeria: An Appraisal Report on the Human Rights NGO Community in Nigeria* (Copenhagen, Demark: The Danish Centre for Human Rights, 2001), 10–40.
149. See Swedish NGO Foundation, "The Status of Human Rights Organizations in Sub-Saharan Africa: Nigeria," on-line: http://www1.umn.edu/humanrts/africa/nigeria.htm (visited 20 October 2000).
150. See P. Wapner, "Defending Accountability in NGOs" *Chicago Journal of International Law* 3 (2002): 197, 201.
151. See P.J. Spiro, "Accounting for NGOs" *Chicago Journal of International Law* 3 (2002): 161, 163.
152. See J. Ezeilo, *Gender, Politics and the Law* (Enugu: WACOL, 1999), 12–15.
153. See *Legislative Mandate* (a CAPP publication) 1:1 (1999): 38.
154. See B. Ibhawoh, *supra* note 17 at 44.
155. See *Action Woman* (A WACOL Publication) 1:1 (2002): 25. Emphasis added.
156. Ibid.,10–12.
157. See R. Fatton Jr, "Africa in the Age of Democratization: The Civic Limitations of Civil Society," *African Studies Review* 38 (1995): 67-94. Emphasis added.

CHAPTER 4

BETWEEN CARE AND ELITISM
THE PROGRAMS AND METHODS
OF THE HUMAN RIGHTS NGOS IN NIGERIA

I. INTRODUCTION

As part of the book's broader attempt to understand the character and impact of the NGO community in Nigeria,[1] it is pertinent, at this point, to inquire into the strengths and deficiencies of the programs mounted and methods deployed by the organizations that constitute this NGO community. The character of these groups cannot otherwise be fully appreciated.

That some conceptual and practical diversity exists in the programs and methods of the various groups that constitute this NGO community is evident from the following lengthy passage from Tunji Abayomi's early essay on the nature of these organizations. This passage is so important as to deserve extensive reproduction here. According to Abayomi:

> ...Human Rights organizations in Africa [i.e., including Nigeria] fall into three broad categories. The first group may be described as the *negative proclaimers* of abuses or perceived abuses. The Nigerian Civil Liberties Organization and the London based Africa Watch [now referred to as Human Rights Watch Africa] fall within this category. It can be said that of this group [sic] no news is worth proclaiming except bad human rights news. They justify their method on the ground that the only business of a human rights group is to proclaim abuses. This negative proclamation is what is commonly described as human rights monitoring. The second group may be described as *remote institution protectors*. As non-activists, the work of this group is very rarely heard of in the media. The approach [sic] is often institutional in nature, non-confrontational and generally quiet. The members of the group are often respected outside Africa because of long established nexus with the outside world academic community. They often have budgetary support from governments though reasonably autonomous. Within this category are human rights institutes and education centers such as the Centre for Human Rights of

the University of Cairo, the Institute of Advanced Legal Studies in Nigeria and the African Centre for Democracy and Human Rights Studies in the Gambia. The third category is typified by an organization like Human Rights Africa....This is a category made up of *"Systematic Value Infusers"*. They often have subjective sympathy for Africa, both in content and approach. There is a clearer distinction between its work and that of the negative proclaimers since its declared mission is not to show how bad Africa is (negative proclamation) but to show how good it can be (positive inspiration) through the efforts of Africans, and friends of Africans. The main criticism of the "systematic value infusers" is that it is often in discourse with perceived human rights abusers such as governments in Africa.[2]

Viewed from the perspective of the character of their programs and methods, NGOs in Nigeria tend to fall within the first and the last of the three categories that have been outlined and described by Abayomi. While most of these NGOs tend to combine the two kinds of approaches suggested by Abayomi's categories, one approach usually predominates. As such, it is reasonable to classify a given NGO either as "negative proclaimer" or "systematic value infuser." The best examples of the NGOs that mostly operate as systematic value infusers are Human Rights Africa (HRA), the Institute of Human Rights and Humanitarian Law (IHRHL), the Empowerment and Action Research Center (EMPARC), and the Center for Law Enforcement Education (CLEEN).[3] Examples of the NGOs that tend to function for the most part as negative proclaimers are the Civil Liberties Organization (CLO), the Constitutional Rights Project (CRP), Media Rights Agenda (MRA), and the Women's Rights Advancement and Protection Alternative (WRAPA). However, as almost every one of these NGOs now tends to double as both a negative proclaimer and a systematic value infuser, Abayomi's typology is no longer as useful as it once was.[4] A range of programs and methods have been adopted and deployed by these NGOs during the period that is of concern to this book. These programs and methods tend to reflect the approaches that have been typical within the global human rights NGO community.[5] Accordingly, Abayomi's typology is not adopted here.

Instead, this chapter is devoted to an examination and assessment of the strengths and the deficiencies of the various specific programs and methods that have been adopted within this NGO community. In the end it should become clear that while these organizations have mounted creative programs and applied useful methods in pursuit of their activist vocation, many significant conceptual and practical problems continue to dog their efforts.

2. THE NATURE OF THE PROGRAMS AND METHODS OF NIGE-RIAN HUMAN RIGHTS NGOS

The major types of NGO programs and methods to be discussed here are monitoring, research and reporting; strategic impact litigation; legislative advocacy; campaigns, mass mobilization, and human rights education; election monitoring; microcredit lending; prison reform and decongestion; coalitions and networks; international collaboration; gender-focused activism; minority/environmental rights activism; social/economic rights activism; and civil/political rights activism.

2.1. MONITORING, RESEARCH, AND REPORTING

The monitoring, research, and reporting work that almost all the relevant NGOs do consists of the surveillance, investigation, documentation, and publicizing of human rights violations. A quotation from George Shepherd captures the salience of this mode of activism to the work of most NGOs around the world. Shepherd is of the view that "NGOs act as investigative and warning systems."[6] Claude Welch has also noted that:

> NGOs are, in large measure, *providers of data*. They seek to gather, verify, and above all disseminate information. They fight with pen, not sword, believing in the efficacy of the written word to change government policies. NGOs are involved in "promoting change by reporting fact".[7]

Almost every one of the NGOs that concern us here has at one time or another adopted this approach. A number of examples will suffice to illustrate this point. Media Rights Agenda (MRA) has been running a broadcast monitoring project for many years. The objective of this project is to monitor and assess the media's coverage of:

> Political and human rights issues [in order] to ascertain the extent of coverage given to such issues, the pattern of reporting of events affecting government officials, the fairness of allocation of airtime to various political parties and the efforts made to reach the rural and illiterate population.[8]

MRA also publishes a monthly report articulating its observations,[9] and specifically conducted this kind of monitoring during the 1999 transitional period.[10]

The Constitutional Rights Project (CRP) has conducted in-depth research and issued reports on topics such as juvenile justice and press freedom in Nigeria.[11] The Socio-Economic Rights Initiative (SRI) has completed studies on housing, health, and education that provided the basis for recommendations to the Nigerian government for policy change and constitutional reform.[12] Specifically, SRI undertook a review of the Nigerian constitution and all laws and policies pertaining to housing, health, and education, and has evaluated them in terms of their compliance with international standards.[13]

SERAC has conducted research and hosted conferences designed to advance the promotion and protection of the human rights of persons living with HIV/AIDS in Nigeria.[14]

In the same spirit, the Committee for Defense of Human Rights has "through its newsletter exposed extra-judicial killings by state agents."[15] It has also reported on the Lagos state government's cruel dispossession of the residents of Maroko of their land.

As the oldest of this generation of NGOs, it is not surprising that the CLO has conducted countless research projects and published a large number of reports. For instance, the organization has published several annual reports on the state of human rights in Nigeria and also produces two major journals, *Liberty* and the *Journal of Human Rights Law and Practice*.[16] What is more, in August 1991, the CLO launched a groundbreaking book-length report captioned *Behind the Wall* that exposed the dehumanizing conditions in Nigerian prisons.[17] The exposure that this book gave to the deplorable state of Nigeria's prisons generated a lot of debate, forcing the federal government to "take measures to improve prison conditions."[18]

Partly as a result of the ensuing heightened national awareness about the problematic state of Nigeria's prisons, Prisoners' Rights and Welfare Action (PRAWA), a full-time prisoner's rights NGO, has now emerged. To its credit, PRAWA has visited over 100 of the 142 prisons in the country.[19] It has also assisted the African Commission on Human and Peoples' Rights' Special Rapporteur on Prisons and Centers of Detention in visiting and monitoring prisons in the rest of Africa.[20] PRAWA has also established "Prison Links Units" in 89 prisons across the federation to assist it in its monitoring work.[21] Some of the goals of this program include the facilitation of prison decongestion and of improved living conditions for prisoners.[22]

The Institute of Human Rights and Humanitarian Law (IHRHL) runs a library and documentation center at its offices in Port Harcourt. Established in August 1998, this library's purpose is to acquire, process, store, and disseminate information towards empowering the masses to identify and assert their interests.[23] This library has established networks with other libraries and human rights groups around the globe.[24] It also collects evidence of abuse from the institute's nationwide network.[25] The IHRHL has also published a number of human rights books, reports, and pamphlets.[26]

In terms of its contributions to such human rights research efforts, Human Rights Africa (HRA) has established a book center at its headquarters—as an extension of its African Library for Human Rights and Democracy. Books on human rights, democracy, constitutional law, and other related areas are housed at this location.[27] It has also produced a number of human rights publications.[28]

The Empowerment Action and Research Center (EMPARC) has on occasion commissioned relevant research and has published the results of such research, mostly in an annual lecture series. For instance, the first such annual lecture was on "Africa and the Challenge of Empowerment", and was delivered by Omafume F. Onoge—a university professor.[29] The fourth annual lecture was on "Human Rights and Social Justice: An African Perspective", and was delivered by Osita C. Eze – also a university professor.[30]

It is worthy of note here that although a portion of the monitoring, research and reporting work that these NGOs have done has been concerned with social/economic rights, women's rights, and minority/environmental rights, the lion's share of their efforts has, as usual, been devoted to the advancement of civil/political rights activism.

2.2. STRATEGIC IMPACT LITIGATION

The expression "strategic impact litigation" refers to the use of particular "test cases" to broaden the general access of members of the society to the enjoyment of their human rights. This strategy has been widely used by progressive social forces around the world.[31]

Not surprisingly, the bulk of the work that has been done within the NGO community in Nigeria in terms of strategic impact litigation has concerned the protection of civil/political rights. An important aspect of the civil/political rights litigation that has been undertaken by these NGOs is their legal struggle against police brutality. For instance, many of these NGOs have championed the prosecution of police officers who have are involved in the unlawful killing of innocent Nigerians. In one important 1991 case, the CLO saw to the prosecution of police officers who unlawfully killed one Dr. Nwogu Okere.[32] In similar cases, the same organization also saw to the prosecution of the police officers responsible for the deaths of Colonel Israel Rindam on 6 September 1992 and of the Dawodu brothers on 17 November 1987.[33]

The promotion and protection of press freedom has also formed another important trajectory of the strategic impact litigation programs and methods of many of these NGOs. For instance, Media Rights Agenda (MRA) has been "undertaking a program of litigation for the purpose of promoting and protecting media freedom in Nigeria."[34] This program has also managed to provide legal aid to approximately 50 distressed journalists.[35] About forty-seven of the journalists involved filed civil actions against the relevant authorities, while two others facing criminal prosecution were provided with free defense counsel.[36] MRA has also challenged successfully the legal validity of the *Nigerian Press Council (Amendment) Decree No. 60 of 1999* (promulgated on 26 May 1999.[37] In the same vein, it has successfully sued the Code of Conduct Bureau, contending and establishing that:

> The Bureau had denied them access to the declaration of assets made by the public officers in disregard of Section 3(c) of part 1 of the Third Schedule to the 1999 Constitution. The section gives every Nigerian citizen an uninhibited right of access to assets declarations made by public officers.[38]

As part of this strategic litigation program, MRA has similarly instituted a suit that challenges the legal validity of the Nigerian *Official Secrets Act of 1962*.[39]

For its part, HURILAWS has established and run a more general strategic impact litigation program. The objectives of this project are:

- Advancing human rights in Nigeria through litigation
- Securing decisions of superior courts and setting judicial legal standards for human rights in Nigeria
- Enhancing the enjoyment of human rights by citizens of Nigeria as litigation compels the government and its agencies to apply human rights norms in the conduct of public affairs
- Creating measures by which government compliance with human rights standards can be ascertained[40]

Through this program, HURILAWS has helped shape government policy and has even secured some notable judicial pronouncements. For instance, in 1998, the Supreme Court of Nigeria dismissed an appeal brought by HURILAWS, urging that court to declare unconstitutional the imposition of the death penalty under the Nigerian criminal code.[41] However, the case led to some salutary penal reforms in Nigeria.[42] The President, the Speaker of the House of Representatives, and a few other top government functionaries have since announced their strong support for the abolition of the death penalty in Nigeria.[43] Similarly, this NGO has challenged the constitutionality of the "holding charge" practice in Nigeria (where accused persons are charged in courts that lack the jurisdiction to try them and are then remanded in prison custody pending the full investigation of the charge).[44] It has contended that the practice is at variance with the provisions of sections 32 and 33 of the 1979 constitution.[45] It has also lined up cases designed to secure direct and clear judicial pronouncements that *fully* incorporate the "Miranda Principles" into criminal prosecutions in Nigeria.[46]

Other NGOs have also mounted similar programs. For example, the IHRHL has assisted numerous individuals and organizations in filing petitions before national and international bodies concerned with the protection of human rights.[47] It has usually done so without charging any fees for its services. So has the CDHR.[48]

Another important aspect of the strategic impact litigation programs and methods of these NGOs is its social/economic rights dimension. For instance, the SRI and the Social and Economic Rights Action Center (SERAC) have both filed actions in court against the Nigerian government on behalf some former residents of Maroko whose shantytown was forcibly demolished by the government in 1990. SERAC's lawsuit charged the government with violating the International Covenant on Economic, Social, and Cultural Rights, which establishes rights to housing, education, food, health, and safe environment.[49] Similarly, the Committee for the Defense of Human

Rights has sued the federal government over the latter's plans to raise the price of motor fuel by a very steep margin.[50]

2.3. LEGISLATIVE ADVOCACY AND LAW REFORM

The legislative advocacy and law reform work of most of these NGOs involves both lobbying federal and states legislatures on the content of particular legislation and attempting to influence the direction of other law reform efforts. In both cases, the aim has been to produce a legal environment that is much more human rights-friendly.

Most of these NGOs have mounted legislative advocacy and law reform projects of one kind or the other. For example, HURILAWS has been involved in several projects that have entailed the preparation of draft legislation and the mounting of lobbying efforts designed to secure the enactment of such bills.[51] HURILAWS has claimed the credit for drafting the bill that forms the basis of the current Anti-Corruption Law.[52] It has also embarked on a justice sector reform project that aims at decongesting the courts,[53] as well as on a campaign to ensure the domestic incorporation of all the treaties that Nigeria has ratified.[54] Since its presentation of the Freedom of Information Bill to the National Assembly in 1999, MRA has continued to lobby for its enactment.[55] The objectives of the bill are (a) to make public records and information more freely available; (b) to provide for public access to public records and information; (c) to protect public records and information to the extent consistent with the public interest and the protection of personal privacy; (d) to protect serving officers from the adverse consequences of disclosing certain kinds of information without authorization; and (e) to establish procedures for the achievement of these and related purposes.[56] MRA has also embarked on a project of law reform aimed at removing from the statute books all anti-press legislation, some dating as far back as 1917 (when Nigeria was still a colonial state).[57] Similarly the Constitutional Rights Project (CRP) has organized training sessions for lawyers working in the Legal Department of the National Assembly[58], and has submitted two separate bills for legislation to protect the welfare of the disabled.[59] For it own part, IHRHL has initiated a "Listening Session" program designed to bring members of the States Houses of Assembly within the so-called South-South zone of Nigeria into face-to-face contact with ordinary citizens from their constituencies.[60] And CAPP publishes *Legislative Mandate*—a quarterly newsletter that serves as a forum for the expression of ideas regarding legislative reform in pro-human rights directions.[61] As importantly, many of these NGOs fought hard (and successfully) against some provisions of the then Anti-Corruption Commission Bill (which has now been passed into law in a more human rights -friendly form).[62]

2.4. CAMPAIGNS, MASS MOBILIZATION, AND HUMAN RIGHTS EDUCATION

Campaigns, mass mobilization, and human rights education projects are intimately related and overlapping modes of human rights activism. However, in the ways in which they have been applied in the Nigerian context they can be treated as semi-distinct categories. The term *campaigns* is used here to refer to the efforts made by these NGOs to motivate the general public to focus attention on and eventually force an end to a particular form of human rights violation or blight on the fabric of the polity (such as military dictatorship, corruption or police brutality). The term *mass mobilization* is distinguishable from campaigns because it focuses on the mobilization of very large numbers of people at the grassroots to take direct action against a perceived human rights violation within the polity. Related as it is to campaigns and mass mobilization projects, the expression *human rights education* is used here to describe those projects that are largely aimed at imparting knowledge about human rights and are not directly focused for the most part on getting people to rise up and take action against the human rights abuses that afflict the society.

I. CAMPAIGNS:

The Civil Liberties Organization (CLO) has always maintained a prominent campaigns program. Such campaigns have been a very visible aspect of its programs and methods, largely because of the widespread nature of the abuses inflicted upon Nigerians by successive military regimes. As the CLO has itself noted:

> The years preceding 2000 were years of "war." It was a period when the CLO had to battle the dictatorship of late General Sani Abacha [and previous military rulers] on an almost daily basis. Then, we had to fight from the trenches using not the weapons of war, but the weapons of persuasion....During the Abacha period, the Campaigns and Media Project maintained its position as the CLO's voice on issues relating to human rights, transparency and good governance, and the struggle for democracy. With the return to civilian rule, the Campaigns Directorate sought to use expanded democratic space. In the last year the Campaigns Directorate joined the Human Rights Law Service (HURILAWS), *ThisDay* newspaper, Channels Television and Transparency International in organizing two public hearings which aimed at articulating civil society's input into the government's fight against corruption, and the battle to recover Nigeria's money looted by erstwhile military dictators and their cronies. The project plans to hold similar public hearings in future.[63]

For its own part, CAPP has tended to be even more campaign-oriented than the CLO. For instance, it has mounted accountability programs in different parts of Nigeria (mostly in the Northern Nigerian regions of Abuja,

Kano, Niger, and Plateau. In the words of one commentator on CAPP's activities:

> Essentially these programs brought together the electorate and public officers ... During the meeting, these elected representatives give a report of their activities [sic] after which the public then asked questions with respect to the accounts presented as well as on what was not said. In this process, often the issue of the cost of projects have to be revealed and discussed [sic]. Sometimes also, people make demands to know [sic] the amount available to the local government and pass judgment on both the level and quality of execution of projects.[64]

CAPP has also launched campaigns aimed at pressuring the relevant governments to ensure the de-contamination of polluted water in certain areas of the country.[65]

As importantly, as part of their campaign against military dictatorship, many of these NGOs fought relentlessly (and successfully) against the trial of civilians by military tribunals.[66]

II. MASS MOBILIZATION

Although most of these NGOs have tended to avoid *partisan* political struggles, and have (in general) been extremely reluctant to use grassroots (or mass) mobilization strategies as ways of advancing their work, such strategies have sometimes been employed. What is more, many such NGOs have begun to appreciate the value of employing such a strategy. MOSOP's routine grassroots activities, WACOL's recent work (as per market rallies), and CAPP's grassroots involvement (as per community forums), eloquently testify to the existence of this emerging, if still marginal, trend.

The CLO has sometimes used this strategy to direct local and international attention to the excesses of the military dictatorships that ruled pre-1999 Nigeria. During that military era, the CLO's Democracy Action Project (now the Democracy and Governance Project) spearheaded the CLO's mass mobilization efforts.[67] It did this through its participation in prodemocracy coalitions such as the Campaign for Democracy (CD) and the United Action for Democracy (UAD) and also through its own independent activities.[68] As military rule drew to an end, the project became an important partner in the Transition Monitoring Group (TMG), the civil society coalition that monitored the elections that ushered in civilian rule in May 1999.[69]

SERAC has utilized this strategy in a different way. It has worked at the grassroots with local communities in order to:

> ...educate and mobilize them to become active participants in the defense and advancement of their rights [and as part of this work] is championing demands for the full resettlement of the more than 300,000 people forcibly evicted from their homes when Maroko, formerly Nigeria's largest slum community was demolished by the

military government in July 1990 without compensating or resettling 97% of the evicted families.[70]

However, one of the most notable instances of the deployment of this strategy was its utilization in the 1990s by the Campaign for Democracy (CD) – a coalition of the CLO and a number of other civil society groups. Julius Ihonvbere's account of the process is so accurate as to deserve elaborate reproduction here:

> [Following the political miscalculation of the Babangida regime in annulling the presidential election results, the CD] decided to mobilize [Nigerians]… [to] make the country ungovernable, and to force the regime out of power by the previously agreed date of 27 August 1993. Massive protests were organized across the country.…Hundreds of thousands of leaflets were printed by the CD.…urging Nigerians to take a final stand against military dictatorship and against the subversion of the popular will.…..The CD capitalized on the presence of over 80,000 soccer fans at the World Cup qualifying match at the National Stadium, Surulere, on 3 July 1993, to distribute leaflets calling on all Nigerians to embark on "one week of national protest to force Babangida to go and to enforce the result of the June 12 election".….The five-day nonviolent protests held during July 5–9 1993 were a huge success. The CD had done its homework by having meetings with special interest groups—meat sellers, market women, shopkeepers, students, trade unions, and road transport workers – and by enlisting their co-operation and support. The country became paralyzed as banks, markets, schools, and government offices were closed, while many streets in the major cities were deserted.[71]

It must be pointed out that this example stands with a handful of others as being among the very few instances in which the NGO community in Nigeria was able to deploy and pursue effectively this kind of mass mobilization strategy.

III. HUMAN RIGHTS EDUCATION

The kinds of human rights education (HRE) strategies that have been adopted by most NGOs in Nigeria are exemplified by the "strategic value infusion" approach that has been taken by HRA.[72] As this approach was described at some length on the first page of this chapter, there is no need for a further discussion of the nature of that approach here.

The CLO—regarded by HRA as a classic example of a "negative proclaimer"—has described its HRE objectives as being aimed at making "Nigerians conscious of their rights, and of the practical steps available to them to defend and promote them."[73] The objectives of its HRE program are:

- To make Nigerians aware of their rights and empower them to assert these rights

- To encourage more Nigerians to be effective in the struggle for human rights
- To develop a collaborative scheme with various sectors of Nigerian society in educating the public on human rights issues
- To make government accountable to the people and to respect their rights
- To create a Nigerian society founded on the observance of human rights and democratic values[74]

The project claims that it "goes out" to meet Nigerians and educate them in human rights wherever they are found. Hence, the major programs being implemented by the CLO's HRE Directorate are human rights education for religious bodies, for students, for trade unionists, and activists.[75] To help meet these objectives, the CLO has instituted a number of projects. These includes its projects on the Church and Human Rights, Islam and Human Rights, and on Human Rights Education for Trade Unions and Other Social Groups.[76] The CLO has also mounted Radio/Television projects;[77] and has trained journalists on reporting skills that are relevant to human rights work.[78]

Similarly, the Constitutional Rights Project (CRP) has run a HRE program. It has in the main used radio broadcasts to promote rights awareness. Its former Executive Director explained that "in the radio programs, discussions are focused on issues that people encounter on daily basis such as police abuse of rights, bail rights, inheritance rights, discriminatory practices, land rights, employment rights etc."[79] In the same vein, the CRP has organized a workshop for the training of law students regarding the application of their legal skills and resources to legislative work at the National Assembly in order to advance human rights.[80]

Other such groups have also undertaken HRE programs. For instance, MRA have organized several workshops for journalists aimed at training them in reporting on human rights issues.[81] Numerous Nigerian journalists, mostly political and human rights reporters, have had this kind of opportunity.[82] CLEEN has mounted a series of HRE programs designed to train law enforcement personnel and help in "reorienting their attitude and world view regarding their profession."[83] The IHRHL has engaged in human rights education practices and has published a manual to facilitate this aspect of its work.[84] In an effort to advance the economic and social rights of the victims of forced eviction in the Ijora Oloye community, SERAC organized a workshop in 1998.[85] The aim of this workshop was to use "existing social and traditional networks to inject the people's real-life experiences into its human rights education program."[86] The workshop was utilized by SERAC to outline the steps they have taken to secure redress and remedies for the victims of Ijora Oloye and Ijora Badiya communities, and to stop further evictions from being carried out.[87] As importantly, it is noteworthy that between 1995-2000, PRAWA, succeeded in training over 2,600 prison officers on the human rights of prisoners.[88] For its own part, the CDHR has organized Leadership Training Workshops for student union leaders on ways of effectively combating intra-campus violence and creating a conducive atmosphere for the enjoyment of the right to education.[89] Human Rights Africa (HRA) has also trained the principals of some secondary schools at its library at Ota, and used the occasion to discuss the need for the infusion of human rights education in the curriculum of secondary schools.[90] However, the HRA is somewhat unique in the extent to which it has devoted its energies to the utilization of the HRE approach. Few of the HRA's peers have, like that NGO, chosen to all but abandon the classic human rights monitoring approach in favor of "value infusion." Its justification for all but abandoning monitoring is captured in another important passage from Tunji Abayomi's essay on the subject:

> Within the organization I represent, that is, *Human Rights Africa* we chose to abandon human rights monitoring. The choice is based on our conviction that a group like Amnesty International is doing all that is needed to be done in this area. We chose to work towards bringing systematic change through education, information, exchange of ideas. Negative proclamation, where necessary, is chosen by us as the last strategy. Our choice is dug out of several principles which in our view are crucial for honest service to promote happiness in Africa. These principles are as follows:
>
> • An Africa focused human rights NGO must win credibility in Africa through objective, just, mature and painstaking efforts
>
> • In the effort to bring a lasting change, no human rights NGO should disregard the African tradition, culture, customs, community rights and rites, family ties, religion, the effect of poverty, illiteracy or the consequences of colonialism and modernity
>
> • Every human rights NGO in Africa must emphatically hold it a sacred duty to prevent, expose and fight abuses of human rights of any kind but in doing so it cannot, without worsening the position of Africans in the world, base its approach on negative proclamation alone. The mission must emphatically move from showing how bad Africa is to how good it can be through our efforts
>
> • Every human rights [NGO] in Africa should be multidimensional in approach. A human rights NGO should not put itself in "an enemy camp" to the extent it is considered irrelevant either by the government or the non-governmental sector of Africa

- For lasting effect, we consider the "systematic infusion of human rights democratic values" at all institutional levels, decision making processes and policy motivator [sic] as a preferred approach to the monitoring of individual abuses[91]

2.5. ELECTION MONITORING AND EDUCATION:

As Karen Jackson has noted:

> The trend [of election observing by NGOs] began in the early 1980s, predominantly in the United States, when NGOs were formed with the aim of engaging in electoral assistance programs.... Since then, organizations in other countries have become involved in election observing, but the main NGOs remain U.S-based with non-Americans often choosing to participate in these groups.[92]

The NGO community in Nigeria has slowly become accustomed to this mode of human rights activism. So far, their most important election monitoring work was in relation to the 1999 elections that ended a fifteen-year era of military rule in Nigeria. These NGOs actively monitored that election's fairness and compliance with human rights standards, and issued an important report on these issues. They did so in a collaborative way, under the auspices of the Transition Monitoring Group (TMG) — a coalition that was made up of sixty-three (63) civil society groups.[93] The TMG was formally launched on the 1 September 1998 at a meeting held in Lagos and attended by 16 representatives from 12 groups. It drew its strength from the varied interests of its members. These interests spanned the human rights, environmental protection, prison reform, women's development, and democratization, fields. The TMG's member organizations were drawn from the six geo-political zones of the country.[94]

Individual NGOs have also engaged in such monitoring efforts. For its own part, MRA has conducted print and electronic media monitoring exercises designed to help assess the fairness of the context in which particular elections were held. One important example concerns the six-month period before the 1999 were held.[95] HRA has monitored elections in several African countries including Angola, Republic of Benin, Cameroon, Ghana, and Nigeria.[96] The IHRHL, the CLO, The CPR, and CAPP have also organized community-based programs geared towards raising the consciousness of the general populace regarding the need to insist on their democratic and voting rights being respected.[97]

2.6. MICRO-CREDIT LENDING

Popularized by Bangladesh's now famous Grameen Bank, micro-credit lending has not been the forte of human rights NGOs the world over. Indeed, until fairly recently, such activities was not considered by most mainstream human rights scholars and activists to be human rights work. Not surprisingly, such activities have been all but absent from the programs and methods of NGOs in Nigeria.

Commendably, SERAC has led the way in ensuring that some of Nigeria's poor have enjoyed the benefits of micro-credit lending. For instance, in May 1999, SERAC established a micro credit program for the purposes of granting soft loans to some of the very impoverished women who had been the victims of the forced eviction of Maroko residents. Similarly, in April 2000 SERAC initiated another micro-credit project "to benefit the women of Ijora Badiya", a slum community whose experiences had formed the basis of SERAC's June 1998 "request for inspection" at the World Bank's Inspection Panel.[98]

Regrettably though, this highly innovative and much needed program has not been emulated by most of the NGOs with which we are concerned here.

2.7. PRISON REFORM AND DE-CONGESTION:

The urgency of prison reform and de-congestion in Nigeria is evident from the following passage taken from a speech by Chimezie Ikeazor, the founder of Nigeria's official legal aid scheme:

> Over 5000 Nigerians were languishing in various jails across the country by February 1999 simply because of their inability to procure legal services during their court trials. Several thousands more....fail to obtain justice in Nigerian courts annually for lack of funds, despite the promulgation of the Legal Aid Decree and establishment of legal aid councils since 1974.[99]

NGOs have played an important role in the attempts to redress this problematic situation. The CLO has been a principal actor in this area. Indeed, it was the CLO's very influential 1996 report on the state of Nigeria's prisons that heightened national consciousness about the deplorable status of prisoners' rights in Nigeria. In the admittedly self-interested but nevertheless essentially accurate words of Lanre Ehonwa, the author of that report:

> Indeed until the emergence of the Civil Liberties Organization.... indifference to the plight of prisoners permeated all segments of Nigerian society, including, regrettably, the legal profession. Even now, with the active and vocal presence of the CLO and other human rights NGOs, prisoners' rights jurisprudence in Nigeria remains a largely virgin terrain. Prisoners, their families, or other interested persons cannot, understandably, go to court to enforce rights about who's [sic] existence they are oblivious. Even if they were minded so to do, very few prisoners can muster sufficient resources to instruct competent counsel to represent them because the majority of prisoners in Nigeria are persons who, prior to imprisonment, lived in poverty.[100]

All available evidence supports this conclusion.

For its own part, HURILAWS has been engaged in a multi-year project to help reform and decongest Nigerian prisons. It has been particularly involved in the effort to decongest the Enugu prisons. Consequently, HURILAWS has filed a number of cases in an effort to advance this project.[101] For instance, in *Arthur Onyejekwo v. Comptroller, Prison Services (Enugu) and another* (unreported), HURILAWS sought to enforce the fundamental rights of prisoners, who were being ill-treated there.[102]

As will be made clear in chapter 6, prison reform has been one of the areas in which these NGOs have made important strides.

2.8. DOMESTIC COALITIONS AND NETWORKS

All over the world, NGOs of all types have tended to form coalitions/ networks with like-minded groups. For instance, in the Niger Republic, at least one umbrella organization of "development" NGOs exists.[103] In Burkina Faso, an umbrella organization of development NGOs was established in 1976.[104] A similar group exists in Ghana.[105]

In the case of Nigeria, a number of important coalitions of domestic human rights NGOs have been established at one time or the other in order to advance the struggle against military rule. As Bonny Ibhawoh has put it:

> [In the 1990s] the human rights community realized that to be effective in their campaign for human rights and democracy in the country, there was need for them to cooperate, coordinate their activities and pool their collective efforts towards their goals. This need led to the formation in 1992, of the Campaign for Democracy (CD), an umbrella organization for 42 human rights organizations and pressure groups working for the enthrone-ment of democracy in Nigeria. The declared objective of the CD included the campaign for the termination of military rule, campaign for the right of Nigerians to choose their government and promotion of fundamental human rights and the rule of law in the country.[106]

Later on, during the dying days of the Abacha junta, a similar group styled United Action for Democracy (UAD) was formed.[107] This organization—a coalition of twenty-nine human rights and prodemocracy groups—campaigned very courageously against the attempt by General Abacha to transform himself into an "elected" civilian ruler. Abacha's sudden death in 1998 put an end to that cynical self-succession bid.[108] This regime change in Nigeria led to the establishment in 1998–99 of a grand coalition of sixty-three (63) human rights NGOs referred to as the Transition Monitoring Group (TMG).[109] The TMG monitored the elections that in May 1999 ushered in Nigeria's fourth republic.

Other smaller coalitions have been established regarding more specific concerns such as prison or police reform and women's rights. For instance, twenty-two NGOs have united under the rubric of the Network on Police

Reforms in Nigeria (NOPRIN).[110] This network aims at not only identifying areas of police reform, but also to liaise with the Police Affairs Ministry, the Nigerian police force, the National Assembly, and other stakeholders to facilitate police reform and to provide civil society with an opportunity to participate in that reform process.[111] Similarly, in August 1997, a group of these NGOs established the National NGO Coalition on Prison Reform.[112] This group is involved in the provision of legal and medical assistance to prisoners, in the rehabilitation of prisoners and ex-prisoners, and in the training of both prisoners and officers on their human rights.[113] As importantly, a diverse group of NGOs that work on women's rights issues in Nigeria have formed the Nigerian NGO Coalition for a Shadow Report on the Implementation in Nigeria of the Convention on the Elimination of all Form of Discrimination against Women (or the CEDAW). Spurred by BAOBAB's initiative, this coalition was formed by a number of NGOs in May 1998. Its principal purpose is to serve as a platform for these NGOs to collaborate in the researching and writing of "shadow" or "alternative reports" regarding the extent to which the Nigerian government has implemented or failed to implement its obligations under the CEDAW.[114]

On an even smaller scale, many of these NGOs have also engaged in bilateral or trilateral NGO coalitions. For instance, Environmental Rights Action (ERA) and the Human Rights Law Service (HURILAWS) have a partnership initiative called the Environmental Defense Fund for Nigeria (EDFN). The aim of this partnership is: (a) to defend environmental activists whose human rights are abused by the Nigerian governments, and (b) to defend and advance the environmental rights of Nigerian communities and citizens who are victims of environmental pollution by the Nigerian regime.[115] In the same vein, HURILAWS has formed a partnership initiative with the CLO and Transparency International (Nigeria) aimed at recovering some of the wealth that has been stolen from Nigeria by corrupt leaders and stashed in foreign banks.[116] And WACOL has worked closely with the Widows Association of Nigeria (WAN) in order to find lasting solutions to the practice of degrading widowhood rites in Nigeria.[117] What is more, groups such as the IHRHL have established useful human rights linkages with some of Nigeria's more powerful faith-based groups.[118]

Given the fragmentation that characterizes the human rights NGO scene in Nigeria, the efforts that these NGOs have sometimes made to network with each other and to form united fronts are particularly commendable, especially in an atmosphere of scarce resources and great need. However, as Emma Ezeazu—a prominent human rights activist—has noted, if these networks are to optimize their potential to serve as catalysts of the human rights transformations that these NGOs so greatly desire, they must not merely be "network[s] of prominent human rights activists but that of *people's* organizations."[119]

2.9. INTERNATIONAL COLLABORATION AND ADVOCACY

It is now widely recognized that *domestic* human rights NGOs all over the world are indispensable to the *international* human rights movement and vice versa.[120] In this light, it is commendable that many domestic NGOs have collaborated formally or informally with their foreign counterparts in seeking to advance their mutual interests. For example, as Virgil Wiebe has noted that:

> Quite often, [domestic] NGOs provide the information for urgent actions in response to gross violations of human rights by contacting UN Special Rapporteurs or instituting the 1503 and 1235 procedure.[121]

The NGOs in Nigeria have not been an exception to this trend. Over the years, they have formed fruitful though almost always unequal relationships with foreign NGOs. As Ibhawoh has pointed out, many domestic NGOs in Nigeria have, at one time or another, been involved in some form of collaboration with a foreign NGO. This kind of partnership includes the work that Media Rights Agenda's (MRA) has done with Article 19 (the London-based International Center against Censorship).[122] The CLO has had a close working relationship with the U.S.-based International Human Rights Law Group,[123] and has also collaborated with the Network of Independent Monitors (NIM) and the NGO-style Kenya Human Rights Commission (KHRC).[124] Similarly, many of these NGOs have benefited from their collaboration with the Canadian Inter-Church Coalition on Africa (ICCAF).[125]

Moreover, for good or for ill, groups like HURILAWS, the CLO, and the CDHR have had regular contacts with the embassies of European and American countries in Nigeria, providing them with information on an ongoing basis and receiving financial and other support from these embassies.[126] According to one CLO executive, often the staff of these embassies:

> … contact CLO officers to obtain or clarify information. These embassies also obtain important information from our Annual Reports and web sites. It is also not uncommon for our leaders to be invited to meetings and luncheons at these embassies for important discussions.[127]

In the words of another leading activist:

> We do provide information [to foreign embassies etc]. In fact, we made it a point of duty to exchange information on cases we are working on. Sometimes we call them and schedule meetings and at other times we go over and see them. There are also times when they have requested specific information from us. I must say that it was very effective to some extent depending on the country and the issue at the material time. Walter Carrington, former US Ambassador, showed exceptional concern with regard to human rights violations in Nigeria.[128]

These NGOs have also worked within what I have referred to elsewhere as a "virtual human rights network."[129] They have done so in collaboration with a few international human rights institutions, particularly the institutions of the African Human Rights system.[130] A few examples will suffice here. The CRP successfully used the African Human Rights System as a resource in its successful battle to prevent the execution of General Zamani Lekwot and other Kataf leaders by the Babangida administration.[131] Second, in response to a petition filed by MRA at the African Commission on Human and Peoples Rights against that same military dictatorship, the Commission held that Decree No.43 of 1993 was illegal and violated certain provisions of the African Charter on Human and Peoples Rights, including the right to freedom of expression.[132] The military government later repealed the offending decree.[133] Similarly, as a result of another petition filed by MRA, the same commission declared that the seizure in January 1994 of about 50,000 copies of Tell magazine by the government violated of Article 9 (2) of African Charter.[134]

Regrettably though, the international collaborative efforts of these NGOs have focused far-too-much on linkages with the NGOs and charities of the so-called developed countries.[135] Only rarely have these NGOs formed active, sustained and fruitful networks or exchanges with other *African* human rights NGOs.[136] One of the few instances of such inter-African collaboration is AFRONET (An inter-African NGO network).[137] Another is WADNET (the West African Democracy Network).[138] However, these inter-African networks have been of limited utility. This situation has obviously hindered the ability of these NGOs to benefit from the possible dividends of such inter-African NGO cooperation.

2.10. GENDER-FOCUSED ACTIVISM

It is trite to state that Nigerian women and female children have, in general, not enjoyed all of the same advantages as their male counterparts. As Bolanle Awe has noted:

> Even the constitution that gave them [Nigerians] independence excluded women in the North from participating in the decision making that affected their lives; they were denied the franchise along with lunatics and children. The various development plans of the period expressed pious hopes for the development of a just, fair, and egalitarian society, but the opposite was the case.[139]

Similarly, participants in a seminar in 1999 organized by the African Commission on Human and Peoples' Rights noted that:

> Gender discrimination affects women [in Nigeria and other African states] in accessing justice as prospective litigants, accused in criminal trials, victims of crime, witnesses and as legal representatives before judicial bodies. Women are not adequately

represented in judicial positions and legal procedures are not sufficiently sensitive to issues that affect them.[140]

In relation to the specific Nigerian context, Joy Ezeilo—a leading Nigerian women's rights activist—has argued, quite correctly, that:

> In Nigeria … women continue to face numerous barriers hindering their participation in public life in general … In fact, it has been a political world without women.[141]

This assertion is buttressed by the following facts.[142] In 1979, during Nigeria's second republic, only one woman was elected into the senate, and only two into the House of Representatives.[143] In the Third Republic, only one of the ninety-one Senate seats was occupied by a woman, and only thirteen women were elected into the five hundred and ninety-three seat House of Representatives.[144] During the fourth parliament (1999–2003), of the one hundred and nine seats in the senate, women occupied only three, and only twelve women held seats in the three hundred and sixty-six seat House of Representatives.[145] Of the fifty federal cabinet ministers, only six were female.[146]

Yet this problem is not a peculiarly Nigerian or African one. As the CRP has noted, all over the world, a significant differential exists between the status of men and women, one that is hardly ever in women's favor.[147] So deep seated is this problem that even human rights NGOs have themselves *not* historically prioritized women's issues within their praxis. As Henry Steiner and Phillip Alston have concluded:

> Of the several blind spots in the development of human rights movements from 1945 to the present, none is as striking as that movement's failure to give violations of women's (human) rights the attention, and in some respects the priority, that they require. It is not only that these problems adversely affect half of the world's population. They affect all of us, for a deep change in women's circumstances means corresponding change throughout social life.[148]

With respect to the attitude of the NGO community in Nigeria to gender concerns, it is important to state, as two senior women's rights activists have noted, that:

> Mainstream human rights NGOs in Nigeria do not generally prioritize gender perspectives. We have to remind them continuously to do so. This is probably because from the beginning the primary concern of the human rights NGO community in Nigeria was with military rule and state violence against Nigerians generally. We always have to remind these mainstream NGOs that domestic violence is as important as state violence meted out by the police.[149]

As part of the efforts to address this problem of gender inequity in the country, a number of women's rights projects have been formed within the more established of the male-dominated NGOs. A number of women-run gender-focused NGOs have also emerged. These women's rights NGOs and the women's rights departments of the mainstream NGOs have mounted a range of programs and deployed certain methods in this connection. We will now examine some of these programs and methods in some detail in order to understand and expose their character.

I. CONFERENCES AND SEMINARS ON WOMEN'S RIGHTS

An important part of the gender work that has been done by NGOs in Nigeria has concerned the organization of conferences and workshops to discuss some of the problems that affect Nigerian women and consider possible ways of ameliorating these problems. While many of these conferences have been convened by the "gender programs" of the mainstream groups, the bulk of the work on the human rights of Nigerian women have still been done by the emergent women's rights NGOs. A number of examples of these programs will now be considered.

For its part, WACOL has, in collaboration with the John D. and Catherine T. MacArthur Foundation, convened an expert meeting on the design of a new curriculum for the introduction of reproductive rights and maternal health education within Nigerian faculties of law. This expert meeting was attended by the author and held in April 2002 at Iworo, near Badagry (in the Lagos area of Nigeria).[150] During the 1991 conference on human rights convened by HRA, the participants observed that adequate guarantees or protections did not exist in most African countries for women, children, and the disabled.[151] They also pointed out the need for more political participation by women and the eradication of traditions that treat women as second-class citizens.[152]

The CRP has also striven to some extent to address the gender deficit within the NGO community in Nigeria. In May 1995, the CRP convened a seminar on discriminatory laws and practices against women in Nigeria.[153] Participants at this seminar concluded that:

- existing laws protecting women's rights are inadequate; and even then certain practices violate the legally protected rights of women.
- although section 39 of the 1979 Constitution guarantees protections against discrimination, its provisions are too general to sufficiently guarantee the rights of women.
- ignorance, low levels of education among women, and differences in socialization patterns are the reasons why such discriminatory practices exist.
- the undue importance of money in Nigeria politics has proved disadvantageous to women who are traditionally and generally economically marginalized in seeking elective posts.[154]

The CRP also organized a similar seminar two years later.[155]

For its own part, SRI has convened a few conferences on the same theme. For instance, in June 1998, its Gender Action Project organized a workshop with the following objectives:

- To sensitize civil society, particularly the legal community, on the issues of violations of women's rights and to seek practical measures of redress within the law
- To raise awareness on national and international standards protecting gender specific rights and mechanism for redress of violation
- To develop and impart litigation and practical realization strategies for the protection of gender-specific rights[156]

The Women's Rights Project of the CLO has also done important work in this area. It has organized a number of roundtable discussions in commemoration of International Women's Day. The focus of such discussions has often been on women's participation in politics and the economy.[157]

II. CAMPAIGNS, EDUCATIONAL PROJECTS, AND MOBILIZATIONAL EFFORTS REGARDING WOMEN'S ISSUES

Most campaigns, educational projects, and mobilizational efforts on women's issues have been mounted and waged by specifically gender-focused NGOs such as BAOBAB and WACOL. BAOBAB is deeply involved in the ongoing effort to sensitize the public to the need to make the sharia criminal laws that have been instituted in parts of Northern Nigeria much more women-friendly.[158] WACOL has been quite active in campaigning against certain obnoxious widowhood practices that abridge women's rights.[159] It has worked very assiduously and visibly in assisting women who have been victims of state/military repression, rape, and torture in the Choba community of Nigeria's Niger Delta region.[160] It has also set up a shelter for battered women and established a women's resource center.[161]What is more, WACOL has trained peer health educators, paralegals, counselors, and social workers on human rights standards and reproductive health matters.[162]

However, mainstream NGOs like CLEEN and the CLO's women's rights department have also done important work in this respect. CLEEN is currently championing a campaign against certain police regulations that discriminate against women in the police force.[163] CLEEN contends that these discriminatory laws and practices violate Nigeria's obligations under domestic and international human rights law.[164] For instance, it argues that police regulations that prevent women from marrying until after two years of service on the force violates both the Nigerian Constitution and the International Covenant on Civil and Political Rights (ICCPR) – a treaty that was ratified by Nigeria in 1993.[165] For its part, the CLO has long waged a campaign against the denial or abridgement of women's inheritance rights and such other issues.[166] As importantly, IHRHL has worked at the grassroots on the issue of widow's rights. For instance, in March 2001, it inaugurated a Widowhood Association at Okechi in Etche Local Government Council of Rivers state. The idea behind the formation of the association was to work with widows in the town in order to educate them about their human rights.[167]

III. MICROCREDIT LENDING TO WOMEN

SERAC is the only one of the sample of NGOs of concern in this book that has established a sizeable microcredit program for purposes of granting soft loans to impoverished women.[168] This program has been discussed at length in section 2.6 of this chapter.

IV. LITIGATION ON WOMEN'S RIGHTS

A few examples will suffice here to illustrate the efforts by the NGO community in Nigeria to advance women's rights through litigation.

WACOL has, for example, filed a number of court petitions aimed at advancing the status of women in Nigeria. In 1998, WACOL and a number of other women's groups sued the government of Enugu state of Nigeria for completely excluding women from its cabinet.[169] In a press conference issued by this coalition, it declared as follows:

> We want this government to note that we have very many quali-
> fied women in Enugu State that have demonstrated considerable
> leadership in community and informal organizations, as well as in
> public office. There is no single woman elected into [sic] the House
> of Assembly. It is now worse that in the Executive, no woman
> has been appointed [sic]. We therefore, demand that the govern-
> ment of Enugu State should take immediate measures to ensure
> women's equal access to and full participation in power structures
> and decision-making in the state. The current discriminatory poli-
> cies and practices in appointments to State executives at the dawn
> of the 21st Century are unacceptable to us. To achieve a transparent
> and accountable government, women's participation in power and
> decision-making must be full not mere tokenism [sic].[170]

WACOL has also striven to provide legal aid services to many women whose human rights have been abused.[171]

As importantly, the Women's Rights Advancement and Protection Alter-native (WRAPA) has litigated a number of "violence against women" cases in the Nigerian courts. For instance, WRAPA initiated criminal proceedings against one Mr. Chibueze Stone for battering his wife.[172]

For its own part, the SERAC, has been actively involved in litigating on behalf of women. In July 2000, it filed a suit on behalf of a woman who had been unlawfully dismissed from her job because she had tested positive for the HIV virus.[173] In the course of the hearing of an application for the accelerated trial of the matter, the presiding judge, Caroline Olufawo of the Lagos High Court, delivered a ruling barring the plaintiff from entering the courtroom during the hearing of her case.[174] According to SERAC sources, the judge went further to prevent the plaintiff from having access to the official records and certified copies of her ruling to enable her launch an appeal.[175] SERAC petitioned the chief judge of Lagos state, threatening to file an application for a writ of mandamus to compel the judge to release the case file. Following this incident the case file was released, and an appeal was launched.[176]

V. LEGISLATIVE ADVOCACY ON WOMEN'S ISSUES

A number of the organizations that make up the NGO community in Nigeria have mounted programs aimed at influencing the content and course of legislation in Nigeria in ways that advance women's rights. Below are a number of examples.

For some time now, HURILAWS has promoted the enactment of legislation for the establishment of a Commission on Gender Equality (GCE).[177] Furthermore, HURILAWS has lobbied the government to enact specific legislation prohibiting the abuse of women and children and penalizing such abuse with appropriate sanctions.[178]

Similarly, the Women Non-Governmental Organizations Coalition Group (WNGOCG) - of which WACOL is a part - has sponsored a bill on the elimination of widowhood practices in Enugu state.[179] The Bill was aimed at protecting the fundamental rights of widows by making unlawful all the dehumanizing widowhood practices in the state.[180] This effort was, as will be seen in chapter 6, successful.

VI. MONITORING, RESEARCH, AND REPORTING ON WOMEN'S ISSUES

Virtually all human rights NGOs in Nigeria have engaged in monitoring, research, and reporting as a mode of human rights activism, and many of these organizations have monitored, researched, and reported violations of women's rights. A few examples will suffice.

For instance, BAOBAB has done a lot of monitoring and reporting work regarding the ill effects on women of certain aspects of the sharia criminal law that applies to a dozen or so Northern Nigerian states (of a possible thirty-six). Its founding executive director, Ayesha Imam, has been honored in Canada with the John Humphrey Human Rights Prize for her excellent work in this connection.[181] BAOBAB also worked to prevent, and did condemn later, the conviction and flogging of a teenage mother in Zamfara state for having had extramarital sex.[182] It has continued to research, monitor, and report on the issues that affect women in the so-called sharia states of Nigeria as well as on the issues that affect other Nigerian women. WACOL has published an important pamphlet on the laws and practices relating to women's inheritance rights in Nigeria.[183] It has also researched and produced many other such pamphlets.[184] In a similar vein, WRAPA has also engaged in a series of collaborative research projects on the rights of female children. In this connection, it has collaborated with the National Human Rights Commission and some Nigerian universities.[185] EMPARC has published a number of important pamphlets relating to the rights of women in Nigeria.[186] EMPARC also publishes a bulletin that is styled *Insight and Impact* in which women's rights issues are addressed. The maiden edition of the bulletin was mostly devoted to women's issues. Similarly, the CLO has researched and reported on the status of women's rights in Nigeria. In a report of a 1998 study carried out by the organization's Women's Rights Project, it was observed that there is a need for the creation of adequate social structures within which the legal provisions guaranteeing women's rights in Nigeria can be enforced.[187] As importantly, CAPP has published an important report on the low percentages of women in the mid-northern Nigerian Plateau state's civil service.[188]

VII. INTERNATIONAL COLLABORATIONS AND ADVOCACY CONCERNING WOMEN

In pursuit of their gender work, many of these NGOs have collaborated with like-minded foreign institutions. For instance, WACOL has been supported by the Center for Reproductive Rights in New York, and has also received funding from the United Nations High Commissioner for Human Rights.[189] BAOBAB has received much external support for its work on women's rights in Nigeria's sharia states.[190]

Similarly, many of these NGOs have also used the African Human Rights System to further their own work on women's rights in Nigeria. For instance, the CLO and the CRP have each sent petitions to the African Commission on Human and Peoples' Rights. Thus, Florence Butegwa's admittedly dated conclusion that most human rights NGOs in Africa that work on women's issues do not know how to make use of the African Charter in order to advance the cause of African women is not entirely inapplicable to the Nigerian situation.[191]

2.11. MINORITY/ENVIRONMENTAL RIGHTS ACTIVISM

As noted in the preceding chapters, a number of minority/environmental rights NGOs do exist in Nigeria. However, only two such NGOs are of concern to us here. These are MOSOP and the ERA.

As part of efforts to redress the historic neglect of minority/environmental rights activism within the NGO community in Nigeria, some other NGOs like the SRI, the CLO, the IHRHL, the CDHR, the SERAC and CAPP have begun to work on these issues, albeit almost always as a marginal aspect of their overall agenda.[192] Some of these efforts will be discussed later on this subsection. However, the bulk of the work in this area is still done by self-described minority/environmental rights NGOs. It is only these specialized groups that have dedicated themselves almost exclusively to this aspect of human rights activism.

On the minority rights side, these specialized NGOs have continued to struggle on behalf of the Niger Delta peoples for greater control by the latter over their oil resources, as well as for the more equal participation of these peoples in oil partnership arrangements among themselves, oil companies, and the Nigerian state. These NGOs have also advocated the convening of a sovereign national conference of Nigeria's constituent nationalities in order to fashion (for the first time ever) a *popularly legitimated* constitutional arrangement for the country.[193] Remarkably, although the book's temporal scope does not allow for its detailed consideration here, it is nevertheless important to note that a less potent version of the suggested conference was convened in 2005 by the Nigerian government.

On the environmental rights side, these NGOs seek to rectify the painful history of environmental exploitation and damage suffered by many Niger Delta communities, mostly at the hands of oil companies. As Ikelegbe has put it:

> The other front of considerable agitation and activity in relation
> to the MNOCs [Multi-National Oil Companies] is environmental.
> The agitation here is at three levels. The first is protest against
> oil spillages and the compensation practices of the MNOCs. The
> second is more general protest against environmental damage and
> irresponsibility by the MNOCs and the quest for cleaning and
> post-impact assessments. The third is the monitoring of environ-
> mental degradation, and the advocacy of environmental standards
> and actions on behalf of affected communities.[194]

More specifically, MOSOP has mass mobilized the Ogoni as well as built considerable international pressure around these issues as they affect their target population.[195] Its activities in this regard have largely consisted of consciousness-raising among the masses of Ogoni people and the waging of international sensitization campaigns. As Steven Cayford has correctly put it:

> Contrary to the top-down strategies of Nigerian elite politics,
> the MOSOP leadership attempted to raise awareness of injustice
> among the clans and to secure the involvement of the Ogoni
> people ... by giving them a stake in real results, even by promising
> them "material progress and lump sum monetary compensation
> if the struggle succeeded," in the form of royalties for oil and
> damages for ecological destruction.[196]

In pursuit of its mass mobilization programs, MOSOP has organized election boycotts, rallies, and seminars.[197] It has also formed very fruitful international alliances with important groups such as the Congressional Black Caucus of the U.S. Congress and Oxfam.[198]

Similarly, the ERA has conducted studies, brought civil actions, and campaigned in the press in favor of much greater respect for the minority and environmental rights of the Niger Delta peoples.[199] In the words of one of its senior activists, the execution of ERA's programs is heavily reliant on the creation of "awareness in the media about what is going on in the communities in which we work."[200] It also undertakes "education campaigns" and attempts to mobilize the people of these communities.[201] In the course of such community work, ERA also undertakes what it refers to as "field monitoring."[202] Such monitoring work is geared toward the collection of what it refers to as "environmental testimonies." This entails the systematic documentation of the experiences of the women and men who live with the consequences of environmental pollution. [203] All this work then leads to the periodic production of so-called alter reports.[204]

It is also important to note and consider the work that has been done in this area by nonspecialist NGOs. For example, following the widespread violations of the human rights of the peoples of the Niger Delta region by multinational oil companies operating in that region, SERAC and the New York-based Center for Economic and Social Rights (CESR) filed a complaint before the African Commission on Human and Peoples' Rights, contending that the actions of these multinational oil companies constituted violations of certain provisions of the African Charter on Human and Peoples Rights.[205] And although a detailed discussion of the outcome of this case is beyond the scope of this chapter, it is important to note here that this petition was successful. Similarly, SERAC's has filed an action against Shell at the Federal High Court of Nigeria (Benin Division) on behalf of Erovie community of Edo state, seeking among other things, an order directing SPDC to commence forthwith the evacuation of the toxic substances it dumped in Erovieland, to undertake a comprehensive clean-up of the dump site, and to execute postevacuation procedures prescribed and supervised by the panel of scientists and environmentalists appointed for that purpose.[206] For their own part, the CRP and twenty-eight other NGOs have visited and issued reports on the destruction of Odi – a Niger Delta town – by Nigerian soldiers, following the killing of some police officers by militant youths protesting the destruction of the Niger Delta's environment.[207] The CRP and a number of other groups also worked tirelessly (albeit unsuccessfully) to prevent the execution of Ken Saro-Wiwa and the rest of the Ogoni nine.[208] The SRI has also been involved in this kind of work—although mostly on the environmental side. It is in fact the African NGO Habitat Caucus' Thematic Focal Point on habitat issues.[209] It has organized seminars, taken out domestic lawsuits, and petitioned international institutions as part of its environmental rights work.[210] CAPP has similarly advocated that certain urgent measures be taken (including legislation) toward redressing the environmental and minority rights problems that have featured prominently in the Niger Delta, Jos tin mine pitches, and in the Enugu and Okaba coal fields.[211] CAPP has also campaigned for much more attention to be paid by the government to the desertification problems in the extreme north of the country as well as to similar issues that have resulted from the hydro-electric and irrigation schemes in the Shiroro, Goronyo, Bakalori and Kadawaare areas of Nigeria.[212] CAPP also publishes *Environmental Alert*—a monthly newsletter that deals with environmental issues. Following the exit of the ERA from the CLO, the CLO has continued to maintain an important but relatively marginal environmental/minority rights project.[213] The concern of the CLO in this area has been to prevent the human rights abuses arising from environmental degradation.[214] It does this by encouraging community efforts aimed at maintaining and controlling the environment and its resources; by monitoring the state of the environment; and by encouraging the government to enforce existing laws and guidelines on environmental protection.[215] For its own part, the IHRHL has mounted campaigns and education projects designed to help redress the environmental/minority rights problems in the Niger Delta region.[216] For instance, it has organized a national workshop on the extractive industries in Nigeria that was attended by representatives of NGOs from thirteen countries.[217] It has launched and undertaken an awareness campaign in the same region that was geared toward raising the peoples' consciousness regarding indiscriminate refuse disposal practices, improper sewage disposal methods, and the application of hazardous chemicals in waters for fishing.[218]As importantly, the IHRHL has published a detailed report on the genesis, nature, and effects of the serious environmental and minority rights crises that currently affect the Niger Delta region.[219] The CDHR has also participated to a limited extent in the struggle for minority and environmental rights in Nigeria: it has organized seminars and spoken out quite strongly against laws, policies, and practices that tend to hinder the full enjoyment of these rights.[220]

As importantly, while the main concerns of these NGOs are obviously local, they have often plugged into a more global environmental rights movement. As Lipschitz has correctly noted:

> One political space in which global civil society is particularly visible is that surrounding environmental politics. In the sphere of environmental activities, we see a growing number of transnational networks oriented around common strategies and goals.[221]

2.12. SOCIAL/ECONOMIC RIGHTS ACTIVISM

Despite the historical neglect of this form of activism by most NGOs in Nigeria, a number of specialized social/economic rights NGOs have been established in the country with the goal of redressing effectively this imbalance in the human rights praxis of the NGO community in Nigeria.

For instance, in one of the cases that it has filed on behalf of the Maroko eviction victims, *Farouk Atanda v. The Government of Lagos State and 4 Others*, SERAC asked the court to determine whether the resettlement housing provided to less than 3 percent of the evicted families is adequate and habitable as required by applicable human rights standards.[222] Likewise, in *Akila v. The Lagos State Government and Others*, the SERAC is challenging the denial of the right to primary education to over 9,000 pupils of the eleven Maroko schools demolished as part of the eviction process. The suit also seeks to compel the Lagos state government to institute a remedial educational program to address the needs of the displaced students. The action is premised on the government's obligation to provide free and compulsory primary education as guaranteed under the International Covenant on Economic Social and Cultural Rights, the African Charter on Human and Peoples' Rights, and other human rights instruments ratified by Nigeria.[223]

The SRI has of course done a huge amount of work in this area. A few examples will suffice to illustrate this point. In 1996, the SRI initiated a health education program. The objectives of the program are to conscientize the Nigerian public (particularly slum dwellers and persons living in degraded environments) on the linkages among the state of a human settlement and the health of its residents; to empower the populace on the methods of ensuring and enhancing health in human settlements; and to focus popular attention on the conditions of degraded human settlements with a view to initiating a program of reforms.[224] That same year, the SRI gave a one-month notice to all the chairpersons of the local government councils in Lagos state to rid the streets of the refuse that littered their respective council areas. At the expiration of the ultimatum, the SRI filed an action in court asking the court to declare that these councils were in violation of their constitutional duties.[225] Also of some importance is the SRI's work in the area of housing rights. For instance, it has petitioned the Lagos state government regarding that government's provision of substandard schoolhouses that has led on occasion to incidences of death or bodily harm caused by collapsing buildings.[226] The SRI has also utilized the processes of the UN Committee on Economic, Social, and Cultural Rights in order to further its housing rights activism. For instance, in October 1997, it wrote to that committee protesting the arbitrary demolition of some houses in the Lagos area by the Lagos state government in execution of the World Bank's slum drainage project.[227] Similarly, in April of that same year, the SRI was able to make an oral intervention before the same committee in Geneva concerning similar incidents of forced evictions in Nigeria.[228] Also worthy of note here is the SRI's innovative work in the area of budget monitoring and participatory budgeting. The SRI has led the human rights NGO community in Nigeria in their emergent turn to budget monitoring and participatory budgeting as important forms of human rights activism. Illustrative of the SRI's leadership in this area is its establishment of the South East Budget Network (SEBN) in the Southeastern States of Abia, Anambra, Ebonyi, Enugu, and Imo.[229] In its own words:

> The central object of SEBN is to introduce a rights based approach to budget advocacy, monitoring and analysis—the budget is a tool to enforce, protect and vindicate rights.[230]

What is more, the SRI has (in association with other NGOs) also organized NGO workshops that study and comment on the government's budget proposals.[231]

The CRP (in association with the Friedrich Naumann Foundation) has also engaged to some extent in economic and social rights activism. For instance, it has organized a seminar on the realization of economic, social, and cultural rights.[232]

For their part, the gender-focused NGOs have tended to engage in a significant level of social and economic rights work in Nigeria. After all, as Ayo Atsenuwa has correctly pointed out:

> .... any project of furthering women's rights/women's empower-
> ment or gender equality, howsoever it is called, must necessarily
> tackle the institutionalized discrimination against women in the
> area of education [and other ESC rights]. The denial to women of
> equality in terms of access to education is, itself, an expression of
> institutionalized gender inequality.[233]

As many others have also recognized, females do constitute the majority of the urban and rural poor in Nigeria.[234] This underscores the importance of economic and social rights activism for those concerned to advance women's rights in Nigeria.

2.13. CIVIL/POLITICAL RIGHTS ACTIVISM

As has been demonstrated in chapters 2 and 3, the NGO community in Nigeria is dominated by civil/political rights-focused NGOs. As is clear from the foregoing discussion, their programs are equally dominated by civil/political rights activism. This tilt is so clear as not to warrant further discussion here.

3. THE DEFICIENCIES OF THE PROGRAMS AND METHODS OF THE HUMAN RIGHTS NGOS IN NIGERIA

The strengths and deficiencies of the programs and methods of these NGOs tend to mirror their overall institutional strengths and deficiencies, an issue discussed more fully in chapter seven. Having already exposed the nature and strengths of these programs and methods, the rest of this chapter is devoted to a discussion of some of their conceptual deficiencies. These problems are discussed under several discrete headings.

3.1. THE CIVIL/POLITICAL RIGHTS CENTRISM OF THESE NGOS

That the work of most (not all) of these NGOs has been largely focused on the protection of civil/political rights is no longer in reasonable doubt, and does not bear detailed consideration here. Suffice it to note that, as has been acknowledged in the literature produced by at least one of these NGOs:

> The Nigerian human rights community would seem to have been
> influenced by the Western concept of human rights as they have
> over the years concentrated their energy in the area of respect for
> the political rights of citizens at the detriment of their economic
> and social rights.[235]

Another important reason for the existence of this kind of bias is the historical dominance of these NGOs by lawyers and such other professionals, what Ibhawoh has referred to as "the significant involvement in human rights initiatives of lawyers, journalists and other professionals whose interests and activities tend to be substantially affected by infringements of civil rights."[236]Given the structure and character of most of these NGOs (which, in general, lack both a significant membership base and a powerful board and which are controlled by their core management) the conceptual biases and priorities of these lawyers, journalists, etc., have loomed large over the program design of these organizations. This factor has meshed with the international human rights climate[237] and donor pressure to foster the civil/ political rights orientation of most NGOs.

The general civil/political rights centrism of these NGOs is, on balance, objectionable. This is so because it has often resulted in the serious neglect of other important though hitherto marginalized aspects of human rights work such as social/economic rights, women's rights, and minority/environmental rights work.[238] This neglect of these popular issues has in turn helped to lengthen the distance between these organizations and most average Nigerians.

3.2. A DEMOCRATIC DEFICIT IN THE AGENDA-SETTING AND PROGRAMING DESIGN OF THESE NGOS

Given that most of these NGOs do not have a powerful community-based membership, their structural linkage with the broader community is often very shallow. This is so in the sense that the broader community does not have a significant input into the decisions that are taken within these organizations.[239] As a result, the process of agenda-setting and programing design of most of these NGOs tends to suffer from a democratic deficit. More specifically, most of these NGOs have consistently failed to involve in their agenda setting and programming design, the very people whose interests they seek to advance via those programs. Consequently, the agendas of most such NGOs are hardly ever the products of a participatory or democratic process involving a significant portion of the wider community. Instead, the agendas of these NGOs tend to reflect agendas that have been set in other lands by other peoples. When the agendas of these NGOs have not in effect been set by some foreign donor or NGO, they are set by the elite cadre of Nigerian activists who run these NGOs. Very little (if any) consultation is undertaken by these NGOs with the rural and underclass communities in which the vast majority of Nigerians live. In relation to "development NGOs," Johnson and Johnson have noted that such NGOs have too often served mostly as a vehicle for the promotion of foreign (read mostly Western) values and interests.[240] These same scholars have also reported that Western NGOs (often the source of the funds that are the life sap of most local NGOs) are only just beginning to recognize the need for local NGOs in Africa to formulate their own agendas based on *local needs* (as opposed to *foreign dictates*).[241] In the specific case of Nigeria, Gathii and Nyamu have reported that as knowledgeable as they are about the constraints set by their donor dominated operational environment, the CLO and its peers have tended to "tailor their agendas to focus on issues in which the foreign donors are interested."[242]

The result of this kind of democratic deficit in the agenda-setting and program design process of NGOs in Nigeria has been very serious. For instance, in the 1980s and 1990s, most of these NGOs either focused entirely on or largely emphasized civil/political rights activism precisely at a time when the vast majority of Nigerians were being grossly impoverished in a way that they had never known. Had the agenda-setting and program-design processes of these NGOs been more connected to the voices of suffering of Nigerians, such a terrible if obvious mistake would not likely have been made.

The point, of course, is not that these NGOs should have *abandoned* their civil/political rights work. They were right to fight gallantly against military rule in Nigeria. After all, military rule itself contributed to the impoverishment of Nigerians. Rather, the point is that these NGOs should not have relegated the struggle for social/economic rights to the margins of their human rights activism. Had the local population had even a slight say about the way these organizations were run, it would have been extremely unlikely that these organizations would have relegated ESC rights to the margins.

3.3. RELATIVE SUBORDINATION TO FOREIGN NETWORK PARTNERS

Worthy of note here is the fact that these NGOs have tended to have more contact and collaborations with organizations in Europe and North America than with the many hometown based development organizations that quite effectively cover the length and breadth of the Nigerian sociopolitical landscape—a linkage that could have "grounded" many of these NGOs. Neither have they tended to link up effectively with their counterparts in other African countries.[243] While this may be due in part to the absence of sufficient opportunities and resources, it is regrettable nevertheless.

Moreover, as can be expected, the collaborations these NGOs have forged with largely Western NGOs and grantmakers have tended to be unequal. One reason for the dominance of foreign NGOs in these collaborative relationships, and for the ensuing marginalization of local populations in the decision-making processes of most of the local NGOs, is the power imbalance that exists between the resource-rich Western NGO community and resource-poor third world NGOs. Local NGOs, including the Nigerian ones, tend to be attracted to the relative power of these Western NGOs. The reasons are obvious. [244] As William Korey has noted:

> Weaker NGOs in the developing countries can win a quick show of support from....more powerful colleagues in the United States or United Kingdom. American-based or British-based NGOs can impact on the international [read Western] media and mobilize support from their own governments on behalf of human rights interests of NGOs in developing countries.[245]

The relative power of these Western NGOs has allowed them an extraordinary amount of influence within the NGO community in Nigeria—a situation that has either led to ambivalence within the NGO community in Nigeria about their relative dependence and subordination to foreign actors,[246] or that has in fact been sometimes decried as counter-productive by local activists. For instance, one senior Nigerian activist has warned fairly recently that:

> National civic groups are becoming more and more marginalized in the consolidation politics [of post-military ruled Nigeria] as *international NGOs and agencies* are moving in fast to usurp the space created by the [local] groups …. It is now time for talks of trade and investment in a 'conducive' environment for democracy, no more roles for national civic groups it seems.[247]

The relative power that such foreign actors have enjoyed has translated into an undue level of influence on the programs of the Nigerian groups.

3.4. THE URBANCENTRISM OF THESE NGOS

The earlier survey of the programs and activities of these NGOs discloses that most such NGOs have paid insufficient attention to the rural areas where most Nigerians live. While most of the programs and activities of these NGOs have been conceived of with a national audience in mind, they have tended to be most relevant to the relatively more endowed urban population. This has been so largely because these programs have almost always been mounted in urban locations, by and for urbanized Nigerians. In addition, few rural-oriented programs have been initiated by these NGOs. This is hardly surprising given the rural/urban split that has characterized human rights activism in Nigeria.[248] As one of the newer NGOs has itself noted, most of these NGOs are "urban-based, leaving the majority rural poor ignorant about their civic responsibilities."[249] As importantly, the available evidence indicates that this tendency is not peculiar to the Nigerian scene.[250]

However, this urban bias has not festered without some negative consequences for the overall relevance and effectiveness of the NGO community in Nigeria. Bonny Ibhawoh, a keen observer of the Nigerian human rights scene, is convinced that the result of such an urban bias has been that these NGOs "have made much less impact in addressing human rights issues that affect rural populations than they have been in addressing urban issues."[251] Chidi Odinkalu, a thoughtful veteran of the Nigerian human rights struggle, has put this charge of rural irrelevance even more succinctly. In his view, the result of the urban bias of these NGOs has been that even today:

> ….the real life struggles for social justice [in Nigeria] are waged *despite* human rights groups—not by or because of them—by people who feel that their realities and aspirations are not adequately captured by human rights organizations or their language.[252]

There are, of course, some notable exceptions to this general trend within the human rights NGO community in Nigeria. For instance, the Abuja-based CAPP has often engaged in grassroots mobilization in several areas of Nigeria aimed at enhancing the consciousness of rural dwellers about their rights and freedoms.[253] And although largely parochial, MOSOP's work has also been heavily oriented toward the majority rural population of the Ogoni people.

3.5. INSUFFICIENT ATTENTION TO GRASSROOTS WORK

A corollary to the urbancentrism of most of these NGOs is their lack of adequate attention to actual grassroots work. Only a handful of these NGOs work in a meaningful way *within* and *with* local communities, whether urban or rural. Most such NGOs largely work from offices in Lagos, or - in comparatively fewer cases - in other large urban centers such as Abuja, Port Harcourt, Kaduna, or Enugu. Grassroots organizing and mobilization on the streets has featured as the exception and not as the rule.[254]

The more notable exceptions here are CAPP, EMPARC, MOSOP, SERAC, and SRI. Each of these organizations has made some attempt (at a level that is well beyond that which is normal within the NGO community in Nigeria) to actively work within and engage local communities. Indeed, MOSOP is by definition a community-based organization. CAPP has also attempted, with some appreciable success, to define itself as an organization that works primarily within local communities. In CAPP's case, Ibhawoh has noted that it:

> ….has been involved in organizing community and town hall meetings aimed at promoting grassroots democracy and good governance in local communities in some Northern states. The organization has particularly worked with local groups to campaign for the rights of the indigenous people of Abuja. The creation of Abuja as the new capital of Nigeria in 1967 (sic), led to the dislocation of the indigenous communities of the area who were not been adequately resettled or compensated.[255]

The SERAC is another such NGO that has made significant strides in cultivating a linkage with the local communities on whose behalf it struggles.[256] In EMPARC's case, its work in the Ibeju-Lekki area is instructive.

3.6. THE NEGLECT OF PRO-HUMAN RIGHTS TRADITIONS

Another important problem with the programs and methods of these NGOs is that they have almost always paid scant attention, if any at all, to those aspects of the cultures that constitute Nigeria's social fabric that tend to support their struggle for human dignity, and that can help legitimate that struggle. They have instead tended to devote almost all their considerable energies to learning, sometimes by rote, the languages and cultures of Europe and North America. No NGO that is known to this author or to his research team has bothered to issue one report or conduct a single seminar on the aspects of Nigerian culture that would support their human rights catechism. In some cases, hidden not very far below the surface of this story of neglect are indications of the lingering presence of a disturbing disdain for African culture, a studied ignorance of African history, and a knee-jerk marvel for almost all things European. These attitudes were fostered during Nigeria's colonial era, and despite some progress in the direction of their abandonment, have been sustained to varying degrees among Nigeria's post-colonial elite. This is of course not a problem that is peculiar to Nigeria. Makau Mutua and Shedrack Gutto have decried the prevalence of this sort of attitude within the international human rights movement.[257]

Happily, this attitude has, under sustained criticism, begun to change. For instance:

> Women's groups in Africa, while campaigning against such cultural practices as female genital mutilation, degrading widowhood rites and discriminatory customary rules of inheritance, have emphasized the need for human rights work to focus more on traditional systems of support for women in the family. Additionally, they assert that human rights work should consider the reciprocal relationship between rights and social responsibilities and traditional methods of conflict resolution that emphasizes more of reconciliation than retribution.[258]

The fact that the human rights agenda in Africa need not always lead to the wholesale abolition (as opposed to internal modification) of African tradition has been so effectively argued by scholars like Celestine Nyamu and Makau Mutua as to be almost beyond reasonable dispute today.[259] Concrete examples of how nonabolitionist progressive human rights praxis may proceed in Africa are important and some have been offered by Ibhawoh. According to him:

> The idea of circumcision through words as an alternative to the practice of FGM [i.e., so-called female genital mutilation or what many discerning Africans prefer to refer to as female circumcision] grew out of collaborations between rural families and the Kenya national women's group Maendeleo ya Wanawake (MYWO), which is committed to ending FGM in Kenya. It follows years of research and discussion with villagers by MYWO field workers with the close cooperation of some NGOs which have served as technical facilitators to the MYWO program.[260]

Elsewhere, the same author has reported that:

> A similar ritual by which the girl [who would otherwise be circumcised] is declared a woman without being maimed is now carried out in parts of Uganda. The case of Uganda is particularly interesting because the new ritual was promoted not only by the women themselves but also by the male elders in the clan

who formed an Elders' Association for the purpose of discussing changes to this and other cultural traditions.[261]

3.7. SCANT ATTENTION TO THE EXTERNAL SOURCES OF HUMAN RIGHTS VIOLATIONS IN NIGERIA

Historically speaking, the NGO community in Nigeria has paid insufficient attention to the external sources of human rights violation in the country.[262] This has (with a few notable exceptions such as in the cases of MOSOP and SERAC) resulted in their programs tending to neglect the often very urgent need to tackle these sorts of violations head on. Given the frequency with which locally generated human rights abuses have occurred within Nigeria itself, this historical tendency is somewhat understandable. Yet, given the historic continuity of externally induced or perpetrated violations within Nigeria, this attitude is surprising nevertheless. However, since most of these NGOs are (as we shall see in chapter 5) financially dependent on many of the very same foreign governments that often perpetrate, facilitate or benefit from such abuses in Nigeria, their historic reluctance to tackle these issues is at another level not all that surprising.

In any event, these NGOs will do well to heed the advice of Justice Chukwudifu Akunne Oputa, one of Nigeria's most respected former Supreme Court judges, and the Chair of the Human Rights Investigation Panel of Nigeria between 1999 and 2002, that:

> Any one who wants to work for social justice in Africa [or elsewhere] has to begin by conducting some sort of social analysis that will help him [or her] to *locate* the structures that maintain injustice, for as long as those structures remain intact social justice will continue to be an illusion.[263]

Some notable exceptions here are the MOSOP, the ERA and SERAC. But even then, their work on the external sources of human rights violations in Nigeria has been concentrated on the environmental devastation that have been caused in the Niger Delta region of Nigeria by foreign multinational corporations such as Shell. SERAC has also done some commendable work on the effects of World Bank policies on slums in Nigeria.

4. OVERALL ASSESSMENT

Overall, while the range, diversity, and appropriateness of the programs and methods of the organizations that constitute the NGO community in Nigeria has been impressive, most such NGOs have still suffered from a number of important (even serious) deficiencies in the character and basis of their program-design and implementation.

NOTES

1. This expression is used here in the same sense as in chapter 1.

2. See T. Abayomi, "Non-Governmental Organizations in the Protection and Promotion of Human Rights in Africa: Critique of Approach and Methods," in A. U. Kalu and Y. Osinbajo, eds., *Perspectives on Human Rights* (Lagos: Federal Ministry of Justice, 1992), 173, 173–174. For more on the diversity in the nature of the programming of these NGOs, see B. Awe, "Conflict and Divergence: Government and Society in Nigeria," *African Studies Review* 42 (1999): 1, 14.

3. As Abayomi has noted, the work of Human Rights Watch Africa – a USA-based NGO – is a classic foreign example of this kind of approach. And according to Richard Dicker, its mandate is basically to monitor and report human rights violations in Africa. See R. Dicker, "Monitoring Human Rights in Africa" *Journal of Modern African Studies* 29 (1991) 505, 505-506.

4. It is important to remember that he published this essay over eleven years ago, when most existing NGOs had not even been established.

5. For a list of some of the approaches adopted internationally, see D. Weissbrodt, "The Contribution of Nongovernmental Organizations to the Protection of Human Rights," in T. Meron, ed., *Human Rights in International Law: Legal and Policy Issues* (Oxford: Clarendon Press, 1984), 403, 403-404.

6. See G.W. Shepherd, "Transnational Development of Human Rights: The Third World Crucible," in V.P. Nanda, J.R. Scarritt, and G.W. Shephard, eds. *Global Human Rights: Public Policies, Comparative Measures, and NGO Strategies* (Boulder, CO: Westview Press, 1981), 213.

7. C.E. Welch, Jr., "NGOs and the Universal Declaration of Human Rights" *Human Rights Quarterly* 22 (2000): 298, 299. Emphasis added.

8. See Media Rights Agenda, *A Harvest of Blooms* (Lagos: Media Rights Agenda, 2000), 129.

9. Ibid.

10. See Media Rights Agenda, *Media Scorecard: Report of the Print Media Coverage of the Political Transition Program* (Nigeria: Media Rights Agenda, 1999), 2.

11. CRP, *The Crisis of Press Freedom in Nigeria* (Lagos: CRP, 1993); and ibid., *Administration of Juvenile Justice in Nigeria* (Lagos: CRP, 1997).

12. See M. Shifter and P. Hayner "Laying the Groundwork: Uses of Law-Related Research," in M. McClymont and S. Golub, eds., *Many Roads to Justice: The Law-Related Work of Ford Foundation Grantees Around the World* (New York: The Ford Foundation, 2000), 315, 318.

13. Ibid.

14. See *Access Quarterly* 1 and 2:2 (2000): 4, 9–12.

15. See N. Aduba, "The Protection of Human Rights in Nigeria," in O.A. Obilade et al., eds., *Text for Human Rights Teaching in Schools* (Lagos: Constitutional Rights Project, 1999), 109.

16. See *Prison Watch* 10 (2000): 2.

17. Ibid.

18. See C.A. Odinkalu, ed., *A Harvest of Violations: Annual Report on Human Rights in Nigeria—1991* (Lagos: CLO, 1991), 64.

19. See PRAWA, *About PRAWA* (Lagos: PRAWA: 2001).

20. Ibid.

21. Ibid.

22. Ibid.

23. IHRHL, "IHRHL Documentation Center" (Port Harcourt: IHRHL, undated).

24. Ibid.

25. Ibid.

26. For instance, see A. Nsirimovu, *Human Rights: An Umblical Cord of Participatory Democracy* (Port Harcourt: IHRHL, 1997).

27. See HRA, *Annual Report 1991/1992* (Lagos: HRA, 1992), 15.

28. See HRA, *The Nigerian Police and Human Rights: Limitations and Lamentations* (Lagos: HRA, 1993); and ibid., *Annual Report 1993/1994* (Lagos: HRA, 1994), 5.

29. See EMPARC, *Annual Lecture Series No.1* (Lagos: EMPARC, 1995).

30. See ibid., *Annual Lecture Series No.4* (Lagos: EMPARC, 1998).

31. See C.R. Epp, *The Rights Revolution: Lawyers, Activists, and Supreme Courts in Comparative Perspective* (Chicago: University of Chicago Press, 1998), 142.

32. CLEEN and the National Human Rights Commission, *Policing a Democracy: A Survey Report on the Role and Functions of the Nigeria Police in a Post-Military Era* (Lagos: CLEEN, 1999), 27–28.

33. Ibid.

34. See Media Rights Agenda, *A Harvest of Blooms* (Lagos: Media Rights Agenda, 2000), 141.

35. Ibid.

36. Ibid.

37. Ibid., 17.

38. See *Media Rights Monitor* 5:4 (2000): 17.

39. Ibid., 16.

40. See *The HURILAWS Newsletter* 1:3 (1998):13, 15–18.

41. See *Constitutional Rights Journal* 9:30 (1999): 19.

42. See *The HURILAWS Newsletter* 1:3 (1998):13, 15–18.

43. See *Daily Trust*, 1 August 2003, on-line: http://www.mtrustonline.com/daily-trust/obasanjo01082003.htm (visited 19 August 2003; and Daily Champion, 4 August 2003, on-line: http://allafrica.com/stories/200308041044.html (visited 19 August 2003).

44. See HURILAWS, *1997-1998 Annual Report* (Lagos: HURILAWS, 1999), 13–14.

45. Ibid.

46. See *The HURILAWS Newsletter* 1:9 (1999): 31.

47. See IHRHL, *Human Rights Education Techniques in Schools: Building Attitudes and Skills* (Port Harcourt: IHRHL, 1994), viii; and *Human Rights Defender* (an IHRHL publication) 4:1 (2000): 15.

48. See CDHR, *Path to a People's Constitution* (Lagos: CDHR, 2000).

49. See H. Hershkoff and A. McCutcheon, "Public Interest Litigation: An International Perspective," in M. McClymont and S. Golub, eds., *Many Roads to Justice: The Law-Related Work of Ford Foundation Grantees around the World* (New York: The Ford Foundation, 2000), 283, 293.

50. See *Liberty* (a CLO publication) 9:3 (1998): 12-13.

51. See B. Ibhawoh, *Human Rights Organizations in Nigeria: An Appraisal Report on the Human Rights NGO Community in Nigeria* (Copenhagen, Denmark: The Danish Center for Human Rights, 2001), 31.

52. See transcripts of interview with AO, 17 August 2001 (on file with the author).

53. Ibid.

54. See HURILAWS, *1999 Annual Report and Accounts* (Lagos: HURILAWS, 2000), 12.

55. See *Constitutional Rights Journal* 10:35 (2000): 37–38.

56. Ibid.

57. See transcripts of interview with DT, 24 May 2000 (on file with the author).

58. See transcripts of interview with NC, 21 August 2001 (on file with the author).

59. See the [Nigerian] *Guardian* on-line: http://ngrguardiannews.com/news2nn811628.html, 5 February 2001 (visited 19 February 2001).

60. See *Human Rights Defender* (an IHRHL publication) 4:1 (2001): 28.

61. For instance, see *Legislative Mandate* (a CAPP publication) 1:1 (1999): 12.

62. See HURILAWS, *The Governance Scorecard: Review of Democratic Governance in Nigeria* (Lagos: HURILAWS, 2000), 53.

63. See Civil Liberties Organization, *Accounts and Activities for 2000* (Lagos: CLO, 2001), 21–22.

64. See Y.Z. Ya'u, "Monitoring and Influencing the Management and Allocation of Public Expenditure in Nigeria—The Experience of CAPP," *Journal of Economic, Social, and Cultural Rights* 1 (2001): 54, 57–58.

65. Ibid., 59.

66. See O. Oko, "Lawyers in Chains: Restrictions on Human Rights Advocacy under Nigeria's Military Regimes," *Harvard Human Rights Journal* 10 (1997): 257, 283–284.

67. See Civil Liberties Organization, *Accounts and Activities for 2000* (Lagos: CLO, 2001), 11.

68. Ibid.

69. Ibid.

70. See *Access Quarterly* 1 and 2:2 (2000): 34, 35-36.

71. See J.O. Ihonvbere, "Are Things Falling Apart? The Military and the Crisis of Democratization in Nigeria" *Journal of Modern African Studies* 34 (1996): 193, 201–202.

72. See Abayomi, *supra* note 2.

73. See CLO, *Training Manual on Human Rights for Trade Unions and Other Social Groups* (Lagos: CLO, 1997), xi.

74. Ibid.

75. See Civil Liberties Organization, *Accounts and Activities for 2000* (Lagos: CLO, 2001), 13–14.

76. Ibid. See also J.E. Odah, ed., *The Church and Human Rights: A Human Rights Education Training Manual for Churches in Nigeria* (Lagos, CLO: 1995).

77. Ibid.

78. See *Liberty* (a CLO publication) 9:3 (1998): 26 and 29; *Liberty* (a CLO publication) 8:3 (1997): 27–31; and *Liberty* (a CLO publication) 7:1 (1996): 11.

79. See C. Nwankwo, "Human Rights and the Challenges of NGOs in Nigeria" in O.A. Obilade et al., eds., *Text for Human Rights Teaching in Schools* (Lagos: Constitutional Rights Project, 1999), 255, 262–263. See also *Constitutional Rights Journal* 8:26 (1998): 15.

80. See Assembly Watch 2:8 (2001): 1-2.

81. See Media Rights Agenda, *A Harvest of Blooms* (Lagos: Media Rights Agenda, 2000), 8.

82. Ibid.

83. See *Law Enforcement Review* 8 (1999): 4.

84. See IHRHL, *Human Rights Education Techniques in Schools: Building Attitudes and Skills* (Port Harcourt: IHRHL, 1994), viii.

85. See SERAC@WORK 2:1 (1999): 6.

86. Ibid.

87. Ibid.

88. See PRAWA, *About PRAWA* (Lagos: PRAWA: 2001).

89. See CDHR, *Citadels of Violence* (Lagos: CDHR, 1999), 199.

90. See HRA, *Annual Report 1993/1994* (Lagos: HRA, 1994), 6.

91. See Abayomi, *supra* note 2, 190–191. Emphasis in the original.

92. See K. J. Jackson, "The Role of Non-Governmental Organizations in International Election Observing" New York University Journal of International Law and Politics 24 (1992): 1795, 1796.

93. See B. Ibhawoh, *supra* note 51, 12.

94. See TMG, *Final Report on the 1998/1999 Transition to Civil Rule Elections in Nigeria* (Lagos: TMG, 2000), 42–46.

95. Ibid., 47.

96. See HRA, *Annual Report 1993/1994* (Lagos: HRA, 1994), 8; and HRA, *Annual Report 1991/1992* (Lagos: HRA, 1994), 12.

97. Ibid.

98. See *Access Quarterly* 2:2 (2000): 30–31.

99. See CRP, *Nigeria: Human Rights Report 1999* (Lagos: CPR, 2000), 34.

100. O.L. Ehonwa, *Behind the Wall: A Report on Prison Conditions in Nigeria and the Nigerian Prison System* (Lagos: CLO, 1996), 52.

101. See *The HURILAWS Newsletter* 1:3 (1998): 15.

102. Ibid.

103. W.R. Johnson and V.R. Johnson, "West African Governments and Volunteer Development Organizations: Priorities for Partnership (Lanham, MD: University Press of America, 1990), 27.

104. Ibid., 42.

105. Ibid., 82.

106. Ibhawoh, *supra* note 51, 10.

107. Ibid., 11.

108. See *Liberty* (a CLO publication) 9:1 (1998): 1, 5.

109. Ibid., 12.

110. Ibid., 35.

111. Ibid.

112. See *The HURILAWS* Newsletter 1:5 (1998): 14.

113. Ibid.

114. See Nigerian NGO Coalition For A Shadow Report To CEDAW, *NGOs' CEDAW Report For Nigeria* (Lagos: Nigerian NGO Coalition For A Shadow Report To CEDAW, 2001), v and vii.

115. See *The HURI-LAWS Newsletter* 1:3 (1998): 21–22.

116. See HURILAWS, *Annual Report and Accounts, 1999* (Lagos: HURILAWS, 2000), 2–3.

117. See *Action Woman* (a WACOL publication) (2002) 1:1 (2002): 6.

118. See *Human Rights Defender* (an IHRHL publication) 4:1 (2001): 31.

119. See *Community* (a CAPP publication) 2:1 (1997): 3. Emphasis added.

120. See H. Fruhling, "From Dictatorship to Democracy: Law and Social Change in the Andean Region and the Southern Cone of South America," in M. McClymont and S. Golub, eds., *Many Roads to Justice: The Law Related Work of Ford Foundation Grantees around the World* (New York: The Ford Foundation, 2000), 55, 63. For an analogy with "developmental NGOs, see E. Sandberg, "Introduction: The Changing Politics of Non-Governmental Organizations and the African State," in E. Sandberg ed., *The Changing Politics of Non-Governmental Organizations and African States* (Westport, Connecticut: Praeger, 1994), 1, 3-4.

121. V. Wiebe, "The Prevention of Civil War Through the Use of the Human Rights System" *New York University Journal of International Law and Politics* 27 (1995): 409, 443.

122. See Ibhawoh, *supra* note 51, 37.

123. See J. Gathii and C. Nyamu, "Reflections on United States-Based Human Rights NGOs' Work on Africa," *Harvard* Human Rights Journal 9 (1996): 285, 294.

124. See *Media Rights Monitor* 5:2 (2000): 13.

125. See ICCAF, *Nigeria—The Struggle for Justice, Democracy and Human Rights* (Toronto: ICCAF, 1999).

126. See transcripts of interview with AO, 17 August 2001 (on file with the author); See also transcripts of interview with OA, 20 August 2001 (on file with the author); and transcripts of interview with FF, 25 August 2001 (on file with the author).

127. See interview with OA, ibid.

128. See interview with FF, supra note 126. See also, transcripts of interview with AO, ibid; and transcripts of interview with NC, 21 August 2001 (on file with the author).

129. O.C. Okafor, "Do International Human Rights Institutions Matter? The African System on Human and Peoples Rights, Quasi-Constructivism, and the Possibility of Peacebuilding within African States" *International Journal of Human Rights* 8 (2004): 1–38.

130. This issue will be dealt with more fully in chapter 6 of this book.

131. See *Constitutional Rights Journal* 9:32 (1999): 15.

132. See Media Rights Agenda, *A Harvest of Blooms* (Lagos: MRA, 2000), 16.

133. Ibid., 16–17.

134. Ibid., 87.

135. See J.O. Ihonvbere, "Where is the Third Wave: A Critical Evaluation of Africa's Non-Transition to Democracy" *Africa Today* 43 (1996): 343, 362.

136. See *Liberty* (a CLO publication) 4:3 (1993): 33.

137. See *Liberty* (a CLO publication) 6:3 (1995): 26.

138. See *African Human Rights Newsletter* 9:4 (1999): 1.

139. See B. Awe, "Conflict and Divergence: Government and Society in Nigeria," *African Studies Review* 42 (1999): 11.

140. See *The HURILAWS Newsletter* 1:9 (1999): 21.

141. See J. Ezeilo, *Gender, Politics and the Law* (Enugu: Women's Aid Collective, 1999), 12–15.

142. Ibid.

143. Ibid.

144. Ibid.

145. Ibid.

146. Ibid.

147. See *Constitutional Rights Journal* 7:25 (1998): 30.

148. See H.J. Steiner and P. Alston, *International Human Rights in Context: Law, Politics, and Morals* (Oxford: Clarendon Press, 2000), 887.

149. See transcripts of joint interview with FM and OC, 2 May 2002 (on file with the author).

150. See WACOL/Macarthur Project, "Expert Meeting on the Designing of Curriculum for the Introduction of the Teaching of Reproductive Rights and Maternal

Health in Nigerian Faculties /Law Schools," unpublished resource pack, vol. 1 (on file with the author).

151. See HRA, *Communiqué of the 1991 African Human Rights Conference* (Lagos: Human Rights Africa, 1991), 5–6.

152. Ibid.

153. See *Constitutional Rights Journal* 10:34 (2000): 39.

154. See *Final Communiqué of the Seminar on Discriminatory Laws and Practices Against Women in Nigeria* (Lagos: CRP, 1995).

155. See *Constitutional Rights Journal* 7:25 (1998): 26.

156. See *Gender Action* 1:2 (1998): 16–18.

157. See *Liberty* (a CLO publication) 12:6 (2000): 6–7.

158. BOABAB's literature.

159. See *Action Woman* (a WACOL publication) 1:1 (2002): 4.

160. Ibid., 10–11.

161. See J. Ezeilo, *Reproductive Rights, Maternal Health Education, and Advocacy Project* (Enugu: WACOL, 2002).

162. Ibid.

163. See *Law Enforcement Review* (a CLEEN publication) 8 (1999): 21.

164. Ibid.

165. Ibid.

166. See T.U. Akumadu, *Women's Reproductive Health Rights: A Training Manual for Communities of Eastern Nigeria* (Lagos: CLO, 1999).

167. See *Human Rights Defender* (an IHRHL publication) 4:1 (2001): 30.

168. See *Access Quarterly* 1 and 2:2 (2000): 30–31.

169. See J. Ezeilo, *supra* note 141, 15.

170. See WACOL, *Legislative Advocacy for Women's Rights* (Enugu: WACOL, 2001), 44.

171. See J. Ezeilo, *Reproductive Rights, Maternal Health Education, and Advocacy Project* (Enugu: WACOL, 2002).

172. See *Post Express wired,* on-line: http://www.postexpresswired.com/postexpr... 31ea33c60df852568ff0057f799?openDocument_(visited 16 June 2000).

173. See *SERAC @ Work* (July 2001): 1–2.

174. Ibid.

175. Ibid.

176. Ibid.

177. HURILAWS, *Annual Report and Accounts, 1999* (Lagos: HURILAWS, 2000), 12.

178. Ibid.

179. See *Grassroots News* 1:2 (2000): 11.

180. Ibid.

181. See Rights and Democracy's web site, on-line: http://www.ichrdd.ca/english/ commdoc/humphrey2002/presentationAyeshaImamEng.html (visited on 17 March 2003).

182. See http://1w3fd.law3.hotmail.msn.com/c...t=341196&len=7712&msgread=
1&mfs=340 (visited 31 January 2001).

183. See WACOL, *The Laws and Practices Relating to Women's Inheritance Rights in Nigeria*
(Enugu: WACOL, 2000).

184. For instance, see ibid., *Gender, Politics and the Law* (Enugu: WACOL, 1999); J.
Ezeilo, *Women's and Children's Rights in Nigeria* (Enugu: WACOL, 2001); J. Ezeilo,
Voices from Below (Enugu: WACOL, 2002); and WACOL, *Women's Socio-Economic
and Legal Rights* (Enugu: WACOL, 2001).

185. See B. Ibhawoh, *supra* note 51, 36.

186. See S.C. Ogbuagu, *Gender and the Democratic Process in Nigeria: Issues of Concern*
(Lagos: EMPARC, 1999).

187. T.U. Akumadu, *Beasts of Burden: A Study of Women's Legal Status and Reproductive
Health Rights in Nigeria* (Lagos: CLO, 1998), 104.

188. See CAPP, *Figures of Marginalization* (Abuja: CAPP, 1996).

189. See *Action Woman* (2002): 23–24.

190. See chapter 5 of this book.

191. See F. Butegwa, "Using the African Charter on Human and Peoples' Rights to
Secure Women's Access to Land in Africa," in R.J. Cook, ed., *Human Rights of
Women: National and International Perspectives* (Philadelphia: University of Pennsyl-
vania Press, 1994), 495, 510.

192. See *Living Newsletter* 2:2 (1998): 22; *Liberty* (a CLO publication) 11:5 (1999): 10;
Legislative Mandate (a CAPP publication) 1:1 (1999): 14; *Human Rights Defender* (an
IHRHL publication) 4:1 (2001): 24; *The Vanguard*, 22 September 1999; and *Access
Quarterly* 1 and 2:2 (2000): 21.

193. See A. Ikelegbe, "Civil Society, Oil and Conflict in the Niger Delta Region of
Nigeria: Ramifications of Civil Society for a Regional Resource Struggle" *Journal
of Modern African Studies* 39 (2001): 437, 455.

194. Ibid., 452.

195. See transcripts of interview with WJ, 1 April 2003 (on file with the author).

196. See S. Cayford, "The Ogoni Uprising: Oil, Human Rights and a Democratic
Alternative in Nigeria," *Africa Today* 43:2 (1996): 183, 187.

197. See transcripts of interview with WJ, *supra* note 195.

198. Ibid.

199. See transcripts of interview with NP, 12 January 2003 (on file with the author).

200. Ibid.

201. Ibid.

202. Ibid.

203. Ibid.

204. Ibid.

205. See *Access Quarterly* 1 and 2:2 (2000): 21, 25; Dinah Shelton, "Decision Regarding Communication 155/96 (*Social & Economic Action Center/Center for Economic
and Social Rights v. Nigeria*) Case No. ACHPR/Comm/A044/1," The American

Journal of International Law 96 (2002): 937. For an imaginative and thought-provoking discussion of this case, see, J. Oloka-Onyango "Reinforcing Margin-alized Rights in An Age of Globalization: International Mechanism, Non-State Actors, and the struggle for Peoples' Rights in Africa," (2003) 18 American University International Law Review 851, 866–71.

206. See *SERAC @ Work* (July 2001): 4 and 6.

207. Constitutional Rights Project, *Nigeria: Human Rights Report—1999* (Lagos: CRP, 2000), 21–22.

208. See *Constitutional Rights Journal* 5:17 (1995): 4, 7–9.

209. See *Living Newsletter* 2:2 (1998): 19–20.

210. In suit no FHC/L/CS/663/97 (*Ray Onyegu v. The Minister of Works & Housing and another*), the SRI sought an injunction in order to restrain the federal government and its agents from continuing the sand filing of the Ilubirin and Osborne lands on Lagos Island without first carrying out an environmental impact assessment. The SRI thus petitioned the court to order the federal government to comply with its own environmental laws. See *Living Newsletter* 2:2 (1998): 22; and *Shelter Watch* 1:3 (1997): 53. In October 1996, the SRI filed a petition at the African Commission on Human and Peoples' Rights Commission on behalf of the residents/owners of properties at Harvey/Moore Roads, Lagos, accusing the Nigerian government of violating Articles 7 and 14 of the African Charter on Human and Peoples' Rights. The basis of the complaint was that the Nigerian government had commenced the demolition of the properties at this location without following the due process of the law. See *Shelter Watch* 1:2 (1996): 10, 11.

211. See *Legislative Mandate* (a CAPP publication) 1:1 (1999): 14

212. Ibid.

213. For instance, see *Liberty* (a CLO publication) 6:3 (1995): 22.

214. Ibid.

215. Ibid.

216. See *Human Rights Defender* (an IHRHL publication) 4:1 (2001): 24.

217. Ibid.

218. Ibid., 30.

219. See IHRHL, *Poverty in Wealth* (Port Harcourt: IHRHL, 2002).

220. See *The Vanguard*, 22 September 1999.

221. R.D. Lipschutz, "Reconstructing World Politics: The Emergence of Global Civil Society," *Millennium: A Journal of International Studies* 21 (1992): 389, 393.

222. See *Access Quarterly* 1&2:2 (2000): 34, 35–36.

223. Ibid.

224. See *Shelter Watch* 1:2 (1996): 57.

225. Ibid.

226. See *SRI Petition on the Death of Opeluwa Olarewaju at Iyana Ipaja*, 15 May 2000 (on file with the author).

227. See *SRI Letter to the UN Committee on Economic, Social and Cultural Rights*, 6 October 1997 (on file with the author).

228. See Concluding Observations of the Committee on Economic, Social, and Cultural Rights: Nigeria, 13 May 1998, E/C.12/1/Add.23 (paragraph 12 of this document seems to indicate that the committee was persuaded by the intervention of SRI and other NGOs).

229. See *SEBN News* 1:1 (2002): 1.

230. Ibid.

231. Ibid., 3.

232. See Constitutional Rights Journal 7:23 (1997) 34–35.

233. See A. Atsenuwa, "The Right to Education and Gender Equality," *Journal of Economic, Social, and Cultural Rights* 1:1 (2001): 1, 1–2.

234. See J.U. Achor, ed., *Practical Issues in Human Settlements and Health: Proceedings of a Workshop for Residents of Slum Communities in Lagos* (Lagos: Shelter Rights Initiative, 1997), 47.

235. See *Liberty* (a CLO publication) 6:3 (1995): 2.

236. See Ibhawoh, *supra* note 51, 14.

237. See J. Smith and R. Pagnucco (with G.A. Lopez), "Globalizing Human Rights: The Work of Transnational Human Rights NGOs in the 1990s," *Human Rights Quarterly* 20:2 (1998) 379.

238. See *Liberty* (a CLO publication) 6:3 (1995): 2. See also J.O. Ihonvbere, "On the Threshold of Another False Start? A Critical Evaluation of Prodemocracy Movements in Africa," *Journal of Asian and African Studies* 31 (1996): 125, 126.

239. See C.A. Odinkalu, "Why More Africans Don't Use Human Rights Language" *Human Rights Dialogue* (2000): 3, 4.

240. See W.R. Johnson and V.R. Johnson, *West African Governments and Volunteer Development Organization: Priorities for Partnership* (Lanham, MD: University Press of America, 1990), 2.

241. Ibid., 13.

242. See Gathii and Nyamu, *supra* note 123, 295.

243. Ibid.

244. Ibid., 295.

245. See W. Korey, *NGOs and the Universal Declaration of Human Rights: A Curious Grapevine* (New York: St. Martin's Press, 1998), 23–24.

246. See T.M. Shaw, "Popular Participation in Non-Governmental Structures in Africa: Implications for Democratic Development," *Africa Today* 37 (1990): 5, 14.

247. See *Human Rights Defender* (an IHRHL publication) 4:1 (2001): 7. Emphasis added.

248. See Ibhawoh, *supra* note 51, 19.

249. See *Legislative Mandate* (a CAPP publication) 1:1(1999): 38.

250. See L. Lawson, "External Democracy Promotion in Africa: Another False Start?" *Commonwealth and Comparative Politics* 37 (1999): 1, 15.

251. Ibhawoh, Supra note 51,19.

252. See Odinkalu, *supra* note 239, 4. Emphasis added.

253. See *Legislative Mandate* (a CAPP publication) 1:1(1999): 38.

254. Again, this orientation is not peculiar to Nigerian human rights NGOs. For instance, Jill Crystal has noted that the Arab Organization for Human Rights "has made little effort at street activism." See J. Crystal, "The Human Rights Movement in the Arab World" *Human Rights Quarterly* 16 (1994): 435.

255. See B. Ibhawoh, *supra* note 51, 29.

256. For example, see sections 2.6 and 2.12 of this chapter.

257. See M. Mutua, "The Banjul Charter and the African Cultural Fingerprint: An Analysis of the Language of Duties," *Virginia Journal of International Law* 35 (1995): 335 and S.B.O. Gutto, "Non-Governmental Organizations, People's Participation and the African Commission on Human and Peoples' Rights: Emerging Challenges to Regional Protection of Human Rights," in B. Andreassen and T. Swineheart, eds., *Human Rights in Developing Countries Yearbook: 1991* (Oslo: Scandinavian University Press, 1992), 33, 48.

258. See B. Ibhawoh, "Between Culture and Constitution: Evaluating the Cultural Legitimacy of Human Rights in the African State," *Human Rights Quarterly* 22 (2000): 838, 853.

259. See C. Nyamu, "How Should Human Rights and Development Respond to Cultural Legitimization of Gender Hierarchy in Developing Countries," *Harvard International Law Journal* 41 (2000): 381; M. Mutua, "The Politics of Human Rights: Beyond the Abolitionist Paradigm in Africa," Michigan Journal of International Law 17 (1996): 591.

260. Supra note 258, 858, footnote 46. Emphasis added.

261. Ibid., 859.

262. See O.C. Okafor, "Re-Conceiving 'Third World' Legitimate Governance Struggles in Our Time; Emergent Imperatives for Rights Activism" *Buffalo Human Rights Law Journal* 6 (2000): 1.

263. See C.A. Oputa, "Keynote Address at the 6th Biennial Conference of African Bar Association at Abuja, Nigeria, 18–22 March 1992," 12, quoted in E.K. Quashigah "Protection of Human Rights in the Changing International Scene: Prospects in sub-Saharan Africa," RADIC 6 (1994): 93, 105. Emphasis added.

BETWEEN THE PIPER AND THE TUNE:
FUNDING PATTERNS AND THE CONSTRUCTION OF THE HUMAN RIGHTS NGO COMMUNITY IN NIGERIA

Without question, funders affect the goals of human rights NGOs…NGOs are resource-driven.
— Claude Welch[1]

Local human rights groups exist to please the international agencies that fund or support them.
— Chidi Odinkalu[2]

1. INTRODUCTION

Chapter 3 was devoted to understanding in some detail the composition, structure, and geopolitical location of the NGO community in Nigeria.[3] That chapter also developed the argument that, much to its disadvantage, this NGO community has tended to exclude from its ranks and internal processes the very people whose interests it strives to protect. Following this analytical exposé, the character and deficiencies of the programs and methods of this NGO community were discussed in chapter 4. It was argued that while these NGOs have mounted reasonably well-conceived programs and adopted many appropriate methods, their programs and methods were still afflicted by a number of important conceptual and strategic problems. It was suggested that each of these problems is attributable in some way and to some extent to the tendency to exclude average Nigerians from active ownership and participation in the internal processes of these NGOs.

As intimately connected to the character of these NGOs are a number of crucial questions related to the sourcing of the funds that have been vital to the execution of their programs. Who makes available the funds and other resources that sustain these NGOs? To what extent have these NGOs made efforts to raise a significant portion of their funds from the local community? To what extent have these NGOs become dependent on foreign funding? What are the consequences for these NGOs of the current structure of their funding regime?[4] These are the major questions that this chapter will address.

The evidence will show that the, relatively speaking, far easier access to foreign funding that these NGOs have enjoyed has tended to relieve them of the admittedly more difficult burden of canvassing the local population for membership fees and other kinds of financial support. The pursuit of this alternative and much more localized fund-raising strategy would most likely have led to the much greater involvement of average Nigerians in the internal decision-making processes and activities of these NGOs. This would likely have led to a sense of "ownership" among ordinary Nigerians concerning these groups and their work. In this way would this NGO community have become a much more integral part of the local populations within which they function. The obvious benefit that such popular integration and validation would have conferred on these NGOs would have been their capacity to command much more readily a dedicated following among ordinary Nigerians (much in the same manner that most faith-based groups and labor unions do). This kind of popular validation and commitment would have in turn enabled the NGOs to exert a far greater degree of influence within the polity. Thus far, despite the modest impact that they have had within the country, these NGOs have mostly been unable to effect the widespread mobilization of average Nigerians to their cause. In this connection, it is most instructive that the NGOs that have had the most marked, appreciable, and visible impact in altering the behavior of the executive branch of the Nigerian government have tended to be those that have been able to catalyze popular grassroots movements in the Niger Delta region.[5]

The point, then, is that the effectiveness of these groups has been markedly affected by their dependence on foreign (as opposed to local) funding. But demonstrating this connection between the NGO funding regime, on the one hand, and the nature and impact of these groups, on the other hand, will not be an easy task. As Karen Jason has remarked in another context, "the influence of funding ...upon the nature and extent of NGO activity is [often] neither obvious nor clearly measurable."[6] However, I am also in agreement with her that the influence of patterns of funding upon the agenda, character and development of these organizations must nevertheless "be taken into account."[7] For, as students of human rights NGOs have increasingly recognized, the funds made available by such Western donors as the Ford Foundation, the MacArthur Foundation, the Rockefeller Foundation, the Canadian International Development Agency, the International Development Research Center, and the European Union have in fact functioned to *constitute* most of these NGOs in specific ways. In the context of the Ford Foundation, William Carmichael has quite correctly noted that this charity has been:

> .... a major actor in the *construction* of the burgeoning global community of nongovernmental organizations (NGOs) in human rights and related fields ....The importance of the Ford Foundation's role in the human rights arena derives in part from the

disturbingly fragile nature of the financial underpinnings of most human rights NGOs.[8]

Thus, even many of the largest international human rights NGOs have been significantly dependent on the funding that they receive from these foundations. The notable exception to this trend among such groups is Amnesty International (AI), which to this day refuses to accept money from governments and is quite wary of foundation grants.[9] As Claude Welch has put it, "[a]mong major human rights organizations, *the AI formula is unique.* Its membership base provides a substantial portion of the annual budget."[10] These Western donors have also exerted significant influence on the development of human rights NGOs in Africa. Indeed, their influence has had a deeply constitutive effect on these groups.[11]

In the Nigerian context, it will be particularly ill advised *not* to take adequate stock of the extent to which the foreign funders that contribute almost all of the funds available to the NGO community there have shaped the character, behavior and development of these NGOs.[12] Indeed, as Julius Ihonvbere has correctly noted, these groups have over the years received millions in the form of dollars, electronic and communications equipment, vehicles, and training facilities from Western donors.[13] The need to undertake such an analysis is further underscored by the fact that in the course of providing financial assistance to these NGOs, the relevant foreign donors have always pursued their own institutional agendas and priorities. As Akin Mabogunje has noted:

> This issue of the sources of funding for [Nigerian] NGOs is of fundamental importance because of the way it often exercises an undue, and perhaps unintended, influence on their priorities, their planning and the development of their institutional capacity.[14]

The necessity for such analysis is also justified by the key roles that financial resources often play in the institutional behavior and development of these NGOs. The urgency with which many of these NGOs have always sought to acquire such resources, usually from foreign donors, is easily gleaned from the following passage, culled from the newsletter of the CLO - the leading such NGO in Nigeria:

> ....what democratic forces in civil society [including NGOs] *need most* is resources, especially money and equipment ....These groups need more financial support [usually from foreign donors] to sustain and expand their operations, and to improve their technologies of communication within Nigeria and between Nigeria and the outside world.[15]

The point this chapter makes is *not* that their far easier access to foreign (as opposed to local) funding has been entirely responsible for the inability of these NGOs to become as adequately integrated and popularly validated within the broader Nigerian society as they could. That would be an incorrect proposition. Rather, the precise point that will be demonstrated is that their far easier access to such foreign funding has played a critical role, among a number of factors, in providing a very *strong disincentive* for these NGOs to regularly cultivate the local population for funds, resources, and other forms of support and has thus stunted their ability to develop into the kinds of popular organizations that can exert far more influence within the country. As such while their dependence on foreign funding has had its obvious advantages, it has been far from an unqualified good.

Chiefly for organizational purposes, the evidence that grounds these propositions will be discussed using the same NGO typology that was applied in preceding chapters. As such, individual NGOs will be considered under the following heads: civil/political rights NGOs, social/economic rights NGOs, women's rights NGOs, and minority/environmental rights NGOs. Thereafter, the chapter will offer a constructive critique of the current NGO funding regime in Nigeria—one that is based on the empirical findings that are reported in preceding sections of the chapter.

2. THE FINANCING OF NIGERIAN CIVIL/POLITICAL RIGHTS NGOS

This section considers questions related to the financing of eleven civil/political rights NGOs: the Civil Liberties Organization (CLO); the Constitutional Rights Project (CRP); the Committee for the Defense of Human Rights (CDHR); the Center for Law Enforcement Education (CLEEN); Media Rights Agenda (MRA); the Institute for Human Rights and Humanitarian Law (IHRHL); Community Action for Popular Participation (CAPP); the Human Rights Law Service (HURILAWS); Human Rights Monitor (HRM); and Human Rights Africa (HRA).

As in other chapters, this one considers these groups respectively, seeking to flesh out the nature of each organization's funding structure, the extent to which it is donor-dependent, and the effects of donor dependence on its institutional development and effectiveness.

2.1. THE CIVIL LIBERTIES ORGANIZATION (CLO)

As is typical within the NGO community in Nigeria, the vast majority of the CLO's funds have been sourced from foreign donors.[16] As one of its senior activists has noted, the main funders of this NGO have been European and North American governments and charities. In his own words:

> We have been funded on a project-by-project basis. Our funders include, the National Endowment for Democracy (NED), Ford Foundation, the Open Society Institute, MacArthur Foundation, the Danish Centre for Human Rights, the British and American Embassies in Nigeria, among others.[17]

The Norwegian Human Rights Fund;[18] the Heinrich Boll Foundation of Germany;[19] the Canada Fund;[20] the British Council;[21] the International

Centre for Human Rights and Democratic Development;[22] the Dutch Reformed Church;[23] the Dutch Inter-Church Aid;[24] the Protestant Association for Cooperation in Development of Germany;[25] and the Swedish NGO Foundation for Human Rights[26] have also funded many of its projects.

This pattern of funding is also confirmed by its annual reports. For instance, its annual report for the year 2000 observes that:

> Grants are received *principally* from foreign donors. Grants received from the foreign bodies are for the following projects:
>
> (a) Legal Assistance Network
>
> (b) Democracy Action Projects/Liberty Magazine
>
> (c) Administration of Justice (Training of Lower Court Judges)
>
> (d) Campaigns and Monitoring Project
>
> (e) Prison Watch and Penal Reforms
>
> (f) Human Rights Education for Religious Groups
>
> (g) Women Rights Projects
>
> (h) Annual Report – State of Human Rights in Nigeria
>
> (i) Human Rights Education with Trade Unions and other Social Groups
>
> (j) Transparency and Accountability Project with Civil Society Groups
>
> (k) Police and Law Enforcement Project
>
> (l) Niger Delta Monitoring Project
>
> (m) General Purpose and Capacity Building
>
> (n) Academic Freedom and State Repression."[27]

According to this same report, in the year 1999, the CLO received mostly foreign grants amounting in Nigerian (Naira) currency to N31,462,153 (worth approximately US$350,000 at that time). In the year 2000, it received a total of N51, 602,436 (worth approximately $400,000) in mostly foreign grant money.[28]

As such, even though the CLO has on occasion received some funds from local sources[29], and especially from its founding members,[30] at no time in its life has it sourced a significant portion of its funds from Nigerian members or donors. As is typical of the NGOs that are of concern here, the CLO is so heavily reliant on foreign funding that it has for almost all of its life scarcely bothered either to raise funds locally or to collect the fees it had levied on its membership. As one of its most senior activists put it:

> When we started there wasn't [sic] any membership dues, but that was subsequently introduced. Initially, there was no urge to collect the dues. *We were receiving funding from donors and weren't, as it were, in*

a hurry to collect the dues. But with the exit of the military and the enthronement of civil rule, funders seem to have their interests elsewhere and have not been paying much attention to funding our programs. Now there is a restructuring going on to re-validate our membership and collect membership dues. We placed adverts in the newspapers and have fixed the membership dues at N1, 000 (one thousand naira); students will pay N350 (three hundred and fifty naira). *We are yet to start collecting these* and so I cannot say how successful we will be or its percentage to our expenditure.[31]

Clearly evident from this passage is this CLO activist's striking recognition of a close linkage between the influx of and reliance on foreign funding into the CLO and its inability to maintain an active and financially supportive membership. Also evident, at least implicitly, is the linkage between the availability of foreign funding and the ability of the CLO to run its programs effectively. It is also evident from this passage that these foreign funders tend to have their own agendas, and that these do not always fit neatly into the priorities of the CLO. For instance, this senior CLO activist pointedly laments that the foreign entities that funded the organization at its birth have now all but abandoned it because of the end of CLO's struggle against military rule (a civil/political rights struggle).[32] Yet, even if one were to concede that the human rights climate in Nigeria has improved somewhat—especially in the area of massive civil/political rights abuses—at the very least, egregious violations of social/economic and minority/environmental rights remain as wanton today as they have ever been! [33]

These funding patterns have negatively affected the CLO's ability to command the kind of mass following that would afford it a critical amount of leverage as it struggles to exert influence on both Nigeria's domestic governance institutions and the body politic. The CLO's heavy reliance on foreign funding has—as admitted by one of its senior activists—served as a strong disincentive for it to cultivate the local population for resources, support, and the commitment that invariably results. Without far more widespread support and commitment among ordinary Nigerians, the CLO stood little chance of optimizing its capacity to influence the play of local politics.

2.2. THE CONSTITUTIONAL RIGHTS PROJECT (CRP)

Like virtually every such NGO, foreign governments and charities have funded the vast majority of the CRP's activities. The CRP's first receipt of such financial support came in1991in the form of a grant from the Canadian government.[34] Following this donation, they received a grant from the Ford Foundation that was specifically earmarked for the funding of the CRP's provision of legal services to the victims of civil/political rights abuses[35] as well as the publication of the CRP's first book on the bail process in Nigeria.[36] Since then it has received hundreds of thousands of U.S. dollars from similar foreign sources. For instance, the publication of its *Constitutional Rights Journal* has been made possible by the generous support of the Royal

Dutch Embassy in Nigeria;[37] and the establishment of its Abuja office, which opened in October 2000, was made possible by the grant of funds by the Canadian government. [38] Similarly, the USA-based National Endowment for Democracy has supported many of its programs, including the publication of a number of important reports,[39] The Friedrich Naumann Foundation sponsored its May 2000 seminar that brought together members of Parliament from both the National Assembly and the various state legislatures. The seminar was aimed at identifying, for reform or repeal, laws made before the current civilian dispensation that violate both the Nigerian constitution and international human rights standards.[40] The same foundation has funded both a training seminar for law students[41] and a conference on the repeal of laws and practices that discriminate against women in Nigeria.[42] It is also noteworthy that the USA Embassy in Nigeria funded the publication of its important 1997 report on the administration of juvenile justice in Nigeria.[43]

The CRP is also like most of its peers in that it has not been able to raise a sizeable portion of its funds locally. Indeed, in the course of its existence as an organization, almost all its funds have come from foreign sources.[44] However, the CRP has sourced small amounts of money from the personal funds of its founder/CEO and from Tayo Oyetibo, a prominent activist lawyer.[45]

Since foreign donors usually have their own set programs of funding that target certain areas of human rights work during each funding cycle[46] and since the vast majority of the CRP's funds have come from these foreign sources, it is only logical to deduce that the CRP's successful grant proposals have been tailored to fit the priorities set by these foreign donors. While these priorities have often coincided with some of the real needs of Nigeria's people, the point remains that one of the critical factors that has shaped the agenda of the CRP has been the priority areas determined by the boards of the foreign bodies that provide its funds. The CRP's expressed desire is to help advance the real needs of abused Nigerians, but since it has hardly cultivated the financial support of Nigerians and is not really a true membership organization, it has so far not afforded much of an opportunity to any significant domestic constituency to help shape its agenda. An important negative consequence of this institutional distance from the formative pressures that could be exerted by average Nigerians has been the CRP's tendency in the severely depressed Nigerian economy to concentrate on civil/political rights to the detriment of social/economic rights. Another such negative consequence has been the CRP's inability to create a deep connection between it and the Nigerian public. Whatever its other strengths, it is clear that the CRP cannot claim the widespread allegiance and commitment of ordinary Nigerians—at least not in the apparent and demonstrable way that the anticolonial organizations that operated in Nigeria in the early to mid-1900s could. That this kind of popular connection can be established by civil society groups in Nigeria is demonstrated by the successful record of many Nigerian faith-based groups and labor unions—one that is discussed in more detail in chapter 7.

2.3. THE COMMITTEE FOR THE DEFENSE OF HUMAN RIGHTS (CDHR)

The CDHR's initial funding was provided by Beko Ransome Kuti, one of its founders.[47] Even though it attempts to raise some of its funds locally, the CDHR is—like almost all of its peers—heavily dependent on foreign funding. As one of its senior activists has admitted, it raises the lion share of its funds from major foreign donors, such as the Ford Foundation, and from many of the more affluent foreign missions in Nigeria.[48] It has also received financial support from other foreign sources such as the Westminster Foundation for Democracy and the National Lottery Charity Board (both UK-based entities).[49] In fact, the CDHR itself acknowledges that almost every single one of its publications and annual reports on the state of human rights in Nigeria since its inception has been funded by some foreign organization.[50]

The CDHR has received some modest funding from local sources. However, it does not rely very much on this source of funding. This is evident from the statement by one of its senior activists that the organization's "members are required to pay dues. [But that] *whether or not they pay at all or regularly is a different matter. But some do pay.*"[51]

Again like its peers, the CDHR's work has been influenced to a significant degree by the agenda of the foreign funders that support the work of these NGOs. As it has been successful in receiving funds from such funders, and such funders have openly set their own criteria for funding such NGO programs, it is only reasonable to deduce that the CDHR's agenda (as evidenced by its programs) has tended to conform to the priorities set by those foreign organizations. In the same sense, it is also clear that outside the contributions of its core management team, contributions that must have been shaped by the prospect of success at obtaining foreign funding, there has been relatively little participation from the broader community in determining the nature of the programs of this NGO. This is in part attributable to the strong disincentive against embarking on the difficult process of popular mobilization and local fund-raising that has been instituted by the readier access to foreign funding that the CDHR has enjoyed.

2.4. THE CENTRE FOR LAW ENFORCEMENT EDUCATION (CLEEN)

CLEEN is not unlike most of its peers in terms of the structure of the financial aspects of its institutional life. The bulk of its funding comes from foreign sources and very little of its financial resources are raised locally. For example, it had to rely on foreign donors such as the Norwegian Human Rights Fund for the financial resources it needed to embark on an extensive survey on the role and functions of the Nigerian police service in the post-military era.[52] Further evidence of this organization's dependence on foreign donors for its operations and activities is found in its own acknowledgment that the generous funding of the Ford Foundation makes possible the publication of its quarterly magazine *Law Enforcement Review.*[53]

While other factors have helped shape CLEEN's social impact in Nigeria, the nature of this organization's funding regime has had some obvious negative repercussions for its ability to establish deep connections with the very populations whose interests it does wish to advance. Freed almost entirely from the necessity of cultivating the kind of local financial support and commitment that a membership base or local fundraising efforts can often ensure, it has not involved the local population in its internal agenda-setting and program design processes, with the result that, like almost every one of its peers, it has remained a typical core management-led NGO, having neither widespread nor committed followership among ordinary Nigerians.

2.5. MEDIA RIGHTS AGENDA (MRA)

MRA is almost entirely funded by foreign donors, and almost all of its projects have been made possible by funding provided by such donors. For instance, the 1999 edition of its "broadcast monitoring project" was executed with a grant from the USA-based National Endowment for Democracy.[54] Its "print media monitoring project" was funded and supported by the United States Information Service (now a part of the U.S. Embassy in Nigeria) and the London-based International Center against Censorship.[55] Likewise, the Ford Foundation has funded its "human rights reporting workshops for journalists."[56] Its workshops on "media law reform," organized in collaboration with the International Centre against Censorship and the Nigerian National Human Rights Commission, were funded by the European Union Commission and the Swedish International Development Agency.[57] In 1999, it organized "voter enlightenment programs," which were funded by the Canadian Catholic Organization for Development and Peace.[58]

There is no evidence in its annual statements of accounts that it has received funds from any Nigerian source. In any case, since it has no real members at all, membership fees cannot be said to contribute in any way to its income.

Given the similarity of its funding regime to those of the NGOs examined above, it is not surprising that MRA also suffers from the same kinds of problems as those groups. The nature of these funding related problems has already been explained in detail above and does not warrant repetition here.

2.6. THE INSTITUTE FOR HUMAN RIGHTS AND HUMANITARIAN LAW (IHRHL)

The funding pattern of the IHRHL has been similar to that of the NGOs discussed thus far: most of its financial resources have sourced from foreign donors. For instance, the John D. and Catherine T. MacArthur Foundation has been a consistent and important donor to many of its projects and activities, including the publication of *Poverty in Wealth*, a 2000 report.[59] The USAID funded the production of the IHRHL's book on human rights education, and the Stitching European Human Rights Foundation provided financial support to the IHRHL for its community-based structural paralegal resources project.[60]

What is more, aside from the resources that were initially expended by Anyakwe Nsirimovu, its founder and current executive director, there is little real evidence to suggest that this organization has made any great effort to raise a reasonable percentage of its resources locally.[61] As importantly, this organization does not have a base of active members from which it can raise such funds.

As such, it has suffered from the same kinds of foreign funding-related negative consequences that afflict almost all of its peers.

2.7. PRISONERS REHABILITATION AND WELFARE ACTION

Like most of its peers, PRAWA has sourced most of its funds from foreign donors. As such, it is as donor-dependent as almost every such NGO in Nigeria. Its major donors have included the Ford Foundation, VPM Zurich, the British Council, and the Office of the UN High Commissioner for Human Rights. The Ford Foundation funded its production of a film entitled *the Rights of Prisoners* (aimed at increasing awareness of the condition of Nigerian prisons and the plights of the inmates); sponsored the attendance of its staff attorney at the Twenty-third Session of the African Commission on Human and Peoples' Rights; and provided funds to enable PRAWA activists attend a training workshop in Switzerland. [62] VPM Zurich financed its executive director's trip to an important 1998 conference in Austria; and has supported PRAWA's training and capacity development projects.[63] PRAWA has also received a grant from the British Council in support of its training programs and has benefited from the UN Voluntary Fund for Victims of Torture.[64]

Concomitantly, PRAWA has not raised a significant portion of its finances from Nigerian sources, be they public or private sector entities. Also, since it is not a membership organization, it has *not* been able to raise a significant portion of its financial needs from a committed membership base. This has of course denied it the opportunity to canvass the bulk of the Nigerian masses (for resources, memberships, and support) in a regular and sustained way.

As such, PRAWA's internal governance mechanism does suffer from the same kind of relative distance from most ordinary Nigerians that almost all its peers have experienced – a distance that has negatively affected its development into an organization with deep roots at the grassroots, one that enjoys widespread validation and legitimacy.

2.8. COMMUNITY ACTION FOR POPULAR PARTICIPATION (CAPP)

In terms of the structure of its funding regime, CAPP is a typical Nigerian NGO. It relies rather heavily on foreign funders for the bulk of its revenues. The Danish Fund for International Development and the British Council have financed many of its projects, including its 1999 human rights education and advocacy campaign in some Northern states, as well as its publication of a report on that campaign.[65] Earlier, in 1996, with a generous donation from the British Overseas Development Agency and the National Endowment for Democracy, it published *Figures of Marginalization: Women in Plateau State Public Service*, which detailed the unacceptable conditions of work of women in that state's public service.

Like virtually all of its peers, there is little evidence that it either solicits or receives a significant percentage of its revenues from Nigerian sources.

Not surprisingly, even though it has most commendably worked with and within local communities in order to cultivate limited mass movements around certain issues such as land dispossession in Abuja (Nigeria's new federal capital), like most of its peers, this organization has not really advanced to a stage where it can command a sufficiently widespread allegiance either throughout the country or among most average Nigerians. For instance, even though it deserves much credit for its role in helping to advance grassroots human rights advocacy and education to the Northern regions of Nigeria thereby encouraging other NGOs to follow suit[66] (and for thus helping to defuse the "dangerous campaign that human rights advocacy is a power tool of southern elites"),[67] its growth into a popular movement has remained limited. This is in part attributable to its failure to deepen its connection to the grassroots by building enough widespread commitment among ordinary Nigerians that it can attract some of the admittedly scarce financial resources of these people. It is noteworthy that most hometown development groups and the vast majority of faith-based groups in Nigeria have been able to raise billions of dollars in this way.

2.9. THE HUMAN RIGHTS LAW SERVICE (HURILAWS)

HURILAWS is largely dependent on foreign charities and governments for the funds needed for its work. Nearly every single one of its projects has been funded by one foreign organization or another. Its work has been supported by many Europe-based, Australia-based, and U.S.-based governmental and private organizations.[68] For instance, the Australian government funded its recent study on the state of democratic governance in Nigeria.[69] HURI-LAWS' legal aid project has been financed by German Catholic Bishops' Conference[70]; and its "court procedures reform project" has been cofunded by the United States Embassy in Nigeria, the British Council, and the Royal Danish Embassy.[71] Its campaign for the abolishment of the death penalty in Nigeria has been generously funded by the Royal Norwegian Embassy (including funding for its "test case" on the matter).[72] The diplomatic missions of the Netherlands and Norway have at one time or another funded HURI-LAWS. It has also received funding from Bread for the World, Irish Aid, the UK-based Westminster Foundation for Democracy, the USA-based National Endowment for Democracy, the European Union, and the Canada-based International Centre for Human Rights and Democratic Development.[73]

However, in contrast to most other such NGOs, HURILAWS has been able to raise a significant (if much smaller) portion of its funds locally. It has received N3, 000,000 (approximately US$30,000) from the United Bank for Africa (UBA) – one of Nigeria's largest banks – in order to advance its judicial reform work.[74] It has also raised N125, 000 (at the time about US$11,000) from another Nigerian company—the Investment Banking and Trust Company; and US$1,000 from a group of Nigerians in the Diaspora led by Dr. Acho Emeruwa.[75]

In recognition of the deep historical and strategic significance of this modest success at local fund raising, HURILAWS appended the following statement to its report on these donations from Nigerian sources:

> HURILAWS is grateful to Hakeem Bello-Osagie, [the then] chairman of UBA, for his visionary generosity. This grant is particularly significant for several reasons, not the least of which is the hitherto difficult relationship between the Nigerian private sector and the human rights community during the last decade and half. We hope and believe that this grant may mark the closing of an unhappy chapter in this relationship, which was often characterized by mutual suspicion and acrimony. A government-private sector-civil society partnership is critical for sustainable democracy and good governance in Nigeria. *Historically, one of the greatest weaknesses of the human rights movement in Nigeria is the pervasive external donor dependency.* This dependency has exposed the movement to constant criticisms of external motivation and control. Donor dependency will not necessarily end overnight but it is time for the human rights movement to deepen its roots among the Nigerian people and this process includes seeking a larger proportion of support for our work from Nigerian donors. The United Bank for Africa has opened the door; the human rights community must be bold enough to enter and sit at the table. For our part, HURILAWS is committed to seeking a greater proportion of support for its work from the Nigerian private sector.[76]

As is noticeable from this otherwise inspiring statement, its efforts at local fund raising are largely geared towards the Nigerian *private sector* (read corporations and the like). For, as is typical of Nigerian NGOs, HURILAWS has neither a large nor an active membership base. Moreover the few members that it has laid claim to do not, by its own admission, "pay anything at all" to it in the form of membership fees.[77] This situation has made it very difficult for HURILAWS to raise more of its funds from among the Nigerian masses in ways that directly tie and commit ordinary Nigerians to its work while allowing them to enjoy, and be moved to action by, a sense of "ownership" of the organization.

Thus, despite this remarkable and commendable record of local fundraising (a record that testifies eloquently to the vision, dynamism, and commitment of Olisa Agbakoba and the rest of its leadership), the bulk of its funding has nevertheless been obtained from foreign donors.[78] Overall, its lack of a significant membership base, and its reliance on foreign donors for the bulk of its funds, has meant that it has also been faced with the same kind of obstacles to its growth into a popularly connected and legitimated human rights organization that most of its peers have experienced over the years.

2.10. HUMAN RIGHTS MONITOR (HRM)

The funding structure of HRM is typical of its peers. It has been funded according to the same foreign-dominated funding regime as have virtually all of Nigeria's human rights NGOs. Evidence of this dependence on foreign funds can be gleaned from the contents of own its reports. For instance, the development of its web site was funded by the European Union[79]; and its January 2000 workshop on civil society groups in Northern Nigeria was funded by the USA-based National Endowment for Democracy.[80]

What is more, as far as the author could learn, HRM has not reported receiving a significant amount of financial support from either the Nigerian private sector or the Nigerian people.

Accordingly, it has been as negatively affected by the structure of the prevalent NGO funding regime in Nigeria as has any other such organization—an important explanation for its failure so far to optimize its potential to develop into a popularly legitimized and thus far more influential activist organization.

2.11. HUMAN RIGHTS AFRICA (HRA)

Despite its choice of "systematic value infusion" (as opposed to "monitoring") as its main approach to human rights activism in Nigeria, HRA has not behaved differently from its peers in terms of its dependence on foreign donors for the bulk of its funds. This fact was acknowledged by one of its senior staff in an interview with one of the researchers involved in this study. This officer admitted that, as with most such NGOs, between 80 and 90 percent of its funds have been donated by foreign entities.[81] As far back as 1992, HRA received a grant of about one hundred thousand kroner (NOK100,000), i.e., about US$16,000, from the Norwegian Human Rights Organization.[82] This grant constituted over 95 percent of the organization's revenue for that year.[83] In the year before that over 90 percent of its funds were donated by sources in the U.S. and Canada; the remainder came from the family funds of its founder/CEO.[84] This shows a steady progression in the extent of this organization's reliance on foreign benefactors, because, in 1990 for instance, only about 60 percent of its revenues came from foreign sources; the rest came from its founder/CEO, Tunji Abayomi.[85] The attendance of its representatives at the biannual sessions of African Commission on Human and Peoples' Rights has been regularly funded by both the British Council and the then United States Information Service in Nigeria.[86] The Robert F. Kennedy Center in New York and Books for the World Inc. of the

USA, have also extended aid to HRA by donating and shipping books to it.[87] The heavy dependence of HRA on such foreign funds and resources and the corresponding leverage enjoyed by foreign donors on HRA are highlighted by its complaint in its *1991/92 Annual Report* that most of its activities had to be shelved because it was not able to secure any grants to support such activities from its largely foreign donors.[88]

It is reasonably clear from the foregoing that although it has tried to do so, the organization has not been as successful as it could in raising funds from the Nigerian people—the community in which it operates and in whose interests it works.[89] And this is so despite the fact that as early as 1994, it had convened a two-day reflective workshop which resolved to "look inwards" in terms of its resource-generation drives.[90]

And since the necessity to raise funds locally almost always provides an incentive to these NGOs to cultivate the Nigerian people much more closely, the failure of HRA to raise more of its funds locally has had a negative impact on its ability to cultivate widespread recognition and commitment among ordinary Nigerians. In this way has it indirectly limited its own capacity to wield substantial influence within Nigeria.

3. THE FINANCING OF NIGERIAN SOCIAL/ECONOMIC RIGHTS NGOS

This section deals with questions related to NGO funding patterns as they affect three organizations: the Shelter Rights Initiative (SRI); the Social and Economic Rights Action Center (SERAC); and the Empowerment and Action Research Center (EMPARC). The aim, as in the previous sections, is to understand the consequences of such funding patterns on their effectiveness and growth potential. One overarching point that is clear from interviews conducted with many of the leading activists within these organizations is that while the proportion (not amounts) of foreign/domestic funding that these NGOs have received is similar to that received by civil/political rights NGOs, the NGOs that are discussed in this section did not initially find it easy to secure funding from foreign donors. This is attributed to their focus on social/economic rights activism—an area that has suffered historically from donor insensitivity. However, this situation eventually changed as foreign funders began to alter their funding agendas to respond to convincing critiques of their civil/political rights centeredness. While this is clear evidence of the leverage that foreign funders have exerted on the development of the NGO community in Nigeria, it is also clear evidence of the conceptual clarity and resilience of many nonmainstream activists in Nigeria.

3.1. THE SOCIO-ECONOMIC RIGHTS INITIATIVE [FORMERLY SHELTER RIGHTS INITIATIVE] (SRI)

As innovative as its brand of activism has been the SRI is, like most NGOs in Nigeria, dependent for most of its funds on the grants it receives from foreign donors. For one, almost every single one of its publications, seminars, and other activities has been funded by a foreign entity.[91] Its attendance in March 1998 at the Addis Ababa, Ethiopia, meeting of African NGOs working in the areas of human settlements and the environment was made possible by funds provided by the Netherlands Ministry of Foreign Affairs, the United Nations Economic Commission for Africa (UNECA), and the United Nations Centre on Human Settlements (UNCHS).[92] In addition, the U.S. Government, the Ford Foundation, and the Austrian Government, have financed many of its publications.[93] The SRI's excellent *Manual on the Judicial Protection of Economic, Social and Cultural Rights* was funded by the Ford Foundation[94]; while its *Manual on Gender Specific Rights Litigation and Protection Strategies* was funded by the U.S. embassy.[95] And lastly, its series of workshops have been sponsored by a number of different foreign donors such as the Dutch embassy and the International Human Rights Internship Program.[96]

Even though the SRI has reported receiving a grant from the Community Development Project based in Jos, Nigeria, there is little evidence that an appreciable proportion of its funds has been raised locally (either from the private sector or from ordinary Nigerians).[97] What is more, as the SRI is not really a membership organization, it is unable to raise funds locally by collecting membership fees.

Thus, while its social/economic rights message and work resonates very much with the bulk of Nigeria's discerning masses, its potential growth into a popular organization that enjoys widespread following around the country has been hindered severely by its reliance on readier foreign funding, and its resulting reluctance to engage in the far more difficult task of cultivating the local population for both memberships and financial support. Given the dynamism of its leaders, had the SRI not had such access to foreign funding, it would have had a strong incentive to innovate strategies for more effective local mobilization and fund-raising.

3.2. THE SOCIAL AND ECONOMIC RIGHTS ACTION CENTRE (SERAC)

Like the SRI and almost all other NGOs in Nigeria, SERAC receives the bulk of its funds from foreign donors. Its projects have almost always been made possible through the financial support of these foreign donors. For instance, the Ford Foundation financed its important nation wide study of the experiences of those living with HIV/AIDS in Nigeria.[98] Likewise, its groundbreaking microcredit program (aimed at giving small loans to poor, urban women) has been received funding from both the Canadian Catholic Organization for Development and Peace and the Ford Foundation.[99] While the U.S.-based Institute of International Education's International Human Rights Internship Program funded its participation in the micro-credit program officer training session run by the Grameen Bank in Bangladesh,[100] the John D. and Catherine.T. MacArthur Foundation, the Ford Foundation, the Royal Netherlands Embassy, and other foreign agencies have funded many its numerous workshops.[101] SERAC's project on the improvement of the capacity of African Commission on Human and Peoples' Rights to protect economic and social rights was sponsored by the John D. and Catherine T. MacArthur Foundation.[102] In addition, SERAC's annual human rights debate competition (involving various Nigerian universities) has been funded by the Ford Foundation.[103]

Much like its peers, SERAC has not been successful at raising a significant portion of its funds locally. Moreover, as it does not have a membership base, it cannot acquire some of its funds by charging membership fees.

As such, while it is one of the few NGOs that routinely work at the grassroots level, and while it does enjoy a remarkably committed following among the displaced Maroko population and in one or two other localities, it still has not built a sufficiently national following and a widespread allegiance among ordinary Nigerians. Thus, its optimal growth into a much more popular organization that is much more rooted in the wider community has been stunted not just by the absence of an active membership but also by its inability to effectively cultivate the local population for funds.

3.3. THE EMPOWERMENT AND ACTION RESEARCH CENTRE (EMPARC)

The structure of EMPARC's funding regime is not all that different from that of most other such NGOs. A cursory glance at the list of the major donors who financed its activities between the years 1992–1997 reveals the extent to which its fund-raising efforts have been skewed towards the outside world, especially toward Europe and North America. In the course of those years, it received funding not only from the New York-based International Women's Health Coalition (1992, 1994–1996) but also from the Ford Foundation (1993–1994) and the Canada-based Inter Pares (1994).[104] The Friedrich Ebert Foundation and the MacArthur Foundation are also mentioned as having provided funds in the years 1993 and 1995–1997 respectively.[105]

Other than a grant made by the Nigerian Bottling Company in support of Lecture No.4 in its Annual Lecture Series, the available evidence provides little indication that EMPARC has been able to raise a sizeable portion of its funding from Nigerian sources.[106]

Despite is commendable emphasis on community action, popular mobilization, and grassroots (including rural) activism, EMPARC's dependence on foreign donors has had some negative consequences on its development into a much more popular organization. This gap between its goals and its attainment has, however, not been for want of effort on the part of its leadership.

4. THE FINANCING OF NIGERIAN WOMEN'S RIGHTS NGOS

Here, we will consider similar questions related to the funding of three Nigerian women's rights NGOs: Baobab for Women's Human Rights (BAOBAB), the Women's Aid Collective (WACOL), and the Women's Rights Advancement and Protection Alternative (WRAPA). A study of these organizations reveals that their revenue generating schemes are as reflective of a heavy reliance on foreign donors as do those of most other such NGOs. Very little of their funds are raised locally. As well, it is important to note that enough evidence exists to suggest that similar claims can be made with respect to the other self-described women's rights NGOs that operate in Nigeria.[107]

4.1. BAOBAB FOR WOMEN'S HUMAN RIGHTS (BAOBAB)

In terms of the nature of its funding patterns, BOABAB is a typical Nigerian NGO. Foreign entities have provided the necessary financial support for almost all of its reports, publications, conferences, and projects. The foreign donors that have funded its activities include the John D. and Catherine T. MacArthur Foundation, the Ford Foundation, the Swedish NGO Human Rights Foundation, the Global Fund for Women, and the International Women's Health Coalition.[108] More specifically, it was the generous funding provided by the Royal Danish Embassy in Nigeria and the Global Fund for Women that made it possible for BOABAB to attend a session of the Committee for the Elimination of Discrimination against Women (CEDAW).[109] The U.S. Information Service in Nigeria funded its subsequent report on that CEDAW session.[110]

In addition, not being a membership organization, BOABAB cannot really raise revenues by levying membership dues.

Consequently, although BAOBAB has tended to work with the local communities whose interests it wants to advance, and though it is one of the few NGOs in Nigeria with a relatively national spread, freed as it has been from the great difficulties of canvassing the local population for funds and other resources, it has not had much of an incentive to involve the broader community in its internal decision-making processes. As such, like most of its peers, its growth as a popular organization has remained stunted and its full potential unrealized.

4.2. WOMEN'S AID COLLECTIVE (WACOL)

Like virtually all its peers, WACOL is dependent on foreign funding. For instance, the Swedish NGO Foundation for Democracy generously finances the publication of its reports and human rights manuals, including *Legislative Advocacy for Women's Human Rights*[111] and *Women's Socio-Economic and Legal Rights*.[112] The U.S. embassy has funded its constitutional advocacy workshops.[113] And its program of offering humanitarian aid to victims of rape and torture has received the support of the UN Voluntary Fund for Victims of Torture.[114]

This reliance on foreign donors is made all the more necessary because it is not a membership-based organization. Thus, it lacks a pool of dedicated members from whom revenues can be generated by levying membership fees.

Its lack of a membership base and the disincentive to the cultivation of community financial support that is in part attributable to the *relative* ease with which foreign funding can be secured, have combined to ensure that its huge potential of becoming an important popular organization remains unrealized as yet.

4.3. WOMEN'S RIGHTS ADVANCEMENT AND PROTECTION ALTERNATIVE (WRAPA)

Despite being founded by a sitting "first lady" (i.e, the wife of the then Nigerian Head of State), the bulk of its funding has been sourced from foreign donors. In this sense WRAPA is typical of its peers.[115] Thus, in terms of its fund-raising efforts, it is more European- and North American-focused than Nigerian-oriented. This has been so mostly because the readier availability of foreign funds has to a large extent "freed" it from the much more difficult task of garnering funds locally. But while the availability of foreign funds has "freed" it in this way from concentrating on canvassing the local population for funding, it has at the same time provided an important disincentive to efforts at cultivating the active support of average Nigerians. While WRAPA is a membership organization, it has not been able to raise an appreciable portion of its funds locally. It is noteworthy though that it has made some most commendable attempts to secure partial local community funding for some of its grassroots projects.[116] However, the amounts of money that is has been able to raise from such local counterpart funding has been relatively small.[117]

5. THE FINANCING OF NIGERIAN MINORITY/ENVIRONMENTAL RIGHTS NGOS

This section is concerned with questions related to NGO funding patterns in Nigeria as they affect two NGOs: the Movement for the Survival of Ogoni People (MOSOP) and Environmental Rights Action (ERA). As will become evident in this section, while the funding structure of ERA is typical of other such NGOs in Nigeria, MOSOP's funding pattern is not as typical.

5.1. THE MOVEMENT FOR THE SURVIVAL OF OGONI PEOPLE (MOSOP)

While MOSOP has sought and relied on foreign funding,[118] its dependence on such foreign monies has not been as heavy when compared to most other NGOs.

Part of the reason for this less than typical reliance on the part of MOSOP on foreign funding has been its large pool of extremely dedicated, highly mobilized, community-based members, many of whom give freely of their time and resources. Another reason is that, at least in its early years, its top leadership donated a significant portion of its financial resources. For instance, the late Ken Saro-Wiwa spent a lot of his own resources on MOSOP, traveling around the world to publicize the MOSOP-led Ogoni struggle.[119]

Consequently, within the confines of its narrow focus on the Ogoni, MOSOP has not been as stunted as most such NGOs in its growth into a popular organization. It has been able to become a mass movement among the Ogoni (its target population) and has as such tended to pose a formidable challenge to those who would oppress and abuse the Ogoni people – a feature that *in part* explains the extremely violent reaction of many Nigerian regimes to its demands and activities.[120] Its success at becoming an integral part of the broader community; its involvement of this larger community in its internal decision-making processes; its deep systematic connection to their "voices of suffering"; and its leadership by extraordinarily courageous activists have combined with its *relative distance* from excessive reliance on foreign funding to promote its development into a popularly legitimized movement (within the Ogoni segment of Nigeria's population) that seems to have realized more of its potential than most of its peers. Yet, on the whole, MOSOP has still failed to capture the support and devotion of the vast majority of Nigerians.

5.2. ENVIRONMENTAL RIGHTS ACTION (ERA):

Like almost all NGOs in Nigeria, ERA is dependent on foreign funding for the execution of its projects. The Ford Foundation and the Netherlands-based NOVID are all mentioned as being significant contributors to the programs and activities of the organization.[121] One of its senior activists has indicated as well that revenues are further generated through the local sales of its publications. Although the specific percentage of its revenues that is raised this way was not made clear,[122] it is most unlikely to constitute a significant percentage of its income.

Given the nature of its heavy reliance on foreign funding and its consequent marginalization of local fund-raising, and given its lack of an active and committed membership base, it is no wonder that, in spite of its genuine efforts at grassroots activism, the ERA has had some difficulty in optimizing its capacity to enjoy widespread popular legitimacy across Nigeria. Yet such popular legitimacy, such a capacity to command the loyalty of large sections of the population, is absolutely crucial if it is to optimize its political influence in Nigeria. It must be added, however, that the ERA is reasonably popular in sections of Nigeria's Niger Delta.

6. OVERCOMING A PROBLEMATIC FUNDING PATTERN

From the evidence supplied and analyzed above it is clear that almost all NGOs in Nigeria are heavily dependent on foreign (as opposed to local) funding. It is fair to say that almost every single one of these NGOs has been almost entirely beholden to foreign (read Western) governments, foundations, NGOs, and/or charities for almost all of their funds. What is more, this fact is increasingly being acknowledged both in the extant scholarly literature and in the reports of the more insightful Nigerian activists.[123]

However, this situation is not surprising at all. For one, it accurately reflects the nature of the global resource distribution map. The vast majority of the world's resources are in the hands of the tiny minority of the world's population who live in the "west." As such, very little of either the aggregate resources available in the world or the portion of it that is available to fund human rights work can be found in a developing country such as Nigeria. And given the difficulties of raising funds from an already impoverished local population and the far easier access to foreign funds enjoyed by NGOs in Nigeria, it was only rational for them to become almost entirely "Western-facing" in their fund-raising strategies and tactics. They have responded quite rationally to the pressures of what Upendra Baxi has referred to as the "human rights market".[124] This is the underlying "political economy" of the fund raising behavior of these NGOs. The following passage, culled from an interview with a senior Nigerian activist, captures this tough situation quite well:

> One basic problem that NGOs in Nigeria face is funding. Eighty to ninety percent of our funding is foreign sourced, and so we are dependent on these donors. Ideally an enlightened Nigerian public should be able to fund us. But …most Africans are themselves still struggling to survive….[Thus, for most of them] donating funds to NGOs [not a luxury]?[125]

Yet, as logical as their behavior seems on one level, it is also clear that on another level the harsh nature of the political economy context within which these NGOs have had to operate has helped impose certain severe costs on their ability to fulfill their potential as possible agents of a fundamental human rights transformation in Nigeria. As Akin Mabogunje has noted, the dependence of these NGOs on foreign donors has tended to "jeopardize the program integrity and credibility of [these] NGOs."[126] Addicted as many of them have certainly become to the far more accessible pots of foreign funding, and relieved as they have been from the much more difficult (albeit far more rewarding) task of canvassing the local population for membership fees and other funds, most of these NGOs have faced a very powerful disincentive to their serious pursuit of the imperative task of immersing and rooting themselves among average Nigerians. Consequently, most of these NGOs have almost always been unable to mass mobilize, in a sustained and effective way, the millions of Nigerians whose lives of daily impoverishment and oppression make them extremely ripe for mobilization. The evidence thus clearly supports Ihonvbere's 1996 claim that these NGOs have been "unable to mobilize their members, generate resources through membership drives, or persuade patriotic and pro-democratic elites to fund their activities at home."[127] Yet this distance and distancing between most of these NGOs and the ordinary Nigerian has severely impeded their ability to optimize their influence on Nigeria's domestic governance institutions. Without the leverage provided by widespread popular support, these NGOs have faced an uphill task indeed as they strove to exert influence on the Nigerian state. Thus, their distance from average Nigerians has translated into a virtually equal distance from the attainment of their primary goal of exerting influence on state and society in Nigeria.

Thus, notwithstanding the clearly expressed preference of most of these NGOs for the adoption of the institutional forms and attitudes that have been common among Western-based watchdog organizations (a preference that was demonstrated in earlier chapters), if these NGOs are going to play a much more central and effective role in the everyday struggles of most Nigerians against oppression and impoverishment, it is imperative that most of them should begin to attempt more seriously the twin and symbiotic tasks of local funding raising and grassroots mobilization. In this connection, Chidi Odinkalu's admonition to African human rights NGOs is so relevant and well articulated as to deserve reproduction in full here:

> Throughout history, the protection of human rights has been won by struggle, and struggle requires mobilization. *The process of mobilization validates the movement, connecting it with the needs of the people and earning their commitment.* To be successful, such struggles must be biased without being unfair and political without being wedded to a particular party. However, it is the practice of today's human rights organizations to claim to be "impartial," "unbiased," "neutral," and "non political." Fashionable though they may be, and *donor-friendly* though they certainly are, such expressions do not describe the complex realities of the struggle for human Rights in Africa.[128]

Explicitly articulated in the foregoing quotation is the imperative for these NGOs to become much more inward-looking in the interest of their own eventual development into a much more popularly validated and therefore far more powerful pressure group.

However, this drive to acquire much more popular legitimization and sharply increased leverage will not be successful unless the powerful disincentive for grassroots mobilization created by the excessive dependence of most of these NGOs on foreign donors is sufficiently reduced through more innovative, and therefore much more effective, local fund-raising efforts. Yet such efforts will themselves be unsuccessful unless these NGOs are able to earn widespread commitment among ordinary Nigerians (in the fashion of the home-town development associations and faith-based groups that have had relatively little trouble raising billions of dollars from the same impoverished constituency).

That effective human rights activism in Nigeria is possible outside the foreign donor funded NGO model is demonstrated by reference to the life-long work of Gani Fawehinmi, Nigeria's most famous human rights activist.[129] Fawehinmi's consistent refusal to accept funding from virtually all foreign donors and his corresponding, if peculiar, innovations in local fund raising are critical components of his rather unique brand of what might be styled the "non-NGO style" of human rights activism in Nigeria. Although Fawehinmi's model of raising his considerable financial resources through his law publications and law firm businesses may not be all that generalizable and does not involve the kind of grassroots canvassing that is essential in validating an NGO within the local community, the point that is being made here is that viable partial alternatives to heavy foreign donor-dependence can, with some effort and creativity, be found.

Happily, this possibility is increasingly being recognized and taken seriously within the NGO community in Nigeria, as is evidenced by the local fund-raising successes that HURILAWS has recently begun to enjoy.[130] What is more, some Nigerian thinkers have, over the years, called for precisely this kind of re-orientation within the NGO community in the country.[131]

Overall, it has been argued in this chapter that the almost exclusively foreign-facing fund-raising strategies and tactics adopted by most NGOs in Nigeria have been important obstacles on their path to popular legitimization. It was emphasized as well that as a result their collective development into a community of much more effective NGOs has been hindered. This last point will be considered in more detail in chapter 7.

NOTES

1. See C.E. Welch, Jr., "Conclusion," in C.E. Welch, Jr., ed., *NGOs and Human Rights: Promise and Performance* (Philadelphia: University of Pennsylvania Press, 2001), 267.

2. See C.A. Odinkalu, "Why More Africans Don't Use the Human Rights Language," *Human Rights Dialogue* (2000): 3, 4.

3. Please refer to the definitions in chapter 1 of this and related concepts.

4. It is important to note here that this line of investigation will *not* be concerned with the claims made by successive military regimes in Nigeria that these NGOs have been "sponsored by external elements who want to destabilize Nigeria". This claim is so incredible as not to deserve serious consideration here. See P.O. Agbese, "The State versus Human Rights Advocates in Africa: The Case of Nigeria," in E. McCarthy-Arnolds, D.R. Penna, and D.J. Cruz Sobrepena, eds., *Africa, Human Rights and the Global System: The Political Economy of Human Rights in a Changing World* (Westport, CN: Greenwood Press, 1994), 166.

5. See A. Ikelegbe, "Civil Society, Oil and Conflict in the Niger Delta Region of Nigeria: Ramifications of Civil Society for a Regional Resource Struggle," *Journal of Modern African Studies* 39 (2001): 437, 438.

6. K.J. Jason, "The Role of Non-Governmental Organizations in International Election Observing," *New York University Journal of International Law and Politics* 24 (1992): 1795, 1796.

7. Ibid.

8. See W.D. Carmichael, "The Role of the Ford Foundation" in C.E. Welch Jr, ed., *supra* note 1, 248. Emphasis added. See also C. E. Welch Jr., "Introduction," in C.E. Welch Jr., ed., ibid., 11.

9. See also C. E. Welch Jr., ibid., 11–12.

10. Ibid. See also M. Mutua, "Human Rights International NGOs: A Critical Evaluation," in C.E. Welch Jr., ed., ibid., 154; and W.D. Carmichael, *supra* note 8, 248.

11. See T.M. Shaw, "Popular Participation in Non-Governmental Structures in Africa: Implications for Democratic Development," *Africa Today* (1990): 5, 8-9.

12. A prominent activist newsletter has noted that it is an indisputable fact that "virtually all the NGOs receive funds for their activities from *foreign* pro-democracy, religious, educational and research organisations." See *Community* (a CAPP newsletter) 2:1 (1997): 6–7. Emphasis added.

13. See J.O. Ihonvbere "Where is the Third Wave? A Critical Evaluation of Africa's Non-Transition to Democracy," [hereinafter "Third Wave"], *Africa Today* 43 (1996): 343, 349.

14. See A. Mabogunje, "Civil Society and the Environmental Quality of African Human Settlements," *Shelter Watch* 1:2 (1996): 47, 51. See also J. O Ihonbvere, "On the Threshold of Another False Start? A Critical Evaluation of Africa's Prodemocracy Movements," [hereinafter "False Start"], *Journal of Asian and African Studies* 31:1-2 (1996): 125, 131.

15. See *Liberty* (a CLO publication) 7:1 (1996): 30. Emphasis added.

16. For early recognition of this pattern, see P.O. Agbese, *supra* note 4, 168. Given the CLO's status as one of the largest *membership* NGOs in Nigeria, one that does at least attempt to levy membership fees, it is interesting in the present respect to note that Agbese has reported that in 1990 only about *1 percent* of the CLO's income was derived from local sources—that is, membership fees. As the rest of this subsection shows, this funding pattern has not changed significantly since then. See Agbese, ibid. It appears, however, that this pattern of foreign funding is not at all peculiar to Nigerian NGOs. See K. Sikkink, "Human Rights, Principled Issue-Networks, and Sovereignty in Latin America," *International Organization* 47 (1993): 411 (contending that a handful of private and public foundations have been active in funding human rights organizations around the world); and J. Smith and R. Pagnucco (with G. A. Lopez), "Globalizing Human Rights: The Work of Transnational Human Rights NGOs in the 1990s," *Human Rights Quarterly* 20 (1998): 379, 410.

17. See transcripts of interview with OA, 20 August 2001 (on file with the author). See also the Civil Liberties Organization, *The Nigerian Military and the Crises of Democratic Transition: A Study in the Monopoly of Power* (Lagos: CLO, 1999).

18. For example, see I. Chukwuma and A. Ibidapo-Obe, eds., *Law Enforcement and Human Rights in Nigeria* (Lagos: CLO, 1995), 7.

19. See CLO, *Annual Reports and Accounts, 1995* (Lagos: CLO, 1995), v.

20. See transcripts of interview with OU, 23 April 2000 (on file with the author). See also CLO, *Annual Reports and Accounts, 1994* (Lagos: CLO, 1994), 16.

21. See *Liberty* (a CLO publication) 6:3 (1995): 29.

22. Ibid.

23. See *Prison Watch* 7 (1998): 3.

24. Ibid.

25. See *Church and Society* 2:3 (2000): 3.

26. See *Liberty* (a CLO publication) 6:3 (1995): 28.

27. See Civil Liberties Organization, *Accounts and Activities for 2000* (Lagos: CLO, 2001), 28. Emphasis added.

28. Ibid, 26.

29. For instance, a local businessman underwrote the production costs of the CLO's 1992 Annual Report. See CLO, *Annual Reports and Accounts, 1994* (Lagos: CLO, 1994), 16.

30. The CLO has received funds from local individuals and organizations such as Olisa Agbakoba, Alex Ibru, and the Justice, Development, and Peace Commission in Ijebu Ode, Nigeria. See transcripts of interview with OA, 20 August 2001 (on file with the author); and transcripts of interview with AO, 17 August 2001 (on file with the author).

31. See transcripts of interview with OA, 20 August 2001 (on file with the author). Emphasis added.

32. See interview with OA, ibid.

33. That those who provide the funds that support the work of NGOs often have a huge amount of influence on the policy directions and behavior of these organizations is no longer a controversial proposition. William Korey has reported the existence of this kind of relationship among the different national sections of Amnesty International, so that those national sections that provide the most funding to that NGO tend to exert the most influence. See W. Korey, *NGOs and the Universal Declaration of Human Rights: "A Curious Grapevine"* (New York: St. Martin's Press, 1998), 305. Similarly, Upendra Baxi has also theorized on the existence of this kind of "market logic" among within most human rights NGO communities in the world. See U. Baxi, *The Future of Human Rights* (New Delhi: Oxford University Press, 2002), 121–131.

34. See *Constitutional Rights Journal* 10:37 (2000): 27.

35. Ibid.

36. Ibid.

37. See *Constitutional Rights Journal* 10:36 (2000): 34.

38. Ibid., 32.

39. See C. Nwankwo, et al., *The Crisis of Press Freedom in Nigeria* (Lagos: CRP, 1993); and CRP, *Nigeria: Human Rights Report, 1999* (Lagos: CRP, 2000).

40. See *Constitutional Rights Journal* 10:35 (2000): 38.

41. See *Constitutional Rights Journal* 5:17 (1995): 26.

42. See CRP, *Eliminating Discrimination against Women: The Report of a Conference organized by the Constitutional Rights Project and the Friedrich Naumann Foundation* (Lagos: CRP, 1995).

43. See C. O. Okonkwo, C. Nwankwo, and B. Ibhawoh, *Administration of Juvenile Justice in Nigeria* (Lagos: CRP, 1997).

44. See *Constitutional Rights Journal* 10:37 (2000): 26–31.

45. See transcripts of interview with NC, 21 August 2001 (on file with the author).

46. For example, the Ford Foundation's website makes it clear that since its resources are relatively modest, i.e., in comparison to societal needs, it focuses on a limited number of problem areas and program strategies within its main objectives (i.e., strengthening and building organizations and networks that can make a contribution towards the goal of strengthening the institutional and cultural foundations of human rights and democratic governance, etc). See http://www.fordfund. org/global/office/Lagos (visited 15 March 2003). The Friedrich Naumann Foundation, for example, makes it clear that it "acts on the basis of Liberalism." It is therefore safe to conclude that those human rights NGO activities (such as the protection of many economic and social rights) that are not seen as furthering "Liberal" values would not be supported. See http://www.fnstusa. org/2002%20Where%W%Stand.htm (visited 15 March 2003).

47. See transcripts of interview with FF, 25 August 2001 (on file with the author).

48. Ibid.

49. See CDHR, *Citadels of Violence* (Lagos: CDHR, 1999), i.

50. See for example, CDHR, *Citadel of Violence* (Lagos: CDHR, 1999); and ibid., *Path to People's Constitution* (Lagos: CDHR, 2000).

51. See transcripts of interview with FF, 25 August 2001 (on file with the author). Emphasis added.

52. See CLEEN, *Policing a Democracy: A Survey Report on the Role and Functions of the Nigeria Police in a Post-Military Era* (Lagos: Center for Law Enforcement Education and the National Human Rights Commission, 1999), vii.

53. For example, see *Law Enforcement Review* 8 (October-December 1999): 1.

54. See MRA, *A Harvest of Blooms* (Lagos: MRA, 2000), 129.

55. Ibid., 130.

56. Ibid., 131.

57. Ibid., 133–34.

58. Ibid., 148.

59. See IHRHL, *Poverty in Wealth* (Port Harcourt: IHRHL, 2000).

60. See A. Nsirimovu, *Human Rights Education Technique in Schools: Building Attitudes and Skills* (Port Harcourt: IHRHL, 1994), viii.

61. Ibid.

62. See PRAWA, *Annual Report 1998* (Lagos: PRAWA, 1998), 29.

63. Ibid., 30.

64. Ibid.

65. See CAPP, *Selling the Message: A Report of Voter Education Campaign in Kano and Jigawa States* (Abuja: CAPP, 1999).

66. Ibid., 29–30

67. Ibid.

68. See transcripts of interview with AO, 17 August 2001 (on file with the author).

69. See HURILAWS, *The Governance Scorecard: Review of Democratic Governance in Nigeria* (Lagos: HURILAWS, 2000), x.

70. See *The HURILAWS Newsletter* 1:3 (1998): 20.
71. See ibid.; and *The HURILAWS Newsletter* 1:5 (1998): 29.
72. See HURILAWS, *Annual Report and Accounts 1999* (Lagos: HURILAWS, 2000), 5; and ibid., *Annual Report 1997-98* (Lagos: HURILAWS, 1999), 11.
73. See HURILAWS, *Annual Report and Accounts, 1999* (Lagos: HURILAWS, 2000), 7.
74. Ibid.
75. Ibid.
76. Ibid.
77. See transcripts of interview with AO, 17 August 2001 (on file with the author).
78. Ibid.
79. See on-line: http://www.hrm.kabissa.org (visited 26 February 2003).
80. See on-line: http://www.hrm.kabissa.org/communiq.htm (visited 26 February 2003).
81. See transcripts of interview with OD, 25 May 2000 (on file with the author).
82. See HRA, *Annual Report 1991/1992* (Lagos: HRA, 1992), 18.
83. See ibid., *Annual Report 1993/1994* (Lagos: HRA, 1994).
84. See ibid., *Annual Report 1991/1992* (Lagos: HRA, 1992), 31.
85. Ibid.
86. See transcripts of interview with OD, 25 May 2000 (on file with the author).
87. See HRA, *Annual Report 1991/1992* (Lagos: HRA, 1992), 4.
88. Ibid.
89. Ibid., 18.
90. Ibid., *Annual Report 1993/1994* (Lagos: HRA, 1994), 16.
91. See infra note 93.
92. *Laser Contact* 2:3 (1998): 9.
93. See for example *Manual on Judicial Protection of Economic, Social and Cultural Rights* (Lagos: SRI, 2000); *Economic, Social and Cultural Rights: A Compilation of International Standards* (Lagos: SRI, 2001). See also O. Eze and E. Onyekpere, *Study on the Right to Health in Nigeria* (Lagos: Shelter Rights Initiatives, 1998), ii; O. Eze, *Study on the Right to Education in Nigeria* (Lagos: Shelter Rights Initiative, 1998), ii; J.U. Achor, ed., *Immunization Guide for the Family* (Lagos Shelter Rights Initiative, 1998), ii; and *Journal of Economic, Social and Cultural Rights* 1:1 (2001): v.
94. See E. Onyekpere, ed., *Manual on the Judicial Protection of Economic, Social and Cultural Rights* (Lagos: SRI, 2000), iii.
95. See *Manual on Gender Specific Rights Litigation and Protection Strategies* (Lagos: Shelter Rights Initiative, 1998), ii.
96. For instance, the Dutch embassy funded SRI's workshop on human settlements and health. See J.U. Achor, ed., *Practical Issues in Human Settlements and Health: Proceedings of a Workshop for Residents of Slum Communities in Lagos Organized by Shelter Rights Initiative* (Lagos: Shelter Rights Initiative, 1997), ii. Also, the International Human Rights Internship Program funded the attendance of one of

SRI's executive directors at an eight week workshop organized by the Center on Housing Rights and Evictions in Geneva. See transcripts of interview with OR, 22 May 1999 (on file with the author).

97. See J.U. Achor, *Improving the Living Environment in Slum Settlements* (Lagos: Shelter Rights Initiative, 1998), ii–iii.

98. See *Access Quarterly* 1and 2:2 (2000): 4.

99. Ibid., 30.

100. Ibid., 31.

101. Ibid., 40.

102. See *SERAC@WORK* 2:2 (1998): 6.

103. Ibid., 2:1 (1999): 4.

104. See *Five Year Report on Activities, 1992–1997* (Lagos: EMPARC, 1997), 43.

105. Ibid.

106. Ibid. See also EMPARC, *Annual Lecture No.4* (Lagos: EMPARC, 1998), 61.

107. See *Community* (a CAPP newsletter) 2:1 (1997): 6 (arguing that "all grants that have come to WIN—one such group—so far have come [sic] from foreign sources, which are German, American or British by their origin or base"); and the Nigerian NGO Coalition for a Shadow Report to CEDAW, *NGOs CEDAW Report for Nigeria* (Lagos: Nigerian NGO Coalition for a Shadow Report to CEDAW, 2001) (which notes that the Global Fund for Women and the Danish embassy in Nigeria provided funding for members of this coalition to attend the CEDAW's sessions; the United States Information Services also funded the printing of the report; and that BAOBAB and its coalition partners provided the free labor that made the report possible).

108. See BAOBAB, *Annual Report, 1999* (Lagos: BAOBAB for Women's Human Rights, 1999), 36.

109. See SRI, *NGO's CEDAW Report for Nigeria* (Lagos: SRI, 1999).

110. Ibid.

111. See WACOL, *Legislative Advocacy for Women's Human Rights* (Enugu: WACOL, 2001).

112. See WACOL, *Women's Socio-Economic and Legal Rights* (Enugu: WACOL, 2001).

113. See J. Ezeilo, J. C. Udenta, and I. Orakwue, *Voices From Below (Vox Populi): Popular Participation, Better Constitution* (Enugu: Women's Aid Collective, 2002), 1.

114. See *Action Woman* 1:1 (2002): 20.

115. See transcripts of interview with MS, 7 March 2003 (on file with the author).

116. Ibid.

117. Ibid.

118. For instance it has received a grant from the World Council of Churches. See http://www.wfn.org/2000/12/msg00055/html . See also http://www.sussex.ac.uk/units/CDE/archive/archive/publish/cdenews/99aut.html (visited 28 May 2003).

119. See generally, K. Wiwa, *In the Shadow of a Saint* (South Royalton, VT: Steerforth Press, 2001).

120. Ibid.

121. See transcripts of interview with NP, 10 January 2003 (on file with the author).

122. Ibid.

123. For instance, see B. Ibhawoh, *Human Rights Organizations in Nigeria: An Appraisal Report on the Human Rights NGO Community in Nigeria* (Copenhagen, Denmark: The Danish Centre for Human Rights, 2001), 39–40; and C.A. Odinkalu, "Why More Africans Don't Use the Human Rights Language" *Human Rights Dialogue* (2000) 3, 4;

124. See U. Baxi, *supra* note 33, 121–131.

125. See transcripts of interview with OD, 25 May 2000 (on file with the author).

126. *Supra* note 14, 51.

127. See J.O. Ihonvbere, "Third Wave," *supra* note 13, 358.

128. See C.A. Odinkalu, *supra* note 2, 3. Emphasis added.

129. Amnesty International has described him as "Nigeria's most renowned human rights lawyer and campaigner." See on-line: http://www.amnesty.org/ailib/intcam/nigeria/fawehinm.htm (visited 26 February 2003).

130. See HURILAWS, *Annual Report and Accounts, 1999* (Lagos: HURILAWS, 2000), 7.

131. See *Democracy Review* (a CLO bulletin) 1:1 (1997): 14–15 (noting that Yima Sen and Pam Sha had called on human rights NGOs in Nigeria to find creative ways to raise much needed funds and resources primarily from within the country).

CHAPTER 6

MODEST HARVESTS:
ON THE LIMITED BUT SIGNIFICANT INFLUENCE OF HUMAN RIGHTS NGOS IN NIGERIA*

1. INTRODUCTION

The evidence that has been adduced thus far does suggest that the institutional form/structure, composition, geopolitical location, conceptual orientation, and funding patterns of the NGO community in Nigeria[1] have each tended to inhibit its advancement into a popular movement (about which most ordinary Nigerians would feel a strong sense of "ownership" and to which they regularly demonstrate their allegiance). This evidence also suggests that the unfortunate result of this state of affairs is that the capacity of this NGO community to achieve a high degree of leverage and influence in their dealings with both state and society in Nigeria has been greatly diminished. These insights will be developed more fully in chapter 7.

The present chapter is devoted to the important task of mapping, contextualizing, and highlighting the significance of the *modest* achievements that have been made by these NGOs.[2] As has been noted all along, as limited as the development of these NGOs into much more popularly legitimized and therefore more influential movements has been, they have nonetheless been able to exert significant, albeit modest, influence on state and society within Nigeria. These NGOs have also been able to exert a significant though quite limited degree of influence on certain international human rights institutions (IHIs). Given the fact that these NGOs have been able to exert a limited degree of influence within and without Nigeria, the overall argument of the book itself is *not* therefore that they have not had any impact whatsoever within and beyond Nigeria. Rather, the overarching point of the book is that despite the modest impact that these NGOs have had both inside and outside an admittedly harsh Nigerian context, they have for identifiable reasons been unable thus far to optimize their capacity to influence state and society in Nigeria.

More specifically, the present chapter shows that these NGOs have helped foster modest harvests of subtle human rights transformations within the Nigerian polity. To put it in Susan Waltz's terms, these NGOs have helped foster "subtle but important [pro-human rights] alterations"[3] in the nature of judicial, legislative and executive thought and action in Nigeria. Subtle alterations—*even transformations*—have occurred in the nature of the "logics of appropriateness"[4] that had hitherto been prevalent in the country. In Kathryn Sikkink's terms, "reformulations in understandings"[5] have definitely occurred in Nigeria, in part as a result of the sustained efforts of these NGOs. In effect, these activist organizations have played a critical role in generating the *correspondence* that has sometimes occurred between the thinking and actions of judicial, legislative, and executive officials in Nigeria (on the one hand) and the norms espoused and promoted by these NGOs (on the other hand).[6]

Largely because of the courageous and often creative advocacy of these NGOs, many judges have transformed conventional jurisprudence in ways that have offered concrete justice to thousands of vulnerable people. Largely because of the activist work of these NGOs, the very conception of legislative process has altered to accommodate ever-deepening consultations with civil society groups; some existing legislation has been changed; and new laws have been proposed and/or passed. And mostly as a result of the humanist efforts of the NGOs, executive action and behavior has now become more human rights sensitive. As well, the efforts of these NGOs have influenced to some extent the character of the media discourse as well as the nature and direction of the political and social debates that have raged among the urban literate elite in Nigeria. As importantly, in part as a result of their efforts at delegitimizing military rule, the hitherto widespread perception of that form of governance as a sometimes necessary option in Nigeria has virtually given way (at least among the literate elite) to a far less benign view of that phenomenon.[7] In a nutshell, widespread understandings of military rule have been reformulated. In the end, this chapter demonstrates that these NGOs have had more impact on the judiciary than on any other arm of the Nigerian state.

Beyond Nigeria's borders, NGOs have often been instrumental in catalyzing progressive improvements in the direction and development of the jurisprudence, decisions and actions of a number of IHIs (especially the institutions of the African Human Rights System), and in creatively mediating the impact that such institutions have sometimes had within Nigeria. This last feat has invariably been the result of the sustained efforts of a "virtual human rights network" that has been formed among the many NGOs that have acted as the go-betweens (or intelligent transmission lines) between the African system and Nigeria's domestic governance institutions (on the one hand) and a range of progressive actors such as activist judges, journalists, lawyers and even politicians (on the other hand). In the ensuing process of *transjudicial communication*, these NGOs have tended to play the role of brainy relays that did not merely transmit, but also contributed actively to the development and strengthening of both the Nigerian state and the African human rights system itself. Here I am reminded of Sikkink's insight regarding the ways in which our appreciation of the workings of IHIs is immediately deepened and expanded once we factor in "the role of nongovernmental actors in developing norms and helping to create, monitor, and strengthen some regimes."[8] As might be expected, these NGOs have had their most significant external influence within the African human rights system.

A note of caution is appropriate, however, at this juncture. It is realized that, as Laurie Wiseberg and Harry Scoble have long noted, the impact that NGOs achieve cannot always be measured with precision in multicausal situations.[9] As I agree with John Gerard Ruggie that the paradigm of causality is now in a state of epistemological chaos,[10] the argument advanced here is not that the work of these NGOs simply "caused" the Nigerian judiciary, legislature, and executive to behave in certain ways. The modest argument being advanced is that the sustained efforts of these NGOs have constituted one critical factor in the production of the pro-human rights alterations and reformulations that have been observed in Nigeria during the relevant period. As such, the chapter does not attribute to these NGOs a very high degree of impact. On the contrary, as the next chapter clearly shows, the overall conclusion of the study is that these NGOs have not yet attained their full potential, largely because almost all of them are steeped in a popular legitimization crisis that has, over time, affected rather negatively their capacity to exert a much greater degree of influence within Nigeria.

Similarly noteworthy is the special analytical difficulty that is involved in accounting for the influence of human rights NGOs in our time. Given the "moral plateau" that the human rights movement has now attained,[11] it is often tempting to accept the autoevaluations and self-assessments of these NGOs with less skepticism than might be warranted. For, as Susan Dicklitch has correctly noted:

> Nongovernmental organizations (NGOs) have a certain mystical, venerable quality to them. They are often portrayed as fighting for the poor and helpless, especially in developing countries,....It is thus sometimes difficult to develop a clear, unbiased, and realistic understanding of what role NGOs really do play in the context of democratic transition and human rights protection.[12]

As Nelson Kasfir has suggested, most scholars and donors have to varying degrees, been guilty of this pitfall.[13] However, a social scientist's search for a tolerable level of scholarly distance must always be pursued if the NGO impact assessments that are offered here are to be credible.

Again, while NGOs may consciously or unconsciously tend to overstate their effectiveness, many governments often understate the impact and value of these NGOs. For instance, in the Nigerian context, NGOs have tended to claim that:

> The NGOs in Nigeria have made *tremendous* contributions toward the expansion of the country's democratic space, through mobilization of the people to appreciate civil, democratic values and governance.[14]

Yet government officials have tended to disagree strongly with this admittedly overstated self-assessment. While most of these officials may not go as far as he has, many of them have historically agreed with Senator Ibrahim Kura Mohamed that these NGOs have been:

> ....nothing but armchair politicians....[and that] you cannot be dining and wining in Geneva and make noise about democracy in Nigeria. To be candid with you they are nothing but a bunch of hypocrites.[15]

Although the reality is much closer to the NGO account than to this senator's hypercritical conclusion, a realistic assessment of the impact of these NGO within Nigeria must locate it somewhere between these two poles. The challenge here is to map, with as much precision as is possible, the location of this phenomenon along that continuum.

Furthermore, it is also important to note here that an accurate understanding of the level of influence that these NGOs have exerted within Nigeria cannot be achieved without taking adequate notice of the extremely harsh conditions under which they have had to function.[16] For much of the period under study, these NGOs functioned under a form of military rule that was novel in orientation, frightening in the extent of its brutality, and suffocating in the degree of its repression. As Ayo Olutokun has recently noted:

> It is generally agreed that, for most of the 1990s, Nigeria regressed to a form of military autocracy, which abandoned the consensual format of the military governments of the 1970s and 1980s in favor of personalized military power marked by state violence.[17]

Thus, to be meaningful, any scholarly assessment of the significance of the influence exerted by these NGOs must situate the relevant data within this harsh context.

In order to demonstrate systematically the validity of the propositions defended herein, the rest of this chapter is organized into seven sections. Section 2 considers the question of the extent to which these NGOs have influenced judicial reasoning and action in Nigeria. Section 3 examines the nature of the modest influence that these NGOs have exerted on legislative process and action in Nigeria. Section 4 focuses on their impact on executive thought and action in Nigeria. Following these segments, section 5 considers the extent to which these NGOs have influenced elite public discourse within Nigeria. Section 6 examines the extent of the impact that these NGOs have had within the African human rights system while section 7 offers an account of their much more modest influence on other international institutions. Section 8 will conclude the chapter, offering a brief overall assessment of the nature and extent of the influence exerted by these NGOs both within and beyond the country and setting the stage for the discussion undertaken in the next chapter (by posing crucial questions regarding the reasons for the modest and limited nature of the impact that these NGOs have thus far exerted within Nigeria).

2. THE INFLUENCE OF NGOS ON JUDICIAL REASONING AND ACTION WITHIN NIGERIA

Given the over forty-year assault on its independence that was waged by the various military regimes that it has endured, significant segments of the Nigerian judiciary have remained remarkably resilient and dynamic—even progressive. Indeed, many activist judges have worked in a virtual (not necessarily actual) alliance with other (aspiring or actual) popular forces such as some NGOs and many labor unions to resist the excesses of military rule. NGOs have both pushed for and benefited from this virtual alliance. Many of these judges have courageously used "the spirit of the law to engender non-violent change"—a function that scholars like Osita Ogbu have correctly identified as crucial to their effectiveness within Nigeria.[18] As one of these activist judges has declared:

> ….it is not enough that we [Nigerians] ratified the African Charter on Human and Peoples Rights or some universal human rights. We must move with the rest of the human race in the implementation of those rights. While the Executive may take steps to examine, or to set in motion, ways of improving the human rights situation [in the country], *the judiciary should actively show its impetuous readiness to complement or indeed surpass the efforts of the Executive* by an inspiring judicial approach to, or definition and recognition of, circumstances of human rights where appropriate and feasible.[19]

NGOs have played a critical role in the constitution of this relatively impressive pattern of judicial activism and resistance under harsh conditions of militarist, dictatorial rule. These NGOs have been an important factor in ensuring that activist judges have, in their own quiet jurisprudential ways, continued to offer conceptual and practical resistance to governmental excesses and abuses. More specifically, these NGOs have carefully supplied to the courts the cases that have presented important opportunities for activist judges to limit executive excesses and abuses; they have educated these judges as to the creative uses to which the African human rights system could be put within Nigeria's domestic legal order; they have developed many of the creative legal arguments and strategies that these activist judges have eventually deployed; they have catalyzed the judicial release of thousands of Nigerians from prison; and they have helped sensitize hundreds of judges on the application of certain human rights norms and strategies. It is with each of these instances of the influence that these NGOs have exerted on judicial reasoning and action in Nigeria that this section will be concerned.

2.1. CATALYZING THE DEVELOPMENT OF INNOVATIVE HUMAN RIGHTS JURISPRUDENCE

Catalyzing innovative human rights jurisprudence has been one of the most important contributions of NGOs to the human rights struggle in Nigeria. Overall, these NGOs have fostered subtle but nevertheless significant reformulations in then prevalent understandings regarding: the superiority of draconian military decrees to the norms of the African human rights system; the applicability of the African Charter on Human and Peoples' Rights within Nigeria's domestic legal order; the validity of clauses in military decrees that seek to oust the capacity of the courts to review actions taken under such decrees; and the circumstances in which the courts may assume jurisdiction over important human rights cases. These NGOs have achieved this by catalyzing the production of correspondence between the norms that they espouse and the attitudes and decisions of many Nigerian judges. The nature and extent of this NGO-led contribution to the development of progressive judicial thought and action in Nigeria is best demonstrated by a case-by-case analysis. The following sample of cases, which have mostly concerned the innovative uses of the African charter and African commission within Nigeria's legal system, will suffice to illustrate the overall point that is being made here.

2.1.1. THE ZAMANI LEKWOT CASE[20]

In 1993, seven prominent leaders of the Kataf ethnic minority in the Northern Nigerian State of Kaduna were arrested, detained, tried before a military tribunal headed by Justice Benedict Okadigbo,[21] convicted, and sentenced to death.[22] Upon a communication to the African Commission on Human and Peoples' Rights filed on their behalf by the Constitutional Rights Project (CRP)—a prominent Nigerian human rights NGO, the commission (an institution of the African human rights system) indicated "interim measures" to the effect that the Nigerian military government should suspend the implementation of the sentence pending the outcome of this application. The Nigerian military government was duly notified of this decision. The ruling was also given extremely wide local publicity by the CRP, which had also instituted an action at the Lagos High Court asking the court to compel the Nigerian military government to respect the commission's request that the planned executions be stayed. In technical legal terms, the CRP asked for an interlocutory injunction restraining the Nigerian military government from executing the seven convicted persons pending the determination of their communication before the African commission.[23] The communication was itself based on the rights that had been guaranteed to them under the African charter (the constitutive document of the African human rights system). The court, per Justice Onalaja, granted the CRP's application and dismissed the government's objections that the court had no jurisdiction to hear the matter. It held that it was necessary to grant the injunction in order to preserve the subject matter of the communication before the commission, i.e., the lives of the convicted persons. Without this injunction, the court reasoned, the government could go ahead and execute them, thereby rendering the anticipated decision of the commission nugatory. The military government did not execute the convicted persons. At the conclusion of the parallel matter before the African commission in 1996, the commission found grave violations of the due process guarantees of the Charter. It also requested the Nigerian military government to release the convicted persons from prison. They regained their freedom that same year.

It is important to note here that the injunction granted to the CRP suspending the executions would not have been possible under Nigerian law had the CRP not deployed the charter and the commission as a major part of its struggle to stop the executions and free the convicted persons. This was because Decree No. 2 of 1987[24] (establishing the military tribunal that convicted the relevant persons as well as ousting the supervisory jurisdiction of courts) and Decree No. 55 of 1992[25] (reiterating this ouster of jurisdiction) both clearly ousted the court's jurisdiction to inquire into the matter. The only way the court could have assumed jurisdiction under the prevalent mode of legal reasoning in Nigeria was for the NGO to deploy the charter, which had been incorporated into Nigerian law, and then approach the commission in the way it did. The court regarded Chapter X of the Laws of Nigeria 1990, (which incorporates the charter into Nigerian law) as a "decree with a difference" and a "decree with international flavor." In the court's view, Chapter X is deemed to be a decree under Nigerian law and binds the Nigerian Government as long as Nigeria remains a part of the African system. In that case, since Chapter X (on the one hand), and Decrees Nos. 55 of 1992 and 2 of 1987 (on the other hand), stood in conflict as laws of Nigeria, the court decided to rely on the particular legal instrument that preserved its jurisdiction (as against the ones that ousted such jurisdiction), i.e., it relied on Chapter X. But the court could not have granted the injunction had the CRP not approached it with a request for that relief: for Nigerian courts do not act *suo motu*, i.e., of their own motion. And the CRP would have stood on much shakier ground had they not approached the court with notice of an interim measure that had been indicated by the commission: for no matter how progressive a Nigerian judge is, s/he is usually committed to one form or the other of the legalistic mode of reasoning and needs to be offered a cogent legal argument on which to found her/his decision. In such cases, it only makes sense that the stronger the legal argument the greater the chance of success. This is especially so when the anticipated decision would be novel, challenging to the government of the day, and directed at the decision of a dictatorial military government. In the end, the interim measure indicated by the commission *at the request of the CRP* was the legal excuse the court needed to act in the way it did and yet remain relatively secure in an atmosphere where the judiciary was already under siege from the military government. The court felt safer in the knowledge that it could always claim to be bound by the legal logic that was initiated when the CRP approached the African Commission and obtained the indication of interim measures. This argument was eminently convincing given that section 1 of Chapter X explicitly demands that all the state institutions of Nigeria comply with the provisions of the charter—the very document that establishes and empowers the Commission. It was in this context, as well as in the more general context of socio-political struggle, that the CRP creatively deployed the charter, the commission, the Nigerian courts, and the mass media (its virtual network partners), as resources in its successful struggle to actualize the rights of seven citizens of Nigeria and save them from the gallows. In effect, the CRP catalyzed the development of innovative judicial reasoning on the part of an activist judge, one that contributed immensely to the overall success of the struggle to save the life of Zamani Lekwot and six other leaders of a Nigerian minority ethnic group. In this way did it critically contribute to the transformation of one aspect of judicial reasoning and action in Nigeria.

2.1.2. THE NEWSPAPERS REGISTRATION DECREE CASE[26]

In 1993, the then Babangida-led military government of Nigeria annulled the democratic election on 12 June that year of Moshood Abiola as president of Nigeria. The mass media was vociferous in its condemnation of this dictatorial action. In response to the hostile posture of the mass media, the Babangida regime promulgated Decree No. 43 of 1993. This decree set out a number of extremely stringent conditions that had to be met before a newspaper could lawfully operate in Nigeria. These conditions included payment of huge sums of money by newspaper publishers, the registration afresh of all newspapers circulating in Nigeria, and the subsequent registration of these same newspapers at periodic intervals. Two Nigerian NGOs, Media Rights Agenda (MRA) and the Constitutional Rights Project (CRP), collaborated and filed a communication at the African commission alleging that this decree was charter-illegal. The commission held that the decree violated several provisions of the African charter. The collaborating NGOs then filed a matter in the Lagos High Court asking it to declare the decree null and void. A massive media campaign was also begun. One of the resources that these NGOs relied on in making their case before the Nigerian courts and before the court of public opinion in Nigeria was this decision of the African commission. At the Lagos High Court, Justice Humponu-Wusu dismissed the preliminary objections of the military government and found for the NGOs. In dismissing this objection, the court held that since the African charter was a part of Nigerian law, vide Chapter X (which has the force of a decree), and that since Chapter X conferred jurisdiction on the court, it had jurisdiction to try the case. More importantly, the court also held that any domestic legislation (including Decree No. 43 of 1993) that was in conflict with the charter was void to the extent of that conflict. This was a momentous decision in the league of the decision of another Lagos High Court judge in the Zamani Lekwot case.

It is important to note that following the decisions of the commission and the Nigerian court, Decree No. 43 was very rarely enforced by the military government and was soon repealed. It is a thing of regret though that the Press Council Decree No. 60 of 1995, which contains similar provisions, was promulgated by the government on the very day that Decree 43 was repealed. However, this later decree has not been enforced at all to date. MRA has chal lenged the legal validity of this last decree in the law courts.[27] However, for all intents and purposes, the decree is a dead letter. This fact is a testimony to the delegitimizing effects of the court's decision, a ruling that would have been extremely unlikely without the empowering earlier decision of the commission and, most importantly, the catalytic role played by two NGOs.

Here again, the success enjoyed by the MRA and the CRP in getting this Decree repealed was a result of their creative deployment of a number of resources to that struggle: the charter, the commission, the mass media, and the courts (a virtual network of "like-minded" institutions). In moves that bore a striking resemblance to those made in the Zamani Lekwot case, the commission and the mass media were approached by these NGOs as a way of strengthening the hands of a local judge. The commission ruled in favor of the NGOs. The commission's decision and other arguments based on Nigerian law were cited to the local judge. This judge then held in favor of the NGOs. All the while, a massive press campaign had been waged to sensitize the public and embarrass the ruling military regime. A combination of these measures worked (if only partially in the last case).

And although many factors were obviously at play, the supportive inter- vention of a Nigerian judge who had been convinced by these NGOs of the validity and social utility of a set of novel legal arguments was clearly central to the generation of the happy end result in this case. In this way, therefore, did two NGOs effectively catalyze the development of Nigerian jurisprudence in ways that advanced and continue to advance the search for human dignity in the country. Here again, the contribution of NGOs to transformations in judicial reasoning to—reformulations in understandings—is palpable.

2.1.3. FRANK OVIE KOKORI V. GENERAL SANI ABACHA AND FOUR OTHERS (NO.3)[28]

In this case, Frank Kokori, the president of the Nigerian Union of Petro- leum and Gas Workers (NUPENG) and an important leader of the opposi- tion to the annulment by then military regime of the 12 June 1993 presidential polls, was arrested and detained in order to frustrate a long-lasting strike by NUPENG that was threatening to cripple the economy and force that regime from power. Kokori's arrest and detention was justified by the military gov- ernment as a nonreviewable state security action taken under the infamous State Security (Detention of Persons) Decree No. 2 of 1984. This decree contained an "ouster clause." Kokori then brought a suit before the Federal High Court (Lagos division), seeking to enforce his fundamental rights under Articles 4, 6, and 7 of the African charter. In seeking to assume jurisdiction over this matter in an atmosphere of massive political upheaval and great risk, and in the face of a clearly worded ouster clause in the text of Decree No. 2, Ojutalayo, J felt empowered by the charter in particular, and by the African system as a whole. At the urging of the human rights lawyers who appeared for the defendants in that case, he held that the African charter was autonomous from, and superior to, all local laws in Nigeria, including the decrees issued by the then ruling military regime. In the words of this federal judge:

> Therefore the African Charter on Human and Peoples' Rights (Ratification and Enforcement) Act is superior to our local or domestic legislations and if there is any conflict in the provisions of any of our domestic legislations and the Charter, the latter shall prevail.[29]

Importantly, the judge in this case relied on precedent in respect of the status of the African charter within Nigeria's domestic legal order that had been laid down in previous cases by other judges. As we have seen, this innovative logic regarding the superiority of the African charter and the uses to which such status could be put was developed as a result of the pioneering work of NGOs. In this way have these NGOs helped to foster significant reformulations in judicial understandings in Nigeria.

2.1.4. MUOJEKWU AND OTHERS V. MUOJEKWU AND OTHERS[30]

In its decision in this case, which had been brought with the active support of a number of women's human rights groups and NGOs, the Court of Appeal (per Justice Niki Tobi *et al.*) invalidated a customary practice of the Nnewi Igbos of Anambra state of Nigeria. These practices were the *Oli-ekpe* and *Nrachi* customs. The words of the court are so instructive as to be quoted in extenso. In their view:

> ....the Nnewi custom relied upon by the respondents which permitted them to inherit the estate of Rueben merely because he had no male child is repugnant....And what is more, such a custom has clearly discriminated against Virginia, the daughter of Rueben and therefore is unconstitutional in the light of the provisions of section 42 of the Constitution of the Federal Republic of Nigeria, 1999....Article 18 of the African Charter on Human and Peoples' Rights specifically provides for the elimination of discrimination against women, a provision which is consistent with the Convention on the Elimination of All Forms of Discrimination against Women (CEDAW).[31]

Here, at the suggestion of NGO supported counsel for the women, the court obviously felt a need to legitimize or reinforce its reasoning (its conclusion that this age-old custom was inherently a violation of the rights of women to equality under the Nigerian Constitution) by making reference to the prohibition of discrimination in the African charter as well as in other such instruments. In effect, the charter helped to strengthen the court's hands as it moved to adopt a progressive view of the Nigerian Constitution. Using this decision as a very valuable *delegitimization resource*, a number of women's rights groups in the relevant area of Nigeria have begun a drive to gradually transcend these practices.[32] The issue has gained visibility and has led to a sense of empowerment among many members of the relevant women's groups. If they succeed fully, both the NGOs (that had pioneered the innovative use of the charter within Nigeria's courts) and that human rights treaty itself (that has served as an important resource), cannot but receive some of the credit. Again this reformulation—nay transformation—in judicial understandings bears the palpable imprimatur of these NGOs.

2.1.5. THE RIGHT TO PASSPORT CASE[33]

In this case, the respondent, Olisa Agbakoba, then the president of the Civil Liberties Organization (CLO), was invited to attend a human rights conference in the Netherlands in April 1992. Officers of the Nigerian State Security Service (SSS) intercepted him at the airport on the day that he was scheduled to depart Nigeria. These officers impounded his travel passport, thereby effectively preventing him from traveling to the conference. The officers did not offer any reasons as to why his passport was being impounded. After repeated but futile attempts to obtain his passport from the office of the SSS, he petitioned the Attorney-General of the federation and later filed a suit in the High Court, seeking to enforce his fundamental rights. This suit was researched, argued and supported by Agbakoba's NGO as well as by a number of other NGOs. The trial court dismissed his suit on the basis that the inscription on the back of the passport (that the passport was the property of the Nigerian Government) showed that Agbakoba had no legal right to the passport. On appeal, the Court of Appeal, especially per Justice Ayoola, quashed the ruling of the trial court and held that not only was Agbakoba's passport unlawfully impounded, the correct legal position was that every Nigerian had a right to a travel passport. This legal entitlement was founded on the right to enter and leave Nigeria, a right that was recognized by the operative Nigerian Constitution. The Supreme Court affirmed the decision of the Court of Appeal. In addition, a majority of the relevant panel of Supreme Court justices explicitly upheld Justice Ayoola's reasoning regarding the constitutional entitlement of every Nigerian to a travel passport. Furthermore, Supreme Court Justice Sylvester Umaru Onu felt empowered by the recognition in Article 12 (2) of the African charter (as incorporated under Nigerian law) of a right to enter and leave one's own country. In his view, the right of Nigerians to hold a travel passport is a logical corollary not only of a similar provision in the Nigerian Constitution, but also of similar provisions in both the charter and the Universal Declaration of Human Rights.

Given that Justice Onu could have reached the same decision while relying entirely on the unsuspended portion of the Nigerian Constitution, it becomes reasonably clear that reference to the charter's provisions in the development of his arguments must have been empowering; must have served the purpose of *justifying* or *legitimizing* his legal reasoning. The charter was a resource that he saw as capable of strengthening his hand. Justice Ayoola's repeated references to the Charter (in the Court of Appeal) could be explained similarly. As such, these judges seem to have benefited from the innovative introduction by NGOs into Nigerian jurisprudence of this kind of reliance on the African charter. What is more, the courts would not have even had the opportunity to pronounce on this matter had it not been for the courage, perseverance, and skills of the NGO activists who pursued the matter. This is further evidence of the positive contributions of these NGOs to the subtle alterations in judicial attitudes that have occurred in Nigeria.

2.1.6. THE FAILED BANKS TRIBUNAL CASE[34]

In this case, Dr. Femi Adekanye and twenty-six other persons had been arrested and detained for over thirty months under the Failed Banks (Recovery of Debts) and Financial Malpractices in Banks Decree No.18 of 1994. They were charged before the Failed Banks Tribunal with various financial offences that had plunged Nigeria's financial sector into a serious crisis. Subsequently, they sued the present appellants (the comptroller of prisons and the attorney-general) at the High Court, asking the court to order their release from detention. The appellants challenged the High Court's jurisdiction to entertain the suit or to order the release of the detained persons on the basis that Decree 18 of 1984 ousted the court's jurisdiction to review any matter or proceedings before the Failed Bank Tribunal. At the urging of the human rights attorneys that appeared in the case, the trial court dismissed this challenge to its jurisdiction, assumed jurisdiction over the suit, and ordered the release of the detained persons. The Court of Appeal, per Justices Oguntade, Galadima, and Aderemi, upheld (on another ground) the lower court's refusal to accede to the ouster clause in Decree No. 18 of 1994. In so doing, the CA affirmed a long line of cases that had up to that point in time held that the African Charter on Human and Peoples' Rights was superior to the decrees passed by the Federal Military Government of Nigeria. More importantly though, the Court of Appeal relied entirely on the provisions of the Charter both for the purposes of assuming jurisdiction over this sensitive case and for the purpose of invalidating certain substantive provisions of Decree No.18. And as has been shown, this innovative strategy was introduced to the Nigerian courts by human rights lawyers affiliated with certain local NGOs.

On the matter of the ouster clause in this Decree, the Court of Appeal held that the attempt to oust the High Court's jurisdiction was ineffectual basically because the ouster clause contravened the African charter. One is immediately reminded of the African commission's decisions and resolutions, reached at the urging of Nigerian human rights NGOs, condemning such ouster clauses.[35] In the Court of Appeal's own very clear words on this specific issue:

> If I had to consider the issue of jurisdiction of the High Court in
> this matter without reference to the African Charter on Human

[and Peoples'] Rights … *I would not have had the slightest hesitation in concluding that the High Court had not supervisory jurisdiction in this matter.*[36]

The Court of Appeal then went on to hold in equally clear terms that the African charter empowered the High Court to assume jurisdiction over the matter even in the face of an ouster clause that was clearly designed to shield the "emergency" Failed Bank Tribunal from the prying eyes of the regular courts of law. In their view, the charter had this empowering effect because the relevant provision in Decree 18 did not explicitly oust, and indeed could not have effectively ousted, the jurisdiction of the High Court under Chapter X—the local legislation that had domesticated the African charter in Nigeria. In Ogundade JCA's own words:

> The ouster of the supervisory jurisdiction of the High Court cannot attach to acts done under a law so patently in conflict with the African Charter … In the instant case, the trial court rightly invoked and assumed the supervisory jurisdiction of the court over the Failed Banks Tribunal as the statutory protection shielding the Failed Banks Tribunal from the supervisory jurisdiction of the High Court is ineffectual.[37]

On the issue of the invalidity (under the African charter) of some sections of the relevant Decree 18, the court began its process of judicial reasoning by making reference to the provisions of section 7 of the African Charter as a critical factor in its decision-making process. In Justice Ogundade's words, "Article 7 of the Charter is *eye-opening.*"[38] The Court of Appeal went on to hold that section 26 of Decree No.18 is oppressive in its effect and "totally destroys the presumption of innocence in favor of the accused" that is guaranteed by Article 7 of the African charter.[39] That section was also pilloried and invalidated for ensuring in practice that anyone charged with an offence under Decree No.18 could not be granted bail.[40] The Court of Appeal also found that the provisions of sections 4(2) and 5(1) of the same decree in effect violated Article 7 of the charter.

One of the most instructive things about this decision is the very explicit ways in which the court was able to rely on the African charter for jurisprudential legitimization and empowerment. The court was thereby able to reach a conclusion that it clearly wanted to reach, but which—as it clearly stated—would have been impossible to justify and rationalize (in a legal sense) without invoking the African charter. A passage from Aderemi JCA's concurring judgment confirms the court's progressive orientation in this case. In his own words:

> In the instant case, with disturbing facts starring one in the face it will be a tragedy to the society for a Judge to demonstrate timidity under the municipal law and thereby in cheap obedience to its wordings refuse to assume jurisdiction when faced with the provisions of the *African Charter.*…A refusal to assume jurisdiction

will make the judge more executive than the executive themselves. The trial Judge of the court below by assuming jurisdiction held himself out as one who is governed by the rule of law."[41]

It is also highly instructive that the CA openly showed the extent to which the goals, norms, and practices of the African system and of those who founded that regime had inspired its orientation and impacted its jurisprudence. According to Oguntade JCA:

> A law that does not discriminate in the award of punishment between the guilty and the innocent is a modern-day anachronism. No nation should tolerate it. And this is one of the reasons that informed the need for African nations to come together for an *African Charter of Human [and Peoples'] Rights*.[42]

Particularly instructive here is the fact that in adopting all of these jurisprudential strategies, and in reaching all of these conclusions, the Nigerian courts benefited tremendously from the fruits of the activist work that local NGOs had done in terms of the domestic application of the charter. The contribution of these NGOs to this reformulation in judicial understandings in Nigeria is therefore no longer in doubt.

2.1.7. THE TREATY SUPREMACY CASES[43]

In a long line of cases, many of which were brought as a result of the gallantry and efforts of NGOs, almost all of which have benefited from the pioneering work of these NGOs, and a few of which are cited and discussed here, some Nigerian courts— anxious as they were in most cases to circumvent the military's claim to absolute unreviewable power—have affirmed at least one of the following propositions: (a) international treaties that have been ratified by Nigeria are *sui generis* in character and cannot be subsumed under the hierarchy of domestic laws; (b) treaties that have been ratified by Nigeria (and the local legislation that incorporates them into Nigerian law) are international agreements that cannot be unilaterally modified or abrogated by the Nigerian government; (c) such treaties can only be modified by the Nigerian government if they are renegotiated with the other states parties, and only if the necessary agreements are thereby secured; (d) such treaties are hierarchically superior to domestic legislation in Nigeria; (e) in the event of a conflict between a provision of a domestic law and a treaty provision, the treaty will supersede the domestic law and the conflicting domestic law provision will be invalidated as a result; (f) the African Charter, as one such treaty, and its incorporating domestic law (i.e., Chapter X), is superior to all domestic laws in Nigeria (including military decrees), and cannot be unilaterally modified or abrogated by Nigeria; and (g) the African Charter is superior to the Nigerian Constitution. Hereafter, all of these propositions are referred to as the "supremacy propositions."

Most notable among these cases is Fawehinmi v. Abacha [Court of Appeal] (now partly overruled by the Supreme Court).[44] In that case, the CA (per Justices Musdapher, Mohammed and Pats-Acholonu) had held, inter alia, that not only is the African charter superior to all domestic laws in Nigeria, it is also superior to decrees of the military government and, in effect, to the then Constitution of Nigeria.[45] It also held that the charter is "in a class of its own" and does not fall within the hierarchy of local laws in Nigeria.[46] Consequently, the Court of appeal held that no Decree of the Military government can oust the jurisdiction of the courts in matters pertaining to the African charter.

Similarly, in *Chima Ubani v. the Director of State Security Services and the Attorney-General*,[47] the same court affirmed the proposition that the African charter is superior to all of Nigeria's domestic legislation, including the decrees made by military regimes that have been widely regarded as dictatorial. The Court of Appeal also ruled that, as such, the lower court ought to have assumed jurisdiction over the extant matter that concerned the judicial review of the detention of a prominent human rights activist by the inspector-general of police under powers purportedly conferred on that officer by the infamous State Security (Detention of Persons) Act (the so-called Chapter CCCCXIV Laws of Nigeria, 1990).

These "supremacy propositions," were most important resources in the hands of many members of the judiciary (and other network partners) during the long period of military dictatorship in Nigeria. The propositions strengthened the hands of many members of the judiciary in their somewhat subtle "cold war" struggle to retain some amount of independence and dignity in the face of military absolutism. This much is evident from the evidence already supplied and especially from the declaration of Oguntade JCA (as he then was) that:

> *It is a clear manifestation of gallantry* and judicial innovativeness to be able to assert jurisdiction over matters which the military rulers tried to shield the judiciary away [sic] from.[48]

Because the cold war was *subtle*, because this war was a struggle for the hearts and minds of Nigerians, such propositions were very potent delegitimization weapons in the hands of such judges, enabling them on many occasions to reach conclusions that they deemed appropriate—conclusions that would otherwise have been virtually impossible to reach (according to the legalistic logic to which Nigerian judges are practically wedded). Crucially, these propositions would have been almost impossible to formulate and "sell" during most of the relevant period had it not been for the creative deployment of the charter (and on some occasions the commission) by the relevant NGOs. For one, the charter was during the relevant period the only relevant international human rights treaty that had been incorporated into the corpus of our domestic laws. Moreover, in the context of a widespread sensitivity even within the Nigerian human rights community, to often overbearing and sometimes hypocritical foreign lectures on human rights, given its eminently African pedigree, the charter was far more potent a delegitimization device than alternative human rights treaties. It was not open at all to the charges, so often levied by successive military governments, that a particular human rights document or proposition was alien and imperialist.

It is noteworthy that early on in this period the African commission had itself decided that the obligations assumed by Nigeria under the African charter are unaffected by the attempts by the military regime to emasculate the domestic law that incorporates the charter into Nigerian law.[49] This stance of the commission was well known to most activist lawyers and judges in Nigeria and helped consolidate their sense of the legitimacy of their strategies and decisions. As well, the commission's resolution on this matter and its influence on local NGOs and judges created a form of correspondence between the decisions of some Nigerian courts and those of the African commission. In most of the relevant cases, these Nigerian courts did not simply complying with a decision of the commission but benefited nevertheless from the commission's jurisprudence and orientation.

An important point to note is that, as has been shown previously, these NGOs have been almost entirely responsible for introducing and popularizing such reliance on the African system (charter or commission) by Nigerian courts in order to circumvent dictatorial or abusive domestic legislation. Many judges deserve some credit, however, for adopting this innovation even when such a strategy placed them at risk of paying a price of one sort or the other for offending the relevant military regime.

However, the potency of these supremacy propositions has been much reduced, since the end of military rule, by the decision of the majority of Nigeria's Supreme Court in *Abacha v Fawehinmi* (already discussed). In that case, the court held, *inter alia,* that Chapter X, the local law that incorporates African charter into Nigerian law, was a domestic law with a difference, possessing greater vigor and strength than any other domestic statute, including a decree. However, the majority of the Supreme Court also held that: Chapter X was *not* superior to the Constitution of Nigeria; it could be amended or even repealed by a decree of a military regime; it could be effectively emasculated by an ouster clause contained in a decree; and it does not necessarily invalidate the conflicting provisions of another domestic law. This decision of the Supreme Court might have represented a serious roll back of the protective shield that had been woven around the human rights of Nigerians by the courts had it not been for the fact that the decision was reached under the new democratic dispensation. Had it been reached under a military regime it would have been even more devastating to the human rights community, and would have seriously compromised the capacity of the African system to serve as a force for progressive social causes in Nigeria. Nevertheless, the above evidence still reinforces the argument that NGOs have contributed quite significantly to reformulations in understandings within the Nigerian judiciary.

2.1.8. OTHER MORE MARGINAL CASES

Realization of the significant extent to which the African charter has penetrated Nigeria's judiciary is reinforced by an examination of some more marginal cases. In *Ogugu v. the State*, and in *Opeyemi Bamidele and Others v. Alele Williams and Another*, various activists affiliated to various NGOs persuaded the courts to gloss over the nonprovision within Nigerian law of a specific procedure for the domestic enforcement of the African charter.[50] Instead, the courts adopted the reasoning of the relevant NGOs that litigants intending to enforce the African charter within Nigeria's legal order can approach the courts through a related constitutional procedure.[51] This is evidence of the liberal attitude of many Nigerian courts in matters related to the enforcement of the charter, one that was fostered to a large extent by the innovative work that NGOs have done on this question.

2.2. CATALYZING THE RELEASE OF DETAINEES AND THE COMPENSATION OF VICTIMS

This is an area in which NGOs have achieved some of their most visible success stories. Civil/political rights NGOs such as the CRP, HURILAWS, and the CLO have been at the forefront of successful efforts to persuade the judiciary to release from detention thousands of poor and vulnerable Nigerians who had been detained (sometimes for years) without trial. In so doing, these NGOs reinforced the power of the idea of the human right to liberty and freedom of movement and, over time, helped foster a subtle and modest alteration in the impunity that had attended the curtailment of such freedoms in Nigeria. In this way did these NGOs contribute to a reformulation in human rights understandings within Nigeria. While it is impossible to recount all the stories of all the prisoners that have been released from jail largely as a result of the efforts of these NGOs, an ample number of examples are supplied below. These examples are organized around the work of particular NGOs.

For its own part, the Constitutional Rights Project (CRP) has enjoyed many such successes. For instance, in January 1999, a Lagos High Court judge, Justice Olu Obadina, ordered the unconditional release of twenty-four ATPs (awaiting trial persons) from the Ikoyi and Kirikiri maximum security prisons. This order was granted as a result of two separate suits [Suit No. M/596/97 and Suit No. M/606/97] filed on the behalf of these persons by legal officers of the CRP.[52] The efforts of the CRP have also led to the release of many other arbitrary detainees by the courts. In Suit M/196/98, which was filed and prosecuted by the CRP, a Lagos High Court ordered the release of some persons who had been in detention without trial for over eleven years.[53] In Suit M/48/98, thirteen persons who had been detained for several years while awaiting their trials were released from jail as a result of legal arguments made on their behalf by the CRP.[54] In Suit M/505/97, the CRP persuaded a Lagos High Court judge to order the release of ten detainees who had been arrested and kept in custody on suspicion of having committed felonies and who had been in detention for between three and eights years without trial.[55] In 1997, as a result of the intervention of CRP, a poor and vulnerable Nigerian who had been arrested and detained without trial for twelve years finally secured his freedom.[56] In 1999, the CRP was able to persuade a court to acquit and release from jail a number of persons who had been arrested and accused by the erstwhile Abacha military regime of being responsible for various bomb blasts that had rocked various parts of the country at the time.[57] Even more strikingly, in 1999, the CRP was able to persuade a Federal High Court to order the release from detention of a number of junior soldiers who had allegedly been involved in a coup attempt.[58] Thus, even in the context of military rule and even with respect to certain "sensitive" matters, the CRP was able to persuade the relevant courts to release the relevant persons from unlawful detention. In the end, this NGO was able to make a dent, even if so slightly, on the explicit and implied arguments of the relevant military regimes that the detention of these persons had been "appropriate."

As young as it is, HURILAWS has also earned a few accolades in the battle to secure the freedoms of poor and vulnerable Nigerians. A few examples will suffice here. In March 1999, 579 prisoners were reportedly released from Enugu prison as a direct result of lawsuits filed on their behalf by HURILAWS. According to this NGO, most of the released prisoners were (ATPs).[59] According to its independently verifiable records, it has since 1998 secured the release from detention of over two thousand detainees.[60] There is no published evidence that contradicts these figures. As such, HURILAWS has also contributed, albeit modestly, to the gradual fostering of alterations in the public's understandings as to the appropriateness of the detention practices of the relevant military and civilian regimes in Nigeria.

Media Rights Agenda (MRA) has also enjoyed similar successes. For instance, in 1999, it persuaded a court to award a relatively huge sum of money to a journalist who had been unlawfully arrested and detained by the much-dreaded Police Rapid Response Squad.[61] Here again, the efforts of this NGO contributed, however modestly, to the delegitimization of the arguments of successive military and civilian regimes that these detention practices were appropriate.

2.3 CATALYZING THE JUDICIAL REVIEW OF THE DECISIONS OF MILITARY TRIBUNALS AND IRREGULAR COURTS

This is another area in which NGOs have played a very important progressive role, especially during the era of military rule in Nigeria. Here are a number of examples of the ways in which this role was played.

As has already been noted above, during the military era, the CRP persuaded a Lagos High Court to stay the death sentence imposed on Zamani Lekwot and several other Kataf leaders by an irregular tribunal which composed of four civilians and one soldier and supervised directly by the ruling military junta. Again, as has already been shown, in the Failed Bank Tribunal case, two NGOs persuaded both the Lagos High Court and the Court of

Appeal to hold that Nigerian courts enjoy supervisory jurisdiction over the so-called Failed Banks Tribunal that had been established by military decree with the intention of depriving the courts of this power.

In the course of the new civilian political dispensation in the country, Nigerian courts have, at the instance of some of these NGOs, taken similar actions. For instance, in 2000, the CRP succeeded in persuading Justice Bode Rhodes-Vivour of the Lagos High Court to quash the judgment of an armed robbery tribunal that had sentenced two men to death on the ground that the tribunal lacked the necessary jurisdiction since Decree No. 62 of 1999 had abrogated the tribunal. This court's decision was reached in the course of exercising its supervisory jurisdiction over such tribunals.[62]

In all of these cases, particular NGOs succeeded in persuading the relevant courts to, in effect, debunk and de-legitimize the Nigerian military's attempts to shield the activities of their irregular tribunals from the prying eyes of the regular courts. The courts sided with the NGOs in holding that such "shields" were inappropriate.

2.4. OTHER IMPORTANT SUCCESSES BEFORE THE COURTS

NGOs have also enjoyed other important successes in persuading the courts to deliver justice to abused and/or vulnerable Nigerians. These cases are so numerous that only a small illustrative percentage of them will be noted here. For instance, in 1999, the CRP was able to persuade a Rent Control and Recovery of Residential Premises Tribunal sitting in the Lagos area to reinstate a poor tenant who had been unlawfully evicted by his landlord.[63] This success may seem minor unless one is conversant with the desperation for housing that characterizes the life of many residents of Lagos, a sprawling city of over eighteen million people. The enormous leverage enjoyed by landlords over tenants and the tendency of the judicial and quasi-judicial institutions to empower landlords rather than tenants must also be kept in mind. In 2000, through Suit FHC/L/CS/1412/97, the CRP was able to persuade a judge of Nigeria's Federal High Court to reinstate a prison officer who had been unlawfully dismissed from his job.[64] Again this success may seem minor unless the severe power imbalance between workers and employers in the paramilitary or police-like agencies in Nigeria is recognized. As importantly, in Suit M/370/2000, the CRP was able to persuade a judge to order the West African Examination Council (WAEC) to issue a graduation certificate to a high school graduand who had been denied the certificate by that body without a fair hearing.[65] As this certificate tends to be crucial for success in the lives of most Nigerians, and as this was one of the first times in which this examining body has been compelled on human rights grounds to rescind its denial of a certificate of graduation, this otherwise minor decision is rendered significant.

In each of these cases, the work of an NGO contributed appreciably to the production of correspondence between the norms espoused by that NGO and the relevant judicial decision—leading to an important positive, if minor, alteration not just in the circumstances of the relevant victims of abuse but also in the character of related norms. Through this process, that NGO helped advance the increasingly successful attempts to alter the prevalent sense of the appropriate judicial response to each of these forms of victimization.

2.5 TRAINING OF JUDGES

Establishing formal training seminars and workshops for lower and upper court judges is a strategy that has been commonly employed by NGOs to advance their work and help produce important alterations in the prevalent understandings of human rights issues in the country. A few examples will suffice. For instance, in the first couple of years of the new civilian dispensation (especially between 1999 and 2000), the Legal Directorate of the Civil Liberties Organization (CLO) trained hundreds of lower court judges in "train-the-trainer" style human rights workshops.[66] The Socio-Economic Rights Initiative (SRI) has also mounted a number of such workshops to educate some Nigerian judges on the adjudication of social/economic rights issues.[67] In all of these cases, the mere fact that the judges did participate in these time-consuming workshops, very often for very little or no financial gain, bears testimony to the increasing though still limited influence of these NGOs on the Nigerian judiciary.

2.6. OVERALL ASSESSMENT OF NGO INFLUENCE ON JUDICIAL REASONING AND ACTIVISM IN NIGERIA

As some of the evidence supplied above shows, many activist Nigerian judges have often gone out of their way to rule in the favor of these NGOs, often adopting the innovative arguments advanced by them. An obvious contributing factor to this willingness on the part of many judges, *even under conditions of military dictatorship*, to risk career advancement and the like in adopting the anti-government arguments advanced by these NGOs, is their sensitization both within and without the courtroom to the human rights imperatives that animate these NGO struggles, as well as to the human rights norms that exist to address them. Outside the courtroom, the sensitization strategies adopted by these NGOs have ranged from radio campaigns to training seminars specifically targeted at judges. As such, while these training seminars have not been the exclusive factor that shaped the positive (if modest) results that these NGOs have often enjoyed in their engagement with the courts, they have nevertheless played an important role. The CLO's own analysis of the evaluation forms of its judicial training workshops reveals some evidence for this proposition.[68] And while this cannot be regarded as conclusive proof of the utility of such workshops, it corroborates other signals to the same effect.

3. THE INFLUENCE OF NGOS ON LEGISLATION AND LEGISLATIVE ACTION WITHIN NIGERIA

One remarkable historical feature of the state-NGO relationship in Nigeria is that even during the harshest days of military rule in that country, NGOs were still able to exert a *modest* measure of influence on legislation and legislative action there. Laws were repealed or modified by various military regimes in part as a result of sustained campaigns launched by many of these NGOs. The legislative process itself was also positively affected. NGOs have also been able to achieve the same modest measure of success during the period of civilian rule between 1999 and 2001. This section of the chapter discusses a number of examples of the kind of influence that these NGOs have been able to exert on legislation and legislative action in Nigeria.

3.1. DURING THE 1987–1999 ERA OF MILITARY RULE

Even under the various military regimes that ruled Nigeria during the period under study, NGOs managed on a number of occasions to contribute appreciably to the success achieved by a coalition of various oppositional forces in forcing the relevant military regimes to alter publicly their own expressed logics regarding the appropriateness of certain legislative provisions. The following are some accounts of such cases.

3.1.1. THE CIVIL DISTURBANCES (SPECIAL TRIBUNAL) ACT OF 1987[69]

This legislation was enacted by the Babangida military regime in March 1987. It provided for the establishment of a special tribunal to conduct the trial of persons charged with offenses related to communal or civil disturbance. The tribunal was to be composed of a serving or retired superior court judge as its chair and four other members, "*one* of whom shall be *a serving member of the Armed Forces.*"[70] It also provided for the confirmation of any conviction or sentence passed by the tribunal by the Armed Forces Ruling Council, the military junta that controlled both the executive and legislative branches of government in Nigeria during the relevant period.[71] Thus, persons convicted and/or sentenced by the tribunal had no right of appeal to another judicial body. As importantly, this law had also ousted the supervisory powers of the High Courts over the proceedings of the tribunal.[72]

As a result of communications filed and arguments advanced by NGOs, the presence on the tribunal of a serving member of the armed forces, the ouster of the jurisdiction of the regular courts to review the decisions of the tribunal, and the absence of a judicial right of appeal from the decisions of the tribunal were repeatedly pilloried in very explicit terms in a number of decisions issued by the African Commission. In the Zamani Lekwot case, that commission found that all of these features were clear violations of the African charter.[73] The commission also expressed similar views on one of these features in *Civil Liberties Organization v. Nigeria*[74] (which was filed and argued by the CLO). Similarly, in a number of decisions and resolutions, the commission has pilloried and declared charter-illegal the kind of "ouster clause" that was contained in the relevant legislation.[75] At its second extraordinary session, primarily convened in order to deal with the execution of the Ogoni Nine and with other aspects of the Ogoni matter, the commission also expressed similar concerns regarding the compatibility of this law with the African charter.[76]These features of the law were also criticized at a number of other international fora.[77]

On 5 June 1996, the notorious Abacha-led military government promulgated the Civil Disturbances (Special Tribunal) (Amendment) Decree. This decree removed the armed forces member of the tribunal and provided for the right of appeal to a Special Appeal Tribunal. This was a great victory for the NGOs that had brought and pursued several cases related to these matters before the African commission and before international public opinion; and that had campaigned so fiercely in the Nigerian courts of law and in the court of public opinion against these provisions. Surely, a sizeable portion of the credit for this important alteration in official understandings regarding the appropriateness of these kinds of special tribunals is attributable to the work of these NGOs.

3.1.2. THE STATE SECURITY (DETENTION OF PERSONS) ACT OF 1984[78]

This legislation was passed by the Babangida military regime in 1984. It aimed to "empower the Federal Military Government to detain persons for acts prejudicial to State Security for a period not exceeding six months at a time, and to provide for a periodic review of such detention."[79] This law was subsequently amended by the State Security (Detention of Persons) (Amendment) (No.2) Decree No. 14 of 1994. Passed into law by the Abacha military regime, this latter decree introduced a new section 2A into the existing legislation that precluded courts from issuing the writ of habeas corpus or any other such writ aimed at the production in court or release from detention of any person detained under the 1984 law (formerly referred to as Decree No. 2 of 1984).

As a result of communications brought before it by some NGOs, the African Commission specifically characterized this legislation (as amended) as charter-illegal.[80] Its prohibition of the issuance of the writ of habeas corpus by the courts clearly offends the guarantees of the right to liberty under the African charter. Similarly, the law contained an ouster clause.[81] The Commission also condemned this sort of clause as, *inter alia*, a violation of the charter's guarantee of the right to a fair trial.[82]

On 7 June 1996, the Abacha military regime promulgated the *State Security (Detention of Persons) (Amendment) (No.2) (Repeal) Decree No. 18 of 1996*. This last Decree repealed Decree No. 14 of 1994, thus restoring the legal capacity of the courts to issue a writ of habeas corpus or the like so as to order the production in court or release from detention of a person detained under the 1984 law. In addition, that military regime ordered a wholesale review of the cases of all those detained under that law. About twelve persons regained their freedom as a result of this particular review.[83]

This is another example of the ways in which the efforts of NGOs have helped in direct and indirect ways to produce a very valuable form of correspondence[84] between the dictates of human rights norms and the laws passed by the Nigerian military government of the time. The sustained pressure brought to bear on this government by these NGOs through publicity campaigns and law suits filed both in the Nigerian courts and at the African commission did bear some legislative fruit.

3.1.3. THE NEWSPAPERS REGISTRATION DECREE NO. 43 OF 1993

The circumstances surrounding the repeal of this decree have already been explained at some length in section 2.1.2. of this chapter. Suffice it to point out that in this case as well, the efforts of NGOs helped to foster a level of correspondence between the actions of the Nigerian military "legislature" of the time and the dictates of the human rights norms espoused by these NGOs. Partly as a result of the work that these NGOs have done, an offensive antipress decree was eventually repealed and was, in any case, never enforced. The work of these NGOs both led to the repeal of the offensive decree and, before then, the failure to enforce it. This is a significant fact given the widely acknowledged penchant of the relevant Nigerian military regimes to repress press freedoms.[85] Indeed, the repression of the independent press was one of the key "survival" strategies deployed by those regimes. Similarly, partly as a result of the efforts of these NGOs, the decree enacted to replace the repealed one was also never enforced.

3.2. DURING THE NEW CIVILIAN DISPENSATION (BETWEEN 1999 AND 2001)

Under the somewhat more favorable conditions of civilian rule, many of these NGOs have managed to insert themselves and their values more firmly into the process of legislation in Nigeria. This has helped to produce subtle alterations of pre-existing attitudes regarding the appropriateness of civil society and popular participation in the Nigerian legislative process.

With the inauguration of elected civilian governments at all levels of governance in Nigeria, the need to monitor the processes and institutions of civil rule warranted the establishment of the CLO's Democracy and Governance Project.[86] The project monitors developments at the national and state legislative assemblies and publishes *Democracy Review*, a quarterly newsletter.[87] It also works with other NGOs in the drive to consolidate Nigerian democracy through the instrumentality of constitutional and legislative reform.[88] This has led to the CLO's modest success (in partnership with a number of other NGOs) in ensuring that a number of proposed and already enacted pieces of legislation became much more human rights friendly. For instance, the content of the so-called Anti-Corruption Act, and the yet to be enacted Freedom of Information Bill have, from the observations of a number of key legislators, benefited from the input of NGOs such as the CLO and MRA.[89] Indeed, the Freedom of Information Bill was drafted by a group of NGOs led by MRA.[90] Similarly, HURILAWS participated in the drafting of the Anti-Corruption Act.[91] These NGOs were also successful in helping to keep up the public pressure that was mounted on the National Assembly to pass the Anti-Corruption Act.[92] Indeed, as a senior activist has noted, the Nigerian President met with the leaders of some of these NGOs and specifically asked for their help in raising the tempo of public pressure on the National Assembly, so as to ensure the speedy enactment of this law.[93] Given their awareness of the severe repercussions that could flow from its implementation (and which has recently began to flow), the National Assembly enacted this law with *relative ease and speed*.

It is also most noteworthy that one of the very first legislative acts of the new civilian administration was to repeal certain notoriously harsh military decrees that in the twelve years before 1999 had been the focus of an extraordinary level of activism and criticism by NGOs. By an *Extraordinary Gazette* (official government notice) issued on Wednesday, 9 June 1999, only ten days into the new regime, the following military decrees were repealed with effect from 29 May 1999 (the first day of the new regime): the Suspension and Modification Decree No. 1 of 1984 (which virtually abrogated all the human rights guarantees in Chapter IV of the Constitution); the States Security Detention of Persons Decree No. 2 (which allowed the previous military regimes to detain anyone without the possibility of judicial review); and the Students' Union Activities (Control and Regulation) Decree No. 22 of 1998 (which prohibited any form of student unionism on Nigerian campuses).[94]

Similarly, the Senate has repealed a number of antimedia legislation enacted by various past regimes.[95] These recently repealed laws include the Newspapers (Amendment) Act of 1964, and the Defamatory, Offensive Publications Decree No. 49 of 1966.[96] This important legislative action was a clear, if partial, response to a sustained media, lobbying, and legal campaign that had been mounted for several years by a coalition of actors led by NGOs such as MRA.[97]

Also noteworthy here is the central role played by NGOs in the passage into law of the National Agency for Traffic in Persons (Law Enforcement and Administration) Bill of 2001.[98] While the chief moving spirit behind the bill was an NGO known as the Women Trafficking and Child Labor Eradication Foundation (WOTCLEF), many other NGOs also participated in the struggle to draft, publicize, and eventually pass this bill into law.[99] The House of Representatives passed this bill in the very same year as it was presented, which is quite remarkable in the Nigerian context.[100]

Importantly, certain members of the National Assembly (the federal Parliament), including many who have championed some of these human rights-friendly legislation, have noted the educational benefits that have accrued to them from the lobbying that NGOs have done within the Assembly.[101] For

instance, in the context of the push for the law that outlawed human trafficking, one of the principal legislative proponents of that law has noted that
although the influence of NGOs on the bill may have been suboptimal—
simply because this particular bill was introduced by the government—the
efforts made by these NGOs were nevertheless influential. In his words:

> First and foremost, you should note that this bill and other related
> bills are essentially government bills...Being a government bill,
> the extent of NGOs direct influence remains low level, and
> perhaps insignificant. *However, we (some Hon. Members, including
> myself) did receive educative memos from NGOs in respect of the bill seeking
> to influence our thinking on the issue at stake....*On the influence of the
> NGOs, I am not saying that NGOs may not have had a more
> direct influence or contribution to the bill, perhaps before it was
> introduced on the floor of the House. *Of course you should know that
> Mrs. Abubakar [the wife of Nigeria's Vice President] is involved with an
> NGO that handles Women's and Children's issues.* I only said what I said
> to the extent of my knowledge and involvement.[102]

As importantly, many members of the National Assembly and of some
of the various state legislative houses now seem to be taking the work and
input of many of these NGOs more seriously than they had in the past. A
few examples are offered here. For instance, in October 2000, the Senate
Committee on Human Rights specifically requested memoranda from NGOs
on ways of improving the status of women in Nigeria.[103] The then chair
of this committee, Senator Abubakar Danso Sodangi, had also convened a
stakeholders' roundtable in February 2001 to discuss the proposed Civil Societies Act. Passage of this bill would establish a Civil Societies Commission
and provide for the registration of societies and the incorporation of trustees
for certain communities, bodies, and associations. The CRP, the CLO, CAPP
and many other such groups were represented at this roundtable.[104] Similarly,
Senator Stella Omu, the then chief whip of the Senate, had on at least one
occasion invited many of these NGOs to participate in a public presentation
of the bills that she had brought before the Senate.[105] Each of these moves to
involve these NGOs in the work of the Senate is attributable, in part at least,
to the work that these NGOs have done in sensitizing the Nigerian literate
elite regarding human rights issues, as well as to the growing reputation of
these NGOs among this same literate elite as knowledgeable and useful partners in the human rights area.[106] Certainly, this has not always been the case.

What is more, certain state assemblies now seem to be taking the work
of these NGOs more seriously than they had in the past. For one, some of
these state assemblies have now passed into law, bills that were drafted and
sponsored by NGOs. For example, the law recently enacted by the Enugu
State House of Assembly prohibiting harmful widowhood practices was
initially mooted, drafted, and pushed by a coalition of fifty human rights
NGOs and civil society groups (including WACOL).[107] From the very begin-

ning, this legislation also enjoyed very strong support from a number of state legislators.[108] It took about two years of very hard work to push this law through this legislative house.[109] The Delta State House of Assembly has also enacted legislation prohibiting the practice of female circumcision in the state.[110] This law came into effect in April 2001. Both the Edo State House of Assembly[111] and the Cross River State House of Assembly have enacted similar legislation.[112] In all these cases, the lobbying work of NGOs and other civil society groups was an important factor in the passage of the relevant laws. As importantly, many of the NGOs that have for years lobbied the National Assembly to enact a Freedom of Information Law have, quite remarkably, been able to enlist the very public support of the Lagos State House of Assembly in this effort. For example, at the 10 April 2000 session of the House of Representatives (the lower house of the National Assembly), a resolution of the Lagos State House of Assembly calling for the quick enactment of this Freedom of Information Law was read.[113] This kind of NGO/State Assembly coalition is virtually unprecedented in Nigerian political history. It is noteworthy that the MRA and the CLO (two of the NGOs that constitute the sample of NGOs that are the focus of this study) were largely instrumental in bringing about the consideration of this bill by the National Assembly.[114]

4. THE INFLUENCE OF NGOS ON EXECUTIVE THOUGHT AND ACTION IN NIGERIA

As will be demonstrated here, these NGOs have also helped to produce subtle but nevertheless notable alterations in the thinking and actions of the executive branch of government in Nigeria. They have also helped to foster reformulations in the executive branch's understandings of the appropriateness or otherwise of military rule. This should not surprise discerning observers of the global human rights scene. That governments the world over—even relatively dictatorial regimes—tend to be sensitive to the kind of pressure that is sometimes generated by NGOs has for a long time been widely acknowledged in the relevant literature.[115] For instance, Kathryn Sikkink has, among other points, noted that the nature of the U.S. State Department's "human rights country reports" was positively altered as a result of that department's interactions with U.S.-based human rights NGOs. In her own words:

> Because [USA] State Department officials did not want to offend foreign officials or undermine other policy goals, their early human rights reports were often weak. However, the State Department reports did serve as a focal point for human rights groups, which were able to create annual public events by issuing responses to the reports. The reports and counter reports attracted press coverage on human rights, and the critiques of the State Department reports held the department up to higher standards in its future

reporting. Domestic human rights organizations in repressive countries in turn learned that they could indirectly pressure their governments to change practices by providing information on human rights abuses to human rights officers in US embassies for inclusion in the US annual county-specific reports.[116]

Similarly, Susan Waltz has exposed the modest but remarkable influence that Tunisian human rights NGOs exerted on the executive branch of the Tunisian government (and thus on the society at large) during the regime of President Ben Ali. According to Waltz:

> Activists in Tunisia have gathered enough support from those in authority – and have in fact themselves found their way into seats of power – that even formal rules of political fair play have been largely rewritten. Tunisia's infamous state-security court has been abolished, and the practice of incommunicado pre-trial detention known as *garde-a-vue* has been curtailed; with these changes two of the regime's most effective tools for muffling dissent have at least been diminished.[117]

Waltz has also reported on a similar phenomenon in Morocco of the 1990s, where one of that country's major human rights NGOs "was successful in putting human rights on the agenda constructed and otherwise controlled by the king," demonstrating as a result that the Moroccan governance system "commonly viewed as closed is, in fact, not impervious to social pressure."[118]

NGOs have exerted similar kinds of modest but significant influence on executive thought and action in Nigeria. From influencing the Executive's actions during the days of military rule to having an impact on the new civilian administration, these NGOs have contributed quite appreciably to the production of modest human rights harvests. They have secured the release of administrative detainees by the executive; they have successfully pressured successive military regimes to direct the suspension of certain obnoxious trials and executions; they have been successful at pressuring even military-controlled executives (which also controlled the law making function) to direct that important changes be made in the content of laws; they have been successful at pressuring successive military regimes to refrain from enforcing some draconian laws; they have been partly successful at pressuring the executive to alter its attitude to the struggle of the Niger Delta communities for more control over their own resources and for better environmental protection; their senior activists have secured important and relevant appointments to governmental agencies; they have facilitated many of the important activities of the Nigerian National Human Rights Commission; they have influenced the nature and work of the Nigerian Human Rights Investigation Panel (the so-called Oputa Panel); they have contributed to the atmosphere that led to the formation of human rights units within the federal ministry of justice and within at least one state ministry of justice; they have helped make important changes to Nigeria's national telecommunications policy; and they have (alongside popular social agents such as guerrilla journalists) helped to force a formal end (at least for now) to fifteen years of military rule in Nigeria.

4.1. THE RELEASE OF ADMINISTRATIVE AND OTHER DETAINEES

A few examples will suffice here to illustrate the contribution of NGOs to the release of administrative and other detainees.

In *Constitutional Rights Project (in respect of Wahab Akanmu and others) v. Nigeria*, Communication No. 60/91, the CRP petitioned the African Commission on behalf of one hundred detainees who had been tried, convicted, and sentenced to death for armed robbery in accordance with the Armed Robbery and Firearms Decree, 1974. The decree under which their trial proceeded made no provision for an appeal from this conviction and/or sentence. Finding that the decree violated Article 7(1)(a) of the African charter, the commission recommended that the petitioners be compensated. Because of the efforts of the CRP, which deployed the commission's decisions locally by mounting publicity campaigns and pressing the government to release these detainees, all of the detainees were eventually released.

In the same vein, in 1990, the Committee for the Defense of Human Rights (CHDR) led a campaign that culminated in the release by the then ruling military regime of a number of university lecturers and student union activists who had been arbitrarily detained.[119] Similarly, in the Zamani Lekwot case (already discussed above), and in the matter concerning the Ogoni nineteen (discussed below), a number of detainees were released mostly as a result of the efforts of NGOs. Even more dramatic (although slightly different) is the fact that when the CLO publicized the abuse of detainees held at Ita Oko, a prison colony that had been established secretly one decade earlier, the Nigerian government reacted almost immediately to the reports by removing all the prisoners and shutting down the colony.[120]

4.2. SUSPENSION OF TRIALS AND COMMUTATION OF DEATH (AND OTHER DRACONIAN) SENTENCES

The activist work done by NGOs has sometimes led to relatively dramatic results: trials have been unexpectedly suspended and death sentences commuted to prison terms. This has had extremely important positive effects not just on the lives of those who have benefited directly from these efforts but also on the social climate in the country. These victories have also helped sustain the zeal and momentum required for these organizations to go the distance in their sustained efforts at fostering positive transformations in the human rights situation in the country. A few examples suffice to illustrate this point.

At its second extraordinary session held in Uganda in December 1995, just after the Nigerian government had executed Ken Saro-Wiwa and the rest of the Ogoni Nine, the African commission decided to ask the chair and secretary general, respectively, of the Organization of African Unity (now the African Union) to "express to the Nigerian authorities that no irreparable prejudice is caused to the nineteen Ogoni detainees whose trial is pending."[121]This indication of interim measures was in fact transmitted to the Nigerian government, and followed up with an on-site investigative mission. The proposed trial of the Ogoni Nineteen (the second batch) was stayed, and they were all later released without trial. It would of course be implausible to argue that the trial of these detainees was stayed *only because* of the efforts of NGOs. A number of other factors were clearly at play. There had been a massive international outcry over the execution of the trial and execution of the first batch of the Ogoni detainees. The African commission had also indicated interim measures, the local press had made a lot of fuss in public about the matter, and Nigeria had been clearly embarrassed by the strong public condemnation of its actions issued by South Africa and Zimbabwe (a treatment that is usually reserved for the very worst cases within the Organization of African Unity and even then rarely meted out). Nigeria had also been expelled from the Commonwealth. But here again, NGOs were central players in the generation of each and every one of these other factors. The work that NGOs did in sensitizing the Nigerian and international public, as well as the African commission, about the plight of the Ogoni led to some limited benefits.

In the Zamani Lekwot case, the commission's indication of interim measures was also deployed within Nigeria, by the CRP, in such a way as to lead to the suspension of the planned execution of Zamani Lekwot and other leaders of his Kataf minority ethnic group; the commutation of the death sentences that had been passed on them to five-year jail terms; and to their eventual release by the Babangida-led military junta. This case has already been discussed at length in section 2 of this chapter. Suffice it to say that given the fact that the release of General Lekwot et al. was in fact ordered by the executive, it is reasonable to deduce and conclude that the executive was markedly influenced, albeit indirectly, by the efforts made by NGOs and other human rights forces to secure the release of Lekwot and the rest of the accused.

Again, in 1990, a massive campaign led by the Civil Liberties Organization (CLO) was one of the critical pressure points that persuaded the military government of the time to commute the death sentences that had been passed by one of the military tribunals it had established, and over which it exercised direct supervisory authority. This sentence had been imposed on twelve persons who had allegedly participated in an unsuccessful coup attempt, and whose trial was marred by serious irregularities.[122]

As part of its broad campaign to abolish the death penalty, HURILAWS filed the case of *Onuoha Kalu v. The State*. In this case, HURILAWS challenged the constitutionality of the death penalty. This suit and other aspects of the antideath penalty campaign contributed significantly to the decision of the executive to institute certain penal reforms, culminating in the grant of amnesty to certain categories of prisoners who had been on death row.[123] It is instructive that the Nigerian President has now gone on record as being supportive of the abolition of the death penalty in Nigeria.[124]

The CRP has also been able to persuade the new civilian regime to grant presidential pardons to three persons who were alleged to have been wrongly convicted and sentenced to life imprisonment by the Miscellaneous Offenses Tribunal for dealing in and transporting contraband goods.[125]

The CLO has also had some impact in this respect. For example, in 1994, CLO activists visited three prisons at Enugu, Abakaliki, and Nsukka.[126] This CLO mission found that a lot of people were being detained for far too long without just cause.[127] These findings were widely reported in the press by the journalists who were part of the CLO team.[128] The Chief Judge of Enugu State eventually invited the CLO to be part of his own visit to these same prisons.[129] During his visit, he exercised his powers under the law and ordered the release of eighty or so persons who were being held while they awaited their trials (also known as ATPs).[130] Similarly, in the same year, the CLO was able to persuade a Lagos High Court to order the release of 136 ATPs being held at the Ikoyi prison in Lagos.[131]

In all of the above situations, pressure mounted by one or more NGOs was a critical factor in securing the desired outcome. The efforts of these NGOs led to the infliction of a slight but significant dent on the argument offered by the executive that the extant governmental behavior had been appropriate. In showing just how inappropriate such behavior was, these NGOs have helped to catalyze an ongoing, albeit slow, reformulation of pre-existing understandings regarding the extant matters.

4.3. CATALYZING THE MODIFICATION OF LEGISLATION BY MILITARY GOVERNMENTS

Under the Nigerian military, the executive exercised complete control over the law-making function. Given the nature of Nigeria's governance architecture during this military era, legislative action was in effect executive action. Legislative action could not, and did not, proceed except with the approval of the executive. It is for this reason that the pro-human rights changes that were made to military decrees during this era to are considered here to be both legislative and executive actions (at one and the same time). As these changes have already been discussed elsewhere in this chapter, they will not be recounted here.

4.4. CATALYZING THE NONENFORCEMENT OF DRACONIAN LAWS

In the Newspaper Registration Decree case, the African commission's decision that the relevant decree violated several provisions of the African charter was relied upon by two NGOs in their successful suit before a local High Court to declare the Decree invalid. The charter was creatively deployed by these NGOs as a critical resource in their public debate with government officials about the appropriateness of the decree's provisions. The net effect of the commission's decisions and the work of these NGOs on this issue was that the decree was never enforced by the executive and was later repealed by a military legislative body controlled completely by the executive.

4.5. FOSTERING INCREASED GOVERNMENTAL SENSITIVITY REGARDING THE NIGER DELTA REGION

This is one area in which some NGOs such as the Movement for the Survival of Ogoni People (MOSOP) and Environmental Rights Action (ERA) have, in alliance with other civil society actors (and even politicians), virtually forced the Nigerian executive to make important changes to the policies and actions affecting that region.[132] In their stride, they have also fostered a vastly increased level of sensitivity on the part of the Nigerian government to the abuses that have been wrought on the Niger Delta peoples and on their environment.[133] For instance, in 1992, as a result of much civil society (including NGO) agitation, the then ruling military junta established the Oil Mineral Producing Areas Development Commission (OMPADEC) and increased the percentage of the national revenue that was allocated exclusively to these areas on the basis of derivation from 1.5 percent to 3 percent.[134] As a result of continued agitation in the Niger Delta, this was again raised to 13 percent in 1999. This very steep (nearly 1000 percent) rise reflected the Nigerian government's vastly increased (although still inadequate) sensitivity to the pressing developmental problems of the people of the Niger Delta.[135] In the year 2000, in response to continued agitation, the new civilian government of President Obasanjo set up the Niger Delta Development Commission (NDDC) to accelerate development in that oil-bearing region.[136] The NDDC replaced the OMPADEC.

What is more, the Nigerian government has become much more sensitive to the need to reign in the oil companies that operate (often rapaciously) in the Niger Delta. In Ikelegbe words:

> The government has become *more sensitive* to the environmental and social responsibilities of oil companies to the Niger delta [peoples], and has recently become consistent in calling on MNOCs to negotiate and reach memoranda of understanding with the host communities, honor agreements, and be responsive to Niger delta problems.[137]

The major role that NGOs played in this marked transformation in executive policy and action was mainly to raise the tempo of the public and legal discourse on the abuse of the Niger Delta, thus sustaining that subject's currency as a key national discursive question. This contributed to the mobilization of favorable public opinion. Even more importantly, especially in the case of organizations like the MOSOP, the indigenous inhabitants of the Niger Delta, who have suffered the most from the historical neglect of the area, were mobilized quite effectively at the grassroots level.

This does not of course mean that the goals of the Niger Delta struggle have all or mostly been accomplished. Far from it. In fact, many important setbacks, such as the retaliatory massacre of civilians that occurred at Odi in 1999, illustrate the immensity of the obstacles that stand in the way of the full realization of those goals.[138]

The point, however, is that the attitude, policies, and actions of the government with respect to these problems have improved *markedly* since NGOs (and other civil society groups) began to campaign for fundamental changes in these attitudes, policies, and actions; and that these improvements occurred partly as a result of such campaigns. Indeed, as scholars like Ikelegbe have recognized, the very "authority and legitimacy" of the control and allocation of Nigeria's oil resources by the federal government has been fundamentally challenged and diminished, *in part* as a result of the efforts of a number of NGOs.[139] A reformulation in the understandings of what is and is not appropriate in the circumstances has therefore occurred, however modest its extent.

4.6. THE APPOINTMENT OF ACTIVISTS TO RELEVANT GOVERNMENTAL AGENCIES

The kind of subtle and modest influence that NGOs have often had on executive action in Nigeria is illustrated by this passage from an interview with a senior activist in which he recounts how Ayo Obe, the then president of the CLO, came to be appointed to the Board of the Police Service Commission by the current federal government of Nigeria. [The Police Service Commission (Establishment) Act of 2000 provides explicitly for the appointment of a representative of NGOs to the Board of the Commission].[140] In the words of this senior activist:

> At the inception of his administration, [President] Obasanjo was reluctant to engage with civil society groups. We had a meeting with him after the NGO retreat at Lekki [near Lagos] and we pushed for institutional reforms (e.g., the military and the police) and the need to deepen democracy....Before that meeting (which took place in June 2000), I had earlier written to Mr. President following a chance meeting with him and in the letter I recounted the discussions we had during the chance meeting. That letter was instrumental to the meeting of June 2000. Following this June 2000 meeting...the president of the CLO, Ayo Obe, was appointed to the Police Service Commission."[141]

Senior activists have also been similarly appointed to other government agencies that are clearly important from a human rights perspective. For instance, Tunji Abayomi, the founder/CEO of HRA was initially appointed to the Oputa Panel (but later removed allegedly because of a perceived conflict of interest);[142] two NGO activists were appointed to the National Committee on Prison Decongestion by the Abdulsalami Abubakar regime;[143] and a number of activists have served on the board of the Nigerian National Human Rights Commission (NNHC).[144]

It is deducible from the very fact that a number of activists have now been appointed by the executive to sit on these important agencies that the Nigerian executive has at least begun to treat with these activists on an appreciably more serious basis than in the past. What is more, by sitting at tables where important policy decisions are taken, these activists now have a better chance of influencing the course of the agencies on whose boards they serve. It will now be much harder for decisions to be made by those boards without input from the NGO community.

4.7. INFLUENCE ON THE NIGERIAN NATIONAL HUMAN RIGHTS COMMISSION (NNHC)

Much of the outreach work that the NNHC has done thus far has been facilitated by NGOs. For instance, the CLO has collaborated with the NNHC in mounting training workshops for lower court judges.[145] As a result of CLO-NNHC collaboration, similar training workshops have been held for police and prison officers.[146] The CRP and the NNHC have also worked together to create and disseminate human rights radio jingles and establish a thirty-minute human rights program called "Rights and Duties" on Ray Power Radio.[147]

Overall, these NGOs have enjoyed a symbiotic relationship with the NNHC, one that has ensured that certain government agencies now take these NGOs much more seriously.[148] At the same time, the NNHC's willingness to work with and assist these NGOs has lent that governmental body a measure of (albeit modest) legitimacy within the local and international human rights community. It would not have otherwise acquired such legitimacy given its origins as a child of the infamous Abacha military regime.

4.8. INFLUENCE ON THE COMPOSITION AND WORK OF THE OPUTA PANEL

On 4 June 1999, shortly after the inauguration of the current civilian regime, the executive branch of the federal government established the Human Rights Violations Investigation Commission, otherwise referred to as the Oputa Panel. The panel was charged with investigating and documenting the serious human rights abuses that had occurred in that country between 1966 and 1998.[149] Chaired by Chukwudifu Oputa (a retired Supreme Court judge), the panel was composed of Alhaji Ali Kura Michika, the Rev. Matthew Kuka, Ms. Elizabeth Pam, Mallam Mamman Daura (replaced later by Alhaji Adamu Lawal Bamalli), Tunji Abayomi (later removed because of a conflict of interest and replaced by Modupe Areda), and T.D. Oyelade (who served as the panel's secretary).[150] The Rev. Mathew Kuka and Tunji Abayomi are well known human rights activists. The latter is in fact the CEO of HRA. The very fact that a significant number of commission members was appointed from the NGO community is itself a measure of growing influence of these NGOs on executive action in Nigeria.

The mandate of the panel was to:

- To ascertain or establish—to whatever extent the evidence and circumstances may permit—the causes, nature, and extent of human rights violation or abuses and in particular all known or suspected cases of mysterious deaths and assassinations or attempted assassinations committed in Nigeria since the last democratic dispensation

- To identify the person or persons, authorities, institutions, or organizations that may be held accountable for such mysterious deaths, assassinations or attempted assassinations or other violations or abuses of human rights and to determine the motives for the violations or abuses, the victims and circumstance(s) thereof, and the effects on such victims or the society generally

- To determine whether such abuses or violations were the product of deliberate state policy or the policy of any of its organs or institutions or individuals or their offices, or whether they were the acts of any political organization, liberation movement or other group or individual

- To recommend measures that may be taken, whether judicial, administrative, legislative, or institutional to redress past injustices and to prevent or forestall future violations or abuses of human rights.[151]

The Oputa Panel subsequently appointed the representatives of some NGOs to serve on its six subcommittees. These NGO representatives were asked to assist the commission in researching and probing the serious human rights abuses that had occurred in the six geopolitical regions of the country.[152] Thus, a number of NGOs were thus able to exert some direct influence on the panel's internal activities.[153] They researched the allegations of human rights violations that were brought before the panel and provided an important portion of the "independent" evidentiary basis on which the commission's report is based.

What is more, many other NGOs were also able to influence the work and final conclusions of the panel by submitting memoranda, attending panel sessions, and raising important questions concerning many of the human rights violations that had occurred during the relevant years. In particular, the CLO, CRP, and SRI prepared and submitted memoranda to the panel highlighting the wide-ranging human rights abuses committed against its members and the general public.[154]

4.9. HUMAN RIGHTS UNITS IN FEDERAL AND STATE MINISTRIES OF JUSTICE

One mostly indirect effect of the work of NGOs in securing a more important place for human rights in the thinking and behavior of the Executive branch of government in Nigeria is the increasing willingness of the federal and state governments to set up or strengthen human rights units within their various Ministries of Justice. The federal government has recently strengthened the human rights unit within the Federal Ministry of Justice.[155] What is more, the recent formation of the Directorate for Citizens Rights within the Lagos State Ministry of Justice was one of the fruits of the collaborative efforts of that state's executive branch and certain NGOs and civil society organizations. In Ibhawoh's words: "The Directorate, which includes the office of the Public Defender, is an independent ombudsman-like institution charged with investigating public complaints of human rights abuses in the state."[156]

4.10. CATALYZING CHANGES IN CERTAIN MARGINAL AREAS

NGOs have also been moderately successful at pressuring the new civilian administration to follow transparent governance principles in the telecommunications policy area. Here the point of interest is the struggle of these NGOs for more transparent governance in Nigeria and not the tele-communications business as such. A good example of how this was achieved is the way in which otherwise unsuccessful suits filed by HURILAWS and other such NGOs challenging the transfer of real power from the National Communications Commission (NCC) to a ministerial committee led to the sensitization of the National Assembly on the need for transparency in this area of governance and to the convening by that body of a public hearing on bad telecommunication polices. Subsequently the executive branch restored the relevant powers to the NCC and formulated a new national telecommu-nication policy that was much more transparent.[157]

Other government policies have also been changed due in part to the efforts of these NGOs. For example, HURILAWS has used its contacts within both the executive and legislature branches of the Lagos state government to catalyze the process by which that government accepted that it would as a matter of policy provide housing for about ten thousand poor landowners who had been forcibly evicted by a previous administration from the Maroko area in Lagos.[158]

4.11. CATALYZING THE END OF MILITARY RULE IN NIGERIA

As was noted in previous chapters of this book, NGOs were at the fore-front of the campaign to end military rule (read executive dictatorship) in Nigeria.[159] This campaign was of course eventually successful in achieving its objective of formally ending military rule. As Clement Nwankwo, one of the most senior of the contemporary breed of Nigerian human rights activists, has stated:

> NGOs...played a crucial role in *ameliorating* the harshness of military rule by providing legal assistance to victims of human rights abuse, creating awareness and building up [a measure of] public opinion and opposition to continued military rule in the country.[160]

Ikelegbe, a scholarly observer of the Nigerian civil society scene, agrees with Nwankwo's admittedly interested assessment of the contribution of these NGOs to the delegitimization and eventual abrogation of military rule in Nigeria.[161] In Ikelegbe's words:

> The activities of civil society [of which these self-described human rights NGOs formed an important part] were *to some extent* able to put pressure on "arbitrary military rule, promote the rule of law, protect socio-economic and political rights," circumscribe violations and compel government revisions of economic and political reforms. The activities of civil society maintained the challenge and pressure for democratization throughout the period from 1986 to 1999.[162]

The authors of a recent independent report on the work of human rights NGOs around the world also endorse this assessment of the Nigerian situation.[163]

As suggested by the above quotations, although successful in the end, the struggle waged by these NGOs and other popular forces to end military rule in Nigeria was a long and hard one, with many ups and downs, and many inchoate results. For example, the struggle against the annulment of the results of the 12 June 1993 democratic presidential elections was only partially successful. Nevertheless, that phase of the struggle was a critical factor in the eventual success of the overall anti-military project in Nigeria. As Julius Ihonvbere has correctly noted:

> For the first time since the January 1966 coup, popular organizations [and human rights NGOs] had challenged the military and forced it to make far-reaching concessions. Though failing to achieve their ultimate goal of a full restoration of democracy, a multitude of groups in Nigeria's new civil society had succeeded in expanding the political landscape, checking the hitherto unabridged power of the armed forces, opening up political spaces for deeper penetration and mobilization, and putting issues of democracy, empowerment, and social justice firmly on the national agenda.[164]

Such was the gradual and incremental nature of this struggle—one that was to an appreciable extent catalyzed and led by NGOs.

That the Nigerian political scene has been much more human rights friendly since the end of military rule in 1999 is suggested in a passage from an interview with a very senior and knowledgeable Nigerian activist. In his own words:

> Because there has been a more congenial atmosphere for human rights to thrive, we have taken advantage of the National Human Rights Commission, the Oputa Panel, the various Ministries of Justice, the Human Rights and Petitions Committee of the various

Houses of Assembly and the National Assembly to further push
for the better protection of human rights in Nigeria and to seek
redress for victims of abuse.[165]

As such, if the political climate in Nigeria is now much more human
rights friendly, NGOs ought to take a significant portion of the credit. As
another activist has noted, the end of military dictatorship has opened up
the government more than a crack, creating even more room for NGOs
to engage with and influence government officials and institutions.[166] The
jury is still out, however, on the extent to which this increased wiggle room
can lead to a much more significant increase in NGO influence within the
current civilian government and within the Nigerian polity. In the meantime,
it remains clear that the influence exerted by these NGOs has thus far been
of a rather modest nature.

4.12. WOMEN'S ISSUES

The work of NGOs (especially those devoted to women's issues) has
been responsible in part for some modest alterations in the behavior of the
executive branch of government in Nigeria. A couple of examples will serve
to illustrate this point.

First, the post-1999 Obasanjo-led federal government has appointed more
women ministers than any other regime in Nigeria's political history. This has
in part been in response to a sustained campaign by women's groups (including
women's NGOs) to increase women's political status in Nigeria. Indeed, the
Obasanjo regime's action in this regard was in partial fulfillment of its promise
to allocate thirty percent of its political appointments to women.[167]

Even more striking is the relatively recent experience of WACOL in
Enugu state. In 1998, WACOL and other such groups filed a court action
against the Enugu state government challenging the complete exclusion of
women from that state's cabinet.[168] In a modest response to this suit, the state
governor appointed one woman into his cabinet and reestablished the state's
Ministry of Women Affairs, a department that he had earlier scrapped.

4.13. MISCELLANEOUS INSTANCES

There are many other instances of NGO influence on the executive in
Nigeria that are not easily categorized under one of the above headings. A
few of these will be discussed below.

In the early 1990s, the CLO campaigned against and effectively stopped
the construction of a dam—the Rafin Zaki dam—that would have drastically
affected the rivers, ecosystems, and economy of the people of North-Eastern
Nigeria.[169] The CLO has also helped pressure the Federal Environmental Protection Authority into paying N67 million (worth about US$250,000 at the
time) to the Ulemon community (near Benin) that had suffered some deaths
and illnesses as a result of a faulty urban waste management scheme.[170] Similarly, the CLO pressured the federal government into paying N2.5 million

(worth about US$85,000 at the time) to the families of victims of a wrongful shooting by the police.[171]

5. THE INFLUENCE OF NGOS ON PUBLIC DISCOURSE IN NIGERIA

NGOs have had a modest but nevertheless important impact on the content, character, and development of public discourse in Nigeria. Ibhawoh, a knowledgeable observer of the Nigerian human rights scene, has even lauded what he sees as the "tremendous impact" that these NGOs have had on the human rights attitude of the general Nigerian public."[172] While the evidence on which the present study is based does not lead to as laudatory a conclusion, I agree that these NGOs have exerted a significant measure of influence on *elite discourse* (as opposed to grassroots opinion) in Nigeria.

Important in this connection is the fact that, at least at the level of formal public discourse, the federal government now tends to address these NGOs more as partners than as adversaries. This is a marked change from the, hitherto, far more adversarial discursive attitude of the Nigerian government regarding these NGOs. A few examples serve to illustrate this point. In response to a March 2000 letter written to him by the CLO, President Obasanjo stated that:

> ....there is no doubt that civil society groups, *especially the human rights organisations*, have a cardinal role to play in nurturing and ensuring the sustenance of our nascent democracy. Government [sic] regards all such groups as partners in progress.[173]

Earlier in 1999, the President had declared to a media audience that his administration would "pursue a noble goal to achieve an egalitarian society, where respect for human rights, which I swore to uphold, would be maintained."[174] In the same vein, the then chair of the House of Representative's Judiciary Committee, the Honorable Obetan Obetan, had declared that:

> Every law we make is supposed to be subjected to public hearings so that stakeholders, including civil society groups, would [sic] make input into it. This is to enable these various groups in the society to say what law they are envisioning [sic] for the future of their country."[175]

Similarly, during the consideration of the Police Service Commission Bill in the Committee of the Whole House, the Honorable Ita Enang (a male member of the House of Representatives) pilloried as unreasonable a proposed amendment that sought to replace the representative of women on the commission with a representative of the Federal Character Commission. The male-dominated House of Representatives accepted his human rights-based argument that the slot for a woman on that commission should not be removed.[176]

Further evidence for this changing formal public "face" of the Nigerian government in relation to these NGOs (and to human rights issues more

generally) can be found in the nature of some of the questions directed at the first batch of ministerial nominees screened by the Senate in 1999. Human rights questions did enjoy a relatively higher profile than at any other time in the short history of constitutional democracy in Nigeria. During the screening of these ministerial nominees, Senator Danso Sodangi asked one of the nominees, Senator Onyeabo Obi, what he would do as a lawyer to ensure protection of the fundamental human rights of Nigerians and to prevent human rights abuses.[177] Another nominee, Alhaji Sule Lamido, was asked what he would do, if posted to the Ministry of Internal Affairs, to improve the conditions of the prisons since their present conditions constituted a breach of human rights.[178] Yet another nominee, Dr Amina Ndalolo was asked what contributions she would make to the issue of the empowerment of women in Nigeria.[179] Alhaji Musa Gwadabe was asked what solution he would proffer regarding the Niger Delta minorities question.[180] What is more, the Senate explicitly congratulated the President for having a relatively high number of women on his list of ministerial nominees.[181]

Also of interest here is the observable change in the formal discourses of the Nigerian Prisons Service (a major target of NGO activism during the twelve years under consideration). For example a very senior prison officer has claimed in an address to officers and staff of the service that henceforth "respect for human rights will be the centerpiece of the nation's prisons service".[182]

This kind of impact can also be illustrated, albeit with some difficulty, by the example of the change that has since occurred in the attitude of the vocal and literate sections of the Nigerian public regarding the "appropriateness" of military rule in that country. Few serious observers of the Nigerian political scene now doubt that the attitude of most vocal and literate Nigerians to military rule was significantly altered and changed for the better during the period under study (i.e.,1987–2001). In the old days, most members of this class of Nigerians used to troop out to the streets, bars, or newspaper columns to celebrate the advent of military rule.[183] Quite understandably, they viewed most of the military officers who staged such takeovers of government as heroes who had come to rescue the polity from the largely dysfunctional behavior of many preceding civilian leaders. It was even fashionable for prodemocracy activists to openly call on the military to seize power from an egregiously abusive civilian regime.[184] However, by the last four years or so of the period under study, this largely benign view of, and attitude toward, military rule had begun to give way to a much more skeptical one. In today's Nigeria, no longer are prospective and successful military coup makers invariably viewed as heroes out to arrest the rot in the polity. They are now widely regarded as a major part of the problem.[185]

Again, it is hardly controversial to state that one of the important reasons for this transformation in the orientation of the vocal and literate public was the tremendous effort made by elements of Nigeria's civil society (including NGOs), to expose the rampant abuses and excesses of successive military regimes. Evidence of these efforts has already been provided elsewhere in this chapter.

However, it is important to emphasize that the kind of impact that is observed here is of a modest (though remarkable) kind. The argument that has been made is not therefore that NGOs single-handedly drove the Nigerian military from power. It is also not that the combination of the efforts of these NGOs was the only factor that led to the delegitimization of the "logic" that presented military rule as an appropriate response to civilian misrule. The argument that is being made here is simply that the work of these NGOs made major contributions to the positive reformulation in the understandings of military rule that has definitely occurred in Nigeria.

Of comparative interest is the fact that Susan Waltz has also recorded a similar kind of modest harvest in terms of a transformation of the local elite discourse in certain North African countries. In her own words:

> Roughly over the past decade, North Africa has seen a proliferation of indigenous human rights groups, and the subtle but important alterations in political dynamics they are working merit closer examination. Foremost of these groups is the Ligue tunisienne des droits de l'homme (L.T.D.H.) [the Tunisian League of Human Rights], founded in 1977. Over the past decade it has shepherded profound changes in Tunisian *discourse* and in the rules of the overall political game as well.[186]

6. THE INFLUENCE OF NIGERIAN NGOS ON THE AFRICAN HUMAN RIGHTS SYSTEM

In 1982, during Nigeria's Second Republic, the two houses of Nigeria's National Assembly ratified the African Charter on Human and Peoples' Rights.[187] This treaty had been adopted unanimously in June 1981 at the summit meeting of the Organization of African Unity (now the African Union) in Nairobi, Kenya.[188] The twin actions of the National Assembly in ratifying this treaty and enacting legislation incorporating it into Nigeria's domestic legal regime has had a salutary effect on the work of NGOs ever since. These NGOs have been able to deploy that treaty most creatively both within and without Nigeria's courts. They have also seized on the access to the African Human Rights System (i.e., the African system) that was provided to them by the ratified treaty and have utilized this access to engage most beneficially with both the local courts and the institutions of that system.[189] This should not be surprising to students of the relationships among domestic actors and international human rights institutions (IHIs). As Helfer and Slaughter have put it:

> [E]ven in a political system that is otherwise corrupt or oppressive, it is possible that a particular government institution – a court or administrative agency or even a legislative body – *will choose to*

forge a relationship with a supranational tribunal as an ally in the domestic political battles against corruption or oppression. Whether such an alliance would be efficacious depends on the nuances and sensitivities of local politics, but the larger point is that participation in the "community of law" constructed by a supranational tribunal is open not only to countries but also to individual political and legal institutions, regardless of how the state of which they are part is categorized or labeled.[190]

In the present case, NGOs have been at the forefront of a virtual network of domestic actors (including activist judges, journalists, and scholars) that have sought to forge such a strategic relationship with the quasi-judicial arm of the African system, the African Commission on Human and Peoples' Rights. That these NGOs have been crucial to the development of the African system is in part evidenced by the fact that virtually all of the communications (petitions) that have been brought before the African Commission on Human and Peoples' Rights have been brought or sponsored by (mostly domestic) NGOs.[191]

In the process of engaging with the African system in this way, Nigerian NGOs have had a very significant impact on the development of the institutions of that system. For one, these NGOs have been responsible for: bringing the largest single chunk of cases that have been brought before the African system;[192] mediating between the Commission and the Nigerian domestic order; and presenting much of the innovative arguments that have helped enrich the otherwise sparse jurisprudence produced by the relatively young African system. For instance, as has already been discussed in this chapter, in 1993, the CRP filed a complaint at the African Commission on Human and People's Rights to preclude the Babangida regime from executing Zamani Lekwot and other Kataf people. The commission issued an interim directive (that is, it "indicated interim measures") urging the Nigerian government to suspend the execution of these people.[193] A High Court judge relied on this directive (in explicit terms) in order to reach a legal conclusion that was not otherwise possible under Nigerian law. This was one of the first times that the commission had been moved to use and to develop its charter power to indicate such interim measures. And this was the first time that the commission had been moved to supply its normative energy in this way to a domestic court in order to achieve an otherwise unlikely feat. In this way did the CRP contribute both to the development of the commission's jurisprudence and the growth of the African system.

Similarly, as has already been discussed, in the Newspapers Registration Decree No. 43 of 1993 Case[194], MRA and the CRP utilized a decision of the African Commission in arguments before a Lagos High Court, providing the judge in that case with a critical resource that it would have otherwise lacked, which enabled him to make a decision that accorded with human rights norms. These NGOs were thus able to mediate between the African system and the Nigerian courts in such a way as to enable the African system to have direct relevance in the lives of some Nigerians. Yet again, we see evidence of the form of *transjudicial communication* that has been created and facilitated through the ingenuity and tenacity of local NGOs in Nigeria. Here the communication was transjudicial because ideas, knowledge, information, legal logic, and normative energy, traveled some distance between a quasi-judicial international institution and various institutions within the target nation-state. In this case, it has traveled to the courts and executives of the targeted state, i.e. Nigeria. But this was not a direct form of communication. Rather it has been a mediated form of communication, one that was creatively initiated, brokered, transmitted, oiled, and serviced by local NGOs.

Between 1993 and 1994, the CLO filed two important communications with the African commission that catalyzed the development of aspects of that body's jurisprudence. For the first time the African commission had an opportunity to consider the legality of clauses in military decrees that oust the jurisdiction of regular courts to supervise the executive arms of military regimes and the special tribunals set up by them. For the first time also, the African commission had an opportunity to consider whether the nonconsensual takeover of a private professional association of lawyers by a government violated the African charter. In the first case, the CLO challenged the legality of these ouster clauses and persuaded the African commission to decide that they violated the charter.[195] In the other case, the CLO successfully challenged the federal government's appointment of the body of benchers—the statutory authority that admits qualified applicants to the Nigerian Bar—to assume authority over the affairs of the Nigerian Bar Association.[196] In both cases, the commission advised the Nigerian government to take steps to repeal the offensive laws. This has now been largely done.[197]

These NGOs have, in consequence, also served as the African human rights system's primary source of independent information. By filing the bulk of the communications that have been considered so far by the African commission and by participating so actively in its deliberations and sessions, these NGOs have served as crucial sources of independent data regarding the human rights situation in Nigeria—data that often helps shape the African system's response to the given situation. For instance, the CLO has attended 99 percent of the sessions of the Commission.[198] It has also filed many a "parallel report" at the commission regarding the state of human rights in Nigeria. During the Abacha era, it was a member of an NGO coalition (that included the CRP and MRA) which filed a "joint parallel report" at that commission.[199] This report was in part responsible for the commission's decision to send an investigative mission to Nigeria in early 1998.[200]

To the extent that the African system's relevance to the lives of ordinary Nigerians (and Africans) depends on their own awareness of the system's existence and utility, the domestic uses to which these NGOs have tended to put the African charter (the constitutional document of the African system) is, in itself, another important positive effect that they have had on the development of the African system as a living legal institution. These NGOs and other activist elements in Nigeria now routinely use the resource of the African charter within Nigeria's domestic order in advancing their efforts to promote and protect the rights of Nigerians. Usually as a result of a creative strategy employed by one of these NGOs, progressive lawyers and judges have widely resorted to the use of the African charter as a way to get out of difficult jurisprudential bottlenecks that might hinder the enjoyment of human rights in Nigeria. A few examples will suffice to illustrate this point. In the particular example of its use by the Social and Economic Rights Action Centre (SERAC), one of that organization's senior activists has observed that SERAC uses:

> ....both the African Charter and the ICESCR [as their normative compass] while researching Economic and Social Rights violations in Nigeria. As ESC rights are not justiciable under our 1999 constitution, the African Charter and the ICESCR are our only resources. We refer to the Charter in our suits before the courts. *We also use the Charter to educate the masses on their rights. We have done so in the communities we work with.* We also educate lawyers on the use of African Charter.[201]

Another SERAC activist corroborated this account of their field work.[202] Similarly, a senior activist employed by HRA has affirmed that this NGO uses the African Charter as its basic normative resource.[203]

Overall, these NGOs have tended to be very supportive of an African human rights system that has provided them with a critical set of resources with which to wage their activist struggles. For instance, SERAC has, with the support of the MacArthur Foundation, worked on a nine-month project designed to help improve the capacity of the African commission to protect human rights in general and social and economic rights in particular.[204] According to one SERAC publication, this NGO seeks to help the commission utilize credible paradigms for assessing the implementation of state obligations under the African charter, while establishing effective monitoring standards for states parties to the Charter.[205]

These NGOs have also worked assiduously to pressure the African commission to improve its operational efficiency. For instance, at its Nineteenth Session (in March/April 1996), the NGOs that enjoyed observer status at the commission (including many of these Nigerian NGOs) were in part instrumental in the open criticism levelled against the then Special Rapporteur of the Commission on Summary and Extra-Judicial Executions, for allegedly having failed to do the work assigned to him within his two-year mandate; and for being absent from that session.[206] This commissioner was present at the next session (in October 1996) and did make a presentation on the work that he had done.[207] While welcoming his report, these NGOs still criticized him for not making his report available in written form; for neglecting the situation in Zaire; for not including the Abiola incident in Nigeria; and for his failure to undertake a mission to Burundi.[208] In this way have Nigerian and other NGOs helped keep the African system on its toes.

However, a note of caution must be sounded at this juncture. It is important to note that these NGOs have never treated with the African system as if they expect it to be the *panacea* to Nigeria's human rights problems. Instead, they have creatively utilized it as a *resource* in their overall strategic plans, and on a case-by-case basis. Indeed, as one activist has put it, these NGOs do not necessarily "regard the African system as politically powerful," in itself, that is, in terms of what it can do *for* them.[209] What they see as most powerful and useful about this institution are the extraordinarily creative things that they can do *with* it. In this sense is it clear that while these NGOs have contributed much to the development of the African system, that institution has also contributed in no small measure to the development of these NGOs as human rights defenders.[210]

7. THE INFLUENCE OF NIGERIAN NGOS ON OTHER INTERNATIONAL INSTITUTIONS:

The contributions of human rights NGOs to international—especially United Nations—institutions is now widely acknowledged in the literature. For instance, Felice Gaer has shown how these NGOs have from the very beginning been the engine for virtually every advance made by the United Nations in the field of human rights.[211] They have supplied the evidence that international human rights institutions (IHIs) have depended on in order to do their own work effectively,[212] and have acted as the unofficial research assistants of the members of these IHIs—whose official secretariats are often "understaffed" and "poorly-financed."[213] Overall, it is striking, as William Korey has observed, that:

> The basic truth, which knowledgeable officials at the UN clearly understood [and continue to understand], was that without NGOs, the entire human rights implementation system at the UN would come to a halt.[214]

Nigerian NGOs have now begun to contribute, albeit in modest measure, to this on going global NGO push for a more effective UN human rights system. For instance, at the 53rd session of the United Nations Commission of Human Rights, the first ever "special rapporteur on Nigeria" was appointed by that UN body to investigate cases of human rights violations in Nigeria in all their ramifications.[215] This position was created (at least in part) as a consequence of the relatively intense lobby within and without that forum by these NGOs. The CRP, the CLO, and Community Action for Popular Participation (CAPP) ably represented these NGOs at that session.[216]

Similarly, based in part on a critical and contrary "shadow report" submitted by some of these NGOs (including the SRI and SERAC), the United Nations Committee on Economic, Social and Cultural Rights issued a highly critical 1998 report on the state of economic, social and cultural rights in Nigeria.[217]

As importantly, a petition filed at a World Bank Inspection Panel by SERAC led to a finding by that body that the bank's management had not fully complied with its own resettlement policy, as it had failed to resettle and compensate the people affected by the execution of the World Bank-funded Lagos Drainage and Sanitation Project in the Ijora Badiya and Ijora Oloye communities in the Lagos area.[218]

In all these cases, a Nigerian NGO's efforts contributed appreciably to the utility and local relevance of a given international institution.

8. OVERALL ASSESSMENT: ON THE MODEST BUT SIGNIFICANT NGO HARVESTS IN NIGERIA

Overall, it is clear from the above expose that these self-described human rights NGOs have been influential to some extent within Nigeria. However, it is also clear that they have not exerted as much influence as they could have. Compared to the influence exerted within Nigeria and other countries by some other kinds of human rights movements, these NGOs cannot realistically be said to have achieved their full potential. For instance, unlike the Zambian, labor-led, prodemocracy movement (which actually won political power)[219], and the anti-apartheid movement in South Africa (which has markedly reformed the state),[220] Nigerian NGOs have not to any appreciable degree been able to either install themselves (or like-minded persons) within the government itself or to deeply transform the character of the state. Despite their central role in ameliorating, delegitimizing, and ending military rule in Nigeria,[221] these NGOs have continued to operate from the margins of political power even in postmilitary Nigeria. They have likewise not been able to command the kind of widespread popular allegiance and commitment that they could, and which would have ensured them much more influence on state and society in Nigeria.

The modest extent of the influence that these NGOs have been able to exert within Nigeria is illustrated somewhat by the anecdotal response of one very senior activist when asked about the degree of influence that his organization has had on the government. In his own words, he is "not really sure whether there has been any influence. Probably the influence has been subtle, but [he] can't really say that it has been tangible or overt."[222]

However, it is important to note as well that because of the subtle nature of much NGO influence, it is often a very difficult quantity to observe or to measure. As such, NGOs may have exerted more influence in Nigeria than can ever be attributable to them by a systematic study such as the present one.

The demonstrated capacity of these NGOs to exert a modest but significant level of influence within and without the country is in tune with the global trend. For instance, most human rights NGO scholars now recognize that international organizations, even many states, have become all but dependent on NGOs for the effectiveness of much of their human rights work.[223] Human rights NGOs have also begun to find that they gain much by working in tandem with like-minded governmental regimes.[224] Transnational networks (that have at the very least included human rights NGOs) have also had a significant impact on world politics.[225] Yet, these movements are far from the Promised Land. There still exists a wide gap between their potential and actual achievements.

But as modest as their impact has been, the fact remains that, as has been shown here, these NGOs have exerted a significant degree of influence within Nigeria. This is, in itself, worth celebrating. However, it is in the next chapter that the reasons for the limited nature of this influence will be more fully explored.

NOTES

*   Some of the evidence on which the present chapter is based overlaps with portions of the data discussed in chapter 4 of my forthcoming book which is tentatively titled *The Domestic Promise of the African Human Rights System: International Institutions, Popular Forces, and the Possibility of Correspondence.* As noteworthy is the fact that an earlier version of a small section of the present chapter was published in the *Journal of African Law* 43 (2004): 1.

1.   See chapter 1 for a broad definition of these entities.

2.   Contrast my assessment of the overall impact of these groups (between 1987 and 2001) as "modest" with Peter Agbese's 1994 conclusion that these same groups had by that date "achieved *immense* successes" in Nigeria. See P.O. Agbese, "The State versus Human Rights Advocates in Africa: The Case of Nigeria," in E. McCarthy-Arnolds, D.R. Penna, and D.J. Cruz Sobrepena, eds., *Africa, Human Rights and the Global System: The Political Economy of Human Rights in a Changing World* (Westport, CN: 1994), 167. Emphasis added.

3.   See S. Waltz, "Making Waves: the Political Impact of Human Rights Groups in North Africa" *Journal of Modern African Studies* 29 (1991): 481, 482.

4.   See K. Sikkink, "Human Rights, Principled Issue-Networks, and Sovereignty in Latin America," International Organization 47 (1993): 411, 416–417. See also M.E. Keck and K. Sikkink, *Activists Beyond Borders* (Ithaca, NY: Cornell University Press, 1998), 1–16; and T. Risse, and K. Sikkink, "The Socialization of International Human Rights Norms into Domestic Practices: Introduction," in T. Risse, S.C. Ropp, and K. Sikkink, eds., *The Power of Human Rights: International Norms and Domestic Change* (Cambridge, U.K.: Cambridge University Press, 1999), 5.

5.   See Sikkink, ibid., 437.

6.   In this chapter the term *correspondence* is employed to denote the alterations in conduct within the judiciary, legislature, and executive that can to an appreciable extent be attributed to these NGOs, even when there is no clear evidence that these domestic institutions simply "complied" with the appeals and demands made directly to them by these NGOs. For a fuller explanation of this concept, see O.C. Okafor, "Do International Human Rights Institutions Matter? The

African System on Human and Peoples' Rights, Quasi- Constructivism, and the Possibility of Peacebuilding within African States," (2004) 8 International Journal of Human Rights 1. This article is hereinafter referred to as Okafor, "Peacebuilding."

7. This much is evidenced in the contents of interviews conducted with prominent human rights NGO activists in Nigeria. In those interviews, *these ardent opponents of military rule* tended to at least imply that military rule in Nigeria had suffered a very serious decline in its reputation. For example, see transcripts of Interview with OA, 20 August 2001 and transcripts of interview with FF, 25 August 2001 (on file with the author). See also A. Olutokun, "Authoritarian State," infra note 17, 317.

8. See Sikkink, *supra* note 4, 439.

9. See L.S. Wiseberg and H.M. Scoble, "Recent Trends in the Expanding Universe of NGOs Dedicated to the Protection of Human Rights," in V.P. Nanda, J.R. Scarritt, and G.W. Shephard, eds., *Global Human Rights: Public Policies, Comparative Measures, and NGO Strategies* (Boulder, CO: Westview Press, 1981), 229, 256–257; and H.M. Scoble and L.S. Wiseberg, "Amnesty International: Evaluating the Effectiveness of a Human Rights Actor," *Intellect* (September-October 1976): 79. See also A. Fowler, "Assessing NGO Performance: Difficulties, Dilemmas, and a Way Ahead," in M. Edwards & D. Hulme, eds., *Beyond the Magic Bullet: NGO Accountability and Performance in the Post-Cold War World* (West Hartford, CN: Kumarian Press, 1996), 169.

10. See J.G. Ruggie, "Peace in Our Time? Causality, Social Facts and Narrative Knowing," *American Society of International Law Proceedings* (1995): 93, 94.

11. See M. Mutua, "The Ideology of Human Rights," *Virginia Journal of International Law* 36 (1996): 589, 589.

12. See S. Dicklitch, "Action for Development in Uganda" in C. Welch, Jr., ed., *NGOs and Human Rights: Promise and Performance* (Philadelphia: University of Pennsylvania Press, 2000), 182.

13. See N. Kasfir, "Civil Society, the State and Democracy in Africa," *Commonwealth and Comparative Politics* 36:2 (Special Issue 1998): 123–124.

14. See *Legislative Mandate* (a CAPP publication) 1:1 (1999): 12. Emphasis added.

15. Ibid., 35–36.

16. See O. Oko, "Lawyers in Chains: Restrictions on Human Rights Advocacy under Nigeria's Military Regimes," Harvard Human Rights 10 (1997): 257, 260–261. See also Agbese, *supra* note 2, 165.

17. See A. Olutokun, "Authoritarian State, Crisis of Democratization and the Underground Media in Nigeria," African Affairs 101 (2002): 317–318.

18. See O.N. Ogbu, "The Judiciary in a Polity – A Force for Stability or Instability?: The Nigerian Experience," *African Journal of International and Comparative Law* 11 (1999) 724, 725–726.

19. See Uwaifo, Justice of the Court of Appeal (JCA), as he then was, in *Peter Nemi v. Attorney-General Lagos State & anor* [1996] 6 NWLR 42 [Court of Appeal

of Nigeria], 58, paragraphs F–G. Emphasis added. Incidentally, this suit was brought by the Human Rights Law Service (HURILAWS), and was argued by Olisa Agbakoba (the former president of the Civil Liberties Organization and the current Senior Counsel/CEO of HURILAWS).

20. For this case before the African commission, see Communication No. 87/93, *The Registered Trustees of the Constitutional Rights Project (in respect of Zamani Lekwot and Six Others) v. Nigeria* (Merits) reproduced in *International Human Rights Reports* 3 (1996): 137. For the same case before the Nigeria courts, see *Constitutional Rights Project v. President Ibrahim Babangida and Two Others*, Suit No. M/102/93– Lagos State High Court, per Justice Onalaja (unreported). This case has become something of a *cause célèbre* among observers of the African human rights scene. See E.A. Ankumah, *The African Commission on Human and Peoples' Rights* (The Hague: Martinus Nijhoff, 1996), 72–73; C.A. Odinkalu, "The Individual Complaints Procedure of the African Commission on Human and Peoples' Rights: A Preliminary Assessment," *Transnational Law and Contemporary Problems* 8 (1998): 359, 402–403; I.O. Smith, "Enforcement of Human Rights Treaties in a Military Regime: Effect of Ouster Clauses on the Application of [the] African Charter on Human and Peoples' Rights in Nigeria," *Review of the African Commission on Human and Peoples' Rights* 9 (2000): 192, 204.

21. This was the Zangon-Kataf Civil Disturbances Special Tribunal.

22. The names of these persons are Zamani Lekwot, James Atomic Kude, Yohanna Karau Kibori, Marcus Mamman, Yahaya Duniya, Julius Sarki Zamman Dabo, and Iliya Maza.

23. It is noteworthy that this kind of legal manoeuvre has only recently been discovered in countries like Canada. In January 2002, Barbara Jackman, a famous Canadian immigration and human rights lawyer asked the Canadian courts to stay the deportation of her client, one Ahani, pending the consideration of a communication filed against the Canadian government at the Human Rights Committee (established under the International Covenant on Civil and Political Rights), to which Canada is a party. The application was refused by Canadian courts. For an extensive discussion and critique of the decisions of the Canadian courts in this case, see J. Harrington, "Putting Terrorists, Assassins and Other Undesirables: Canada, the Human Rights Committee and Requests for Interim Measures of Protection," *McGill Law Journal* 48 (2003): 55.

24. Civil Disturbances (Special Tribunal) Decree No. 2 of 1987.

25. See sections 3, 4, and 6 of this Decree.

26. For the African Commission version of this case, see Communications Nos. 105/93 and 130/94. For the same case before the Nigerian courts, see *Richard Akinola v. General Ibrahim Babangida and Three Others*, Suit No. M/462/93 (Lagos High Court). See also transcript of interview with KM, 24 May 2000 (on file with the author). For a second similar case before the Nigerian courts, see *Incorporated Trustees of Media Rights Agenda and another v. Honorable Attorney-General of the Federation*, Suit No. FHC/L/CS/908/99 (Federal High Court, Lagos).

27. See *Incorporated Trustees of Media Rights Agenda and Another v. Honorable Attorney-General of the Federation*, Suit No. FHC/L/CS/908/99 (Federal High Court, Lagos).

28. FHCLR 413 (1995).

29. Ibid., 425.

30. CA/E/7/99, Court of Appeal (Enugu Division), (unreported).

31. Ibid. Emphasis added.

32. The work of the Enugu-based Women's Aid Collective (WACOL) is instructive in this regard. See *Action Woman* 1:1 (2002): 8.

33. For the Court of Appeal decision, which was subsequently affirmed by the Supreme Court, see *Olisa Agbakoba v. Director of State Security Service and Another* 6 NWLR (Pt. 351) 475 (1994). For the Supreme Court decision, see *Director State Security Service and another v. Olisa Agbakoba* 3 NWLR 314 (1999).

34. See *Comptroller Nigerian Prisons v. Dr. Femi Adekanye and Twenty-six Others* 10 NWLR 400 (1999).

35. For instance, see item 3 of the Commission's *Resolution on Nigeria*, Eighth Annual Activity Report of the African Commission on Human and Peoples' Rights, 1994–1995, ACHPR/RPT/8th, Annex VII. See also *Constitutional Rights Project v. President Ibrahim Babangida and Two Others*, *supra* note 16.

36. See *Failed Bank Case*, *supra* note 34, 419.

37. Ibid., 407. Emphasis added.

38. Ibid., 422.

39. Ibid., 423.

40. Ibid.

41. Ibid., 427–428. Emphasis added.

42. Ibid., 422. Emphasis added.

43. See *Oshevire v. British Caledonian Airways Ltd* 7 NWLR 507 (1990); *U.A.C. of Nigeria v. Global Transporte Oceanico S.A.* 5 NWLR 291 (1996); *CRP v. Babangida and Others* (the domestic version of the Zamani Lekwot case) *supra* note 16; the *Failed Bank case*, *supra* note 34; *Fawehinmi v. Abacha* [Court of Appeal] 9 NWLR 710 (1996); and *Abacha v. Fawehinmi* [Supreme Court] 13 NWLR (Pt. 660) 228 (2000). The post-military rule decision in the *Abacha v. Fawehinmi* [Supreme Court] case in effect rolled back the extent to which the charter could invalidate domestic laws in Nigeria. This is understandable in the light of the fact that the threat posed by military dictatorship had substantially abated by the time this decision was issued.

44. See 9 NWLR 710 [Court of Appeal] (1996).

45. Ibid., 746–47.

46. Ibid., 747.

47. See 11 NWLR 129 [Court of Appeal] (1999). This decision was written by Justice Oguntade (as he then was), for himself and Justices Galadima and Aderemi.

48. Ibid.

49. See *Account of the Internal Legislation of Nigeria and the Disposition of the African Commission on Human and Peoples' Rights*, Doc.II/ES/ACHPR/4, 3 (1994-95).

50. See *Ogugu v the State* 9 NWLR 1, 26-27 (1994); and the *Bamidele case*, Suit No. B/6M89 (1989), Benin High Court.

51. Ibid.

52. See CLO, *Accounts and Activities for 1999* (Lagos: CLO, 2000), 42.

53. See *Constitutional Rights Journal* 9:32 (1999): 4.

54. Ibid., 8:28 (1998): 4.

55. Ibid., 8:26 (1998): 15.

56. Ibid., 7:23 (1997): 4.

57. Ibid., 9:31 (1999): 4.

58. Ibid., 9:32 (1999): 14.

59. See *The HURILAWS Newsletter* 1:3 (1998): 15. See also CLO, *Accounts and Activities for 1999* (Lagos: CLO, 2000): 42.

60. See HURILAWS, *Annual Report and Accounts 1999* (Lagos: HURILAWS, 2000), 3

61. See MRA, *A Harvest of Blooms* (Lagos: Media Rights Agenda, 2000), 70–71.

62. See *Constitutional Rights Journal* 10:36 (2000): 4.

63. See *Constitutional Rights Journal* 10:34 (2000): 4.

64. Ibid., 10:35 (2000): 4.

65. Ibid., 4.

66. See CLO, *Accounts and Activities for 2000* (Lagos: CLO, 2001), 5–6.

67. See *Shelter Watch* (an SRI Publication) 1:3 (1997): 52–53.

68. See *Liberty* (a CLO publication) 11:5 (1999): 33.

69. See Chapter LIII, Laws of the Federation of Nigeria, 1990.

70. Ibid., section 2. Emphasis added.

71. Ibid., section 7.

72. Ibid., section 8.

73. See *the Constitutional Rights Project (in respect of Zamani Lekwot and Six Others) v. Nigeria*, Communication No. 87/93, reproduced *in* Institute for Human Rights and Development, *Compilation of Decisions on Communications of the African Commission on Human and Peoples' Rights* (Banjul: The Gambia, 1999) at 38-41 (Hereinafter referred to as "Compilation of Decisions").

74. Communication No. 129/94, *reproduced* in "Compilation of Decisions, ibid., 64–67.

75. For instance, see ibid.

76. See the *Final Communique of the Second Extraordinary Session of the African Commission on Human and Peoples' Rights*, held in Kampala, Uganda, 18–20 December 1995 (on file with the author), paragraph 16.

77. For instance, see the United Nations General Assembly's *Resolution on the Situation of Human Rights in Nigeria*, A/RES/50/199, 22 December 1995.

78. See Chapter CCCCXIV, Laws of the Federation, 1990.

79. See ibid., long title of the Act. Emphasis added.

80. See *the Constitutional Rights Project and the Civil Liberties Organization (on Behalf of Ken Saro-Wiwa) v. Nigeria*, Consolidated Communications No. 137/94, 154/96, and 161/97, reproduced in Institute for Human Rights and Development, *Compilation of Decisions on Communications of the African Commission on Human and Peoples' Rights* (Banjul: The Gambia, 1999), 150–168.

81. Section 4 thereof.

82. See the Zamani Lekwot Communication, *supra* note 73.

83. See *Nigerian Democracy: The Journey So Far* (Abuja: Federal Ministry of Information and Culture, 1998), 188.

84. This concept was defined at the beginning of this chapter. Again, for an extensive development of the concept, see Okafor, "Peacebuilding" *supra* note 6.

85. See K.S.A. Ebeku, "Press Freedom and Democracy in Nigeria" *Review of the African Commission on Human and Peoples Rights* 9 (2000): 44; and A. Olutokun, *supra* note 17.

86. See CLO, *Accounts and Activities for 2000* (Lagos: CLO, 2001), 6.

87. Ibid.

88. Ibid.

89. For instance, see transcripts of interview with IW, 30 August 2001 (on file with the author).

90. See CLO, *Accounts and Activities for 1999* (Lagos: CLO, 2000), 50–51.

91. See transcripts of interview with AO, 17 August 2001 (on file with the author).

92. See B. Ibhawoh, *Human Rights Organizations in Nigeria: An Appraisal Report on the Human Rights NGO Community in Nigeria* (Copenhagen, Denmark: The Danish Centre for Human Rights, 2001), 28.

93. See transcripts of interview with OA, 20 August 2001 (on file with the author).

94. See *National Assembly Debates: Fourth Assembly, First Session - House of Representatives*, Official Report, vol. 1, no. 10. See also *Extraordinary Gazette* of Wednesday, 9 June1999 (Lagos: Federal Government Printers, 1999).

95. See The Guardian, 21 February 2003, on-line: http://odili.net/nes/source/209003/feb/21/22.html (visited 21 February 2003).

96. Ibid. See also http://www.thisdayonline.com/archive/2003/02/19/20030219 edi01.html (visited 16 May 2003).

97. See The Guardian, 21 February 2003 online at http://odili.net/news/source/209003/feb/21/22.html (visited 21 February 2003).

98. See *National Assembly Debates: House of Representatives*, Wednesday, 16 May 2001, 3.

99. See *The Guardian*, 17 May 2001, on-line: http://ngrguardiannews.com.

100. Ibid.

101. See transcripts of interview with IW, 30 August 2001 (on file with the author).

102. Ibid.

103. http://www.nigerianassembly.com/Sen...0hearing%20on%20Human%20 rights.html (visited 19 February 2002).

104. See *Assembly Watch* (a CRP newsletter) 2:10 (2001): 1–2.

105. Ibid., 6.

106. This much was acknowledged in the valedictory speech of the immediate past Senate President Pius Anyim. See http://odili.net/news/source/2003/may/ 29/15.html (visited 10 January 2004).

107. See *Legislative Advocacy* (a WACOL publication) (2001) 35–36 and 41–42. This law was passed on 8 March 2001.

108. Ibid.

109. Ibid. See also *Action Woman* (a WACOL publication) 1:1 (2002): 8.

110. See *The Vanguard*, 11 April 2001, 1.

111. See http://allafrica.com/stories/200105140301.html (visited 16/05/2003).

112. See http://www.vanguardngr.com/news/articles/2001/june/11062001/d2130 601.htm (visited 16 May 2003).

113. See 4th National Assembly, 3d. Session, No. 57, 10 April 2000.

114. See *Liberty* (a CLO publication) 12:6 (2000): 40.

115. See G.W. Shepherd, "Transnational Development of Human Rights: The Third World Crucible," in V.P. Nanda, J.R. Scarritt, and G.W. Shephard, eds., *Global Human Rights: Public Policies, Comparative Measures, and NGO Strategies* (Boulder, CO: Westview Press, 1981), 213, 216. See also D. Weissbrodt, "The Contribution of Nongovernmental Organizations to the Protection of Human Rights," in T. Meron, ed., *Human Rights in International Law: Legal and Policy Issues* (Oxford: Clarendon Press, 1984), 403; and H. Wang and J. Rosenau, "Transparency International and Corruption as an Issue of Global Governance," *Global Governance* 7 (2001): 25, 39–40.

116. See Sikkink, *supra* note 4, 422.

117. See Waltz, *supra* note 3.

118. Ibid., 498–504.

119. See N. Aduba, "The Protection of Human Rights in Nigeria," in O.A. Obilade et al., eds. *Text for Human Rights Teaching in Schools* (Lagos: Constitutional Rights Project, 1999), 109, 135.

120. See D.F. Orentlicher, "Bearing Witness: The Art of Human Rights Fact-Finding," *Harvard Human Rights Journal* 3 (1990): 83 and 84 note 3.

121. See *Final Communiqué* (on file with the author).

122. See Aduba, *supra* note 119, 134.

123. See transcripts of interview with AS, 13 March 2000 (on file with the author). See also HURILAWS, *Annual Report 1997–1998* (Lagos: HURILAWS, 1998), 11–13.

124. See *ThisDay*, 17 October 2002, on-line: http://allafrica.com/stories/2002 10170396.html (visited 20 October 2002).

125. See *Constitutional Rights Journal* 9: 30 (1999): 4.

126. See CLO, *Annual Report 1994* (Lagos: CLO, 1994), 26–27.

127. Ibid.

128. Ibid.

129. Ibid.

130. Ibid.

131. Ibid., 29.

132. See A. Ikelegbe, "Civil Society, Oil, and Conflict in the Niger Delta Region of Nigeria: Ramifications of Civil Society for Regional Resource Struggle," *Journal of Modern African Studies* 39 (2001): 437.

133. Ibid., 460.

134. Ibid.

135. Ibid.

136. Ibid.

137. Ibid. Emphasis added.

138. See Ibiyinka Oluwole Solarin, "Nigerian Federalism: The Lesson of Odi," *Nigeriaworld* on-line: http://nigeriaworld.com/feature/publication/solarin/federalism_odi.html (visited 25 October 2001); "Genocide in Odi" on-line: http://lists.essential.org/shell-nigeria-action/msg00701.html (visited 6 October 2000); and T. David-West Jr., "The Niger Delta: A Call for Reparations" *Nigeriaworld* on-line: http://nigeriaworld.com/feature/publication/david-west/reparations.html (visited 25 October 2001).

139. See Ikelegbe, "Civil Society and Conflict," *supra* note 132, 463.

140. See section 2(1)(a)(iii) of that Act. See also *Assembly Watch* (a CRP newsletter) 6:1 (2000): 5–6.

141. See transcripts of interview with OA, 20 August 2001 (on file with the author).

142. *Newswatch*, 6 November 2000, on-line: http://allafrica.com/stories/200011060060.html (visited 20 February 2003).

143. See PRAWA, *Annual Reports* 1998 (Lagos: PRAWA, 1998), 30.

144. See http://www.nopa.net/Justice/messages/1.shtml (visited 16 May 2003).

145. See transcripts of interview with AC, 27 March 2000 (on file with the author).

146. Ibid.

147. Ibid.

148. For more on this issue, see O.C. Okafor and S.C. Agbakwa, "On Legalism, Popular Agency and 'Voices of Suffering': The Nigerian National Human Rights Commission in Context," *Human Rights Quarterly* 24 (2002): 662, 669–700 and 708.

149. See http://www.africaaction.org/adna/bpn0008.htm (visited 16 May 2003). See also *BBC News* 21 May 2002, on-line: http://news.bbc.co.uk/1/hi/world/africa/2000691.stm (visited: 20 February 2003); and "Truth Commissions Digital Collection," on line: http://www.usip.org/library/truth.html (visited 20 February 2003).

150. See http://www.truthfinder.go.kr/eng/r11.htm#Nigeria (visited 16 May 2003).

151. Ibid. See also *Liberty* (a CLO publication) 11:5 (1999): 5 6.

152. See *Constitutional Rights Journal* 10:36 (2000): 25.

153. Although the Panel's Report was been submitted to the Federal Government on 21 May 2002, it had not been officially published as at May 2005. See also http://news.bbc.co.uk/1/hi/world/africa/2000691.stm (visited 17 May 2005). However, electronic copies of the report have been published unofficially by a group of concerned citizens and activists. See http://www.nigerianmuse.com/nigeriawatch/oputa/?u=TheNews_prologue_oputa_report.htm (visited 24 May 2005).

154. See *Liberty* (a CLO publication) 11:5 (1999): 6.

155. This unit had been established some years ago. See Concluding Observations of the United Nations Committee on the Elimination of Racial Discrimination: Nigeria, A/48/18, 15 September 1993, on-line: http://www.unhchr.ch/tbs/doc.nsf/(Symbol)/A.48.18,paras.306-329.En?Opendocument (visited 17 May 2003).

156. See B. Ibhawoh, *Human Rights Organizations in Nigeria: An Appraisal Report on the Human Rights NGO Community in Nigeria* (Copenhagen, Denmark: The Danish Center for Human Rights, 2001), 37.

157. See HURILAWS, *Annual Report 1997-1998* (Lagos: HURILAWS, 1998), 11–13.

158. Ibid.

159. See also O. Oko, "Lawyers in Chains: Restrictions on Human Rights Advocacy under Nigeria's Military Regimes," *Harvard Human Rights Journal* 10 (1997): 257, 288.

160. See C. Nwankwo, "Human Rights and the Challenges of NGOs in Nigeria," in O.A. Obilade et al, eds., *Text for Human Rights Teaching in Schools* (Lagos: Constitutional Rights Project, 1999), 255, 261. Emphasis added.

161. See A. Ikelegbe, "The Perverse Manifestation of Civil Society: evidence from Nigeria" *Journal of Modern African Studies* 39 (2001): 1.

162. Ibid., 9. Emphasis added.

163. See H. Hershkoff and A. McCutcheon, "Public Interest Litigation: An International Perspective," in M. McClymont and S. Golub, eds., *Many Roads to Justice: The Law-Related Work of Ford Foundation Grantees around the World* (New York: The Ford Foundation, 2000), 283, 287.

164. See J.O. Ihonvbere, "Are Things Falling Apart? The Military and the Crisis of Democratization in Nigeria," *Journal of Modern African Studies* 34 (1996): 193, 204.

165. See transcripts of interview with FF, 25 August 2001 (on file with the author).

166. See transcripts of interview with OD, 25 May 2000 (on file with the author).

167. See R. Oyo, "Politics: Nigeria Forms the Largest Cabinet Since Independence," on-line: http://www.oneworld.org/ips2/july99/11_31_036.html (visited: 20 June 2003).

168. See J. Ezeilo, *Gender, Politics and the Law* (Enugu: WACOL, 1999), 15.

169. See CLO, *Annual Report 1994* (Lagos: CLO, 1994), 225–229. See also *Liberty* (a CLO publication) 6:3 (1995): 23.

170. See CLO, *Annual Report 1994*, ibid.

171. See *Liberty* (a CLO publication) 6:3 (1995): 20.

172. See B. Ibhawoh, *supra* note 156, 17.

173. See *Liberty* (a CLO publication) 12:6 (2000): 6.

174. See *The Post Express*, 11 September 1999, on-line: http://www.postexpresswired.com/postexpr...d1f15c78d3a85256824003796b1?openDocument (visited 9 November 1999).

175. See *Assembly Watch* (a CRP newsletter) 1:5 (2000): 10.

176. See *National Assembly Debates: Fourth Assembly, First Session—House of Representatives*, Official Report, vol. 3 no. 19, Thursday, 23 March 2000, 4.

177. See *National Assembly Debates: Fourth Assembly, First Session—The Senate*, Official Report, vol. 1 no. 10, Tuesday, 22 June 1999, 11, 32, 35, 39, and 57.

178. Ibid.

179. Ibid.

180. Ibid.

181. Ibid.

182. See *The Vanguard*, 20 October 1999, on-line: http://www.afbis.com/vanguard/n1220109.htm (visited 20 October 1999).

183. That military interventions "to save the polity" where once trendy in many African states is implicitly acknowledged by the African Commission in its *Resolution on the Military*, Eighth Annual Activity Report of the African Commission on Human and Peoples' Rights, 1994–1995, ACHPR/RPT/8th, Annex VII.

184. For instance, Bolaji Akinyemi, a one-time foreign minister of Nigeria, notably called on the military to overthrow the Shonekan-led civilian "interim government". The notorious General Sani Abacha had served as the Defense Minister of that government.

185. This conclusion is supported by the author's assessment of the nature of the entire postmilitary context in Nigeria, i.e., since May 1999, and especially by the huge public support for, and consequent success of, the efforts of the present civilian regime to purge the military of all the officers who had served in some political capacity during the long period of military rule in the country.

186. See Waltz, *supra* note 3. Emphasis added.

187. See W. Weinstein, "Human Rights and Development in Africa: Dilemmas and Options," *Daedalus* 112 (1983): 171.

188. Ibid.

189. On such NGO access to the African system, provided under the African Charter on Human Peoples' Rights and related documents, see S.B.O. Gutto, "Non-Governmental Organizations, People's Participation and the African Commission on Human and Peoples' Rights: Emerging Challenges to Regional Protection of Human Rights," in B. Andreassen and T. Swineheart , eds., *Human Rights in Developing Countries—Yearbook 1991* (Oslo: Scandinavian University Press, 1992), 33, 39–42.

190. See L.R. Helfer and A. Slaughter, "Toward a Theory of Effective Supranational Adjudication" *Yale Law Journal* 107 (1997): 273, 335. Emphasis added.

191. See M.A. Olz, "Non-Governmental Organizations in Regional Human Rights Systems," *Columbia Human Rights Law Review* 28 (1997): 307, 372.

192. See *Compilation of Decisions*, supra note 73. An analysis of the cases reported in this compilation supports this claim.

193. See *Constitutional Rights Journal* 9:32 (1999): 15.

194. *Supra* note 26.

195. See *CLO v. Nigeria*, Communication No.129/94, reproduced in *Compilation of Decisions*, *supra* note 73, 64.

196. See *CLO (in respect of the Nigerian Bar Association) v. Nigeria*, Communication No. 101/93, reproduced in *Compilation of Decisions*, *supra* note 73, 43.

197. See O. Agbakoba, "The Role of Lawyers in the Observance of Human Rights" *Journal of Human Rights Law and Practice* 5:1 (1995): 115, 135.

198. See transcripts of interview with OU, 23 April 2000 (on file with the author).

199. Ibid. See R. Murray, "Report on the 1996 Sessions of the African Commission on Human and Peoples' Rights," *Human Rights Law Journal* 18:1-4 (1997): 22.

200. Ibid.

201. See transcripts of interview with NJ, 22 May 2000 (on file with the author). Emphasis added.

202. See transcripts of interview with IS, 21 May 2000 (on file with the author).

203. See transcripts of interview with OD, 25 May 2000 (on file with the author).

204. See SERAC@WORK 2:2 (1998): 6.

205. Ibid.

206. See R. Murray, "Report on the 1996 Sessions of the African Commission on Human and Peoples' Rights: 19th and 20th Ordinary Sessions," *Human Rights Law Journal* 18:1-4 (1997): 16, 18.

207. Ibid.

208. Ibid.

209. See transcripts of interview with AS, 13 March 2000 (on file with the author).

210. An example of how the African system has worked actively to advance the agenda of these NGOs is the African commission's letter to the Nigerian military government (concerning the military's attempt to block the use of the African charter in Nigerian courts). In that letter, the commission declared to that regime that it "finds that the act of the Nigerian Government in nullifying the domestic effect of the [African] Charter constitutes an *affront* to the African Charter on Human and Peoples' Rights." See Letter from the African Commission, Ref. No. ACHPR/COMMU/AO44286, reproduced in *Liberty* (a CLO publication) 6:3 (1995): 16–17. Emphasis added.

211. See F.D. Gaer, "Reality Check: Human Rights Nongovernmental Organizations Confront Governments at the United Nations," *Third World Quarterly* 16 (1995): 389, 389–393.

212. Ibid., 393.
213. Ibid., 394.
214. See W. Korey, *NGOs and the Universal Declaration of Human Rights" "A Curious Grapevine"* (New York: St. Martin's Press, 1998), 9.
215. See *Constitutional Rights Journal* 7:23 (1997): 7, 9–11.
216. Ibid.
217. See SERAC@WORK 2:2 (1998): 3; and *Laser Contact* 2:3 (1998): 4, 5.
218. See SERAC@WORK 2:1 (1999): 1.
219. On the extent of the success of the Zambian prodemocracy struggle in the early 1990s, see J.O. Ihonbvere, *Economic Crisis, Civil Society, and Democratization: The Case of Zambia* (Trenton, NJ: Africa World Press, 1996).
220. On the South African human rights movement's extraordinary influence on the postapartheid state, see M. Mutua, "Hope and Despair for a New South Africa: the Limits of Right Discourse," *Harvard Human Rights Law Journal* 10 (1997): 63; and W. Korey, *NGOs and the Universal Declaration of Human Rights: "A Curious Grapevine"* (New York: St. Martin's Press, 1998).
221. See Agbese, *supra* note 2, 168.
222. See transcripts of interview with OA, 20 August 2001 (on file with the author).
223. See K. Nowrot, "Legal Consequences of Globalization: The Status of Non-Governmental Organizations Under International Law," *Global Legal Studies Journal* 6 (1999): 579; H. Cullen and K. Morrow, "International Civil Society in International Law: The Growth of NGO Participation," *Non-State Actors and International Law* 1 (2001): 7, 13; Korey, *supra* note 214, 291–292 and 545; and Y.K. Tyagi, "Cooperation Between the Human Rights Committee and Nongovernmental Organizations: Permissibility and Propositions," *Texas International Law Journal* 18 (1983): 273, 275.
224. See M.A. Cameron, B.W. Tomlin, and R.J. Lawson, eds., *To Walk without Fear: The Global Movement to Ban Land Mines* (Toronto: Oxford University Press, 1998).
225. See Keck and Sikkink, *supra* note 4, 1–16; and S.D. Burgerman, "Mobilizing Principles: The Role of Transnational Activists in Promoting Human Rights Principles," *Human Rights Quarterly* 20 (1998): 905, 913.

CHAPTER 7

LEGITIMIZATION CRISIS
A CRITICAL REFLECTION ON THE PHILOSOPHY, PRACTICE, AND POTENTIAL OF CONTEMPORARY HUMAN RIGHTS NGO ACTIVISM IN NIGERIA*

Human rights NGOs, especially those in the Third World, need to negotiate the dilemmas of legitimacy and autonomy.
—Upendra Baxi[1]

*There is no future for the human rights movement in Africa unless it can secure domestic, ideological, financial and moral support from interested [domestic] constituencies....*It is crucial that the movement be part of the people; *its leadership and aspirations must reflect the needs and perspectives of ordinary citizens...Otherwise, the human rights movement in Africa will remain marginal, homeless, detached, and ultimately ineffective.*
—Makau Mutua[2]

Throughout history, the protection of human rights has been won by struggle, and struggle requires mobilization. The process of mobilization validates the movement, *connecting it with the needs of the people and earning their commitment.*
—Chidi Odinkalu[3]

1. INTRODUCTION

As the above quotations clearly indicate, there has been some recognition, at least in a small section of the human rights literature, that many of the human rights NGO communities that exist in various African countries (and in other parts of the so-called third world) are beset by popular legitimization crises that have significantly impeded their development into *popularly legitimized* and therefore far more influential mass social movements.[4] Yet, only rarely have existing studies of these national NGO communities treated this subject in a detailed and comprehensive way.[5] To be sure, systematic studies that have arrived at analogous conclusions do exist in relation to other kinds of NGOs in Africa (such as development NGOs).[6] However, as analogous to human rights NGOs as these other kinds of activist groups can often be, viewed from a scholarly perspective, it is rather untenable to rely entirely on studies of these other types of NGOs when attempting to understand and explain the character of specific national human rights NGO communities. There is therefore a need for scholars to examine much more closely the overall character of particular national communities of human rights NGOs in order to provide a much more satisfactory evidentiary basis for the theoretical and conceptual conclusions that have often been reached with respect to these NGO communities.

It is precisely this kind of detailed and systematic analysis of the nature, structure, composition, geopolitical location, programs, impact, and limitations of Nigeria's NGO community[7] that has been offered in the foregoing chapters of this book. From the origins, general character, and the development of these NGOs to their composition, structure, and geopolitical location; from their programs, methods, and impact to their funding patterns, most of the important conceptual and institutional strengths of these NGOs have been located and analyzed. The conceptual and institutional problems that have stood in the way of the development of these NGOs into popularly legitimized (and therefore far more influential) mass social movements have also been painstakingly detailed, mapped, and analyzed.

What remains to be done at this point is to reflect on the nature and negative effects of the popular legitimization crisis that has afflicted these NGOs during the period under study and the existence of which is implied and foreshadowed in the foregoing chapters of this book. It is extremely important that the character of this crisis be clearly explained and understood since it has impaired considerably the development of these NGOs into much more powerful movements.

As such, the present chapter is devoted to a more in-depth consideration and explication of the various ways in which the very nature and conceptual orientation of most of these NGOs (that is, their composition, structure, geopolitical location, programming, methods, and funding orientation) have all too often functioned in ways that have alienated from the internal structures and processes of these NGOs, the very masses of vulnerable and abused Nigerians whose interests these groups want to advance. The chapter also attempts to show that this state of affairs has helped in no small measure to foster and to maintain a (low-intensity) popular legitimization crisis within this NGO community—one that has greatly impeded its capacity to attract the level of popular validation and widespread allegiance that would guarantee it the kind of influence within the Nigerian polity that it does require, if it is to attain its objectives in much larger measure. The claim that is being made in this chapter is *not* of course that any one of the many problems that afflicts this NGO community is entirely responsible for the generation or continuance of this popular legitimization crisis. The claim is that each of these problems (conceptual or institutional they may be) has contributed in some significant way to the generation and continuance of this crisis.

To this end, this chapter is organized into four segments, including this introductory section. In section 2, I attempt to explain more closely the linkages that are observable among certain *conceptual* problems that afflict the operations of these NGOs and the emergence and persistence of the popular legitimization crisis that has been referred to already. Section 3, attempts to explain in similar fashion the linkages that are evident among certain of the *institutional* problems that most of these NGOs face and the popular legitimization crisis that afflicts them as a community. Section 4 concludes the chapter by doing a number of related things. First, an analytical overview of the precise character of the popular legitimization crisis that afflicts these NGOs is offered. The second segment of the section then broaches the point (which for brevity's sake cannot be treated in detail in the present book) that the above-mentioned argument might be much strengthened and reinforced by comparing these NGOs to the far more grassroots-oriented and considerably more influential faith-based groups, labor unions, and hometown development associations that dot Nigeria's civil society landscape. And third, the last segment of the section suggests that, despite the challenging contingencies involved, the same effect might be achievable by comparing these NGOs to two demonstrably more successful human rights movements in other parts of the African continent, namely, the African National Congress (ANC) in apartheid South Africa and the Movement for Multi-Party Democracy (MMD) in Kenneth Kaunda's Zambia.

2. THE CONTRIBUTION OF CERTAIN CONCEPTUAL PROBLEMS TO THE LEGITIMIZATION CRISIS

The important conceptual problems that most of these NGOs have tended to grapple with have already been documented in some detail in a number of the preceding chapters. Consequently, that exercise will not be repeated here. What will be done though is to attempt to explain more closely and exactly the ways in which each specific conceptual problem has contributed to the popular legitimization crisis that continues to afflict this NGO community.

2.1. THE SOCIAL/ECONOMIC RIGHTS DEFICIT

As discussed in some previous chapters, these NGOs have traditionally tended to neglect and marginalize social/economic rights activism as a form of the human rights struggle. The work of the vast majority of these NGOs have tended to be civil/political rights-centered in its orientation.[8] Indeed, it was not until much later in the history of these NGOs that social/economic rights got on the agenda of the established NGOs in a significant (if still marginal) way. It was also at this later point in time that self-described *social/economic rights NGOs* emerged in Nigeria.[9]

As was demonstrated in a number of previous chapters, this historical neglect stemmed in part from the dominant conceptual orientation among the leadership of this NGO community. Most of these senior activists have been, relatively speaking, elite and urbanized. Most have been lawyers and/or journalists whose main interests and activities tended to be more affected by infringements of civil rights than by infringements of social and economic rights. As was also shown in previous chapters, this situation also reflected the priorities of the foreign donors on whom these NGOs were dependent for almost all of their income and resources. In any case, as has been shown before already, this tendency to marginalize social/economic rights activism has never been peculiar to the Nigerian human rights scene. At the very least, the Nigerian experience has always paralleled the age-old marginalization of social/economic rights struggles by the international human rights movement.[10] To be sure, a few NGOs, like the MOSOP, the SRI, the SERAC, and the EMPARC, have always tended to treat social/economic rights struggles as priorities. But these NGOs emerged later on in the history of this NGO community and even then still constitute a small minority among their peers.

Given the unprecedented and very rapid increase in the impoverishment and economic vulnerability of the vast majority of Nigerians over the exact same period during which the NGOs that concern us here emerged, the widespread marginalization of socioeconomic rights activism by the vast majority of these NGOs is a most curious and troubling fact. It is clearly inferable from the near-exclusive nature of their focus on "civil/political rights" during this period that the vast majority of these NGOs could not really be said to have been as deeply connected to the "voices of suffering" of most Nigerians as they ought to have been. Had they been so connected, they would have treated social/economic rights activism as a priority. The fact that they did not is therefore clear evidence of the existence of a considerable level of discordance, at least during this period, between their agenda-setting and program-design processes (on the one hand) and the obvious priorities of most Nigerians (on the other hand). This gulf in priorities threatened to render most members of this NGO community irrelevant to the most pressing needs and aspirations of the vast majority of Nigerians. One consequence of this disconnection was that the capacity of these NGOs to validate their organizations among Nigeria's vast economic underclass; to deeply integrate themselves within the fabric of Nigerian society; and to acquire the kind of widespread allegiance within the community that would have enabled them exert much more influence, remained largely underdeveloped.

It may of course be argued in objection to this argument that since military rule did contribute in no small measure to the economic difficulties that most Nigerians began to experience from the mid-1980s, many of these NGOs had correctly perceived their struggle against military rule as the most important priority to be pursued, and that they were right to do so with a single-minded focus. However, such an objection would not stand up to closer scrutiny since military rule was hardly the only factor that gave rise to these economic difficulties. The global crash of the price of oil—Nigeria's main source of income—and the implementation of an ill thought out and

devastating World Bank-imposed structural adjustment program (SAP) contributed a lot more to the emergence of this severe economic climate in
Nigeria.[11] After all, was it not this same military class that had (in the 1970s
and early 1980s) presided over Nigeria's only era of massive economic boom?
As such, the struggle against military rule could only have been one part of
the broader struggle for socioeconomic rights in Nigeria.

In any case, the argument that is being made is not that these NGOs
ought to have abandoned their heroic struggle to end military rule in Nigeria.
Rather, the point is that had their internal program design processes been
more attuned and sensitive to the voices of the ordinary members of the
communities in which they worked, most of these NGOs would have had
little choice but to accord some priority to social/economic rights at a time
when millions of vulnerable and abused Nigerians (whose interests they want
to protect) were, more than ever before in the country's history, very visibly
concerned with their ability to afford their most basic needs: food, shelter,
clothing, education, and the like. Their distance from the voices of the vast
majority of Nigerians led most of these NGOs to marginalize economic and
social rights activism, and as such limit their own capacity to attract the widespread allegiance of Nigerians. This in turn severely limited their capacity to
markedly exert pressure on the government.

2.2. THE MARGINALIZATION OF GENDER ISSUES

As has been noted in chapter 2, while the genealogy of women's rights
activism in Nigeria is a very long and rich one, it was not until much more
recently that self-described women's rights NGOs emerged as a force to be
reckoned with within Nigeria's human rights NGO community. As noted in
chapter 4, prior to this era, the NGOs that constituted this community had
tended to marginalize women's issues and gender perspectives. Again, this has
not been a peculiarly Nigerian phenomenon. The international human rights
movement had until fairly recently also failed to give violations of women's
rights the attention it deserved.[12]

Of course, this is not to argue that all of the mainstream NGOs in Nigeria
had completely ignored women's rights issues. Even before the emergence,
in the mid to late 1990s, of women's NGOs such as BAOBAB, WACOL,
and WRAPA, some of the traditional civil/political rights NGOs such as the
CLO had established their own women's rights programs. However, even
at this time, women's rights activism had remained marginal to the overall
agenda of this NGO community. The struggle to end military rule was, at
this juncture, the consuming passion of most of these NGOs.

Given the fact that women make up roughly half of Nigeria's population
and, more importantly, the fact that they make up the greater percentage of
the most vulnerable and abused segment of Nigeria's population, the relative
marginalization of women's rights activism by most of these NGOs has in
practical terms meant that these NGOs did miss an opportunity to connect
with, and to validate themselves among, a huge and particularly vulnerable

segment of the Nigerian population. Had they seized this opportunity, these NGOs would have been able to greatly enhance their popular appeal. This would be so since their agenda would have resonated more readily with a greater percentage of the poor and vulnerable in Nigeria. At the very least, although now less so, the marginalization of women's issues by most of these NGOs, has impeded their own capacity to attract the widespread allegiance of the vast majority of Nigerian women. In this way has this conceptual orientation of the dominant NGO praxis been a significant limitation to this NGO community's development into a popularly validated movement that is thus able to command much more influence within the polity.

2.3. THE MARGINALIZATION OF MINORITY/ENVIRON-MENTAL RIGHTS ACTIVISM

As has been shown in chapter 2, despite the long and rich history of minority rights agitation in colonial and postcolonial Nigeria, and despite the establishment in the 1990s of community based minority/environmental NGOs such as MOSOP, it was not until more recently that minority/environmental rights activism gained currency within the NGO community in Nigeria. As noted in chapter 4, most of these NGOs have traditionally failed to accord a pride of place to minority/environmental rights activism. With the exception of a few organizations such as MOSOP and ERA, these NGOs have not tended to adopt this kind of struggle as their central focus. To be sure, some of the mainstream NGOs like the CLO did at one time or the other establish their own "Niger Delta Projects" (reflecting the domination of this area of human rights activism by the concerns of Niger Delta communities). What is more, these mainstream NGOs have since done some important work regarding the minority/environmental rights problems that have troubled that extremely important region of Nigeria. However, the bulk of the work on minority/environmental rights issues in Nigeria continues to be done by a few minority/environmental rights NGOs such as MOSOP and ERA. As such, these issues have remained relatively marginal to the agenda of the mainstream civil/political rights groups that constitute the bulk of this NGO community.

Given the centrality of the enjoyment of minority/environmental rights in the oil-rich Niger Delta area (and beyond) to the well-being of all Nigerians, one would have expected that most of these NGOs (especially the generalist ones) would have historically accorded a pride of place to this aspect of human rights activism. The contrary is of course true. Again, given Nigeria's historical experience as a state that agglomerates hundreds of pre-existing polities that had been hastily thrown together into one political container by a colonial power, and given the long history of minority struggles in the Niger Delta and in other regions of Nigeria, one would have expected these NGOs to have focused more of their attention to this type of work. Here again, the contrary is true.

At a minimum, this is another example of the way in which a partial conceptual deficit or blind spot in the orientation of this NGO community has produced an important gap between this activist community and the needs and yearnings of a very large percentage of the members of the population at large. This gap has impeded the capacity of these NGOs to attract widespread commitment and allegiance even among the ranks of the abused people it wants to protect. This has in turn negatively impacted on the capacity of these NGOs to optimize their influence within the polity.

2.4. THE NEGLECT OF POSITIVE LOCAL CULTURE

As has been argued at the end of chapter 4, the agendas, programs, and methods of these NGOs have been almost entirely lacking in attentiveness and sensitivity to the need to research, understand, mobilize, and deploy those aspects of each of Nigeria's various cultures that support or enhance the content and language of their human rights catechism. For instance, to the best of this authors' knowledge, of the hundreds of human rights reports and publications that these NGOs have issued, and the hundreds of seminars and workshops that they have conducted, not a single one has been devoted in whole or in part to this question. This parallels a similar historical tendency within the larger international human rights movement in which African culture tends to be seen almost exclusively as a source of human rights violations and almost never as a source of the norms that can ground a human rights renaissance on the continent.[13]

In tending to tow this sort of line, these Nigerian NGOs have missed yet another easily available step on the route to their own popular legitimization. Had these NGOs attempted to study and understand the various local cultures in Nigeria, with a view to gleaning those aspects of these cultural systems that support their human rights work, they would be in a much better position today to understand and speak the various languages of human dignity that are widely and continually spoken by most ordinary Nigerians—languages that form part of a rich, long, and continuous tradition of struggle against violations of human rights.[14] They would thus have been in a much better position to truly hear and be heard by these masses of ordinary Nigerians. This would have helped to validate these NGOs at the grassroots and would have increased their chances of securing widespread commitment among ordinary Nigerians, especially the majority rural population. Without such widespread allegiance, they have been hard put to optimize their influence within the polity.

2.5. SCANT ATTENTION TO THE EXTERNAL SOURCES OF HUMAN RIGHTS VIOLATIONS IN NIGERIA

As already explained in chapter 4, unlike their counterparts in the Nigerian labor movement, these NGOs have tended to ignore or downplay the complicity of certain foreign actors (such as certain states, a number of multinational corporations, the IMF and the World Bank) in the production of many of the human rights violations that these NGOs work to redress.[15] The obvious exceptions are the social/economic rights NGOs like the EMPARC, the SERAC, and the SRI. For instance, SERAC has impugned the World Bank's conduct in its Lagos slum development project.[16] Similarly worthy of note is the fact that the MOSOP has directed a considerable portion of its resistance against the activities within Ogoniland of Shell Petroleum (a multinational corporation).

Since the abuses that are *not* attributable to foreign actors are numerous and frequent enough to attract most of the attention of these NGOs, and since many of these same foreign actors (especially governments) are the principal financial benefactors of these NGOs, this marginalization of activism directed against the foreign sources of violations in Nigeria is hardly surprising. For example, it would be impolitic (and for most activists impracticable) for any of these NGOs to focus a substantial portion of its efforts on criticizing a certain foreign actor's complicity in the decimation of social programs in Nigeria (through its insistence on certain economic policies) at the very same time as it approaches that regime's embassy in Nigeria for much-needed funding. It is one thing to criticize the much-pilloried foreign multinational oil corporations on which NGOs are not really dependent for funding, but it is another thing for these NGOs to, as it were, bite the fingers that feed them!

However, given the serious consequences of the activities of many foreign actors in many of the human rights violations that have occurred in Nigeria, it is still troubling that these NGOs do not pay more attention to it.[17] What is more, it is increasingly the case that the framework governance of Nigeria (and of most other third world countries) has all but been seized by foreign entities such as the World Bank, IMF, and the G-8 countries.[18] In any case, this failure to center the complicity of these external sources in many of the human rights violations that have occurred in Nigeria has too often left a gaping hole in attempts to explain the nature of these violations to discerning Nigerians. The impression of insincerity or naivetté is created when such inadequate explanations are offered and when concomitantly unworkable *local* struggles are waged. Such doubts certainly complicate and extend the process of popular validation that these NGOs must undergo if they are to become more influential within the polity.

3. THE CONTRIBUTION OF CERTAIN INSTITUTIONAL PROBLEMS TO THE LEGITIMIZATION CRISIS

Most of the important institutional problems that afflict the vast majority of these NGOs have already been noted and documented in some detail in previous chapters – especially in chapters 2, 3, and 5. This section of the present chapter is thus devoted to explaining more closely how exactly each of these institutional problems has contributed to the emergence and maintenance of the popular legitimization crisis that continues to afflict these NGOs.[19]

3.1. EXCESSIVE FRAGMENTATION AND COMPETITION

As was demonstrated in previous chapters, like its counterparts elsewhere,[20] this ever-burgeoning NGO community has benefited, as well as suffered, from the fragmentation and rivalries that have characterized much of its developmental history. Beginning with the exit of the leader of the Constitutional Rights Project (CRP) from the CLO in 1990, many senior activists have departed from the CLO (and other such organizations) and formed autonomous organizations of *their own*. While the formation of more and more separate and smaller NGOs by more and more activists has had its positive aspects, it has not been altogether a commendable phenomenon.[21]

In some cases, the creation of these separate organizations was at least justifiable on the basis that the CLO and other such "parent" NGOs had marginalized social/economic rights, women's rights, and minority/environmental rights and had favored excessively the promotion and protection of civil/political rights. Where such conceptual difficulties have animated the onset of fragmentation within this NGO community, such fragmentation has seemed understandable. This was, for example, partly the case with the emergence of the SRI, the SERAC, the EMPARC, and some of the gender-focused NGOs.

In other cases, it was the personal dissatisfaction of particular activists with the goings-on in the parent organization that led them to found their own autonomous NGOs, thus increasing the level of fragmentation within this NGO community.

Valid as these reasons often are, given the fact that all too often the emergent NGOs end up doing exactly the same things as the parent NGO, and end up competing for the very same pots of funding with the parent NGO, such fragmentation is more often than not still perplexing. This type of fragmentation can often divert some of the scarce human and financial resources within these NGOs to unnecessary competition for the same grants. It is in such cases that it would be appropriate to describe the NGO fragmentation that occurred, and the ensuing competition, as *excessive*.

What is more, the excessiveness of this fragmentation and competition often leaves many observers with the impression that some activists are insincere and are more concerned about establishing and controlling their own NGOs (a form of careerism) than in the corporate success of the NGO community as a whole.[22] Clearly, regardless of its validity, this kind of negative impression concerning the sincerity of at least some activists must surely impede the ability of these NGOs to fire the mass imagination and foster the requisite widespread allegiance. Yet without a high level of mass mobilization and popular appeal, the popular legitimization of these NGOs would remain an uphill struggle. And without acquiring a high degree of popular legitimization, these NGOs can only continue to exert a very modest level of influence within the country. Happily, this imperative is gaining in recognition, albeit rather slowly, among Nigerian human rights activists themselves. For example, one prominent activist has recently warned that this NGO community must:

> .... quickly recover from marginalization and *fragmentation* and remobilize ourselves and resume our social advocacy campaign with vigor comparable or stronger than during the democratic transition.[23]

3.2. THE "OGA-SHIP" SYNDROME[24]

A related problem is the phenomenon of "Oga-ship". As has been discussed above, when an activist leaves a parent NGO to found her or his own organization, there is all too often no *obvious* good reason for the fragmentation that occurred. The strong impression is often left in the minds of observers that the activist simply craves a much higher degree of personal autonomy. Moreover, as has been made clear in chapter 3, in many such cases, the new NGO ends up becoming much less institutionalized and much more driven by the "personal rule" of one powerful boss (or Oga) than is the case with its parent NGO. This has certainly been the case for many (but not all) of the NGOs that were formed by former CLO activists.

This tendency for separate NGOs to be formed from existing ones for no obvious good reason and in spite of the increased competition for funds that is entailed has led to a widespread perception (at least among highly influential opinion makers in Nigeria) that the real reason for the formation of these new NGOs from the old ones is the oga-ship ambitions and desires of many of the leader(s) of the new organizations who, having cut their teeth dutifully serving the older "ogas", now want to control directly their own portion of the pot of funds available to support the NGO community.[25] In Ikelegbe's perhaps more directly articulated view, these NGOs "have proliferated because of crass opportunism in the competition for donor funds."[26] The question that is therefore entailed is: autonomous control of such donor funds to what ends?

Whatever the answer, as many NGOs themselves have acknowledged, this tendency for NGOs to proliferate in the course of their competition for donor funds has affected negatively their credibility in the wider Nigerian community and has consequently impeded their drive to achieve popular legitimization in Nigeria. For instance, it is disturbing to realize that many Nigerian journalists – an important group of opinion molders – have tended to portray these NGO activists as financial opportunists and profiteers! As the CRP has reported, at a 1998 seminar organized for the media by these NGOs, "the cold war between the Nigerian media and the NGOs became more manifest and public knowledge."[27] At this seminar, many of these journalists openly expressed their perception of NGO activists as preoccupied with jostling for foreign funds for their organizations, funds that, in the view of these journalists usually find their way into the pockets of individuals. It was for this reason that these journalists justified their own claims to be given "the opportunity to share in the loot!" Given the prevalence of this kind of perception among the very same journalists who help to shape the views of the general public, the credibility of these NGOs could not but have suffered a sizeable dent. Even more worrying, from the point of view of the credibility of these NGOs, is the fact that (believing that this was in fact a potent weapon) successive Nigerian governments have tended to take advantage of the presence of this kind of negative perception among the general public as a way of delegitimizing and defusing NGO challenges to their policies and actions.[28]

3.3. EXCESSIVE DEPENDENCE ON FOREIGN FUNDING

The point has already been made in chapter 5 that the understandable but nevertheless problematic overdependence of most of these NGOs on foreign donor funding has on the balance provided a real disincentive for virtually all of them to undertake the imperative but difficult task of cultivating the local population for memberships and resources. It was also shown that partly as a result of their foreign donor-facing orientation these NGO have for the most part not achieved the imperative goal of incorporating into their internal processes the views and even votes of the very peoples and communities whose interests they seek to advance.[29] Most of these NGOs have not even begun to take this task as seriously as they ought to.

Given the obvious fact that mass mobilization is a precondition for securing the high level of popular support that these NGOs do seek, and do most certainly need, in order to optimize their influence within the polity, the fact that the vast majority of these NGOs have often neglected or *not treated seriously enough* the task of canvassing the ranks of ordinary Nigerians in search of memberships and resources is highly problematic. Though this attitude is not of course peculiar to these Nigerian NGOs[30], the neglect of the admittedly difficult task of grassroots mobilization has reduced quite appreciably their capacity to generate the kind of widespread allegiance that they require if they are to optimize their influence on both Nigeria's domestic governance institutions and the body politic itself. This attitude has thus contributed quite significantly to the popular legitimization crisis that these NGOs face today. How can these NGOs be motivated to confront the very difficult task of mobilizing the local population effectively when their dependence on foreign funding provides a strong disincentive to such activity?

What is more, given the widespread skepticism that exists within the body politic, at least among those who primarily shape public perceptions and opinions[31] (and even within the NGO community itself),[32] regarding the sincerity of a significant number of activists, these NGOs already face a difficult journey toward their popular legitimization. The difficulty of the task ahead can be deciphered from an essay that was recently published by Edwin Madunagu - one of Nigeria's most notable social commentators. This

220 Legitimizing Human Rights NGOs: Lessons from Nigeria

passage is so important to achieving an understanding of the extent of the popular legitimization crisis that faces these NGO as to deserve extensive reproduction here. According to Madunagu:

> In Nigeria, the public perception of the NGO industry can be put this way: some white people (*oyibos*) in distant lands, out of sympathy for our material and spiritual suffering or to achieve some aims which are not clear but which no one should in fact bother himself or herself about, send dollars to some people in Nigeria. As demanded by the *oyibos*, these lucky Nigerians then put up organizations which they give funny names like the "Friends and Saviors of the Poor Collective" (for material sustenance) or the "Re-awakened Soldiers of God Incorporated" (for spiritual deliverance). But these organizations are mere clothings [sic] for individuals, or are controlled absolutely and without account-ability by them, which is the same thing. There is nothing one can do about this, and it is, in fact, counter-productive to even attempt to do anything about it as this may result in unintended self-exclusion. What is important is to try to get one's own share of this free money, this *oyibo* money. What of the programs that the "owners" of the NGOs claim to be executing and for which, ostensibly, money is sent by the *oyibos*? The dominant public per-ception is that these programs are essentially fake: They are, at best, profit-yielding undertakings (for the owners), and at worst, mere devices for "chopping" *oyibo* money. *I submit that this public perception is essentially correct. Of course, there are exceptions, but these constitute a very small minority.* What is the perception of NGO workers, the employees in NGOs and their programs? The domi-nant belief in this sector is that the NGO owners together with the "consultants" and "resource persons" they employ, "chop" a large fraction of the *oyibo* money meant for them as workers and deny them their own share of the "profit" accruing from the execution of the advertised programs. More directly, although the workers accept that their employers are non-governmental, they dismiss the "non-profit" claim as mere propaganda.[33]

If Madunagu's assessment is correct – and there is some evidence to suggest that it is not *altogether* inaccurate - then Kathryn Sikkink's generic assumption that "[a]ctivists join NGOs because they believe strongly in the principles of the organizations, *not because of any tangible benefits that they receive from membership*"[34] is not entirely applicable to the NGO scene in Nigeria. To be sure, the majority of Nigerian activists are motivated to varying extents by the principles of the organizations to which they belong. However, far too many of them have been motivated at the very same time by what, Chidi Odinkalu, a senior Nigerian activist, has referred to as the relatively comfort-able, privileged, and visible "lifestyle" of the top leadership (or owners) of these NGOs, a lifestyle that, as Odinkalu has noted, progressively distances too many of these leaders from a life of struggle.[35] Indeed, Odinkalu was even more explicit on this point when he declared pointedly that within many of these NGOs:

> Local problems are only defined as potential pots of project cash, not as human experiences to be resolved in just terms, thereby delegitimizing human rights language and robbing its ideas of popular appeal.[36]

While this may be a strong phrasing of the problem, there is obviously some merit in Odinkalu's conclusions. As such, it is no wonder that this NGO community has not as yet fulfilled its real potential to enjoy widespread allegiance among ordinary Nigerians.

3.4. A DEMOCRATIC DEFICIT

In chapter 3, it was shown in some detail how only very few of these NGOs have a significant membership base.[37] Most of these NGOs are in effect "personally" run by a core management team that is led by a founder/ CEO who is widely regarded as the "owner" of the organization.[38] As such, the vast majority of these NGOs are not accountable *at all* to any local constituency made up of Nigerians. Their accounting responsibilities are in almost all cases owed to the foreign entities that fund their projects.[39] As such, and since most of these NGOs are nonmember organizations, Peter Spiro's generic observation regarding the stranglehold of such foreign donors on the activities of NGOs is apposite. According to him:

> Non-member groups are kept on a tighter leash by sophisticated funders (especially foundations), nor can they wave around membership rolls by way of attempting to enhance their influence. If a non-membership group does not show results *or follow a funder's directive*, discipline can be swift and effective.[40]

This is a picture of local exclusion and foreign domination that reveals just how removed from the local population many of these NGOs tend to be: no real *local* membership base and virtually no accountability to any *local* constituency.[41]

Not surprisingly, this kind of funder imposed market discipline has also affected the behavior of other NGOs around the world NGOs. As William Korey has observed:

> What had prompted the shift [within Amnesty International] from an emphasis on research to an emphasis upon campaigning.... *was pressure from the largest sections of Amnesty, who also provided the largest amount of funding. The U.S. section...was the largest single source of funds and exerted "the biggest clout"*. From the perspective of the U.S. section, confronted as it was by a dynamic and aggressive Human Rights Watch organization, Amnesty had to be equally dynamic

and quick in releasing reports. If research had to be made secondary, so be it.[42]

Clearly, the fact that such pressure for conformity can profoundly affect
a powerful Western NGO such as Amnesty International is indicative of the
extent to which such pressure constrains the behavior of the much weaker
Nigerian NGOs. The real effect of such donor-imposed market discipline has
been that the possible space for local democratic participation in the internal
decision-making processes of these organizations has been quite narrow.

As such, a democratic deficit exists in the internal processes of these
NGOs. Already strongly circumscribed by foreign donor pressures, and
lacking a real membership base drawn from the wider community, the agendas
of most of these NGOs tend not to be formulated with appreciable local
community involvement and participation.[43] Rather, as has been argued, the
priorities of the donors that fund these NGOs tend to have a huge influence
on the nature of the agendas pursued by them. Similarly, other organizational
decisions are not made in a way that renders the given NGO even minimally
accountable to, at the very least, a small segment of the local community in
which it works. As such, Wapner's general claim that "NGOs are accountable
to their members" is largely inapplicable to the human rights NGO scene in
Nigeria, where virtually all NGOs lack any kind of membership base.[44]

This democratic deficit has helped create some distance between the
agenda priorities of these NGOs and the needs of the most vulnerable
Nigerians.[45] For example, the early focus of most of these NGOs on civil/
political rights at a time when Nigerians were beginning to experience the
worst crisis of economic and social rights in their history of independent
statehood is attributable in part to the existence of this democratic deficit.
Given the fact that most of these NGOs exclude from their ranks and decision-making processes the very ordinary Nigerians that they want to protect,
the existence of this kind of distance between the agenda of most of these
NGOs and the palpable yearnings of the bulk of Nigeria's underclass should
not surprise most discerning observers. For, as Gutto has argued, has not the
involvement of the people in rights struggles been central in giving *appropriate
content* to such struggles?[46]

This democratic deficit has also helped exacerbate the popular legitimization crisis that afflicts this NGO community. Without immersing themselves
among the Nigerian people (by massively including within their ranks an
active cadre of members who are drawn from the wider community) without
actively canvassing the local community for members, resources, and programming direction, a communication gap is created between these NGOs
and the ordinary Nigerians whose widespread support they must attract if
they are to optimize their influence within Nigeria.

That similar issues regarding the democratic accountability of such NGOs
are being raised with respect to other NGO communities is illustrated by a
passage from Paul Wapner's recent essay on the subject. In his own words:

[We have]…to ask difficult questions about NGOs: Who elects them? Who appoints them as spokespersons for the world society? To the degree that NGOs seem like conveyors of the global civic-mindedness, on what basis do they purport to understand, let alone embody, the global public interest? Behind these questions sits the issue of accountability. *When we think about political actors and even political structures, we almost always wonder about their legitimacy, and this often rests on their being answerable to a broad-based constituency.* Criticism about NGOs turns largely on the same concern. To whom are NGOs accountable? On what basis should we treat them as legitimate political actors?[47]

If, as has been argued, NGOs in Nigeria are largely accountable to their foreign donors, and owe little accountability to the local population, then this ought to be a source of serious worry for those concerned with democratizing and making more effective the human rights struggle in Nigeria. For, as Kofi Quashigah has observed, "aid of whatever nature from the developed countries is never altogether given out of altruism".[48] Foreign donors, be they governmental or nongovernmental agents, always have an agenda of their own to pursue, and will inevitably bring pressure to bear on the beneficiaries of their funds to conform with, or help advance, those objectives.[49]

3.5. ELITISM AND URBAN BIAS

As has been discussed in previous chapters, the NGO community in Nigeria is dominated (though not exclusively populated) by a cadre of very highly educated, legally trained, and largely urbanized, activists. The vast majority of these NGOs are also located within the Lagos geographical axis. It is thus, in Nigerian terms, a quintessentially elite community. What is more, despite the efforts of a few of these organizations to reach beyond their Lagos-centered and urban-focused orientation, the activities of these NGOs have also tended to be concentrated in the urban areas of the country, largely to the exclusion of Nigeria's majority rural population. This kind of NGO elitism is of course not an exclusively Nigerian phenomenon. Susan Phillips has, for instance, concluded that most NGOs in Africa (foreign or domestic) are elitist in orientation.[50]

Quite obviously, the excessiveness of the elite and urban-facing nature of the NGO community in Nigeria—its effective exclusion of the vast majority of ordinary Nigerians—has severely limited its capacity to canvass for and enjoy the unalloyed allegiance of most Nigerians.[51] This has in turn impeded this NGO community's capacity to acquire the high level of popular legitimization that is imperative for it to optimize its influence within Nigeria. Whatever the advantages that elitism has conferred on other NGO communities in other places,[52] on the balance, it has been an obstacle to the evolution of Nigeria's NGO community into a popular and, therefore, much more influential movement.

4. OVERALL ASSESSMENT: UNDERSTANDING THE POPULAR LEGITIMIZATION CRISIS WITHIN THE NIGERIAN NGO COMMUNITY

From the foregoing analytical exposé, it is fairly clear that the NGO community in Nigeria does indeed face a popular legitimization crisis, i.e., in the sense that its dominant institutional and conceptual orientation has not allowed it to secure the kind of widespread validation and allegiance that is imperative for its popular legitimization within Nigeria (as opposed to its popularity among foreign donors). As a result, this otherwise dynamic NGO community has remained mostly incapable of fulfilling its very real potential of becoming a much more influential movement. It has thus been unable to close the wide gap between its modest attainments and tremendous potential.

While, as has just been demonstrated, a number of factors combine to explain the existence and character of this crisis, one of the most important factors seems to have stemmed from the structural pressures placed on these NGOs by the demands of the political economy in which they have had to work. This NGO community has from its very beginnings faced tremendous structural pressures to become more and more donor friendly and foreign facing in its institutional and conceptual orientation.[53] Thus, one of the most difficult challenges that this NGO community has confronted has been to find ways to legitimize itself within a Nigerian polity from which its does not receive significant funding, at the very same time as it struggles to remain attractive to the foreign donors on whom it is dependent for its vital financial needs.[54] For example, how is this NGO community to determine the nature of its agenda: by reference to the expressed or perceived priorities of the Nigerian people on whose behalf it supposedly works, or in accordance with the expressed or perceived priorities of vital foreign donors? These two priorities do not always coincide. If it chooses to respect the expressed priorities of the Nigerian people, how is this NGO community to fund its work when it is so much more difficult to raise vital funds from relatively scarcer local sources? In the end, this NGO community has almost always preferred to orient itself in ways that would ensure the continued flow to its coffers of the foreign funding that has been its life sap.

Partly as a result of the donor-oriented outlook that this NGO community has tended to exhibit, it has had very little incentive to focus its attention on the far more demanding (but legitimacy-conferring) tasks of raising much more of their funds locally. It has also lacked the incentive to cultivate a significant membership base, democratize its internal decision-making processes, and become much more attentive to the needs of the rural dwellers that constitute the vast majority of Nigeria's population. This NGO community has thus tended to lean away from treading the paths that would normally lead to its popular validation and legitimization and therefore to its acquisition of much greater influence within Nigeria. In this sense is the NGO community in Nigeria very similar in orientation to similar groups that operate elsewhere in Africa. As Nelson Kasfir has observed:

> With notable exceptions, the African organizations specified by conventional civil society notions [including human rights NGOs] are new, *lack social roots*, have objectives unrelated to ongoing political conflicts and are heavily financed by outside donors.[55]

Ihonvbere's work confirms Kasfir's conclusions. According to Ihonvbere:

> Africa's pro-democracy movements [including most human rights NGOs] and new political parties have devoted a lot of time to winning support and legitimacy abroad. True, in some way, this is merely an attempt to capitalize on the character of the new global order. It also reflects a search for necessary funds to operate internally....[but] the search for foreign exchange to set up their political and other declared and undeclared agendas has turned some of the pro-democracy movements into appendages of international funding agencies. The effect of such alignments on the originality, creativity, autonomy and effectiveness of new governments is *damaging*. Yet many movements are unable to mobilize their members, generate resources through membership drives, or persuade patriotic and pro-democratic elites to fund their activities at home."[56]

The Nigerian NGO community's inability to optimize its influence is of course *not* entirely attributable to the relative ease with which it has accessed foreign funding. Other factors such as the mainstream ideological orientation of the bulk of leadership of these NGOs; the elite character of most of its cadres; the grave dangers involved in openly challenging military regimes; and the drive of far too many activists to set up their own mini NGOs have all combined with the "funding incentive factor" to shape this NGO community into an elite-based and foreign-facing (rather than mass-based and popular) social institution. This has in the end impeded its development into a popular movement that can count on the widespread allegiance and commitment of the bulk of the Nigerian people. In this way has the capacity of this NGO community to wield real power within the Nigerian polity been severely constrained.

This gap between the modest achievements of this NGO community and its real potential to become a popular, and therefore far more influential, local actor is further illustrated by briefly comparing this NGO community to certain other types of activist groups. In this case, comparisons to the hometown development associations and labor movements that have exerted tremendous impact in Nigeria; to African church groups; and to two similar movements that have actually been voted into power in other African countries will suffice. Of course, an in-depth examination of the impact that these other groups have had in their respective target societies is well beyond the scope of this book.

So is a detailed comparison of these other groups to the NGO community in Nigeria. Only a cursory illustrative comparison is attempted here.

Regarding the impact of Nigeria's hometown voluntary associations, I agree with Joel Barkan *et al* that:

> A host of private and voluntary associations have historically had a *profound impact* upon individual and collective behavior in both rural and urban Africa. [These organizations] not only provide links between the state and societal interests, but also perform an important mediating role whereby the macro-policy objectives of the state and the particularistic interests of society's groups are adjusted to each other by a process of bargaining.[57]

As Barkan and others have also shown such groups have often transformed the standard of living of their target rural (and even urban) communities.[58] They almost always command far more grassroots loyalty and allegiance and wield much more power than the NGO community. These associations have had such a tremendous level of impact in Nigeria largely because of what can be referred to as their mass social movement character,[59] i.e., their nature as grassroots, member-oriented, democratically-run, and (mostly) locally-funded organizations that are largely in tune with the yearnings and priorities of their target populations.[60] It is of course obvious that these key characteristics are exactly those that tend to be absent in the character of most of the entities that constitute the NGO community in Nigeria.

Regarding the comparatively much more profound impact that the labor movement has had on the Nigerian polity, it is hardly a controversial point (at least among most serious observers of the Nigerian scene) that the labor movement has been one of the most influential civil society groups in the country. From forcing increases in the wages of workers to forcing governments to pay much greater attention to public demands for affordable petroleum products, this movement has at once been taken seriously and despised by successive governments.[61] On the whole, even though it sometimes works in concert with NGOs, this movement has been far more influential than the NGO community. Here again, other then the strike weapon, its comparative advantage is mostly attributable to its mass social movement character—a feature that has hardly defined the operations of most of the relevant NGOs. Indeed, without operating in this mode, its strike weapon would have been impotent against relentless attempts on the part of successive regimes to weaken, and even eliminate, it.

Regarding the tremendous influence of the Christian churches that have all but draped the African landscape with their theological messages, it is well acknowledged in the literature that these churches collectively constitute one of the largest and most effective mass social movements in contemporary Africa.[62] Despite their problems, African church groups tend to be member-oriented, grassroots-based, mass mobilization-focused, and largely locally funded organizations. Many even allow a level of democratic participation in their decision-making processes. It is also widely acknowledged that these churches possess a level of widespread allegiance in Africa that traverses class lines, ethnic differences, associational groupings, and national boundaries.[63] As a consequence, the African church has remained a potent political force within most African states.[64] Importantly, most of the features that have helped church groups gain in popular legitimacy and influence in Africa are in general lacking within the relevant NGO community in Nigeria.

Regarding the tremendous influence that the ANC-led antiapartheid movement has had within South Africa (including taking over the state itself), it suffices for the purposes of this chapter to note that most scholars of South African civil society are agreed that the ANC did indeed wield much popular power in that country even before the end of the infamous apartheid regime.[65] And here again, it is clear that despite being funded to some extent by other African countries, the ANC and its allies basically operated in what has so far been referred to here as a "mass social movement" mode.[66] These organizations were, in general, grassroots-based, member-oriented, democratically run, and community based. As has been shown elsewhere in this book, the NGO community in Nigeria does not, for the most part, fit this description.

Regarding the tremendous influence that the labor-led prodemocracy movement has had on the Zambian polity (including ousting one-party rule and capturing state power), similar points can be made with confidence.[67] The Zambian prodemocracy struggle (as embodied in the Movement for Multi-party Democracy or MMD) was led and dominated by the Zambian labor movement. This labor movement clearly operated in a mass social movement mode.[68] Despite raising a significant percentage of its funds from foreign sources, it raised a considerable portion of its funds locally. It was also a largely grassroots-based, member-oriented, and democratically run movement that succeeded in mobilizing its target population to a very high degree. Here again, it is fair to note that these features are, in general, lacking within the NGO community in Nigeria.

Overall, the clearest example of the gap in achievement that exists between the ANC and MMD (on the one hand), and the NGO community in Nigeria (on the other hand) is the wide variance in their respective records of effecting fundamental state transformations and/or capturing state power. The NGO community in Nigeria has been far less successful than the relevant South African and Zambian social movements in this crucial respect. Unlike the Zambian and South African social movements that literally captured their respective states, the NGO community in Nigeria was mostly sidelined and marginalized from state power after the military regime was eased out in Nigeria. Without deep roots in their target communities, and without widespread allegiance (or even name-recognition) among the Nigerian masses, these NGOs stood little chance of successfully catalyzing a popular takeover of the government. Without such deep social roots, they could not counter effectively the winning (if unpopular) strategies and gimmicks of Nigeria's ruling political/military class.[69] And even though many senior NGO activists have now recognized the need to remedy this deficit by directly canvassing ordinary Nigerians in the mode of mass political struggles, and thus expanding their popular appeal and legitimacy, it remains unlikely that this NGO community will, as currently constituted and operated, be able to engineer a successful, popular, velvet revolt against the excesses of the Nigerian political class.[70] Before this can happen, this NGO community will need to pay much closer attention to the difficult conceptual and strategic lessons that can be learnt from its first fifteen or so years of operation. These lessons are palpable even from the above cursory comparison of this NGO community with other similar movements.

The above analysis provides some preliminary evidence to support the proposition that where a human rights community in Africa has tended to operate in what can be styled a mass social movement mode, it has tended to strengthen tremendously its ability to wield influence within its target polity. While this very preliminary conclusion requires much broader empirical support before it can be firmly proposed as a general theory, it is nevertheless a very promising analytical conclusion with regard to this NGO community. The converse also seems to be true; where a community of human rights NGOs in Africa has not operated in a social movement mode, it has not tended to wield as much influence as it could within its target polity.

As such, it is fair to conclude that the NGO community in Nigeria may have to reinvent itself as a popularly validated and legitimated movement, if it is to achieve its full potential to influence state and society in Nigeria. This reinvention will require it to become or at least aim toward becoming a predominantly grassroots based, member oriented, institutionally democratic, and locally funded, mass social movement. Similarly, it appears that if the NGO community in Nigeria is to transcend the popular legitimization crisis that currently impedes its capacity to realize its full potential, it has to become much more like the other human rights movements to which they have been compared here. And since Neil Stammers has isolated the reliance of a collection of actors on "mass mobilization, or the threat of it, as their main political sanction" as the minimum feature of a mass social movement,[71] the argument that is being made here in effect is that if the NGO community in Nigeria is to grow into a much more relevant and influential movement, it must in effect become a mass social movement.[72] It must therefore shed its currently dominant institutional forms and conceptual praxis and become far more immersed among the Nigerian people than it already is. Without going through this kind of conceptual and institutional transformation, Odinkalu's conclusion that most of "the real life struggles [of ordinary Nigerians] for social justice are waged *despite* human rights groups—*not by or because of them*,"[73] will continue to ring true in the ears of knowledgeable observers of the Nigerian human rights scene. For with or without these NGOs, most ordinary Nigerians (students, workers, market women, farmers, the unemployed, professionals, etc) will continue to wage their daily resistance to the oppressive conditions in which they mostly find themselves.[74]

On a happier note, as Ihonvbere had shown in the mid 1990s, many NGOs in Nigeria have been forced by developments within the last decade or so to "develop or openly support political programs and move toward mass mobilization as a basic activist strategy," albeit in an episodic and ad hoc (rather than systematic and sustained) manner.[75] For example, prior to the collapse of the Abacha regime in 1998, the United Action for Democracy (UAD), a coalition of twenty-nine human rights and pro-democracy groups in Nigeria, had on a single day mobilized an estimated five million Nigerians to express their opposition to General Abacha's self-succession project.[76] Before this, these NGOs had, under the banner of the Campaign for Democracy (CD), undertaken a relatively successful – although ad hoc and short-lived – effort at mobilizing the Nigerian masses to oppose the Babangida regime's annulment of the results of the 12 June 1993 presidential polls.[77] As importantly, WACOL, a women's rights NGO, has integrated "market rallies" into its mode of activism, a fact that is quite significant given the nature of open markets as a site of popular congregation among ordinary Nigerians.[78] In the housing rights area, experienced activists have begun to realize that the formation of community-based organizations is indispensable in realizing the right to housing within the slums. It is only by forming effective community and neighborhood associations that the necessary momentum for improvement in this area can be generated.[79] With respect to the campaign against official corruption in Nigeria, another experienced activist has urged NGOs to seize "the initiative from the government and transform the campaign into a mass based one."[80] And so, although these NGOs have clearly *not* embraced this preferred mode of activism in as sustained and ample a manner as they could and should (after all, these mass mobilization efforts have tended to be ad hoc and episodic and have not resulted from significant alterations in the basic character of individual NGOs),[81] in view of the gist of the previous discussions in this chapter, the moves by some NGOs to adopt the mass social movement mode is most welcome. Nevertheless, this trend must heighten, broaden, and deepen substantially if appreciable progress in the preferred direction is to arrive much more quickly. Given the demonstrated creativity and resourcefulness of the activists that run these NGOs, there is room for optimism in this respect.

NOTES

* The notion of *legitimacy* that is relied on in this chapter and throughout this book is implied in and captured by the following quotation from Charles Taylor's work: "This term [legitimacy] is meant to designate the beliefs and attitudes that members have towards the [institutions] and society they make up." See C. Taylor, *Reconciling Solitudes: Essays on Canadian Federalism and Nationalism* (Montreal: McGill-Queen's University Press, 1993), 64. As such, the "legitimization crisis" frequently referred to in this chapter relates to the (sometimes unacknowledged) crisis that exists within the extant NGO community regarding

their marked inability to secure widespread validation and commitment among the masses of vulnerable and abused Nigerians who constitute a ready and well-primed "market" for the "products" that these NGOs purvey. For an earlier allusion to this kind of crisis, see E.K. Quashigah and O.C. Okafor, "Toward the Enhancement of the Relevance and Effectiveness of the Movement for the Securement of Legitimate Governance in Africa," in E.K. Quashigah and O.C. Okafor, *Legitimate Governance in Africa: International and Domestic Legal Perspectives* (The Hague: Kluwer Law International, 1999), 539, 544.

1. See U. Baxi, *The Future of Human Rights* (New Delhi: Oxford University Press, 2002), 124. Emphasis added.

2. See M. Mutua, "A Discussion on the Legitimacy of Human Rights NGOs in Africa," *Africa Legal Aid Quarterly* (October–December 1997): 28. Emphasis added.

3. See C.A. Odinkalu, "Why More Africans Don't Use the Human Rights Language," *Human Rights Dialogue* (2000): 3. Emphasis added. See also J. Ihonbvbere, "Where is the Third Wave? A Critical Evaluation of Africa's Non-Transition to Democracy," *Africa Today* 43:4 (1996): 343, 358 (hereinafter referred to as "Third Wave").

4. For the minimum definition of *mass social movements*, see N. Stammers, "Social Movements and the Social Construction of Human Rights," *Human Rights Quarterly* 21 (1999): 980, 984. See also B. Rajagopal, "International Law and Resistance: Theoretical Challenges from the Perspective of Social Movements," in A. Anghie, B.S. Chimni, K. Mickelson, and O.C. Okafor, eds., *The Third World and International Order: Law, Politics and Globalization* (The Hague: Kluwer Law International, 2003).

5. One of the very few examples is S. Dicklitch, *The Elusive Promise of NGOs in Africa: Lessons from Uganda* (Houndmills, U.K.: Macmillan Press, 1998). But Dicklitch's book is almost completely focused on a Ugandan case study; is concerned for the most part with the role of NGOs in promoting democratization; and is not exclusively focused on self-described human rights NGOs. Another example is Claude Welch's pioneering study of NGOs in a number of African countries, which Makau Mutua has criticized for generalizing from too few samples. See C. E. Welch, Jr., *Protecting Human Rights in Africa: Roles and Strategies of Non-Governmental Organizations* (Philadelphia: University of Pennsylvania Press, 1995); and M. Mutua, "The Politics of Human Rights: Beyond the Abolitionist Paradigm in Africa," *Michigan Journal of International Law* 17 (1996): 591.

6. For example, see D. Hulme and M. Edwards, eds., *NGOs, States and Donors: Too Close for Comfort* (London: Macmillan/Save the Children, 1999); E. Sandberg, *The Changing Politics of Non-Governmental Organizations and African States* (Westport, CN: Praeger, 1994); and S. Ndegwa, *The Two Faces of Civil Society: NGOs and Politics in Africa* (West Hartford, CN: Kumerian Press, 1996).

7. See chapters 1 and 2 for the definition and limitations of this concept.

8. See B. Ibhawoh, *Human Rights Organizations in Nigeria: An Appraisal Report on the Human Rights NGO Community in Nigeria* (Copenhagen, Demark: The Danish

Centre for Human Rights, 2001), 14. See also *Liberty* (a CLO publication) 6:3 (1995): 25.

9. See chapter 2 of this book.

10. See J. Oloka-Onyango, "Beyond the Rhetoric: Reinvigorating the Struggle for Economic and Social Rights in Africa," *California Western International Law Journal* 26 (1995): 1.

11. P. Lewis, "From Prebendalism to Predation: The Political Economy of Decline in Nigeria" *Journal of Modern African Studies* 34 (1996): 79, 84. See also J. Ihonvbere, "Economic Crisis, Structural Adjustment and Social Crisis in Nigeria," *World Development* 21:1 (1993): 141, 145. See further Y. Bangura "IMF/World Bank Conditionality and Nigeria's Structural Adjustment Programme," in K. J. Havnik, ed., *The IMF and the World Bank in Africa: Conditionality, Impact and Alternatives* (Uppsala: Scandinavian Institute of African Studies, 1987), 95, 110–112.

12. See H. Steiner and P. Alston, *International Human Rights in Context: Law, Politics, Morals* (New York: Oxford University Press, 2000), 887.

13. C. Nyamu, "How Should Human Rights and Development Respond to Cultural legitimization of Gender Hierarchy in Developing Countries" *Harvard International Law Journal* 41:2 (2000): 381.

14. See generally S.B.O. Gutto, "Non-Governmental Organizations, People's Participation and the African Commission on Human and Peoples' Rights: Emerging Challenges to the Regional Protection of Human Rights," in B. Andreassen and T. Swineheart, eds., *Human Rights in Developing Countries Yearbook, 1991* (Oslo: Scandinavian University Press, 1992), 33, 42.

15. See O.C. Okafor, "Re-Conceiving "Third World" Legitimate Governance Struggles in Our Time: Emergent Imperatives for Rights Activism" *Buffalo Human Rights Law Review* 6 (2000): 1.

16. See SERAC@WORK 2:1 (1999): 1.

17. See Okafor, "Re-Conceiving," *supra* note 15.

18. Ibid.

19. The link between a human rights NGO's institutional form and its effectiveness is best illustrated by the experience of Amnesty International, the world's preeminent human rights NGO. See M.E. Winston, "Assessing the Effectiveness of International Human Rights NGOs-Amnesty International," in C.E. Welch Jr, ed., *NGOs and Human Rights: Promise and Performance* (Philadelphia: University of Pennsylvania Press, 2001), 30–31 (arguing that "AI's organizational form—in particular, being first and foremost a membership organization—has enabled it to effectively propagate the human rights ethos within global civil society. AI's sheer number of members and sections sets it apart from other international human rights NGOs and gives it its distinctive identity as an organization of human rights activists, rather than just an elite human rights research institute. AI's basic message—that ordinary people, from every nation, and every walk of life, should and can do something to secure human rights for all—translates well into almost every language, and finds enthusiastic agreement among people nearly everywhere").

20. This is not a novel phenomenon. As far back as the early 1980s, Robert Fried-lander had broached the question of the "potential adverse effects resulting from a proliferation of NGOs." See R. Friedlander, "Human Rights Theory and NGO Practice: Where Do We Go from Here?" in V.P. Nanda, J.R. Scarritt, and G. W. Shephard, *Global Human Rights: Public Policies, Comparative Measures, and NGO Strategies* (Boulder, CO: Westview Press, 1981), 219, 223. More recently, Paul Ghils has alluded to the "unprecedented proliferation" of NGOs on all continents. See P. Ghils, "International Civil Society: International Non-governmental Organizations in the International System" *International Social Science Journal* 44 (1992): 417, 419.

21. This contradicts Martin Olz's implied view that, with regard to the numerical size of communities of NGOs, the more they are the better their situation. See M. Olz, "Non-Governmental Organizations in Regional Human Rights Systems" *Columbia Human Rights Law Review* 28 (1997): 307, 364.

22. See N. Aduba, "The Protection of Human Rights in Nigeria," in A.O. Obilade et al., eds., *Text for Human Rights Teaching in Schools* (Lagos: Constitutional Rights Project, 1999), 109, 136; and E. Madunagu, "NGOs and Problems of Foreign Grants," *The Guardian*, Thursday, 16 May 2002, on-line: http://www.ngrguardiannews.com/editorial_opinion/article2 (visited 16 May 2002).

. Regarding the relevance of this kind of accusation to the broader African context, Shadrack Gutto has pilloried the "opportunism" and "careerism" that he sees as rife within human rights NGO communities in Africa. See S.B.O. Gutto, "Non-Governmental Organizations, People's Participation and the African Commission on Human and Peoples' Rights: Emerging Challenges to Regional Protection of Human Rights," in B. Andreassen and T. Swineheart, eds., *Human Rights in Developing Countries Yearbook, 1991* (Oslo: Scandinavian University Press, 1992), 33, 38.

23. See *Human Rights Defender* (an IHRHL publication) 4:1 (2001): 7.

24. The term *oga* is derived from the Nigerian pidgin English word for *boss.*

25. See E. Madunagu, *supra* note 22.

26. See A. Ikelegbe, "The Perverse Manifestation of Civil Society: Evidence from Nigeria," *Journal of Modern African Studies* 39 (2001): 1, 10. This phenomenon is not of course exclusively Nigerian. In relation to other NGOs, Henrik Marcussen has concluded that they do have difficulty working seriously with each other due to "jealousy, rivalry or simply defending their turf." See H.S. Marcussen, "NGOs, the State and Civil Society," *African Political Economy* 69 (1996): 405, 415.

27. See *Constitutional Rights Journal* 8:29 (1998): 41.

28. See A.C Odinkalu, ed., *A Harvest of Violations: Annual Report on Human Rights in Nigeria, 1991* (Lagos: CLO, 1991), 34.

29. Ironically, Tunji Abayomi, a notable Nigerian human rights activist, had once chastised "Africa Watch" [now Human Rights Watch (Africa Division)] for having more credibility in Europe and the United States than it had on the African continent on which its work focuses. See T. Abayomi, "Non-Governmental Organizations in the Protection and Promotion of Human Rights in

Africa: Critique of Approach and Methods," in A.U. Kalu and Y. Osinbajo, eds. *Perspectives on Human Rights* (Lagos: Federal Ministry of Justice, 1992), 173. The irony here is that, for understandable (though not supportable) reasons, most NGOs in Nigeria tend to be more engaged with and accountable to their European and Northern American donors than with the average Nigerian. See also A. Mabogunje, "Civil Society and the Environmental Quality of African Human Settlements," *Shelter Watch* 1:2 (1996): 47, 51.

30. See P. Wapner, "Introductory Essay: Paradise Lost? NGOs and Global Account-ability," *Chicago Journal of International Law* 3 (2002): 155, 157–158 (arguing that most NGO leaders the world over are not elected, and the few that are elected are not voted into office by the members of the society at large; as well as that to be an NGO these days, it seems one needs only a fax machine and internet access).

31. For instance, during a seminar for the media organized by a network of NGOs in November 1998, the vast majority of journalists in attendance alleged that "the interest of the NGOs in human rights struggles does not transcend beyond [sic] personal aggrandizement" and urged that since NGOs are supported by foreign donors, in writing proposals for funding, these NGOs ought to incorporate the financial needs of journalists. See *Constitutional Rights Journal* 8:29 (1998): 41.

32. Informal interviews conducted with younger activists on this sensitive issue invari-ably led to these activists volunteering comments regarding the insincerity of some (but by no means all) activists. For ethical reasons, I am bound not to disclose the names of those interviewed and those that were accused of being careerists.

33. See E. Madunagu, *supra* note 22, 2 (of internet copy). Emphasis in original.

34. See K. Sikkink, "Human Rights, Principled Issue-Networks, and Sovereignty in Latin America," *International Organization* 47 (1993): 411, 416.

35. See C.A. Odinkalu, "Why More Africans Don't Use the Human Rights Lan-guage" (2000) Human Rights Dialogue 3 at 4.

36. Ibid.

37. Ibid.

38. See Ibhawoh, *supra* note 8, 18.

39. See Odinkalu, *supra* note 35, 4.

40. See P.J. Spiro, "Accounting for NGOs," *Chicago Journal of International Law* 3 (2002): 161, 163–164.

41. Thus, even Paul Wapner's measured theoretical conclusion that NGOs have found themselves embedded in mechanisms that affect a *modicum* of account-ability is largely inapplicable to the Nigerian human rights NGO scene. See Wapner, *supra* note 30, 159. Similarly, Peter Spiro's arguments that the problem of NGO accountability to their members is exaggerated, and that competition among NGOs for members can effect a form of discipline on each individual organization, are inapplicable to the Nigerian scene. To begin with, most of these NGOs do not have a membership base at all. And even in the rare cases where a membership roll is kept by an NGO, the vast majority of members do not regularly pay their dues, are passive, and provide no meaningful check on the activities of their leaders or founder/CEOs. As such, inter-NGO competition

for members is an insignificant factor in orienting the behavior of individual NGOs in Nigeria. See chapter 3 of the present study for a detailed survey of the composition and institutional character of Nigerian human rights NGOs.

42. See W. Korey, *NGOs and the Universal Declaration of Human Rights: "A Curious Grapevine"* (New York: St. Martin's Press, 1998), 305.

43. See A. Ikelegbe, "The Perverse manifestation of Civil Society: Evidence from Nigeria," *Journal of Modern African Studies* 39 (2001): 1, 5–6.

44. See P. Wapner, "Defending Accountability in NGOs," *Chicago Journal of International Law* 3 (2002) 3 197, 201.

45. See Ibhawoh, *supra* note 8.

46. See Gutto, *supra* note 14.

47. See Wapner, *supra* note 30, 155, 156. Emphasis added.

48. See E.K. Quashigah, "Protection of Human Rights in the Changing International Scene: Prospects in Sub-Saharan Africa," *RADIC* 6 (1994): 93, 96.

49. See J. Gathii and C. Nyamu, "Reflections on United States-Based Human Rights NGOs' Work on Africa," *Harvard Human Rights Journal* 9 (1996): 285, 291. See also B. Awe, "Conflict and Divergence: Government and Society in Nigeria," *African Studies Review* 42:3 (1999): 1, 14.

50. See S. Phillips, "Fuzzy Boundaries: Rethinking Relationships between Governments and NGOs," *Policy Options* 15 (1994): 13, 16.

51. See J. Ihonvbere, "On the Threshold of Another False Start? A Critical Evaluation of Prodemocracy Movements in Africa," *Journal of Asian and African Studies* 31 (1996): 125, 140. See also L. Lawson, "External Democracy Promotion in Africa: Another False Start?" *Commonwealth and Comparative Politics* 37:1 (1999): 1, 15 (arguing that "[n]on-governmental organizations (NGOs) are narrow, urban-based and highly fragmented").

52. For example, Susan Waltz has suggested that the success enjoyed by some indigenous human rights groups in Morocco can in fact be attributed in part to the elite character of such groups. See S. Waltz, "Making Waves: the Political Impact of Human Rights Groups in North Africa," *Journal of Modern African Studies* 29 (1991): 481, 502.

53. These groups even have far more contact with funding agencies and NGOs in Europe and North America than with like-minded groups in neighboring African countries (with similar problems and experiences). See Ihonvbere, *supra* note 51, 139.

54. See Gutto, *supra* note 14, 36, where he alludes to the existence of this dilemma:

> It should be appreciated that when NGOs are funded from outside the organizations' own resources, and most are funded in this way, varying degrees of double, though not necessarily equal, allegiance to the funding source on the one hand, and to their members and/or the consumers of their services [i.e., the wider society] on the other hand is to be expected. This is a reality.

55. See N. Kasfir, "Civil Society, the State and Democracy in Africa," *Commonwealth and Comparative Politics* 36 (Special Issue, 1998): 123, 142–43. Emphasis added.

56. See J. Ihonbvbere, "Third Wave," *supra* note 3, 358.

57. See J.D. Barkan, M.L. McNulty, and M.A.O. Ayeni, "'Hometown' Voluntary Associations, Local Development, and the Emergence of Civil Society in Western Nigeria," *Journal of Modern African Studies* 29 (1991): 457, 457–458. Emphasis added.

58. Ibid., 458 and 478.

59. Neil Stammers has noted that the minimum core, the litmus test, for a "mass social movement" is that it uses mass mobilization or the threat of it as its political sanction. See Stammers, *supra* note 4, 984. See also Rajagopal *supra* note 4.

60. Barkan et al., *supra* note 57, 462 and 466.

61. F. Barchiesi, "The Social Construction of Labor in the Struggle for Democracy: The Case of Post-Independence Nigeria," *Review of African Political Economy* 23 (1996): 349.

62. See K. Jenkins, "The Christian Church as an NGO in Africa: Supporting Post-Independence Era State Legitimacy or Promoting Change?" in E. Sandberg, ed., *The Changing Politics of Non-Governmental Organizations and African States* (Westport, CN: Praeger, 1994), 83, 84–85.

63. Ibid.

64. Ibid.

65. See P. Gray, *Modern South Africa* (Boston: McGraw-Hill, 2001); R. Brooks, *When Sorry Isn't Enough* (New York: New York University Press, 1999); T. Binns and R. Robinson, "Sustaining Democracy in the 'New' South Africa," Geography 87 (2002): 1; J. Saul, "Cry for the Beloved Country: The Post-Apartheid Denouement," *Monthly Review* (2001): 1 (Internet copy); D. Mindry, "Non-Governmental Organizations, Grassroots, and the Politics of Virtue," *Signs* 26 (2001) 1187; C.E. Welch Jr., "NGOs and the Universal Declaration of Human Rights," *Human Rights Quarterly* 22 (2000): 298; H. Holland, *The Struggle: A History of the African National Congress* (New York: Braziller Press, 1990); H. Marais, *South Africa, Limits to Change: The Political Economy of Transition* (London: Zed Press, 1998); and W. Korey, *NGOs and the Universal Declaration of Human Rights: "A Curious Grapevine"* (New York: St. Martin's Press, 1998).

66. See E.J. Wood, *Forging Democracy from Below: Insurgent Transitions in South Africa and El Salvador* (Cambridge: Cambridge University Press, 2000); G. Hawker, "Political Leadership in the ANC: The South African Provinces 1994–1999" Journal of Modern African Studies 38 (2000): 4; J. Maree, "The COSATU Participatory Democratic Tradition and South Africa's New Parliament," *African Affairs* 97 (1998): 386; M. Murray, *South Africa: Time of Agony, Time of Destiny – The Upsurge of Popular Protest* (London: Thetford Press, 1987); and Mindry, ibid.

67. J.O. Ihonbvere, *Economic Crisis, Civil Society, and Democratization: The Case of Zambia* (Trenton, NJ: Africa World Press, 1996), 117 and 124–125.

68. Ibid.

69. As the CLO, Nigeria's largest and most successful human rights NGO, has acknowledged, these NGOs were in the beginning not minded to be political. Although they have progressively realized the folly of this approach in the particular Nigerian context, they have till this day failed to become the kind of highly effective political (and yet non-partisan) players within the Nigerian polity that they could have become. See *Liberty* (a CLO publication) 9:1 (1998): 26.

70. A number of senior activists did contest for political office in the April 2003 polls. For instance, Olisa Agbakoba (the founding President of the CLO and the current CEO of HURILAWS) was the unsuccessful presidential candidate of the Green Party of Nigeria. See email copy of Agbakoba's announcement of his intention to seek election as Nigeria's president sent to the author on 16 September 2002 by HURILAWS (on file with the author). Similarly, Femi Falana (the President of the CDHR) unsuccessfully sought election to the office of the Governor of Ekiti state of Nigeria. See transcripts of interview with FF, 25 August 2001 (on file with the author). However, Abdul Oroh, the immediate past executive director of the CLO, did seek and win election into the Federal House of Representatives during the same election season. See transcripts of interview with OA, 20 August 2001 (on file with the author). Although Oroh's victory was on the platform of the relatively conservative ruling Peoples Democratic Party, it is nevertheless a ray of hope. However, the very fact that he chose to contest on the platform of the ruling party, rather than the platform of the leftist National Conscience Party or the Green Party, is instructive with regard to the argument being made here. A couple of other activists, like Uche Onyeagocha, have also won election into a couple of offices around the country. However, a significant proportion of these activists still resist the move to situate the NGO community in Nigeria within the wider community and entrench it firmly as a political player within the polity. As recently as 2001, a senior Amnesty International (Nigeria Branch) officer had argued (at a human rights forum) that since, the world over, the work of human rights activists is purely to serve as a "human rights watchdog" and not to engage in partisan politicking, Nigerian NGOs should avoid becoming political. He was however in the minority on this issue. Prominent activists from the CLO and the CRP were among those who opposed this view. So did Akwasi Aidoo, a senior official at Ford Foundation's West African office. See the Guardian, 17 May 2001, on-line: http://www.ngrguardiannews.com/news2/nn821718.html (visited 17 May 2001).

71. See Stammers, *supra* note 4, 984.

72. There is a conceptual and actual difference between NGOs and social movements. Not all NGOs are social movements and not all social movements are NGOs. See Rajagopal, *supra* note 4.

73. See C.A. Odinkalu, *supra* note 35.

74. See Ihonvbere, "False Start," *supra* note 51, 125.

75. See ibid., "Third Wave," supra note 3, 349

76. See *Liberty* (a CLO publication) 9:1 (1998): 16.

77. See J. Ihonvbere, "Are Things Falling Apart? The Military and the Crisis of Democratization in Nigeria," *Journal of Modern African Studies* 34 (1996): 193, 201–204.

78. See *Action Woman* (a WACOL publication) 1:1 (2002): 26. See also, J. Ezeilo *et al.*, *Voices from Below: Popular Participation, Better Constitution* (Enugu: WACOL 2002), 1.

79. See J.U. Achor, ed., *Improving the Living Environment in Slum Settlements* (Lagos: SRI, 1998), 18–19 and 21. See also Mabogunje, *supra* note 29, 50.

80. See Y.Z. Ya'u, "Monitoring and Influencing the Management and Allocation of Public Expenditure in Nigeria: The Experience of CAPP," *Journal of Economic, Social and Cultural Rights* 1:1 (2001): 54, 64.

81. See Ihonvbere, "Are Things Falling Apart?" *supra* note 77, 201–204.

CHAPTER 8

CONCLUSIONS AND RECOMMENDATIONS

1. CONCLUSIONS OF THE STUDY

The central conclusions of this extensive case study of the nature, impact and limitations of the NGO community in Nigeria between 1987 and 2001 are as follows:

a. The NGO community in Nigeria has, on the whole, been modestly successful in contributing to the remarkable, albeit modest, transformations that have certainly occured in that country in the nature and character of judicial thinking and action, in legislative process and legislation, and in executive thought and action. This limited success is in large measure attributable to this NGO community's dynamism, creativity, and courage.

b. There have been many significant problems with both the very nature of these organizations and their current mode of human rights activism; problems that have undermined appreciably their capacity to attract and secure the widespread commitment and allegiance of average Nigerians. This inability to successfully mobilize most ordinary Nigerians has considerably circumscribed the capacity of these NGOs to optimize their influence on the polity.

c. These NGOs were largely founded by elite, male, urbanized, Lagos-based civil rights lawyers (and other such professionals) who were, during the relevant period, mostly focused on undermining military rule in Nigeria; and who as a result tended to marginalize other equally important human rights issues related to gender equality, socio-economic rights, and minority/environmental rights.

d. Controlled and run as they almost always are by a core management team, virtually all of these NGOs lack an active and effective membership base; rarely canvass the local population for members and financial resources; are dominated by mostly unelected, very powerful founder/CEOs (who are, in practice, only marginally accountable to a governing board or active membership); too often lack sufficiently democratized internal decision-making structures; and too often lack offices and projects in the rural parts of Nigeria where the vast majority of Nigerians live and work.

e.   With a few notable exceptions, these NGOs tend to set agendas and mount programs that are focused on, centered in, and targeted at urban Nigeria; thus tending to marginalize agendas that are rural- or grassroots-centered. What is more, rarely do their agendas bear the democratic imprimatur of an active, community-based membership. As such, these agendas have too often not spoken *adequately* to the priorities of most ordinary Nigerians.

f.   The funding structure of this NGO community (which is in general characterized by a situation where almost every dollar that is spent by each of these organizations is raised from foreign sources) has provided an incredibly powerful disincentive to their engaging in the admittedly much more arduous task of canvassing the local population for donations, memberships, and other resources. This has in turn contributed to the conceptual and physical distance that can often be observed between most of these NGOs and most average Nigerians.

g.   Thus, partly as a result of its very character, the NGO community in Nigeria has almost since its inception, faced a popular legitimization crisis; and has, as a consequence, been largely unable to develop fully, its potential of becoming a highly influential movement.

h.   If it is to grow into a popular movement, this NGO community will have to re-invent itself. It has to recraft its institutional and conceptual praxis by paying far greater attention to the more difficult process of mass mobilization, by becoming substantially more Nigerian-facing in its fundraising drives, and by ceding far more real institutional power to an active membership base that is drawn from the local community. In other words, this NGO community must allow ordinary Nigerians to "own" much more of it.

Overall, the study concludes that despite the fact that this NGO community has been a dynamic, courageous, innovative (and therefore modestly successful group), a visible gap still exists between its actual achievements and its real potential to contribute effectively to the positive transformation of the Nigerian polity. The study also found that the existence of this gap between this community's attainment and its potential is manifestly attributable to the fact that the character of its conceptual and institutional praxis has worked in various ways to distance this NGO community from the vast majority of ordinary Nigerians. Yet the widespread allegiance of these average citizens is imperative for this NGO community's optimal success. It is this gaping distance that marks the outlines of the popular legitimization crisis that this NGO community continues to confront.

2. RECOMMENDATIONS ARISING FROM THE STUDY

Given its findings, the recommendations entailed by this study are that most (but not all) of these NGOs will need to incorporate most of the following imperatives in their agendas if they are to transcend the popular legitimization deficit that they now confront as a community and begin to acquire the desired and desirable level of influence within Nigeria:

a.   Cultivate a broad-based and active membership that is sourced from the grassroots, and that exercises real power within the relevant organization. This process of mass mobilization will help narrow the conceptual and physical distance between these NGOs and the vast majority of Nigerians.

b.   Democratize much more deeply their internal decision-making structures and operations, in a way that cedes far more real institutional power to the membership. This specific reform will enable them attract the commitment of their membership and validate them among the broader public.

c.   Democratize to a much greater extent the process through which they formulate and prioritize their activist agendas.

d.   Seek to overcome their generally elitist, urbanized, and Lagos-centered, institutional character by working much more actively with and within Nigeria's majority rural population.

e.   Ascribe much more importance to economic/social rights activism, gender issues, rural issues, and minority/environmental rights activism. Since these issues remain central to the daily struggles of the vast majority of Nigerians, the more the agendas of these NGOs reflect these concerns, the more their human rights catechisms will resonate with the Nigerian people.

f.   Seek to source much more of their resources locally. Difficult as local fund-raising is in the depressed economic context in which Nigerians currently find themselves, the more these NGOs are able to raise funds from their local constituency, the more likely they are to secure widespread commitment among ordinary Nigerians. While the process of local fund-raising necessitates a prior effort at cultivating and energizing potential local donors, this should not be as difficult as it at first appears. As long as concerned and interested Nigerians are allowed to participate in and exercise real power within these NGOs (and as a result feel a sense of inclusion and commitment), they will most certainly contribute funds to these groups. After all, millions of impoverished Nigerians already contribute regularly to the coffers of the hometown development unions and faith-based groups to which they belong.

3. CONTRIBUTIONS OF THE STUDY TO SCHOLARSHIP

The present study makes a number of important contributions to both general human rights NGO theory and TWAIL[1] human rights scholarship.

One such contribution is its empirical confirmation of the constructivist thesis that, under certain conditions, human rights NGOs are able to exert appreciable influence within a given society by penetrating key domestic institutions in ways that foster subtle alterations in prevalent thinking within them.[2] As importantly, the study confirms the much less popular thesis that the exertion of such influence is possible even in relation to largely dictatorial regimes.

Another one of the study's most important contributions is that it demonstrates *empirically* the various ways in which the conceptual orientation and institutional features of the NGO community in Nigeria have together created and fostered the distance that currently exists between these groups and most ordinary Nigerians, confirming to this extent the sense that is emerging in the conceptual literature that many third world NGO communities are afflicted by popular legitimization crises. This sense of crisis is exemplified by Chidi Odinkalu's hypothesis that:

> The current human rights movement in Africa – with the possible exception of the women's rights movement and faith based social justice initiatives – appears almost by design … to exclude the participation of the [very] people whose welfare it purports to advance.[3]

An intimately related contribution that the present study makes to human rights scholarship is that it also demonstrates, to some extent, the emergent sense in a small segment of the relevant literature that most "third world" peoples continue to express their human rights concerns *outside* rather then *within* the structures of the relevant NGO communities. In other words, that most of the resistance put forward by the average citizens of these countries against the oppressive social conditions that often obtain in their societies proceeds beyond the reach, what more the grasp, of most NGOs.[4] Despite their strong allegiance to faith-based initiatives, labor unions, and hometown development associations, the vast majority of the poor, oppressed, and/or vulnerable third world peoples have not easily found a comfortable home within the relevant NGO communities. Instead, these NGOs have almost always claimed to represent these subalterns without necessarily working to ensure the direct and full participation of average citizens within their internal organizational structures. Yet these average citizens have always sought through their daily acts of resistance to transform positively the oppressive conditions in which they often find themselves. The present study has been able to make this point through its demonstration of the mechanics and effects of the distance that exists between such NGOs and the vast majority of the Nigerian people.

The contributions of this study that have just been discussed entail a further contribution. The study also suggests that rapid transition to a mass social movement model is the most promising way in which the NGO community in Nigeria can overcome their popular legitimization deficit and, as a result, begin to enjoy a much higher level of influence within Nigeria. While this last suggestion is clearly indicated in this study only with respect to the NGO community in Nigeria, given the findings of the excellent work already done by Baxi, Odinkalu, Gutto, Mutua, and Oloka-Onyango, and the tenor of a joint paper written by Gathii and Nyamu, there is strong preliminary evidence to suggest the potential generalizability of this conclusion to other parts of the so-called third world.[5]

Overall, while the study provides further confirmation for the broad thesis that human rights NGOs have exerted a significant level of influence around the world, it also provides some empirical confirmation of the validity of the reservations that have been notably expressed by TWAIL human right scholars regarding the severe limitations of the dominant model of human rights NGO activism in the context of most third world states.[6]

4. SUGGESTIONS FOR A FUTURE RESEARCH AGENDA:

While the results of the study can be applied with confidence to human rights NGO praxis in Nigeria (its primary focus), much further study is required before the theses that are presented in this book can be generalized with confidence to other countries in Africa, what more to the rest of the third world. In particular, the consequential thesis of the book—i.e., that transition to a mass social movement model is required if the relevant NGOs are to achieve the desired and desirable levels of both popular validation and influence in their target societies—needs to be tested much more generally before it can become a general theory of NGO activism in Africa. More detailed comparisons of the NGO community in Nigeria to other NGO communities, as well as to a number of the mass social movements that operate or that have operated at one time in Africa are necessary. And even much more extensive work needs to be done on this subject if that thesis is to apply beyond Africa to the rest of the third world.

NOTES

1. The acronym *TWAIL* stands for the "third world approaches to international law movement." For detailed explanations of these approaches, see M. Mutua, "What is TWAIL?" *ASIL Proceedings* (2000): 31; and J. Gathii, "Alternative and Critical: The Contribution of Research and Scholarship on Developing Countries to International Legal Theory," *Harvard International Law Journal* 41 (2000): 263.
2. For instance, see M. Keck and K. Skkink, *Activists Beyond Borders: Advocacy Networks in International Politics* (Ithaca, NY: Cornell University, 1998).
3. See C.A. Odinkalu, "Why More Africans Don't Use Human Rights Language," *Human Rights Dialogue* (2000) 3, 4.
4. For early recognition of this important feature of the third world human rights scene, see L.S. Wiseberg and H.M. Scoble, "Recent Trends in the Expanding Universe of NGOs Dedicated to the Protection of Human Rights," in V.P. Nanda, J.R. Scarritt, and G.W. Shephard, eds., Global *Human Rights: Public Policies, Comparative Measures, and NGO Strategies* (Boulder, Co: Westview Press, 1981), 229. For a much more current conclusion to the same effect, see Odinkalu, ibid., 3.
5. For example, see M. Mutua, "A Discussion on the Legitimacy of Human Rights NGOs in Africa" *Africa Legal Aid Quarterly* (October-December, 1997): 28. U. Baxi, *The Future of Human Rights* (New Delhi: Oxford University Press, 2002), 124; Odinkalu, *supra* note 3; S.B.O. Gutto, "Non-Governmental Organizations, Peoples' Participation and the African Commission on Human and Peoples' Rights: Emerging Challenges to the Regional Protection of Human Rights," in B. Andreassen and T. Swineheart, eds., *Human Rights in Developing Countries Yearbook 1991* (Oslo: Scandinavian University Press, 1992); J. Oloka-Onyango,

"Beyond the Rhetoric: Reinvigorating the Struggle for Economic and Social Rights in Africa," *California Western International Law Journal* 26 (1995): 1; and J. Gathii and C. Nyamu, "Reflections on United States-Based Human Rights NGOs Work on Africa," *Harvard Human Rights Journal* 9 (1996): 285.

6. Ibid.

SELECT BIBLIOGRAPHY

BOOKS

Adedeji, A, ed. *Africa within the World*. Ijebu Ode: ACDESS, 1993.

Andreassen, B., and T. Swineheart, eds. *Human Rights in Developing Countries Yearbook 1991*. Oslo: Scandinavian University Press, 1992.

Anghie, A., B.S. Chimni, K. Mickelson, and O.C. Okafor, eds. *The Third World and International Order: Law, Politics and Globalization*. The Hague: Kluwer Law International, 2003.

Ankumah, E.A. *The African Commission on Human and Peoples' Rights*. The Hague: Martinus Nijhoff, 1996.

Awe, B., ed. *Nigerian Women in Historical Perspective*. Ibadan: Sankore/Bookcraft, 1992.

Baer, P., H. Hey, J. Smith, and T. Sineheart, eds. *Human Rights in Developing Countries*. The Hague: Kluwer Law International, 1995.

Baxi, U. *The Future of Human Rights*. New Delhi: Oxford University Press, 2002.

Brooks, R. *When Sorry Isn't Enough*. New York: New York University Press, 1999.

Cameron, M.A., B.W. Tomlin, and R.J. Lawson, eds. *To Walk without Fear: The Global Movement to Ban Land Mines*. Toronto: Oxford University Press, 1998.

Cook, R.J., ed. *Human Rights of Women: National and International Perspectives*. Philadelphia: University of Pennsylvania Press, 1994.

Dicklitch, S. *The Elusive Promise of NGOs in Africa: Lessons From Uganda*. Houndmills, UK: Macmillan Press, 1998.

Edwards, M., and D. Hulme, eds. *Beyond the Magic Bullet: NGO Accountability and Performance in the Post-Cold War World*. West Hartford, CN: Kumarian Press, 1996.

Epp, C.R. *The Rights Revolution: Lawyers, Activists, and Supreme Courts in Comparative Perspective*. Chicago: University of Chicago Press, 1998.

Gray, P. *Modern South Africa*. Boston: McGraw-Hill, 2001.

Havnik, K. J., ed. *The IMF and the World Bank in Africa: Conditionality, Impact and Alternatives*. Uppsala: Scandinavian Institute of African Studies, 1987.

Holland, H. *The Struggle: A History of the African National Congress.* New York: Braziller Press, 1990.

Hulme, D. and M. Edwards, eds. *NGOs, States and Donors: Too Close for Comfort.* London: Macmillan/Save the Children, 1999.

Ibhawoh, B. *Human Rights Organizations in Nigeria: An Appraisal Report on the Human Rights NGO Community in Nigeria.* Copenhagen, Denmark: The Danish Centre for Human Rights, 2001.

ICCAF. *Nigeria: The Struggle for Justice, Democracy and Human Rights.* Toronto: ICCAF, 1999.

Ihonvbere, J. *Economic Crisis, Civil Society, and Democratization: The Case of Zambia.* Trenton, NJ: Africa World Press, 1996.

Johnson, W.R., and V.R. Johnson. *West African Governments and Volunteer Development Organization: Priorities for Partnership.* Lanham, MD: University Press of America, 1990.

Kalu, A.U. and Y. Osinbajo, eds., *Perspectives on Human Rights.* Lagos: Federal Ministry of Justice, 1992.

Keck, M.E., and K. Sikkink. *Activists Beyond Borders: Advocacy Networks in International Politics.* Ithaca: Cornell University, 1998.

Korey, W. *NGOs and the Universal Declaration of Human Rights: A Curious Grapevine.* New York: St. Martin's Press, 1998.

Marais, H. *South Africa, Limits to Change: The Political Economy of Transition.* London: Zed Press, 1998.

McCarthy-Arnolds, E., D.R. Penna, and D.J. Cruz Sobrepena, eds. *Africa Human Rights and the Global System: The Political Economy of Human Rights in a Changing World.* Westport, CN: Greenwood Press, 1994.

McClymont, M. and S. Golub, eds. *Many Roads to Justice: The Law-Related Work of Ford Foundation Grantees around the World.* New York: The Ford Foundation, 2000.

Meron, T., ed. *Human Rights in International Law: Legal and Policy Issues.* Oxford: Clarendon Press, 1984.

Murray, M. *South Africa: Time of Agony, Time of Destiny – The Upsurge of Popular Protest.* London: Thetford Press, 1987.

Nanda, V.P., J.R. Scarritt, G. W. Shephard. *Global Human Rights: Public Policies, Comparative Measures, and NGO Strategies.* Boulder, CO: Westview Press, 1981.

Ndegwa, S. *The Two Faces of Civil Society: NGOs and Politics in Africa.* West Hartford, CN: Kumerian Press, 1996.

Obilade, O.A. et al., eds. *Text for Human Rights Teaching in Schools.* Lagos: Constitutional Rights Project, 1999.

Ogbu, O.N. *Human Rights Law and Practice in Nigeria: An Introduction.* Enugu: CIDJAP Press, 1999.

Okafor, O.C. *Re-defining Legitimate Statehood: International Law and State Fragmentation in Africa.* The Hague: Kluwer Law International, 2000.

Oriji, J.N., ed. *Ngwa History.* New York: P. Lang, 1997.

Over, W. *Human Rights in the International Public Sphere: Civic Discourse for the 21ˢᵗ Century.* Samford, CN: Ablex Publishing Corporation, 1999.

Quashigah, E.K., and O.C. Okafor, eds. *Legitimate Governance in Africa: International and Domestic Legal Perspectives* (The Hague: Kluwer Law International, 1999).

Risse, T., S.C. Rupp, and K. Sikkink, eds. *The Power of Human Rights: International Norms and Domestic Change.* Cambridge, U.K: Cambridge University Press, 1999.

Sandberg, E., ed. *The Changing Politics of Non-Governmental Organizations and African States.* Westport, Connecticut: Praeger, 1994.

Shivji, I. *The Concept of Human Rights in Africa.* London: CODESRIA, 1989.

Steiner, H., and P. Alston. *International Human Rights in Context: Law, Politics, and Morals.* Oxford: Oxford University Press, 2000.

Swedish NGO Foundation and International Human Rights Internship Program. *Non-Governmental Organizations in Sub-Saharan Africa.* Stockholm and Washington, D.C., 1994.

Taylor, C. *Reconciling Solitudes: Essays on Canadian Federalism and Nationalism.* Montreal: McGill-Queen's University Press, 1993.

UNESCO, ed. *Philosophical Foundations of Human Rights.* Paris: UNESCO, 1986.

Welch, C.E. Jr., ed., *NGOs and Human Rights: Promise and Performance* (Philadelphia: University of Pennsylvania Press, 2001).

Welch, C.E. Jr., *Protecting Human Rights in Africa: Roles and Strategies of Non-Governmental Organizations.* Philadelphia: University of Pennsylvania Press, 1995.

Wiseman, J.A., ed. *Democracy and Political Change in Sub-Saharan Africa.* London: Routledge, 1995.

Wiwa, K. *In the Shadow of a Saint: A Son's Journey to Understand His Father's Legacy.* South Royalton, VT: Steerforth Press, 2001.

Wood, E.J. *Forging Democracy From Below: Insurgent Transitions in South Africa and El Salvador.* Cambridge, UK: Cambridge University Press, 2000.

JOURNAL ARTICLES

Agbakoba, O. "The Role of Lawyers in the Observance of Human Rights." *Journal of Human Rights Law and Practice* 5:1 (1995) 115.

Anghie, A. "Francisco Vitoria and the Colonial Origins of International Law." *Social and Legal Studies* 5 (1996) 321.

Atsenuwa, A. "The Right to Education and Gender Equality." *Journal of Economic, Social and Cultural Rights* 1:1 (2001) 1.

Awe, B. "Conflict and Divergence: Government and Society in Nigeria." African Studies Review 42 (1999) 1.

Barchiesi, F. "The Social Construction of Labour in the Struggle for Democracy: The Case of Post-Independence Nigeria." *Review of African Political Economy* 23 (1996) 349.

Barkan, J.D., M.L. McNulty, and M.A.O. Ayeni. "'Hometown' Voluntary Associations, Local Development, and the Emergence of Civil Society in Western Nigeria." *Journal of Modern African Studies* 29 (1991) 457.

Baxi, U. "Voices of Suffering and the Future of Human Rights." *Transnational Law and Contemporary Problems* 8 (1998) 25.

Binns, T. & R. Robinson, "Sustaining Democracy in the 'New' South Africa." *Geography* 87 (2002) 1.

Burgerman, S.D. "Mobilizing Principles: The Role of Transnational Activists in Promoting Human Rights Principles." *Human Rights Quarterly* 20 (1998) 905.

Cayford, S. "The Ogoni Uprising: Oil, Human Rights, and a Democratic Alternative in Nigeria." *Africa Today* 43:2 (1996) 183.

Crystal, J. "The Human Rights Movement in the Arab World." *Human Rights Quarterly* 16 (1994) 435.

Cullen, H. and K. Morrow. "International Civil Society in International Law: The Growth of NGO Participation." *Non-State Actors and International Law* 1 (2001) 7.

Dicker, R. "Monitoring Human Rights in Africa." *Journal of Modern African Studies* 29 (1991) 505.

Fatton, R., Jr. "Africa in the Age of Democratization: The Civic Limitations of Civil Society." *African Studies Review* 38 (1995) 67.

Gaer, F.D. "Reality Check: Human Rights Nongovernmental Organizations Confront Governments at the United Nations." *Third World Quarterly* 16 (1995) 389.

Gathii J., and C. Nyamu. "Reflections on United States-Based Human Rights NGOS' Work on Africa." *Harvard Human Rights Journal* 9 (1996) 285.

Gathii, J. "Alternative and Critical: The Contribution of Research and Scholarship on Developing Countries to International Legal Theory," *Harvard International Law Journal* 41 (2000) 263.

Ghils, P. "International Civil Society: International Non-governmental Organizations in the International System" *International Social Science Journal* 44 (1992) 417.

Harrington, Julia. "Practice Made Personal." *Harvard Human Rights Journal* 9 (1996) 333.

Harrington, Joanna. "Punting Terrorists, Assassins and Other Undesirables: Canada, the Human Rights Committee and Requests for Interim Measures of Protection." *McGill Law Journal* 48 (2003) 55.

Hawker, G. "Political Leadership in the ANC: The South African Provinces 1994-1999." *Journal of Modern African Studies* 38 (2000) 4.

Helfer, L.R. and A. Slaughter. "Toward a Theory of Effective Supranational Adjudication." *Yale Law Journal* 107 (1997) 273.

Ibhawoh, B. "Between Culture and Constitution: Evaluating the Cultural Legitimacy of Human Rights in the African State." *Human Rights Quarterly* 22 (2000) 838.

Ihonbvbere J. "Are Things Falling Apart? The Military and the Crisis of Democratization in Nigeria." *Journal of Modern African Studies* 34 (1996) 193.

_____ "A Critical Evaluation of Pro-Democracy Movements in Africa." *Journal of Asian and African Studies* 31 (1996) 125.

_____ "Where is the Third Wave? A Critical Evaluation of Africa's Non-Transition to Democracy." *Africa Today* 43:4 (1996) 343.

_____ "Economic Crisis, Structural Adjustment and Social Crisis in Nigeria." *World Development* 21: 1 (1993) 141.

Ikelegbe, A. "Civil Society, Oil and Conflict in the Niger Delta Region of Nigeria: Ramifications of Civil Society for Regional Resource Struggle." *Journal of Modern African Studies* 39 (2001) 437.

_____ "The Perverse Manifestation of Civil Society: Evidence from Nigeria." *Journal of Modern African Studies* 39 (2001) 1.

Jason, K. J. "The Role of Non-Governmental Organizations in International Election Observing." *New York University Journal of International Law and Politics* 24 (1992) 795.

Kasfir, N. "Civil Society, the State and Democracy in Africa." *Commonwealth and Comparative Politics* 36 (1998) 123.

Lawson, L., "External Democracy Promotion in Africa: Another False Start?" *Commonwealth and Comparative Politics* 37 (1999) 1.

Lewis, P. "From Prebendalism to Predation: The Political Economy of Decline in Nigeria." *Journal of Modern African Studies* 34 (1996) 79.

Lipschutz, R.D. "Reconstructing World Politics: The Emergence of Global Civil Society." *Millennium: A Journal of International Studies* 21 (1992) 389.

Marcussen, H.S. "NGOs, the State and Civil Society." *African Political Economy* 69 (1996) 405.

Maree, J. "The COSATU Participatory Democratic Tradition and South Africa's New Parliament." *African Affairs* 97 (1998) 386.

Mindry, D. "Non-Governmental Organizations, Grassroots, and the Politics of Virtue." *Signs* 26 (2001) 1187.

Murray, R. "Report on the 1996 Sessions of the African Commission on Human and Peoples' Rights." *Human Rights Law Journal* 18:1–4 (1997) 22.

Mutua, M. "A Discussion on the Legitimacy of Human Rights NGOs in Africa." *Africa Legal Aid Quarterly* (October-December 1997) 28.

_____ "Hope and Despair for a New South Africa: The Limits of Rights Discourse." *Harvard Human Rights Journal* 10 (1997) 63.

_____ "Savages, Victims and Saviours: The Metaphor of Human Rights." *Harvard International Law Journal* 42 (2001) 201.

_____ "The Banjul Charter and the African Cultural Fingerprint: An Analysis of the Language of Duties." *Virginia Journal of International Law* 35 (1995) 335.

_____ "The Ideology of Human Rights." *Virginia Journal of International Law* 36 (1996) 589.

_____ "The Politics of Human Rights: Beyond the Abolitionist Paradigm in Africa." *Michigan Journal of International Law* 17 (1996) 591.

_____ "What is TWAIL?" *ASIL Proceedings* (2000) 31.

Nowrot, K. "Legal Consequences of Globalization: The Status of Non-Governmental Organizations under International Law." *Global Legal Studies Journal* 6 (1999) 579.

Nyamu, C. "How Should Human Rights and Development Respond to Cultural Legitimization of Gender Hierarchy in Developing Countries?" *Harvard International Law Journal* 41 (2000) 381.

Obiora, L. A. "Symbolic Episodes in the Quest for Environmental Justice." *Human Rights Quarterly* 21 (1999) 464.

Odinkalu, C.A. "Why More Africans Don't Use Human Rights Language." *Human Rights Dialogue* (2000) 3.

Ogbu, O.N. "The Judiciary in a Polity – A Force for Stability or Instability?: The Nigerian Experience." *African Journal of International and Comparative Law* 11 (1999) 724.

Okafor, O.C., "Re-Conceiving "Third World" Legitimate Governance Struggles in Our Time: Emergent imperatives for Rights Activism" *Buffalo Human Rights Law Journal* 6 (2000) 1.

_____ "After Martyrdom: International Law, Sub-State Groups, and the Construction of Legitimate Statehood in Africa." *Harvard International Law Journal* 41 (2000) 501.

_____ "Do International Human Rights Institutions Matter? The African System on Human and Peoples Rights, Quasi-Constructivism, and the Possibility of Peace building within African States." *International Journal of Human Rights* 8 (2004) 1.

Okafor, O.C. and S.C. Agbakwa. "On Legalism, Popular Agency and 'Voices of Suffering': The Nigerian National Human Rights Commission in Context." *Human Rights Quarterly* 24 (2002) 662.

Oko, O. "Lawyers in Chains: Restrictions on Human Rights Advocacy under Nigeria's Military Regimes." *Harvard Human Rights Journal* 10 (1997) 257.

Oloka-Onyango, J., and S. Tamale. "The Personal is Political' or Why Women's Rights are Indeed Human Rights: An African Perspective on International Feminism." *Human Rights Quarterly* 17 (1995) 691.

Oloka-Onyango, J. "Beyond the Rhetoric: Reinvigorating the Struggle for Economic and Social Rights in Africa." *California Western International Law Journal* 26 (1995) 1.

_____ "Reinforcing Marginalized Rights in an Age of Globalization: International Mechanism, Non-State Actors, and the Struggle for Peoples' Rights in Africa." *American University International Law Review* 18 (2003) 851.

Olutokun, A. "Authoritarian State, Crisis of Democratization and the Underground Media in Nigeria." *African Affairs* 101 (2002) 317.

Olz, M.A. "Non-Governmental Organizations in Regional Human Rights Systems." *Columbia Human Rights Law Review* 28 (1997) 307.

Orentlicher, D.F. "Bearing Witness: The Art of Human Rights Fact-Finding." *Harvard Human Rights Journal* 3 (1990) 83.

Osaghae, E. "The Role of Civil Society in Consolidating Democracy: An African Perspective." *African Insight* 27 (1997) 15.

Phillips, S. "Fuzzy Boundaries: Rethinking Relationships between Governments and NGOs." *Policy Options* 15 (1994) 13.

Power, J. "Like Water on Stone: The Story of Amnesty International." *Human Rights Quarterly* 24 (2002) 830.

Quashigah, E.K., "Protection of Human Rights in the Changing International Scene: Prospects in Sub-Saharan Africa." *RADIC* 6 (1994) 93.

Ruggie, J.G. "Peace in Our Time? Causality, Social Facts and Narrative Knowing." *American Society of International Law Proceedings* (1995) 93.

Scoble, H.M., and L.S. Wiseberg. "Amnesty International: Evaluating the Effectiveness of a Human Rights Actor." *Intellect* (September-October 1976) 79.

Shaw, T. "Popular Participation in Non-Governmental Structures in Africa: Implications for Democratic Development in Africa" *Africa Today* 37 (1990) 5.

Shelton, D. "Decision Regarding Communication 155/96 (Social & Economic Action Center/Center for Economic and Social Rights v. Nigeria) Case No. ACHPR/Comm/A044/1." *American Journal of International Law* 96 (2002) 937.

Sikkink, K. "Human Rights, Principled Issue-Networks, and Sovereignty in Latin America." *International Organization* 47 (1993) 411.

Smith, I.O. "Enforcement of Human Rights Treaties in a Military Regime: Effect of Ouster Clauses on the Application of [the] African Charter on Human and Peoples' Rights in Nigeria." *Review of the African Commission on Human and Peoples' Rights* 9 (2000)192.

Smith, J., and R. Pagnucco (with G. A. Lopez). "Globalizing Human Rights: The Work of Transnational Human Rights NGOs in the 1990s." *Human Rights Quarterly* 20 (1998) 379.

Spiro, P.J. "Accounting for NGOs." *Chicago Journal of International Law* 3 (2002)161.

Stammers, N. "Social Movements and the Social Construction of Human Rights." *Human Rights Quarterly* 21 (1999) 980.

Thomas, D.C. "International NGOs, State Sovereignty, and Democratic Values." *Chicago Journal of International Law* 2 (2001) 389

Tyagi, Y.K. "Cooperation between the Human Rights Committee and Nongovernmental Organizations: Permissibility and Propositions." *Texas International Law Journal* 18 (1983) 273.

Waltz, S. "Making Waves: the Political Impact of Human Rights Groups in North Africa." *Journal of Modern African Studies* 29 (1991) 481.

Wang, H., and J. Rosenau. "Transparency International and Corruption as an Issue of Global Governance." *Global Governance* 7 (2001) 25.

Wapner, P. "Defending Accountability in NGOs." *Chicago Journal of International Law* 3 (2002)197.

_____ "Introductory Essay: Paradise Lost? NGOs and Global Accountability." *Chicago Journal of International Law* 3 (2002)155.

Weinstein, W., "Human Rights and Development in Africa: Dilemmas and Options." *Daedalus* 112 (1983) 171.

Welch, C.E. Jr. "NGOs and the Universal Declaration of Human Rights." *Human Rights Quarterly* 22 (2000) 298.

Wiebe, V. "The Prevention of Civil War Through the Use of the Human Rights System." *New York University Journal of International Law and Politics* 27 (1995) 409.

Wiseberg, L.S. "Protecting Human Rights Activists and NGOs: What More Can Be Done?" *Human Rights Quarterly* 13 (1991) 525.

Ya'u, Y.Z. "Monitoring and Influencing the Management and Allocation of Public Expenditure in Nigeria: The Experience of CAPP." *Journal of Economic, Social and Cultural Rights* 1:1 (2001) 54.

CASE LAW

Abacha v. Fawehinmi 13 NWLR 228 (2000).

Chima Ubani v. Director of State Security Services and Attorney-General 11 NWLR 129 (1999).

CLO (in respect of the Nigerian Bar Association) v. Nigeria, Communication No. 101/93 (1994–95), reproduced in Institute for Human Rights and Development, *Compilation of Decisions on Communications of the African Commission on Human and Peoples' Rights* (Banjul: The Gambia, 1999).

CLO v Nigeria, Communication No. 129/94 (1995–96), reproduced in Institute for Human Rights and Development, *Compilation of Decisions on Communications of the African Commission on Human and Peoples' Rights* (Banjul: The Gambia, 1999).

MRA and CRP v. Nigeria, Communications No. 105/93 and 130/94 (1998–99), reproduced in Institute for Human Rights and Development, *Compilation of Decisions on Communications of the African Commission on Human and Peoples' Rights* (Banjul: The Gambia, 1999).

Comptroller of Nigerian Prisons v. Dr. Femi Adekanye & Twenty-six Others 10 NWLR 400 (1999).

CRP (in respect of Zamani Lekwot and Six Others) v. Nigeria, Communication No. 87/93 (1994–95), reproduced in Institute for Human Rights and Development, *Compilation of Decisions on Communications of the African Commission on Human and Peoples' Rights* (Banjul: The Gambia, 1999).

CRP, International PEN, Interrights, and the CLO (on Behalf of Ken Saro-Wiwa) v. Nigeria, Consolidated Communications Nos. 137/94, 154/96, and 161/97 (1998–99), reproduced in Institute for Human Rights and Development, *Compilation of Decisions on Communications of the African Commission on Human and Peoples' Rights* (Banjul: The Gambia, 1999).

CRP v. President Ibrahim Babangida and Two Others, Suit No. M/102/93 (1993), Lagos State High Court, per Justice Onalaja (Unreported).

Director State Security Service and Another v. Olisa Agbakoba 3 NWLR 314 (1999).

Fawehinmi v. Abacha 9 NWLR 710 (1996).

Frank Ovie Kokori v. General Sani Abacha and Four Others (No.3) FHCLR 413 (1995).

Incorporated Trustees of MRA and Another v. Honorable Attorney-General of the Federation, Suit No. FHC/L/CS/908/99 (1999), Federal High Court, Lagos.

Muojekwu and Others v. Muojekwu and Others CA/E/7/99 (1999), Court of Appeal-Enugu Division.

Ogugu v. the State 9 NWLR 1 (1994)

Olisa Agbakoba v. Director of State Security Service and Another 6 NWLR 475 (1994).

Opeyemi Bamidele and Others v. Alele Williams and Another Suit No. B/6M/89 (1989), Benin High Court.

Oshevire v. British Caledonian Airways Ltd 7 NWLR 507 (1990).

Peter Nemi v. Attorney-General Lagos State and Another 6 NWLR 42 (1996).

Richard Akinola v. General Ibrahim Babangida and Three Others, Suit No. M/462/93 (1993).

U.A.C. of Nigeria v. Global Transporte Oceanico S.A. 5 NWLR 291(1996).

DOMESTIC STATUTES

Civil Disturbances (Special Tribunal) Decree No. 2, 1987.

Constitution (Suspension and Modification) Decree No. 1, 1984.

Defamatory and Offensive Publications Decree No. 49, 1966.

Newspapers (Amendment) Act, 1964.

Newspapers Registration Decree No. 43, 1993.

State Security (Detention of Persons) Act, 1984.

State Security (Detention of Persons) (Amendment) (No.2) Decree No.14, 1994.

State Security (Detention of Persons) (Amendment) (No.2) (Repeal) Decree No.18, 1996.

Students' Union Activities (Control and Regulation) Decree No. 22, 1998.

LEGISLATIVE RECORDS/HANSARDS

National Assembly Debates: Fourth Assembly, First Session - House of Representatives, Official Report, vol. 1, no.10, 22 June 1999.

National Assembly Debates: Fourth Assembly, First Session - House of Representatives, Official Report, vol.3, no.19, 23 March 2000.

National Assembly Debates: Fourth Assembly, First Session - The Senate, Official Report, vol.1 no.10, 22 June 1999.

National Assembly Debates: Fourth Assembly - House of Representatives, Official Report, 16 May 2001 [unspecified volume and number].

INSTRUMENTS, REPORTS AND RESOLUTIONS OF INTERNATIONAL BODIES

African Commission on Human and Peoples' Rights, *Account of the Internal Legislation of Nigeria and the Disposition of the African Commission on Human and Peoples' Rights*, 1994–95. Doc.II/ES/ACHPR/4.

African Commission on Human and Peoples' Rights, *Resolution on the Military*, Eighth Annual Activity Report of the African Commission on Human and Peoples' Rights, 1994–1995. ACHPR/RPT/8th, Annex VII.

African Commission on Human and Peoples' Rights, *Resolution on Nigeria*, Eighth Annual Activity Report of the African Commission on Human and Peoples' Rights, 1994–1995. ACHPR/RPT/8th, Annex VII.

Concluding Observations of the Committee on Economic, Social and Cultural Rights: Nigeria, 13 May 1998. E/C.12/1/Add.23.

Concluding Observations of the United Nations Committee on the Elimination of Racial Discrimination: Nigeria, A/48/18, 15 September 1993, on-line: http://www.unhchr.ch/tbs/doc.nsf/(Symbol)/A.48.18,paras.306-329.En?Opendocument (visited 17 May 2003).

Final Communiqué of the Second Extraordinary Session of the African Commission on Human and Peoples' Rights, Kampala, Uganda, 18–20 December1995 (on file with the author).

Letter from the African Commission, Ref. No. ACHPR/COMMU/AO44286, reproduced in *Liberty* (a CLO publication) 6:3 (1995).

United Nations General Assembly, *Resolution on the Situation of Human Rights in Nigeria*, A/RES/50/199, 22 December 1995.

MANUALS, REPORTS, AND UNPUBLISHED PAPERS OF NIGERIAN NGOS

Achor, J.U., ed. *Immunization Guide for the Family*. Lagos: SRI, 1998.

_____*Improving the Living Environment in Slum Settlements*. Lagos: SRI, 1998.

_____*Practical Issues in Human Settlements and Health: Proceedings of a Workshop for Residents of Slum Communities in Lagos Organized by Shelter Rights Initiative*. Lagos: SRI, 1997.

Akumadu, T.U. *Beasts of Burden: A Study of Women's Legal Status and Reproductive Health Rights in Nigeria*. Lagos: CLO, 1998.

Akumadu, T.U. *Women's Reproductive Health Rights: A Training Manual for Communities of Eastern Nigeria*. Lagos: CLO, 1999.

BOABAB. *Annual Report, 1999*. Lagos: BAOBAB, 1999.

CLO. *Accounts and Activities for 2000*. Lagos: CLO, 2001.

_____*Accounts and Activities for 1999*. Lagos: CLO, 2000.

_____*Annual Reports and Accounts, 1995*. Lagos: CLO, 1995.

_____ *Annual Reports and Accounts, 1994*. Lagos: CLO, 1994.

_____ *The Nigerian Military and the Crises of Democratic Transition: A Study in the Monopoly of Power*. Lagos: CLO, 1999.

_____ *Training Manual on Human Rights for Trade Unions and Other Social Groups*. Lagos: CLO, 1997.

CLEEN. *Policing A Democracy: A Survey Report on the Role and Functions of the Nigeria Police in a Post-Military Era*. Lagos: CLEEN, 1999.

CAPP. *Figures of Marginalization.* Abuja: CAPP, 1996.

CAPP. *Selling the Message: A Report of Voter Education Campaign in Kano and Jigawa States.* Abuja: CAPP, 1999.

CDHR. *1999 Annual Report on the Human Rights Situation in Nigeria.* Lagos: CDHR, 1999.

_____ *Citadel of Violence.* Lagos: CDHR, 1999.

_____ *Path to People's Constitution.* Lagos: CDHR, 2000.

CLEEN and the National Human Rights Commission. *Policing a Democracy: A Survey Report on the Role and Functions of the Nigeria Police in a Post-Military Era.* Lagos: CLEEN, 1999.

Chukwuma, I. and O. Ibidapo-Obe, eds. *Law Enforcement and Human Rights in Nigeria* Lagos: CLO, 1995.

CRP. *Administration of Juvenile Justice in Nigeria.* Lagos: CRP, 1997.

_____ *Eliminating Discrimination against Women: The Report of a Conference organized by the Constitutional Rights Project and the Friedrich Naumann Foundation.* Lagos: CRP, 1995.

_____ *Final Communiqué of the Seminar on Discriminatory Laws and Practices against Women in* Nigeria. Lagos: CRP, 1995.

_____ *Land, Oil and Human Rights in Nigeria's Delta Region.* Lagos: CRP, 1999.

_____ *Nigeria: Human Rights Report 1999.* Lagos: CPR, 2000.

_____ *The Crisis of Press Freedom in Nigeria.* Lagos: CRP, 1993.

Ehonwa, O.L. *Behind the Wall: A Report on Prison Conditions in Nigeria and the Nigerian Prison System.* Lagos: CLO, 1996.

EMPARC. *Annual Lecture Series No.1.* Lagos: EMPARC, 1995.

_____ *Annual Lecture Series No.4.* Lagos: EMPARC, 1998.

_____ *Five Year Report on Activities 1992-1997.* Lagos: EMPARC, 1997.

Eze, O., and E. Onyekpere. *Study on the Right to Health in Nigeria.* Lagos: SRI, 1998).

Eze, O. *Study on the Right to Education in Nigeria.* Lagos: SRI, 1998.

Ezeilo, J., J. C. Udenta., and I. Orakwue. *Voices From Below (Vox Populi): Popular Participation, Better Constitution.* Enugu: WACOL, 2002.

Ezeilo, J. *Gender, Politics and the Law.* Enugu: WACOL, 1999.

_____ *Women's and Children's Rights in Nigeria.* Enugu: WACOL, 2001.

HRA. *Annual Report 1991/1992.* Lagos: HRA, 1992.

_____ *Annual Report 1993/1994* (Lagos: HRA, 1994).

_____ *Communiqué of the 1991 African Human Rights Conference.* Lagos: HRA, 1991.

_____ *The Nigerian Police and Human Rights: Limitations and Lamentations.* Lagos: HRA, 1993.

HURILAWS. *1997-1998 Annual Report.* Lagos: HURILAWS, 1998.

_____ *1999 Annual Report and Accounts.* Lagos: HURILAWS, 2000.

_____ *The Governance Scorecard: Review of Democratic Governance in Nigeria.* Lagos: HURILAWS, 2000.

IHRHL. *Human Rights Education Techniques in Schools: Building Attitudes and Skills.* Port Harcourt: IHRHL, 1994.

_____ "IHRHL Documentation Center" (undated IHRHL Publication).

_____ *Poverty in Wealth.* Port Harcourt: IHRHL, 2002.

MRA. *A Harvest of Blooms.* Lagos: MRA, 2000.

_____ *Media Scorecard: Report of the Print Media Coverage of the Political Transition Programme.* Lagos: MRA, 1999.

Nigerian NGO Coalition for A Shadow Report to CEDAW. *NGO's CEDAW Report for Nigeria.* Lagos: BOABAB, 1999.

Nsirimovu, A. *Human Rights Education and Techniques in Schools.* Port Harcourt: IHRHL, 1994.

_____ *Human Rights: An Umblical Cord of Participatory Democracy.* Port Harcourt: IHRHL, 1997.

Nwankwo, C. et al. *The Crisis of Press Freedom in Nigeria.* Lagos: CRP, 1993.

Odah, J.E., ed. *The Church and Human Rights: A Human Rights Education Training Manual for Churches in Nigeria.* Lagos, CLO: 1995.

Odinkalu, C.A., ed. *A Harvest of Violations: Annual Report on Human Rights in Nigeria, 1991.* Lagos: CLO, 1991.

Ogbuagu, S.C. *Gender and the Democratic Process in Nigeria: Issues of Concern.* Lagos: EMPARC, 1999.

Okonkwo, C. O., C. Nwankwo, and B. Ibhawoh. *Administration of Juvenile Justice in Nigeria.* Lagos: CRP, 1997.

Onyekpere, E., ed. *Manual on the Judicial Protection of Economic, Social and Cultural Rights.* Lagos: SRI, 2000.

PRAWA. *About PRAWA.* Lagos: PRAWA: 2001.

_____ *Annual Reports 1998.* Lagos: PRAWA, 1998.

_____ *Overcrowding in Nigerian Prisons.* Lagos: PRAWA, 1999.

SRI. *Economic, Social and Cultural Rights: A Compilation of International Standards* (Lagos: SRI, 2001).

_____ Letter to the UN Committee on Economic, Social and Cultural Rights. 6 October 1997.

_____ *Manual on Gender Specific Rights Litigation and Protection Strategies.* Lagos: SRI, 1998.

_____ *Manual on Judicial Protection of Economic, Social and Cultural Rights.* Lagos: SRI, 2000.

_____ *NGO's CEDAW Report for Nigeria.* Lagos: SRI, 1999.

TMG. *Final Report on the 1998/1999 Transition to Civil Rule Elections in Nigeria* Lagos: TMG, 2000.

WACOL. *Legislative Advocacy for Women's Rights.* Enugu: WACOL, 2001.

_____ *The Laws and Practices Relating to Women's Inheritance Rights in Nigeria.* Enugu: WACOL, 2000.

_____*The Reproductive Rights and Maternal Health Education and Advocacy Project*. Enugu: WACOL, 2001.

_____ *Women's Socio-Economic and Legal Rights*. Enugu: WACOL, 2001.

WACOL. *Macarthur Project Resource Pack, Volume 1*. Enugu, WACOL, 2001.

NEWSLETTERS OF NIGERIAN NGOS

1:1 *Action Woman* (2002).

1:1 *SEBN News* (2002).

Legislative Advocacy (2001).

SERAC @ Work (July 2001).

2:8 *Assembly Watch* (2001).

2:10 *Assembly Watch* (2001).

4:1 *Human Rights Defender* (2001).

1:2 *Grassroots News* (2001).

1 and 2:2 *Access Quarterly* (2001).

10:34 *Constitutional Rights Journal* (2000).

10:35 *Constitutional Rights Journal* (2000).

10:36 *Constitutional Rights Journal* (2000).

10:37 *Constitutional Rights Journal* (2000).

10 *Prison Watch* (2000).

1:5 *Assembly Watch* (2000).

1:2 *Grassroots News* (2000).

1 and 2:2 *Access Quarterly* (2000).

10:34 *Constitutional Rights Journal* (2000).

10: 35 *Constitutional Rights Journal* (2000).

10:36 *Constitutional Rights Journal* (2000).

10:37 *Constitutional Rights Journal* (2000).

2:3 *Church and Society* (2000).

5:2 *Media Rights Monitor* (2000).

5:4 *Media Rights Monitor* (2000).

6:1 *Assembly Watch* (2000).

12:6 *Liberty* (2000).

9:4 *African Human Rights Newsletter* (1999).

9:30 *Constitutional Rights Journal* (1999).

9:31 *Constitutional Rights Journal* (1999).

9:32 *Constitutional Rights Journal* (1999).

11:5 *Liberty* (1999).

8 *Law Enforcement Review* (1999).

1:1 *Legislative Mandate* (1999).

1:9 *HURILAWS Newsletter* (1999).

2:1 SERAC@WORK (1999).

2:2 SERAC@WORK (1999).

2:3 *PRAWA News* (1999).

11:5 *Liberty* (1999).

2:3 *Laser Contact* (1998).

7:25 *Constitutional Rights Journal* (1998).

8:26 *Constitutional Rights Journal* (1998).

8:28 *Constitutional Rights Journal* (1998).

8:29 *Constitutional Rights Journal* (1998).

7 *Prison Watch* (1998).

1:2 *Gender Action* (1998).

1:3 *The HURILAWS Newsletter* (1998).

1:5 The HURILAWS Newsletter (1998).

2:2 *Living Newsletter* (1998).

2:2 SERAC@WORK (1998).

2:3 *Laser Contact* 4 (1998).

8:26 *Constitutional Rights Journal* (1998).

8:28 *Constitutional Rights Journal* (1998).

8:29 *Constitutional Rights Journal* (1998).

9:1 *Liberty* (1998).

9:3 *Liberty* (1998).

7:25 *Constitutional Rights Journal* (1998).

1:1 *Democracy* Review (1997).

1:1 *Democracy Review* 3-5 (1997).

1:3 *Shelter Watch* (1997)

2:1 *Community* (1997).

8:3 *Liberty* (1997).

7:23 *Constitutional Rights Journal* (1997).

1:2 *Shelter Watch* (1996).

7:1 *Liberty* (1996).

(5:17 *Constitutional Rights Journal* (1996).

6:3 *Liberty* (1995).

4:3 *Liberty* (1993).

NEWSPAPERS

Daily Champion, 4 August, 2003, on-line: http://allafrica.com/stories/200308041044.html (visited 19 August 2003).

Daily Trust, 17 January 2003, on-line: http://allafrica.com/stories/200301170355.html (visited on 13 May 2003).

Daily Trust, 1st August, 2003; on-line: http://www.mtrustonline.com/dailytrust/obasanjo01082003.htm (visited 19 August 2003).

The Guardian, 5 February 2001, on-line: http://ngrguardiannews.com/news2nn81 1628.html (visited 19 February 2001).

The Guardian, 16 May 2002, on-line: http://www.ngrguardiannews.com/editorial_ opinion/article2 (visited 16 May 2002).

Newswatch, 29 January 2001, on-line: http://www.newswatchngr.com/editorial/ allaccess/29012001/ng515.htm (visited: 30 January 2001).

Newswatch 6 November 2000, on-line: http://allafrica.com/stories/200011060060. html (visited 20 February 2003).

Post Express, on-line: http://www.postexpresswired.com/postexpr...31ea33c60df 852568ff0057f799? openDocument (visited 16 June 2000).

Post Express, 11 September 1999, on-line: http://www.postexpresswired.com/post-expr...d1f15c78d3a85256824003796b1 ?openDocument (visited 9 November 1999).

ThisDay, 17 October 2002, on-line: http://allafrica.com/stories/200210170396.html (visited on 20 October 2002).

Vanguard, 20 October 1999, online: http://www.afbis.com/vanguard/n1220109.htm (visited 20 October 1999).

West Africa Review (2000) on-line: http://www.westafricareview.com/war/vol12.1/ orji.html (visited 29 May 2003).

ONLINE SOURCES
BBC News, 21 May 2002: http://news.bbc.co.uk/1/hi/world/africa/2000691.stm (visited 20 February 2003).

David-West, T., Jr. "The Niger Delta: A Call for Reparations," http://nigeriaworld. com/feature/publication/david-west/reparations.html (visited 25 October 2001).

Oronto, D. "A Community Guide to Understanding Resource Control," http://www. waado.org/NigerDelta/Essays/ResourceControl/Guide_Douglas.html (visited 20 June 2003).

Oyo, R. "Politics: Nigeria Forms the Largest Cabinet since Independence," [unspeci-fied date], http://www.oneworld.org/ips2/july99/11_31_036.html (visited 20 June 2003).

Saul, J. "Cry for the Beloved Country: The Post-Apartheid Denouement" Monthly Review (2001) 1 (Internet copy).

Solarin, I.O. "Genocide in Odi," 10 June 2000, online: http://lists.essential.org/shell-nigeria-action/msg00701.html (visited: 10 June 2000).

Solarin, I.O. "Nigerian Federalism: The Lesson of Odi," 25 October 2001, http:// nigeriaworld.com/feature/publication/solarin/federalism_odi.html (visited: 25 October 2001).

Swedish NGO Foundation. "The Status of Human Rights Organizations in Sub-Saharan Africa: Overview-Introduction," http://www1.umn.edu/humanrts/ africa/intro.htm (visited 20 October 2000).

"Truth Commissions Digital Collection" online: http://www.usip.org/library/truth. html (visited: 20/02/2003).

"Truth Commissions Digital Collection, http://www.usip.org/library/truth/truth. html (visited 20 February 2003).

http://www.ichrdd.ca/frame.iphtml? (visited 23 May 2003).

http:///www.srinitiative.org/saboutus.htm (visited 11 March 2003).

http://1w3fd.law3.hotmail.msn.com/c...t=341196&len=7712&msgread=1&mfs= 340 (visited 31 January 2001).

http://allafrica.com/stories/200105140301.html (visited 16 May 2003).

http://news.bbc.co.uk/1/hi/world/africa/2000691.stm (visited 17 May 2003).

http://www.africaaction.org/adna/bpn0008.htm (visited 16 May 2003).

http://www.amnesty.org/ailib/intcam/nigeria/fawehinm.htm (visited 26 February 2003).

http://www.capp.kabissa.org/ (visited 28 February 2003).

http://www.dawuda.net/mosop.htm (visited 4 March 2003).

http://www.hrm.kabissa.org (visited on 26 February 2003).

http://www.hrm.kabissa.org/ (visited 28 February 2003).

http://www.hrm.kabissa.org/communiq.htm (visited 26 February 2003).

http://www.hurilaws.org/about%20us.htm (visited 27 February 2003).

http://www.hurilaws.org/secretariat.htm (visited 7 May 2003).

http://www.internews.org/mra/mra_about.htm (visited 26 February 2003).

http://www.ngprawa.org/prawa/contact.htm (visited 26 February 2003).

http://www.ngprawa.org/prawa/default.asp (visited 2 June 2003).

http://www.ngprawa.org/prawa/programs/recass.htm (visited 2 June 2003).

http://www.nigerianassembly.com/Sen...0hearing%20on%20Human%20rights. html (visited 19 February 2002).

http://www.nopa.net/Justice/messages/1.shtml (visited 16 May 2003).

http://www.odili.net/news/source/2003/apr/325/327.html (visited 13 August 03).

http://www.rightlivelihood.se/recip/saro-wiwa.htm (visited 4 March 2003.).

http://www.righttolivelihood.se/recip/saro-wiwa.htm (visited 4 March 2003).

http://www.srinitiative.org/saboutus.htm (visited 28 February 2003).

http://www.srinitiative.org/saboutus.htm (visited 11 March 2003).

http://www.thisdayonline.com/archive/2003/02/19/20030219edi01.html   (visited 16 May 2003).

http://www.truthfinder.go.kr/eng/r11.htm#Nigeria (visited 16 May 2003).

http://www.vanguardngr.com/news/articles/2001/june/11062001/d2130601.htm (visited 16 May 2003).

http://www.wangonet.org/serac/default.htm (visited 28 February 2003).

http://www.wfn.org/2000/12/msg00055/html (visited 19th August 2001).

http://www.wrapa.org/profile.htm (visited 18 March 2003).

http://www.sussex.ac.uk/units/CDE/archive/archive/publish/cdenews/99aut. html (visited 28 May 2003).

http://www.cleen.kabissa.org/links.htm (visited 16 March 2002).

http://www.ngprawa.org/prawa/about/membership.htm (visited 23 May 2003).

http://odili.net/news/source/2003/may/29/15.html (visited 27 June 2003).

http: www.fordfund.org/global/office/Lagos (visited 13 August 2003).

http://www.fnstusa.org/2002%20Where%W%Stand.htm (visited 3 March 2003).

http//www.newswatchngr.com/editorial/allaccess/2901200/ng515.htm (visited 4 March 2003).

Rights and Democracy: http://www.ichrdd.ca/flash.html (visited 2 August 2003).

INDEX